Goodness and Justice

In *Goodness and Justice*, Joseph Mendola develops a unified moral theory that defends the hedonism of classical utilitarianism, while evading utilitarianism's familiar difficulties by adopting two modifications. His theory incorporates a new form of consequentialism. When, as is common, someone is engaged in conflicting group acts, it requires that one perform one's role in that group act that is most beneficent. The theory also holds that overall value is distribution-sensitive, ceding maximum weight to the well-being of the worst-off sections of sentient lives. It is properly congruent with commonsense intuition and required by the true metaphysics of value, by the unconstituted natural good found in our world.

Joseph Mendola is professor and chair in the Department of Philosophy at the University of Nebraska–Lincoln. He is the author of *Human Thought* and of articles on ethics, metaphysics, and philosophy of mind.

T0370828

CAMBRIDGE STUDIES IN PHILOSOPHY

General Editor WALTER SINOTT-ARMSTRONG (Dartmouth College)

Advisory Editors:
JONATHAN DANCY (University of Reading)
JOHN HALDANE (University of St. Andrews)
GILBERT HARMAN (Princeton University)
FRANK JACKSON (Australian National University)
WILLIAM G. LYCAN (University of North Carolina at Chapel Hill)
SYDNEY SHOEMAKER (Cornell University)
JUDITH J. THOMSON (Massachusetts Institute of Technology)

Recent Titles:

For my daughter,
Lily Griffin

Goodness and Justice

A Consequentialist Moral Theory

JOSEPH MENDOLA
University of Nebraska–Lincoln

CAMBRIDGE
UNIVERSITY PRESS

CAMBRIDGE UNIVERSITY PRESS
Cambridge, New York, Melbourne, Madrid, Cape Town,
Singapore, São Paulo, Delhi, Tokyo, Mexico City

Cambridge University Press
The Edinburgh Building, Cambridge CB2 8RU, UK

Published in the United States of America by Cambridge University Press, New York

www.cambridge.org
Information on this title: www.cambridge.org/9780521353557

First published 2006
First paperback edition 2011

A catalogue record for this publication is available from the British Library

Library of Congress Cataloguing in Publication data
Mendola, Joseph.
Goodness and justice : a consequentialist moral theory / Joseph Mendola.
p.   cm. – (Cambridge studies in philosophy)
Includes bibliographical references and index.
ISBN 0-521-85953-0 (hardback)
1. Ethics.   2. Consequentialism (Ethics)   3. Good and evil.
4. Justice (Philosophy)   I. Title.   II. Series.
BJ1031.M46   2006
171′.5 – dc22   2005019558

ISBN 978-0-521-85953-0 Hardback
ISBN 978-0-521-35355-7 Paperback

Contents

Acknowledgments

I owe special thanks for extensive and helpful criticism during the long unfolding of this project from Tom Carson, Allan Gibbard, Jaegwon Kim, Mark van Roojen, and several anonymous referees. I am also grateful for help from Robert Audi, Bryan Belknap, Tim Black, Dick Brandt, Mark Cullison, Dave Cummiskey, Steve Darwall, Mark Decker, Bill Frankena, Jean Griffin, Russell Hahn, Jennifer Haley, Robert Hanna, Thomas Hill, Jr., Leo Iacono, Clayton Littlejohn, Heidi Malm, Sally Markowitz, Donette Petersen, Peter Railton, Beatrice Rehl, Guy Rohrbaugh, Margaret Skean, Mike Tonderum, Rainer W. Trapp, J. D. Trout, Sheldon Wein, and the students of Philosophy 920 in fall 2004. Thanks to the publishers for permission to reuse material from the articles "Multiple-Act Consequentialism," forthcoming in *Nous*; "Intuitive Maximin," *Canadian Journal of Philosophy* 35 (2005), 429–439; "Consequences, Group Acts, and Trolleys," *Pacific Philosophical Quarterly* 86 (2005), 64–87; "Justice within a Life," *American Philosophical Quarterly* 41 (2004), 125–140; and "Objective Value and Subjective States," *Philosophy and Phenomenological Research* 50 (1990), 695–713. Modified forms of "Intuitive Hedonism," forthcoming in *Philosophical Studies*, and "An Ordinal Modification of Classical Utilitarianism," *Erkenntnis* 33 (1990), 73–88, are used with the kind permission of Springer Science and Business Media.

1

Introduction

Ethicists must deliver intuitive platitudes about lying, murder, theft, injury, and the whole familiar bunch. If we can hope to surprise or advance, it is only in neglected or undeveloped corners of normative consensus. True conclusions in ethics must be mostly boring.

And yet ethicists must deliver a vindication of common moral claims. We must give arguments that should convince all the reasonable that our normative claims are correct. To put it grandly, we must deliver a transcendental vindication of those claims, from the point of view of the universe. To put it less grandly, we must provide a direct argument for the truth of the claims, independent of appeal to common moral intuitions. We need to provide considerations that ought to convince those who are outside normative consensus that we are right and they are wrong. If we merely monger common intuitions, unsupported by argument, evidence, or fact beyond their mere familiarity or warm fuzziness, we will have little to add to the standard wisdom of the street and the sea lanes. And worse, to the immoral, disagreeable, skeptically minded, or just diverse, it may not unreasonably seem that there is nothing to philosophical ethics but so much talk, so much high-minded or sanctimonious but otherwise empty blather.

And so we face two dragons. There may be no sufficiently transcendental vindication of any ethical claims, so that ethics is just a bunch of chatter. Or there may be a transcendental vindication of something, but not of the common platitudes, perhaps rather of something shockingly revisionary like the empty moral equivalence of all human action or the moral insignificance of human life or pain. In either case, philosophical ethics fails. Ethical discourse is committed both to the normative platitudes and to the objective correctness of such claims. Perhaps there are limits to what should be required of an argument in ethics, and perhaps there are limits to the probity of commonsense intuition. But if we can't provide a somewhat transcendental vindication of most moral platitudes, then ethics sinks, with all hands.

Or so I believe. I believe that it is a constraint of the meaning of "morally wrong" that intuitively heinous murder is morally wrong, and yet that there is a robustly objective status to that claim, so that contrary meaning constraints would be incorrect. But if you think I'm wrong in one way or the other, if you think that intuitive moral implications are alone enough to vindicate an ethical theory or that transcendental vindication alone is enough, if you think that one of these constraints is a mere idol of our marketplace, you should still be satisfied if a view meets both tests. And since both tests must be met by any theory that has the ghost of a chance of convincing all sober practicing ethicists, you should still hope that both monsters can be slain by the true theory.

This book tries to develop a moral theory that meets both tests. This chapter will sketch that theory, my arguments, and the structure of the book. Sections I and II introduce the theory and provide some rough motivation for its features. Section III introduces my arguments for it.

I

Classical utilitarianism is one traditional ethical theory.[1] As a form of *consequentialism*, it claims that the rightness of acts depends on the value of their consequences, that rightness depends on goodness in that way. And it claims in particular that value is *utility*, the very earthy happiness of all, pleasure and the absence of pain.

The maximization of everyone's happiness and the minimization of everyone's unhappiness is one humane and reasonably rational grounds for ethics. But there are forceful intuitive objections to such a theory, which suggest that, even in the best case, it must be modified.[2] We should not simply ignore the obvious moral salience of general happiness. But nor should we ignore standard objections to classical utilitarianism.

It may be natural to presume with classical utilitarianism that the best outcome contains the greatest sum of well-being. But this aggregative conception of best outcomes seems improperly indifferent to how well-being is distributed among individuals. If overall utility would be

---

1 Mill (1979).
2 But for a spirited defense of classical utilitarianism, see Tännsjö (1998).

maximized under some arrangement in which goods were distributed to people whose circumstances were already comfortable, while other people were allowed to starve, then that is the arrangement that classical utilitarianism would recommend. And that would be wrong. It would be unjust.

And consequentialism itself, at least in a direct form, which specifies that a right act is one that will produce the best overall outcome, faces serious objection, whatever conception of good outcomes we deploy. Consequentialism seems to require that we perform whatever act will, in a given situation, produce the best overall outcome. And this may require doing something unjust and intuitively horrible, such as murdering an innocent. There is a standard consequentialist response to this difficulty, which is rule consequentialism or some other indirect form. For instance, our duties may not be best acts, but rather acts required by best systems of moral rules, where systems of moral rules are best if their general acceptance would lead to best outcomes. But there is also a standard difficulty with this response. It is hard to understand how indirect consequentialisms, when they differ from simple and direct forms, respect the original intuitive motivation for consequentialism, which is that best outcomes are what morally count.

This book develops a variant of classical utilitarianism that can evade its traditional difficulties, while yet retaining its intuitive motivations. This variant maintains the hedonism of the classical view, the traditional conception that well-being or goodness is the presence of pleasure and the absence of pain, and argues that familiar objections to hedonism are mistaken. But two key modifications of classical utilitarianism will allow the view proposed here to evade the other two familiar intuitive objections to traditional forms of utilitarianism, objections rooted in two sorts of concern about justice.

Classical utilitarianism is a consequentialist view. It holds that the moral status of an act depends on the value of its consequences. And one component of the true ethical theory is, I will argue, a new form of consequentialism. It evades at once the traditional intuitive difficulties of act consequentialism, and the unstable rationale that plagues indirect forms like rule consequentialism. I call this conception of proper action Multiple-Act Consequentialism, or MAC.

The key to this possibility is that there are group acts. Indeed, there is a multiplicity of overlapping group acts. There is often no single fact of the matter that a piece of your momentary behavior is in particular an act you can perform in the moment, rather than a portion of a longer individual act that will take time and require the cooperation of yourself tomorrow, or a portion of a corporate act of some group of several individuals of which you are part. There is, rather, often a multiplicity of things you are doing through a single bit of behavior all at once. These facts allow MAC to perform direct consequentialist evaluation of acts that yet yields intuitive normative implications. This is roughly how it works: There can be a group act of which you are part that requires particular activity by you, which yet conflicts with activity required if you take part in another group act or perform certain individual acts. Direct consequentialist evaluation of these overlapping acts can yield a conflict. And, I will argue, the central consequentialist rationale – which is that the value of consequences is what matters – supports resolving the conflict in favor of the alternative available to you that is your part of the group or individual act with the best consequences.

We are rowing together, in important pursuit, and I can secretly ease up to create a little extra aesthetic utility, to sip my lemonade and rattle the ice cubes. You will all keep rowing and get us where we need to go, around that turbulence, and I can grab a little extra utility on the side, by that slight injustice. But then I would be defecting from an act with a stronger direct consequentialist rationale. I shouldn't do it.

MAC involves four key tenets: (1) There are group agents of which individuals are constituents, and such that an individual may be part of more than one group agent, and their acts constituents of the acts of more than one group agent. (2) Direct consequentialist evaluation of the options of group agents is appropriate. (3) Sometimes, but only sometimes, one should follow one's role in a group act even at the cost of the overall good one could achieve by defecting from that role. One should defect from a group act with good consequences only if one can achieve better consequences by the defecting act alone than the entire group act achieves. (4) When different beneficent group agents of which one is part specify roles that conflict for one, one should follow one's role in the group act with more valuable consequences.

How Multiple-Act Consequentialism works in detail, why it is true, and how it helps deliver intuitive implications with a firm consequentialist rationale are the burdens of Part One. But there are other reasons to worry about utilitarianism and its descendants. Classical utilitarianism seems transparently unjust when it suggests that we should maximize the good irrespective of its distribution. And it does not deploy a conception of human good on which ethicists have reached consensus. These are both worries about the basic normative principle that is applied by consequentialism. The basic normative principle I favor involves the second and third elements of my view, which correspond to these two points of intuitive concern about traditional utilitarianism. This principle amalgamates and reconciles one traditional conception of goodness and one traditional conception of distributive justice. It unites a classical utilitarian conception of goodness rooted in pleasure and pain, and an egalitarian conception of distributive justice requiring special concern for the worst off. I will call this principle the Hedonic Maximin Principle, or HMP for short.

The hedonism of HMP is developed and defended in Part Two. Hedonism is not fashionable, and we will need to examine this prejudice. I will have quite a bit of arguing to do before I can convince most contemporary ethicists that hedonism is viable. But hedonism is a venerable position. For instance, its utilitarian roots are evident. It is the position of the classical utilitarians, of Bentham, the Mills, and Sidgwick. We will see that this venerable view deserves greater respect than it has lately received from philosophers, and we will also see that it fits well with the transcendental vindication of ethical claims that we will eventually need to produce.

But there is a significant modification of the traditional utilitarian normative principle that is the third component of my view. It is a particular distribution-sensitive assessment of the value of overall states of affairs. The Hedonic Maximin Principle reflects another concern than the maximization of hedonic value. It is immediately responsive to the distributive justice of situations, in a way that skews our concern toward the benefit of the worst-off among us. Consequentialists shouldn't just pile up happiness in the world – in hoards of ingots or cities of butter sticks – but should also make sure that it is properly and equitably distributed.

That second aspect of HMP, concerning justice, is developed and defended in Part Three. It is characteristic of some of traditional utilitarianism's competitors, and helpful in disposing of some traditional objections to traditional utilitarianism. For instance, John Rawls's influential theory of social justice, explicitly conceived in opposition to the utilitarian tradition, requires, after certain basic liberties are assured and it is also assured that differences in income are attached to positions open to all, that differences in prospects for monetary income and wealth of representative members of basic social groups satisfy a "Difference Principle", which unites a concern with maximization and a concern with just distribution.[3]

3   Rawls (1971).

According to this principle, any inequalities in birth prospects of income must be to the benefit of the worst-off. This is a kind of "maximin" principle, which tells us to maximize the minimum level of some sort of well-being, to make the worst-off as well-off as possible. HMP is also a kind of maximin principle, but applied within the context of a classical utilitarian value theory. It implies, roughly, that one outcome is better than another when the worst-off are better off, and also that relative well-being is, as the classical utilitarians suggested, a straightforward matter of pleasure and pain.

More exactly, the Hedonic Maximin Principle incorporates two clauses, which specify, respectively, a risk-averse treatment of chances and a distribution-sensitive treatment of outcomes. The details may seem hard to understand, unmotivated, or false until the detailed discussions of the following chapters. But a brief full statement is this:

First, consider two lotteries (that is to say, alternative sets of chancy outcomes where the probabilities of the members of each set sum to one) over complete situations (that is to say, more or less, over possible worlds). When those lotteries consist of the same number of equally probable outcomes, the better lottery is the one that has the better worst-possible outcome. If they have equally bad worst-possible outcomes, then the better lottery is the one that has the better second-worst-possible outcome, and so on. We can always represent a lottery whose possible outcomes have rational probabilities as a lottery over equally probable outcomes, and we can always compare two lotteries over equally probable outcomes by comparing two equivalent lotteries that have the same number of equally probable outcomes, so this method yields a complete ordering of lotteries over complete situations, from worst to best. This ordering implies that of any two lotteries over complete situations, the better lottery is the one that has the better worst-possible outcome.

Second, consider two complete situations. Of two complete situations that contain the same number of momentary bits of experience, the better situation is the one that has the better worst momentary bit of experience. The value of a momentary bit of experience is its level of ordinal hedonic value or disvalue of a sort shortly to be characterized. If two situations have equally bad worst momentary bits of experience, then the better situation is the one that has the better second-worst momentary bit, and so on. And any such situation is equivalent in value to another that has the same number of momentary bits of experience at each level of ordinal value and disvalue as the first plus any number of momentary bits with null value. So this specifies a complete ordering from worst to best of complete situations. It implies, more or less, that of any two such situations that include painful experiences, the better situation is the one that has the least severe most painful experience. It implies, more or less, that of any two situations that contain no painful experiences, the better situation is the one that contains the greater number of positively valuable experiences.

Despite what will seem at the moment the obscurity of some of the specific details of this formulation, a normative principle of approximately this sort is not unprecedented. The value theory incorporated in my account is reminiscent of classical utilitarianism, and the utilitarian Henry Sidgwick thought that, when two states of affairs contained the same overall quantity of happiness, still one state might be preferable because its distribution of happiness was just, and that just distributions were equal ones.[4] There are also nonutilitarian precedents. Of course, there is Rawls. But William Frankena also proposed a deontological theory that incorporates two basic duties, to maximize the good and to be just.[5] Samuel Scheffler has developed a hybrid ethical theory that not only allows agents sometimes to desist from maximizing the good when pursuing individual projects, but also requires that their maximization of the good be tempered with distribution sensitivity, so that the less the relative well-being of a person, the greater the weight that should be given to benefitting him or her.[6] David Brink has built a kind of distribution sensitivity into his modification of utilitarian theory, by specifying that certain sorts of basic well-being have great weight in determining the value of a situation.[7] Thomas Scanlon has developed Rawls's maximin principle in certain ways, and Thomas Nagel has suggested that we need to give greater weight to the interests of those who are less well-off.[8]

So ethical and political theories that mix a concern to maximize well-being with a concern for just distribution, particularly in regard to the worst-off, are not unknown. But HMP is somewhat different from and, I will argue, superior to each of these competitors.

The first difference between my proposal and its close competitors is that, of all these accounts, only Sidgwick's deploys the kind of classical hedonistic value theory, with pleasure the only positive value and pain the only disvalue, that my account will develop. In the current climate,

4   Sidgwick (1907: 416–417).
5   Frankena (1973).
6   Scheffler (1982).
7   Brink (1989: 268–273).
8   Scanlon (1973); Nagel (1991: 73).

that may hardly seem an advantage. The abandonment of classical hedonist value theories by the recent competitors noted is motivated by widespread worries that such traditional hedonist theories are inadequate, in particular because they have certain counterintuitive implications. But we will eventually see that a hedonistic value theory, when properly developed and deployed, is not unintuitive, and that indeed the ethical theory developed here has detailed normative implications that suitably match our commonsense morality. And we will also see that a classical hedonistic conception of value fits far better than its competitors with one key sort of argument that should underwrite ethical theories. It accords far better with our need to provide a reasoned vindication and legitimation of our normative principles and claims over possible competitors.

We will also see that HMP enjoys advantages over Sidgwick's classical alternative. According to Sidgwick's account, justice as equality matters merely in a quite secondary way – for instance, when we are choosing between two outcomes that involve the same overall quantity of happiness distributed among the same number of people. The Hedonic Maximin Principle marries a traditional utilitarian conception of value with the greater distribution sensitivity characteristic of more recent competitors, and in a way that we will see is at once more intuitive and capable of reasoned vindication independent of appeal to ethical intuition.

Still, this greater distribution sensitivity may itself suggest grounds for worry about HMP. That is because even some fans of maximin principles have held that such straightforward application as I propose will yield quite counterintuitive applications.[9] And the novel form of my maximin principle, which maximins over risks to momentary bits of experience, and not over whole people, may suggest further grounds for intuitive objection. But, as I've said, we will eventually see that in fact the theory to be proposed here has plausible ethical implications, despite any apparent threats of intuitive implausibility. In part, as we will see in Part Three, this results from the way in which maximining over risks to momentary bits differs from more familiar sorts. In part, as we will see in Part Two, it is because hedonism is more intuitive than is often presumed. But the intuitive ethical implications of my proposal also stem in part from Multiple-Act Consequentialism as developed in Part One, which would help in the defense of any plausible consequentialist principle, and also from MAC's specific interaction with HMP.

---

9 For instance, Rawls and Scanlon.

Multiple-Act Consequentialism and the Hedonic Maximin Principle together imply the fourth component of my proposal. That fourth component provides an intuitive set of specific moral constraints, requiring intuitively moral actions. I will call it the Proposed Code, or PC for short. MAC and HMP are, I hope, of independent interest, but we will see in Part Four that, in conjunction, they imply this intuitive set of moral injunctions. It incorporates constraints reminiscent of the virtues favored by Aristotelian virtue theories, which specify individual traits whereby momentary individuals become parts of successful continuing agents capable of unitary moral behavior over time. It also incorporates constraints reminiscent of the obligations recognized by deontological theories like Kant's or Ross's, which specify forms of action for individuals whereby cooperative moral behaviors become possible and effective, whereby individuals can constitute groups acting appropriately together. And it also incorporates a properly chastened concern with the pursuit of justly distributed good. We will compare PC with the details of commonsense morality, and see that they properly coincide. We will also discuss two cases that common sense does not resolve, but that this theory does resolve in a plausible way. They are our obligations to the needy and our obligations to refrain from certain sorts of bad corporate activity.

The Hedonic Maximin Principle incorporates one feature of traditional competitors of traditional utilitarianism, and so reflects one intuitive concern for justice. And Multiple-Act Consequentialism and hence the Proposed Code are reminiscent in a second way of some of utilitarianism's traditional competitors, and reflect another intuitive concern for justice. So this moral theory is, in this dually chastened sense, a conception of a just good. But still it is a conception that ultimately roots ethical valuation in *merely* goodness, in *just* good, and indeed hedonic good of a classically utilitarian form. Goodness retains that priority.

II

The theory developed here is a modification of classical utilitarianism to evade pressing intuitive objections. Yet there are other dominant strands in common sense, not just a few intuitive objections to a single dominant utilitarian strand. Mere modification may not seem enough.

Our complex social world is heir to many different ethical traditions. If we are to deliver intuitive normative implications, we need a normative theory that is in some sense a reconciliation of various competing strands in our normative inheritance. Even if we achieve such a reconciliation, it may be hard to see how there can be an argument that should independently convince everyone that such a conciliatory normative view is true, and not just an arbitrary political compromise among competing dominant normative factions. Yet if there isn't such an argument, then there will be no transcendental vindication of such a view. But focus for the moment on the point about reconciliation.

Each of the traditional competing ethical systems – for instance, Aristotle's, Mill's, and Kant's – emphasizes certain strands in our rich and confusing normative heritage, toward which each of us feels some intuitive pull. While such strands can be developed in many ways, and some developments leave them inconsistent and competing like the famous historical systems, still the strands should, it seems, be woven together in a consistent and unified manner, if they can be. Since the various intelligent and conscientious individuals who have prominently represented each of the various strands of our tradition were surely all onto something that is reflected in our commonsense ethical consciousness, and since that common sense should bear at least some argumentative weight, it would be better, other things equal, if an ethical theory drew all the strands together, if it found some way to interpret the various apparently competing elements in our tradition of ethical discussion so that they came out consistent and unified, if it provided some sort of reconciliation of these various elements of our diverse tradition, and not just a patched-up and barely acceptable version of one strand – say, the utilitarian strand. Of course, it is also important that this reconciliation eventually be capable of a proper independent rationale, of a transcendental vindication. But even bare reconciliation may be hard enough.

There are two deep conflicts in our tradition that my proposal can reconcile in a well-founded way, despite its roots in utilitarianism. One reflects the standard teaching division of moral theories. There are consequentialist theories, like utilitarianism, which hold that right action is that which leads to the maximization of value. There are deontological theories, like Kant's and Ross's,[10] which hold that right action is not right solely – nor perhaps even in part – because of the value of its consequences, but rather at least in part because of its intrinsic nature. There are virtue theories, like Aristotle's, which focus first not on the rightness of action but on the goodness of lives. And there are also rights-based theories.

10 Kant (1996a); Ross (1930).

While my account is within the utilitarian tradition, this standard typography isolates four strands that it weaves together, though with a certain spin and emphasis reflecting its utilitarian origin. It is a reconciliation from the perspective of one of the key strands. No doubt there are other reconciliations possible, but this is one. The third component of my proposal, the distribution-sensitive form of HMP, demands a certain kind of equity, and hence respects Kant's central belief that reason demands that we treat like as like. It also constitutes one sort of distributional right. The first component of this theory, Multiple-Act Consequentialism, naturally encompasses basic concerns of deontological and virtue-based theories, as we will see in Part One. This proposal is one legitimate heir to and development of the central concerns of each of these traditional classes of alternative ethical theories, and hence partakes of some of the intuitive rationale of each. We will gradually see this in detail.

A second familiar typography of ethical theories whose threads can be drawn together is Thomas Scanlon's triad of "philosophical explanations of the nature of morality".[11] These are general theories about the nature of the grounds of truth for moral claims, the proper moral epistemology, and the nature of the reasons that morality provides for us. Scanlon distinguishes intuitionism, philosophical utilitarianism, and contractarianism as theories of this sort.

The primary underlying concern for intuitionists is to preserve the full range of intuitive first-order normative judgments about the right, good, and just, which do of course more or less directly engage our motivation. The Proposed Code will seem, I hope, quite hospitable to intuitionists. But consider the other two philosophical explanations of morality.

Philosophical utilitarianism, as distinguished from utilitarianism as a first-order normative doctrine, is the thesis that the only fundamental moral facts are facts about individual well-being. Such facts have obvious motivational significance, because of our at least loosely sympathetic and benevolent inclinations, and hence sympathy is, according to philosophical utilitarianism, the primary moral motivation.

Contractarianism holds that an "act is wrong if its performance under the circumstances would be disallowed by any system of rules for the general regulation of behaviour which no one could reasonably reject as a basis for informed, unforced general agreement."[12] The basic idea is that morality is a scheme of cooperation that should command the informed

11 Scanlon (1982).
12 Ibid., 110.

and uncoerced allegiance of all the reasonable, and that it is supported by the desire to be able to justify one's actions to others on grounds that they could not reasonably reject.[13] It is rooted not in benevolence but in a kind of reciprocity.

While philosophical utilitarianism is not a first-order normative doctrine, it seems to have normative implications. If all that matters morally is individual well-being, that seems to imply that we should maximize the sum of individual well-being. Scanlon once argued that the contractarian conception may support more distribution-sensitive normative principles, since it naturally directs our attention to those who would do worst under a possible system of normative rules. If anyone has reasonable grounds for objecting to that system, it is likely that they will.[14] And there are also other ways in which reciprocity supports forms of moral constraint that seem to conflict with the maximization of well-being, which have become more prominent in Scanlon's later work,[15] and to which we will return.

If both these philosophical conceptions of the nature of morality are present in our normative tradition, and if both are rooted in motivations – benevolence and reciprocity – to which most of us by training or nature are susceptible, then we seem to face a strain in our ethical inheritance. It is a strain not unlike the strain between self-interest and morality that Sidgwick discerned in our practical reason.[16] It may seem that the issue between, on the one hand, philosophical utilitarianism and a concern to maximize the sum of well-being, and, on the other, contractarianism and a concern with distribution and other manifestations of reciprocity, cannot be rationally adjudicated. So some reconciliation of these disparate philosophical conceptions of morality would seem, if possible, desirable. If they could be developed together into one consistent account, that would eliminate the threat of deep incoherence in our normative tradition.

But we will see that they are consistent, and reconciled in the theory proposed here. And so this view can claim the heritage of both the contractarian and the philosophical utilitarian traditions, once they are clarified and rationalized. And as I said, we will also see that my proposal is quite friendly to intuitionists.

Of course, more than loose-limbed motivation is required. The next section sketches and locates my *arguments* for this theory.

---

13 Ibid., 116.
14 Ibid., 123.
15 Scanlon (1998).
16 Sidgwick (1907: 496–509).

III

There are three converging arguments for this ethical theory, all of which I believe are necessary. This reflects that fact that two monsters threaten ethics, and one has two heads.

The first argument does not depend on an appeal to ethical intuitions, and provides the suitably transcendental vindication we require, the necessary argument more or less from the point of view of the universe, which I will call a "direct" argument. It has five broad steps. First, I will argue that a crucial feature of ethical discussion is that it is a form of reason giving in which appeals for a reasoned justification of legitimate normative principles and claims must always be capable of being met. Second, I will argue that this feature of ethical discussion can be plausibly underwritten only by a particular metaphysics of the ethical according to which, first, there are natural and objective properties of pleasantness and painfulness that are yet normative properties and, second, there are certain principles constraining how the value of a whole is related to the values of its parts. Third, I will argue that this entails the Hedonic Maximin Principle. Fourth, I will argue for the truth of Multiple-Act Consequentialism, whatever our moral intuitions. Fifth, I will argue that the Hedonic Maximin Principle and Multiple-Act Consequentialism jointly imply the Proposed Code in the situation in which we find ourselves.

Let me expand the first three steps of this argument, those leading to HMP, so that I can dispose of necessary background, so that I can explain better what I mean by a direct argument, and so that I can properly introduce the final doctrinal element of the book. Here is the expanded form of the first three steps:

Premise One: Normative practice, by which I mean our practice of ethical and political evaluation, has as a central and indefeasible commitment something we might call "justificatory reason giving".

Premise Two: Justificatory reason giving crucially involves

(a) normative claims that express justificatory reasons for or against things, which reasons
(b) are governed by consistency and other logical constraints, and
(c) are capable of something we might call "deep justification".

Premise Three: To give a deep justification of a normative claim is to show that no conflicting claim is appropriate, that there is an objective asymmetry that vindicates a practice of reason giving deploying the first against a practice deploying the second.

13

Premise Four: One form of the necessary objective asymmetry is an objective normative fact to which a normative claim and not its possible competitor is true. It requires a kind of normative realism. Another form supports principles for constructing the value of wholes from the value of their parts that can be vindicated in a properly objective and asymmetrical fashion against possible competitors. But those are the only operative possibilities.

Premise Five: There are certain sorts of objective normative facts, and certain principles of construction that can be given the relevant deep justification with properly objective asymmetry.

Premise Six: These facts and principles entail the Hedonic Maximin Principle.

Two points about this argument require immediate attention. First, it invokes justificatory reason giving. The peculiarly *normative* feature of normative discourse, of ethical and political discourse, is its capacity to provide an articulation of reasons of a certain sort, and not merely reasons as explanations such as we can hope to give of any natural phenomenon. It is *justificatory* reason-giving utterance. It purports to give reasons that justify or condemn, reasons genuinely for or against. Justificatory reason giving is a deep enough commitment of our normative practice that skepticism about its legitimate possibility can generate a kind of corrosive skepticism about ethics and the normative in general. It is arguably the most central and crucial feature of our normative practice. But whether it is most central or not, it is surely central enough that at least many of us would conclude, if this commitment of ethics cannot be vindicated, that ethics is a kind of scam, just a lot of empty talk. This is in fact what many people, including many philosophers, believe, and on something recognizably like these grounds. We can see in this way that justificatory reason giving is quite central to our practice of normative evaluation, that its loss would be enormous and shattering. This fact underwrites the need for our first argument, but also supplies its first premise. An important and central thing about normative evaluation is that it purports to be justificatory reason giving, the giving of genuine justificatory reasons for or against things.

My second point is that it will turn out that legitimate justificatory reason giving has a certain cost, which involves the final doctrinal element of my proposal. This is a metaethical position that, like the normative position it supports, is a confluence of traditional competitors.

Parts Two and Three will sketch an account of normative judgment and language that adopts insights regarding normative discourse of both

14

cognitivist and *noncognitivist* authors, both authors who hold that normative sentences have genuine truth conditions and those who deny this. And this position can indeed claim to reconcile standard metaethical contenders in a second way also, within cognitivism.

Some traditional cognitivists postulate non-natural normative properties, properties in some sense outside the natural order. Some other cognitivists claim that normative features are constituted by natural properties of a non-normative sort. But my proposal is that certain obviously natural and quite concrete properties – for instance, the property of being painful – are in fact normative properties. My view is in that sense midway between naturalist and non-naturalist forms of cognitivism. It has some affinity with "sensibility" theories, like those of Wiggins and McDowell, which claim that normative properties are analogous to allegedly "secondary" properties like color, and are constituted by our sensibilities. But my alternative implies that normative properties are fully mind-independent and objective properties of objects. It is a form of full-blown normative realism. The normative properties it deploys are much as our pre-Galilean ancestors conceived color to be, *not* as Boyle and Locke conceived color to be. Only such normative properties can make proper sense of justificatory reason giving; they will turn out to be necessary to that necessary end. This component of my metaethical proposal is developed in Chapter 5.

But there is also a second component of this metaethical proposal, developed in Chapter 6. This is a set of construction principles that allow us to generate an ordering of wholes from better to worse given information about the value contained in them, and that help provide HMP with its distribution-sensitive form. These elements of my view are underwritten by features of our reason-giving normative discourse that some noncognitivists have developed, and that also find expression in current "practical-reasoning" and "constructivist" conceptions. So the position to be developed here exhibits some affinities with current noncognitivist projects, as well as cognitivist affinities. It is a confluence of familiar competitors. While partisanship has greatly sharpened our understanding of the theoretical alternatives in metaethics as well as in normative ethics, it is implausible that opponents on these matters are simply and straightforwardly mistaken.

My insistence on the need for a direct argument, for a transcendental vindication of normative claims, may itself seem quite unreasonably partisan. If there is now a dominant methodological view in normative ethics, it is that we should seek reflective equilibrium among our firm intuitive ethical judgments, without worrying much about any intuition-independent vindication of those claims, or other metaethical and metaphysical niceties. This methodology shapes much of the best and most interesting current work in ethics. It seems to many contemporary ethicists that it really doesn't matter how or even whether there are robustly objective normative facts that underwrite our intuitive judgments, while I am insisting on their significance. What's more, it is hard to deny that we should have more confidence in the particular commonsense moral judgments that I aim ultimately to vindicate here than in the robust and controversial metaphysical premises of my attempted vindication of those judgments.

But there are three reasons why I think that we need to pursue the transcendental vindication of normative claims, why we need to provide a direct argument for the truth of those claims, independent of appeal to normative intuitions.

First, the meaning of our moral words invokes such an intuition-transcendent basis, I believe. We need to see how the correctness of even such normative judgments as we are all inclined to make is in fact delivered by the world in which we live. There is inevitable controversy about the nature of the world, but there must be some true story about what makes our common intuitive normative judgments correct, or we are mistaken in those judgments. While the metaphysical and metaethical details of the particular story I tell are surely more controversial than the normative claims that I rest on them, still the details are plausible, and would suitably underwrite those normative claims. And if no such true story is available, then those normative claims are in fact inappropriate, whether we like it or not. It surely isn't enough that the words of those claims echo vividly through our hearts and minds. Some horrendous normative sentences have echoed vividly through the hearts and minds of human beings.

Of course, my claim about the meaning of our moral words is controversial, and some will think that this first reason should be granted no weight at all. But my next two reasons are more ecumenical. The second reason to pursue a direct argument for a moral theory is that there are reasonable and rational people who fall outside of our normative consensus, and we need something true to say to those people that should convince them to join the consensus. Objective facts that root a true normative theory would provide it, as would other forms of transcendental vindication.

The third reason to pursue a direct argument is that even those of us inside the relevant intuitive consensus still coherently differ about many practically significant moral matters, and will continue to differ as we refine the coherent equilibrium of our individual normative intuitions.

We need some appropriate means to resolve these disputes that are beyond our reflective consensus, and it seems that only transcendental vindication, only direct argument independent of appeal to normative intuitions, can provide it.

Depending on who "we" are – depending on whether all minimally intelligent and reasonable people in all times and places, or merely the currently dominant community of academic normative ethicists, constitute the relevant community – these two reasons will vary in weight. But they cannot be evaded at once without real cost. The broader the community of normative intuition we seek, the more significant the normative disputes it will leave unresolved. Of course, we may not be able to get everything we want. Maybe we cannot resolve significant moral disputes. But it is surely worth trying.

Some will accept none of these reasons even to attempt the transcendental vindication of normative claims and theories. But I will also provide two more arguments for my theory. The first argument for my proposal, which I have just sketched, does not depend on appeals to ethical intuition. But the second and third arguments do depend on appeals to ethical intuition. As I said, I myself think that all these arguments are necessary. Even if there is a transcendental vindication of some particular normative theory, even if there is a proper normative argument from the point of view of the universe, still ethics and ethical discourse might be bankrupt, since the theory for which there is such a proper direct argument might have morally abhorrent implications. Indeed, I think that in that situation it would be only in a strained sense that there are genuine practical reasons at all, even genuinely normative reasons of self-interest. But if you disagree, you may still think that my second and third arguments, from commonsense moral intuition, are important. Perhaps you think they trump all other forms of argument, even a direct argument. Or perhaps you think that they alone are sufficient in the absence of such a transcendental vindication, or at least in the absence of a unique transcendental vindication of one single moral theory. Or perhaps you think that they are all that could matter in support of such a theory. And even if you think these appeals to intuition should bear no weight, at the very least you should admit that they are important in the eyes of many contemporary ethicists.

My second argument focuses on the first three basic components of my proposal – its hedonism, maximin distribution over risks to bits of experience, and Multiple-Act Consequentialism – which together entail, in our circumstances, its fourth component, the Proposed Code. This argument appeals to commonsense moral intuitions of the same level of generality and abstraction as those first three components. Whose commonsense intuitions? The suitably reflective intuitions of contemporary academic ethicists, since they will provide a quite restrictive test, and since they also generate the common intuitive objections we must consider.

I will argue that hedonism, maximin, and Multiple-Act Consequentialism are each independently at least generally intuitive. That such an argument is possible reflects the fact that my proposal is a confluence of traditional competitors, that it is a legitimate heir of each of the chief and apparently competing normative strands present within our complex and not obviously coherent ethical tradition, the tradition inherited by all contemporary moral philosophers. It also reflects the fact that this proposal is a modification of classical utilitarianism to evade standard intuitive objections.

My argument by appeal to these general intuitions has a positive aspect. But it also involves discussion of what will seem in the current philosophical climate pressing general intuitive objections to such a view, and especially to its apparently controversial hedonism, its extreme distribution sensitivity regarding momentary bits of lives, and its consequentialism. It will also involve detailed discussion of the traditional intuitive objections to more familiar forms of utilitarianism from which my proposal descends.

We will see with confidence that the three basic components of the theory developed here are acceptably intuitive at the somewhat general level in question, that my proposal is not known intuitively to be false in that way. We will also see, though with less certainty, that these three components are, despite current fashion, dominantly suggested by reflective intuition focused at the same level of abstraction, and hence that the theory seems intuitively true at that level of detail.

Our discussion of the general intuitions that in fact support but may seem to undercut hedonism will come in Chapter 4. The intuitive nature of the maximin structure of HMP will be the concern of Chapter 7. The mechanism of Multiple-Act Consequentialism, though founded in fact in Chapter 2, will also flow directly out of standard intuitive objections to consequentialism, which are answered for MAC in Chapter 3.

It also matters, of course, how these parts fit together. The third argument for my proposal is that it yields properly intuitive detailed applications, that it yields properly intuitive judgments about particular cases. This argument depends on the intuitive nature of the Proposed Code, which is implied, in our situation, by the conjunction of Multiple-Act Consequentialism and the Hedonic Maximin Principle. This code is developed, in Chapter 8, with an eye to comparison with reconstructions of commonsense morality by Aquinas, Aristotle, Donagan, Fried, Gert, Kant, Ross, Scanlon, Sidgwick, and four religious traditions, though my dominant focus again will be contemporary academic intuition. We will see that the Proposed Code can withstand the scrutiny of our reflective moral consensus. We will see that it can withstand the very specific objections in application that are the stock-in-trade of intuitionists. But, more positively, we also will see that it provides a plausible and suggestive framework for understanding the detailed content of commonsense moral intuition, once our normative intuitions about cases are drawn together and corrected by reflection for idiosyncracy, inconsistency, incoherence, and vagueness.

Here's a summary map: Part One develops Multiple-Act Consequentialism. In particular, Chapter 2 argues that it is required by the facts, independent of moral intuition, while Chapter 3 shows how it evades familiar intuitive normative objections to act consequentialism.

Part Two concerns the hedonism of the Hedonic Maximin Principle. Chapter 4 argues that hedonism is properly intuitive, while Chapter 5 attempts a direct and intuition-independent argument for hedonism.

Part Three concerns the maximin structure of HMP. Chapter 6 pursues an intuition-independent vindication of that maximin structure, and Chapter 7 argues that it is properly intuitive.

Part Four draws everything together. Chapter 8 develops the Proposed Code as a joint implication of HMP and MAC, and shows that it is properly intuitive in detail.

Part One

A Better Consequentialism

2

Multiple-Act Consequentialism

Act consequentialism – the view that right acts are those individual acts with best consequences available in the circumstances – has an obvious and intuitive rationale. To make the world as good as possible is a plausible moral goal. But indirect forms of consequentialism promise more intuitive normative implications, though at evident cost of intuitive rationale. This chapter will introduce a new form of consequentialism, Multiple-Act Consequentialism or MAC, which combines the intuitive rationale of act consequentialism and the intuitive normative implications of the best indirect forms.

MAC has four key tenets: (1) There are group agents of which we are constituents. (2) Direct consequentialist evaluation of the options of group agents is appropriate. (3) Sometimes we should follow our roles in a group act even at the cost of the overall good we could achieve by defection from those roles. In particular, one should defect from a group act with good consequences only if one can achieve better consequences by the defecting act alone than the entire group act achieves. (4) When different beneficent group agents of which one is part specify roles that conflict for one, one should follow the role in the group act with more valuable consequences.

MAC is a natural response to three standard objections to familiar forms of act consequentialism. Section I sketches these three objections, the indirect consequentialism that is the standard consequentialist response, and standard objections to indirect consequentialism. We need another approach. The rest of the chapter develops MAC. It evades the inherent difficulties of indirect forms largely because it is a new direct form. The next chapter will apply MAC in response to the three standard objections to familiar direct forms. But we will see in this chapter that if a basic consequentialist moral principle is true – for instance, the Hedonic Maximin Principle or a standard utilitarian valuation principle – then MAC is true independent of normative intuitions like those that root these three objections.

I

Consider three standard objections to act consequentialism. First, act consequentialism seems to be "an excessively demanding moral theory, ... [which] require[s] that one neglect or abandon one's own pursuits whenever one could produce even slightly more good in some other way."[1] But it seems morally permissible to spend money on an old sailboat, or to buy your daughter a nice toy knight, even when that money might be put to better use alleviating the suffering of the starving.

Second is the standard deontological objection that act consequentialism seems insufficiently demanding. It doesn't forbid – indeed, it sometimes requires – lying, or injuring or even murdering the innocent, when those things will generate an overall increase in the good. Some of the force of this objection is directed solely against act consequentialisms that deploy a traditional utilitarian value theory. We might evade this element of the objection by adopting a theory of value that ceded weight to death, or even to murder per se. But there is another element of the objection that cannot be evaded by this fix, a fix that in any case seems in questionable accord with some traditional motivations for consequentialism, and won't fit HMP. That second element is that it seems wrong to murder even to prevent several other murders. Even this problem can be evaded by a modification of basic consequentialist normative principles in which the value of states of affairs is relativized to particular agents. The world is worse for me if I murder, but worse for you if you murder. But this may seem a kind of trick that evades the letter of the objection in question only by abandoning the spirit of act consequentialism. And it requires a theory of value that cannot be independently motivated. Consequentialists need another response.

The third standard objection to act consequentialism is that it is in some ways at once too permissive and too demanding. It directs that we ignore our individual *special obligations* – our obligations to our own children or friends and our obligations of gratitude and reparation – and pursue the

---

1 Scheffler (1988: 3).

good of all indiscriminately. Or at least it does that when it is allied with a characteristic nonrelative value theory.

There is a standard consequentialist reply to all these standard objections. It is indirect consequentialism. It does not succeed, but why it fails is important.

Act consequentialism prescribes that each individual agent in each situation act in *direct* accord with the proper ordering of options from worst to best – indeed, in the simplest form of act consequentialism, that each always choose the best.[2] A basic normative principle like HMP or a classical utilitarian principle is applied directly to evaluate individual acts from among individual options. But consequentialism might alternatively assess things other than individual acts by reference to valuable consequences, and then assess individual acts *indirectly*, by reference to those other things. This may evade the three intuitive objections to direct maximization of the good.

There are a variety of possible forms of indirect consequentialism. Individuals have relatively stable motives and characters, which constrain individual acts over relatively long stretches of time and across many situations of choice. So perhaps we are to assess what motives are best on consequentialist grounds, and allow best motives to determine proper actions.[3] Or perhaps we are to focus on the best relatively stable characters.[4] Other forms of indirect consequentialism focus on the actions of many distinct individuals at once. We might focus on relatively universal acceptance of sets of moral rules, and claim that an act is morally permissible if and only if it is allowed by rules whose acceptance by the overwhelming majority of everyone everywhere could reasonably be expected to result in as good consequences as would result from any other code identifiable at the time.[5] Alternatively, we might focus on ideal rules for particular societies in particular local conditions. Or we might focus on act-types, and adopt consequentialist generalization, claiming that "an act is right if and only if the consequences of its being performed by the agent and all other agents similarly situated are at least as good as the consequences of any other

2   There is a distinction between subjective and objective consequentialist theories, which in their simplest direct forms suggest respectively that the right act is that which is best according to the basic normative principle applied upon our conception of our options or the fact of our options. I presume the latter.
3   Adams (1976).
4   Railton (1984). Railton does not endorse an indirect form of consequentialism.
5   Hooker (1995: 20). See also the somewhat different formulation in Hooker (1996) and the most recent version in Hooker (2000: 32).

available act's being performed by the agent and all other agents similarly situated."[6] Donald Regan has proposed yet another sort of indirect alternative, cooperative consequentialism.[7] On this view, each agent ought to cooperate, with whoever else is thus cooperating, in the production of the best consequences possible given the behavior of noncooperators.[8] We focus on the group present in any particular situation that is willing to cooperate in pursuit of the proper consequentialist end in that situation, and act in effective concert with that group.

While indirect forms of consequentialism promise a way around the three standard objections to act consequentialism, they in turn face three crucial objections. Not all of the objections succeed, but their nature and the nature of the replies that they necessitate are important to us.

One classic objection to indirect consequentialism is that the various indirect forms – for instance, rule consequentialism – have the same implications as, are extensionally equivalent to, act consequentialism. This would imply that those indirect forms are no more properly intuitive than the act consequentialism on which they are supposed to be an intuitive improvement.[9] The argument for extensional equivalence seems straightforward. The best and most beneficent rules seem of necessity to allow for exceptions to any general restrictions on behavior that they proffer, exceptions that allow the local maximization of the good.

But in fact this objection is mistaken. None of the standard forms of indirect consequentialism is extensionally equivalent to standard act consequentialism. There are perhaps many reasons for this, but one is important to us. One way in which extensional equivalence fails is instructive, since it suggests that the intuitive normative advantages of indirect forms result from the effects of cooperative behaviors.

This key objection to extensional equivalence is Allan Gibbard's.[10] Here is his case:

Smith and Jones . . . [are] placed in separate isolation booths, so that the actions of one can have no influence at all on the actions of the other. . . . [A] red push-button [is] installed in each . . . booth. The only action of moral significance open to either man will be to hold his push-button down at 10:00 a.m., or to refrain

6 Regan (1980: 94). But perhaps the classic statement is Harrod (1936). Murphy (2000) suggests a new and somewhat analogous form to which we will return.
7 Actually, Regan calls it "co-operative utilitarianism".
8 Regan (1980: 124).
9 For classic forms of this argument, see Lyons (1965) and Brandt (1963).
10 Gibbard (1965).

from doing so. . . . If at 10:00 a.m. both are holding down their push-buttons, they receive cake and ice cream. . . . If only one of them is holding his push-button down, however, they both receive electric shocks. . . . If neither is holding his button down, nothing happens.[11]

This is how the case works: Notice that if at 10 A.M. Smith is not holding his button down, then it is best for Jones not to hold his down. But then the best act consequentialist act for Jones is not that which would be best for each to engage in, nor that which would be best for rules to prescribe to both, nor that which would be best for both to do in similar circumstances.[12] The coordinating effects of joint action block the alleged extensional equivalence of act consequentialism and indirect forms.

Of course, some indirect forms of consequentialism − for instance, character consequentialism − focus not on the acts of more than one agent but on the acts of a single individual over many temporally distinct choice situations. But notice that the phenomenon Gibbard notes has a temporal analogue. It is simply Castañeda's "paradox" of act consequentialism seen from a different angle:[13] If among your options are conjunctive acts − for instance, acts that take some time and require a temporal conjunction of two shorter acts − it may be that the conjunctive act has the best consequences of all temporally extended acts available, but that neither conjunct has good consequences on its own. The conjunctive act may be in effect a cooperative action of two periods of your life.

So the first objection to indirect forms of consequentialism fails. But it fails in an instructive way. Almost everyone grants that indirect forms have more intuitive normative implications as long as they are not extensionally equivalent to act consequentialism. But Gibbard's counterexample to extensional equivalence suggests that it is in particular the coordination of action in cooperative behavior that generates those intuitive advantages for indirect forms. This perhaps reflects the traditional Kantian and contractarian insight that cooperative activity and the respect and reciprocity that support it undergird norms that forbid lies, murder, and injury.

Still, there is an important complication. In Gibbard's counterexample, one of the two individuals *does not* perform their component of the joint act that would have best consequences. If they *had* performed their component, act consequentialism and indirect forms would require the

---

11 Ibid., 214.
12 There is a similar example developed in Gibbard (1990a: 6−7), a reprint of his 1971 dissertation.
13 Castañeda (1973). For extensive discussion, see Feldman (1975, 1986).

same act of the second individual. Act consequentialism and indirect forms are apparently extensionally equivalent in their recommendations for that second individual in that situation. This is relevant because we will eventually see that the best form of consequentialism cedes normative salience to actual forms of cooperative behavior on the part of others. In other words, in the important cases of extensional equivalence or inequivalence for the view to be developed here, the relevant analog of Gibbard's first individual does his part in the cooperative scheme, while in Gibbard's case he does not.

But there are also other sorts of counterexamples, which reflect other aspects of cooperative activity, and which show a failure of extensional equivalence even in the cases most relevant to the view to be developed here. In the familiar Prisoner's Dilemma, there are two individuals who are so positioned that, if each acts directly to pursue their own self-interest, then each will do better in that regard whatever the other does, and yet both will lose relative to an outcome that was available by their joint action. Act selfishness and more indirect forms of selfishness are not extensionally equivalent even when the other prisoner in fact acts in a cooperative manner. This has the structure of the case we need. And there are also moralized versions of the Prisoner's Dilemma, in which two consequentialists are positioned in such a way that, if each acts directly to pursue best consequences, then each will do better whatever the other does, and yet both will lose relative to an outcome that was available by joint action.

It might seem that this could not be, since the two consequentialists, unlike the two selfish prisoners, share a goal. But it can be – for instance, because the options available to someone can depend on how they choose among their options. If someone chooses among options as an individual act consequentialist, a wizard may torture all humans. If they choose as a deontologist or otherwise, the wizard may promote the general welfare of all. Hence all the options of our consequentialist might be worse on consequentialist grounds if they choose as an act consequentialist rather than otherwise. Such a wizard can also assure the characteristic payoff matrix of a moralized Prisoner's Dilemma.[14] Note that my point isn't merely that there can be indirect negative consequentialist effects that result from self-consciously deploying consequentialist decision procedures or having consequentialist motives. In the case at hand, all the options open to an agent will in fact be much worse according to consequentialism if the

14   This case is a slight modification of a case presented in Mendola (1986).

agent in fact acts in accord with consequentialism, whatever their motives or decision procedures. If they take the best option available to them, then all their options will be much worse than they otherwise would have been. Of course, there are no wizards with nasty schemes like that one. But a more realistic counterexample is available whenever acceptance of certain traditional constraints against lying and murder makes better options available than would be available in a world of individual act consequentialists. The consequent reduction in anxiety about the possibility of being murdered or injured, even if only for the common good, would alone sometimes be sufficient. And truth telling allows a kind of cooperative planning in the face of our ordinary ignorance of what others believe and will do under various conditions that is crucial to successful forms of cooperative behavior. And of course in the real world not everyone is an act consequentialist. Others may refuse to admit someone who is an act consequentialist into groups with beneficent goals, or may not be able to sufficiently trust an act consequentialist to allow for the successful cooperative pursuit of some important consequentialist goal. Effective joint action seems also sometimes to require that some of the cooperators abandon independent pursuit of the goal, even where trust is not in question.[15]

Gibbard introduced another class of counterexamples to extensional equivalence of the sort we need, which indeed introduce other phenomena that are crucial for MAC. Gibbard calls these cases of "surplus cooperation".[16] Imagine that we all cooperate in a very beneficial practice of truth telling. It would be very bad if many of us often lied, which would undercut the practice. But given the fact that almost no one ever lies, it may be beneficial for me to tell a few lies. I won't tell enough lies to undercut the practice with its significant general benefits, but I will grab a little extra utility on the side. There are *some* indirect forms of consequentialism that require that I not lie in this circumstance, while familiar forms of act consequentialism suggest that I should. What are

15 Gibbard (1990a: 157–237) argues that in a society of act utilitarians an established convention of agreement keeping might under certain conditions create a coordination point sufficient to allow a practice of agreement keeping among act utilitarians, and that such a convention could be established among such utilitarians by a teaching practice of a certain sort described there. He also argues more generally that in an act utilitarian society, "the agreements that would be kept include almost all the agreements to which act-utilitarians want to bind themselves" (159). But note the qualifications on pp. 201–205. He suggests that the argument extends to truth-telling on pp. 158–159, but does not explain the extension. Still this does not undercut the extensional inequivalences noted in the text.
16 Ibid., 20.

probably the most intuitive indirect forms of consequentialism fall within the relevant space of this counterexample. In the instances most relevant to our eventual concerns, act consequentialism and indirect forms are not extensionally equivalent for this reason also.

So the first objection to indirect consequentialism fails in an instructive way. Indirect forms of consequentialism are not extensionally equivalent to standard forms of act consequentialism, because of the effects of cooperation. Therein lie the intuitive advantages of the indirect forms.

Let's turn now to the second standard objection to indirect forms of consequentialism. That second objection will play a rather specific role here, since it can be evaded by nonstandard indirect forms. It applies to the standard and paradigmatic forms of indirect consequentialism, and reveals a characteristic difficulty with these forms that suggests that they should be developed in a particular direction.

For instance, both standard rule consequentialism and consequentialist generalization imply that one should do what would generate best consequences if at least most people did it, even though in fact most people aren't going to do it. Since in fact they aren't, this may lead one to neglect great goods that one could in fact actually achieve and great harms that one will in fact cause by acting in accord with the ideal rules.[17] Fafner the dragon is asleep on his ingots over there, and we can get them if we act together, which is a great good. But it would be foolish for you to do your part alone.

Cooperative consequentialism does somewhat better in this regard. It realistically focuses on the actual group of consequentialist cooperators. But[18] there are still structural problems even with cooperative consequentialism. In many morally problematic situations, there may not be any other proper consequentialists around with whom to cooperate. Certainly many humanly important forms of cooperation include individuals who are motivated by other than explicit consequentialist concerns.

This suggests that the best form of indirect consequentialism would focus on all forms of actual but normatively positive cooperation, and not just on cooperating consequentialists. It is relevant that only some people in fact cooperate, but it is also relevant that there are normatively significant forms of cooperation that do not rest on any shared

17 There are possible rule consequentialist responses. See, for instance, Hooker (2000: 98–99).
18 At least if I have understood Regan (1980) properly. See, for instance, the key argument on page 138. But in any case, the indirect consequentialism that I vaguely develop is a variant of cooperative utilitarianism in Regan's sense.

and explicitly consequentialist understanding. Some cooperation is clearly toward evil ends, and should bear little normative weight. But still, cooperative activity can be in accord with basic consequentialist strictures – productive of the good and even more productive than any alternative form of cooperation – even if consequentialist motives aren't explicit in the cooperators.

So the second objection has pushed us in a certain direction, toward a specific form of indirect consequentialism. According to such a view, actual cooperative activity toward good consequences has a kind of normative weight that may properly trump individual maximization of the good. Of course, that is a vague conception. For instance, it doesn't tell us when that cooperative activity trumps individual maximization. But it is a rough start. And it fits nicely with our reply to the first objection, which suggested that the intuitive implications of indirect consequentialism stem from cooperation.

Still, there is a third objection to all indirect forms of consequentialism, and I think that it succeeds. Indirect forms lack a coherent normative rationale. For instance, if maximization of the good is the ultimate rationale of rule consequentialism, then it is ad hoc or incoherent to suggest at the same time that individual acts that maximize the good are yet sometimes wrong because they violate rules whose merely hypothetical general acceptance would have good consequences. Even forms of indirect consequentialism that focus on actual cooperation, such as cooperative consequentialism or the vague improvement I just suggested, seem to face a similar incoherence. It is a fact that consequences are sometimes better served if an individual consequentialist defects from a cooperative consequentialist scheme and leaves its success for others to assure. And an indirect form of consequentialism that assesses such a defecting act only by its fit with that best cooperative scheme seems to lack a coherent consequentialist rationale.

It may seem that there can be no middle ground. Nevertheless, there is a form of consequentialism that enjoys at once the intuitive implications of indirect forms – indeed, that closely tracks the intuitively ideal form of indirect consequentialism suggested by my vague improvement of cooperative consequentialism – and that also has a coherent consequentialist rationale. It can hence evade all the objections to indirect forms.

That form is Multiple-Act Consequentialism, or MAC. It will be developed in the next two sections. The key point is that much cooperative activity is in fact group action. And so the ideal indirect form of consequentialism is extensionally equivalent to an unusual direct form.

The normative advantages of the best indirect forms of consequentialism turn on the effects of actual cooperative activity. But many forms of cooperative activity are group acts. Indeed, we will see that the forms of cooperative activity that are normatively significant in the most crucial ways are group acts. And group acts, like individual acts, can have a direct consequentialist rationale.

MAC is a direct form of consequentialism that focuses on all acts, including group acts. A focus on something like group acts has been proposed before, by Postow, Jackson, and Tännsjö.[19] But MAC's new and most characteristic feature is that it propounds a specific way to balance these sometimes conflicting forms of agency. It will take us a little while to understand the rationale and detail of this novelty that principally distinguishes MAC from familiar forms of act consequentialism. But its general structural advantages over indirect forms are already evident. Group actions can be conjunctions of individual acts, and hence can approximate the cooperative activities invoked by the ideal but somewhat vague form of indirect consequentialism previously sketched. And yet group action in accord with a consequentialist principle can have a direct consequentialist rationale.

Some charge that indirect forms of consequentialism, which are apparently intuitive in their normative implications, in fact collapse into unintuitive act consequentialism. That is wrong. Rather, things go the other way. A novel direct form of consequentialism, Multiple-Act Consequentialism, in fact collapses comfortably into extensional equivalence with the best form of indirect consequentialism, the indirect form that has the most intuitive implications. And it carries its coherent and intuitive direct consequentialist rationale along with it when it does so.

In the next chapter we will see in detail that Multiple-Act Consequentialism can evade the three standard objections to familiar forms of act consequentialism, objections rooted in normative intuitions. But it is also relevant that it is true, independent of any standard objections or normative intuitions about cases. That is the central topic of this chapter.

II

Two non-normative facts require Multiple-Act Consequentialism if consequentialism is true and if its proper specific form has a coherent normative rationale. In other words, those non-normative facts require MAC

---

19   Postow (1977); Jackson (1987); Tännsjö (1998).

if a basic consequentialist principle – for instance, HMP or a traditional utilitarian valuation principle – is true. This and the next two sections show why.

The first key non-normative fact is that there are group acts, performed by group agents. I will begin by clarifying the specific conceptions of group acts and agents to be deployed here. Then I will argue that they are the correct conceptions.

The basic cells of group agents in my sense are what I will call atomic agents.[20] These are more or less momentary periods of human agents, which persist for but a short time. I might also say that atomic agents are brief time slices of people, which have correspondingly short sets of options, as long as such language isn't taken to imply a controversial metaphysical thesis about the nature of personal identity over time.

Of course, momentary agents are not the most familiar agents. Familiar agents persist over whole lives. But my analytic convenience is not really revisionary, nor does it invoke controversial metaphysics. And I don't mean to be fighting over the folk word "agent". Clearly, it makes familiar sense to talk of how someone's options change over time, or how they change their preferences or choices among stable options. Familiar agents try different things at different times. Clearly, quite brief periods of someone's life are sufficient to try for certain options over others, and even to succeed at certain things, and hence can constitute agents with options in my perhaps unusually weak sense. That is all that the notion of an atomic agent requires.

But perhaps the notion of a group agent or of a group act seems more problematic. One or both notions may seem mere metaphors.

Still, since atomic agents exist, we should also grant that temporally persisting individual agents, the most familiar and obvious kind of agent, are a type of group agent. Some intuitive individual actions require a temporally extended series of steps, and this is one type of group action in my sense, which requires extended temporal coordination among temporally distinct atomic agents. In such a case there is a single persisting group agent comprised of many cooperating atomic agents.[21]

---

20 Thanks to Mark van Roojen and Guy Rohrbaugh for the phrase.

21 Let me stress again that I do not take this to imply controversial metaphysical theses about the nature of identity over time. The connection between group agents and temporally extended individual agency is proposed in Jackson (1987). It is also a theme of Korsgaard (1996b) and Rovane (1998). If options and actions that someone can perform include conditions that obtain after their death, or after their agency ceases, then this conception

Common sense also recognizes group actions and agents of other kinds, involving several persisting humans. Certainly there are circumstances in which it makes vivid sense to talk of a group such as an army or a family trying one thing or another, or achieving one thing or another. This gives these groups alternative options in the crucial sense.

Even this very common speech may seem metaphoric. But in our messy concrete world, even individual people are built up from messy fleshy bits in such a way that it is sometimes a somewhat soft or indeterminate fact whether they try one thing rather than another at even a particular time. And certainly it is sometimes a somewhat soft or indeterminate fact whether someone tries something continuously over time. And yet intuitive individual agency is no mere metaphor. So too with group agents consisting of many persons. On the other hand, plausible metaphysical presumptions do rule out some things that my denial that group agency is a mere metaphor might seem to suggest or threaten. If literal group agency were to require some strange nonreducible monstrosity on the order of absolute idealism, that would be out of bounds. But literal group agency doesn't require any such thing. There are a variety of more or less reductive accounts of group agency now in play among philosophers.[22]

So let me refine the notions of group agent and group act deployed here by asking this question: What concrete collections of atomic agents constitute intuitive group agents capable of intuitive group action in my sense? And let me begin my answer with a concrete case of Margaret Gilbert's. She asks,

What is it for two people to go for a walk together? . . . Imagine that Sue . . . is out for a walk. . . . Suddenly she realizes that . . . [Jack,] a man in a black cloak[,] . . . has begun to walk alongside her. . . . His physical proximity is clearly not enough to make [it] . . . that they are going for a walk together. . . . Is each one's possession of the goal that they continue walking alongside each other logically sufficient for their going for a walk together? I would say not. Note that it is possible that each one's possession of the goal in question is not known by either one. Sue may look worried and Jack may suspect that she would rather be alone. . . . [Assume then] that is it *common knowledge* between Jack and Sue that each one has the goal

of a continuing agent would need to be augmented in certain ways. But this will not be important in what follows.

22 Gilbert (1989, 1996, 2000). The essay "Walking Together" in Gilbert (1996: 177–194) is a good introduction to this complex project. See also Bratman (1987, 1992, 1993); Tuomela (1995).

in question. By this I mean, roughly, that each one's goal is completely out in the open as far as the two of them are concerned. . . . [Still] a crucial feature of going for a walk together will be lacking. . . . [S]uppose that Jack starts drawing ahead.[23]

Gilbert suggests that this is a crux, and I agree. If Jack draws ahead and that is the end of it, then there is no joint or group action, no going for a walk together. Their activity isn't entwined in the requisite way.[24]

Still, what exactly is lacking? Gilbert focuses on what she calls a normative though not a moral fact, that Sue is entitled to rebuke Jack.[25] For our purposes, this is an unfortunate feature of Gilbert's account, since we want to rest normative evaluations on MAC noncircularly. But it is also apparently unnecessary to the central spirit of her proposal. What seems crucial is not the fact of a (normative but nonmoral) obligation, but rather merely the mutual acceptance that there is such an obligation. We can believe that there are dragons when there are no dragons, and we can accept or believe that there are obligations when there are no obligations. As I will put it, Jack and Sue must accept that there is a reason to continue to coordinate activity. This will serve to stabilize the activity, but without any genuine normative facts being required. It will also explain the normative criticism and discussion we might expect in such a situation if Jack goes blithely on, and which Gilbert stresses as significant. My modification of Gilbert's proposal is also desirable on other than systematic and metaphysical grounds. It will allow us to respect the obvious fact that there can be group action toward abhorrent ends, where people share a hideous project and hence have no true normative obligations of any sort to continue to coordinate on that project, whatever they may believe.

So that is my rough proposal, a variant of Gilbert's view: Group action and agency exists when there is common action by a number of agents rooted in common true belief that there is a shared goal, and in acceptance by all the members of the group that there is a reason to continue to coordinate activity until the goal is adequately accomplished, a reason

---

23   Gilbert (1996: 178–180).

24   More exactly, it isn't entwined in the requisite way for the existence of joint action when they are still in close proximity in this way and they don't have a plan that requires that they ignore one another.

25   Gilbert (1996: 180). This theme is also present in her central original discussion in Gilbert (1989: Chapter IV, 146–236), though not so clearly marked as crucial. Gilbert also discusses the acceptance by the two cooperators of this obligation, but characteristically calls it *knowledge* of the obligation, which implies the existence of the obligation.

whose acceptance we can expect to occasion criticism and the acceptance of criticism for failure to continue coordination until that point, or until the goal is mutually abandoned.

Despite the fact that I will leave much of the vagueness of that rough proposal intact, as sufficient for our purposes, let me add two complications.

The first is occasioned by Aristotle's distinction between processes and actions, where "processes", like making a rudder, characteristically aim at a goal that extinguishes the activity in question, while pleasant "actions", like surfing, do not.[26] This will matter later on. So let it rather be that all the members of the relevant group accept that there is a reason to continue to coordinate activity until the goal is adequately accomplished, or indefinitely if it is not the sort of goal that will be finitely and definitely accomplished, a reason whose acceptance we can expect to occasion criticism and the acceptance of criticism for failure to continue coordination until the point (if any) at which the goal is accomplished or mutually abandoned.

The second complication is further specification of what I mean by "common action", "coordinated activity", and "sharing a goal", which in turn involves claims about the sorts of motives that underlie group action. Let me begin with the last phrase. Participants in a group action must share a goal. This means that they must each have some motive to pursue a certain perceived good. There must be some description of the content of that shared goal that captures the contents of the goals of each. And the goal must be moralized in a certain weak way. It must be taken to be a good by each of the members of the group, which minimally involves accepting it as a positive reason for choice. It also involves a good-pursuant sentiment, motive, or intention, which I will call "beneficence", I hope without too much violence to ordinary usage. But perhaps mere desire for the goal is enough, when the agent accepts the goal as a positive reason, to constitute beneficence in this sense. Even abhorrent group acts pursue some apparent good.

But what about "common action" and "coordinated activity"? Common action results from coordinated activity in pursuit of a shared goal. And "coordinated activity" is at least hypothetically cooperative. You may not be in communication with, or even know in any very specific way, all the participants in the group actions of which you are part, but you must

---

26   Aristotle (1980: Book I, Chapter 1).

be prepared to cooperate with them in pursuit of the goal of the action should you be in position to do so. You must be prepared to work together to achieve the goal. And this disposition must be supported by accepted reasons, and also by a second sort of sentiment, a second sort of normative motivation that is entwined with the beneficence that supports the goal of the joint project. This is a sentiment of reciprocity that supports group action in pursuit of that goal.

If there is a genuine group act in which we participate, then we will have two sorts of normative involvement in that group, both modulated by accepted reasons, and this will be mutually recognized in certain at least hypothetical ways. And indeed, those two sorts of normative involvement will be entwined. A particular group act will have a particular normative goal, which will occasion one sort of normative involvement, involving beneficence. And it is a *group* act, which will occasion another sort, involving reciprocity. And indeed, in group acts these two sorts of normative involvement will be entwined. We should expect criticism of defections from group acts of two different but entwined sorts, as failures to pursue a good and as failures to reciprocate. In group actions in general, beneficence and reciprocity are entwined. But remember that I suggested in Chapter 1 that benevolence and reciprocity are both basic moral motives. And benevolence is a certain sort of expansive beneficence.

There are more complications regarding the nature of group actions in my sense to which we will return in section V, particularly regarding what it is to accept a reason. And we will return in section VI to issues of moral motivation. But let me now resume our consideration of possible alternative conceptions of group action.

There is a related yet still weaker conception of group action than my own that shares some of its advantages over Gilbert's view. But it is not really workable. Gilbert requires genuine normative entitlements where I merely require acceptance of reasons. But we might merely believe that reasons exist without really accepting them, since accepting a reason in my sense does have some motivational implications.

However, belief in such reasons is not enough for plausible group action. Of course, genuine group action requires that there be some action of a group toward its goal. But even if, say, a group of travelers inadvertently stumbles toward some goal and everyone in the group believes in the existence of some relevant reason to continue cooperative activity toward that goal but without accepting that reason, there is no intuitive group action. If everyone cognitively admits the existence of a reason to criticize the others and to accept such criticism for failure to continue cooperative activity toward that goal, but isn't at all motivated to make that criticism or to accept it, then in fact the travelers aren't trying.

That is the key issue, I think: what things literally try. We may talk of a boat trying to right itself, but we don't really mean it. But we do really mean it when we say a person is trying something over an extended period of time, is on a quest; and that is a group act in my sense. And since groups of many people can also try, such groups too can act. As I said before, sometimes it is a somewhat soft or indeterminate fact whether even some individual is trying one thing or another, but it is still a literal fact that they are trying to do something. So it is still a literal fact that they are intentionally acting.

Belief in the existence of reasons is not enough for trying. And Gilbert requires normative facts that are not necessary. But there are also other competing conceptions of group action. Some require weaker conditions than my own, but don't suffice for trying. Some require richer conditions, but which are not necessary for trying. Begin with notable richer conceptions.

Michael Bratman makes this proposal:

> Shared cooperative activity (SCA) involves, of course, appropriate behaviors. . . . Given appropriate behaviors, what else is needed . . . ? Suppose that you and I sing a duet together, and that this is an SCA. I will be trying to be responsive to your intentions and actions, knowing that you will be trying to be responsive to my intentions and actions. This mutual responsiveness will be in the pursuit of the goal we each have, namely, our singing the duet. You may have this goal for different reasons than I do; but at the least we will each have this as a goal. Finally, I will not merely stand back and allow you to sing your part of the duet. If I believe that you need my help I will provide it if I can.[27]

There is a pair of relatively subtle elements of this view that are slight enrichments of the view I prefer, enrichments to which we will shortly return. But Bratman's analysis of the remaining conditions undergoes some refinement until it becomes roughly this: Each of our paired singers sings their part, intends that they sing a duet, intends that they so act in accordance with and because of meshing subplans for action, and this is common knowledge between them. The stability of that intention in each individual, as suggested in Bratman's other work on the notion of

---

27   Bratman (1992: 327–328).

intention as a plan, provides a certain stability of interaction and ensures certain sorts of mutual support.[28]

The relationship between this element of Bratman's account and my model turns on the relationship between stable intentions and accepted reasons. And it seems that in the central cases for humans, these things do not come apart. There may be animals, or even some humans, who have intentions but don't accept reasons. But, as Bratman himself suggests, you and I seem to treat our continuing stable intentions as reasons of at least some weight.[29] And if we were not so to treat them, then they would be insufficiently stable to constitute stable group activity. So while my variant of Gilbert's view deploys a slightly different basic notion than the weakened Bratman view, there is at least a rough confluence between those two accounts.

Nevertheless, there are the controversial enrichments that Bratman incorporates. The elements developed in the two preceding paragraphs are not enough, Bratman believes, for an SCA. Here's the first reason:

You and I are singing the duet. I fully expect you to get your notes right, and so I intend to coordinate my notes with yours so that we sing the duet. But I have no disposition at all to help you should you stumble on your notes; for I would prefer your failure to our success. Were you unexpectedly to stumble I would gleefully allow you to be embarrassed in front of the audience. . . . And you have a similar attitude. . . . [O]ur singing may be *jointly intentional*; but it is not a SCA.[30]

Bratman can do with the notion of an SCA what he wishes. But this enrichment doesn't seem necessary for genuine group action, for genuine group trying. Perhaps I am just not as nice a guy as Bratman. But I can easily imagine conscientiously engaging in a group action whose goal I favor, and yet hoping secretly that it will all fall apart because you will let down your end while I have kept mine up. Perhaps your embarrassment of that sort is a more significant goal to me than the goal of the group action, even though not something I will actively pursue, indeed not something that I *can* actively pursue. And even without such a secret goal, I can imagine being prepared to do my part in a group action, but not being prepared to go beyond my part to bail you out should you stumble in certain ways. I accept the reasons that underlie the group activity and grant them significant weight, enough weight that I am part of the group

28 Bratman (1987).
29 Ibid., 51.
30 Bratman (1992: 336–337).

attempt, but not as much weight, or perhaps not the kind of weight, that Bratman requires. I am prepared to cooperate, but only so far.

There is another enrichment present in Bratman's account. He requires that continuing action be mutually responsive.

Suppose, for example, you and I lay plans for you to go to San Francisco while I go to New York. We might have a web of intentions concerning this joint activity, a web which satisfies . . . [the preceding conditions.] And our activity of prior planning may itself be a SCA. But if when we each go our separate ways there is no mutual responsiveness in action, our activity is prepackaged cooperation, not SCA.[31]

But the prior planning Bratman notes – which, for instance, might have specified the separate trips as part of a clever plot – is sufficient to constitute group activity in this case, as long as the individuals cleave to the plan. Yet it probably wouldn't be enough if they were still in reach of one another and failed to respond together in even minimal ways to changes in conditions. But such response seems assured by the conditions required for group agency in my sense.

Bratman's notion of an SCA is slightly richer than the notion we need in two ways, as is Gilbert's in one. And both alternative accounts overlap more or less in the notion I will deploy. Now consider one more contrast with a richer and more restrictive account.

Tuomela's account of group action is quite complicated. It is in some ways quite close to my proposal. But one of the complexities of Tuomela's view is that it is formulated in such a way as to suggest that there are more and less central cases of group agency, and the core cases are a bit richer than those I treat as crucial. Social group action, Tuomela believes, requires explicit or implicit agreement, and it requires that the group have an authority system, which determines the way in which individual wills determine group will.[32] In the paradigm cases of social group action, according to Tuomela, there is explicit agreement and also a relatively rich authority "system", a characteristic way in which group members transfer their authority "over some issues to the group, and the group . . . use[s] special operative members to form its will or . . . form[s] the group will through negotiation, bargaining, or voting with all its members acting as operative ones."[33] While an informal group carrying a table counts as a

31 Ibid., 339.
32 Tuomela (1995: 171–227).
33 Ibid., 177.

social group engaged in group action, on Tuomela's view, it is only in a peripheral and somewhat degenerate way. It is only because that group can be conceived as having an implicit agreement and a degenerate authority system.

But these complexities are unhelpful, at least in our context. Many group agents that literally try involve neither agreements nor authority systems of any reasonably literal sort. Still, even the central group agents and actions in Tuomela's sense are simply enriched in a fourth direction from the core that my notion specifies. When an authority system is not accepted by its participants as generating reasons, when so-called implicit agreements are not recognized as reasons by the parties involved, the authority system is unstable and perhaps illegitimate, and there really is no implicit agreement.

We have seen that my notion of group action and agency captures a notion in which Tuomela's, Bratman's, and Gilbert's conceptions overlap, and which can be enriched in various different ways to get the more specific forms of group agency that they favor as an analytical focus. That seems an advantage of my account. And yet it seems rich enough to deliver genuine group trying. It seems to be a minimum account that captures all group acts.

But there aren't just richer notions in the rough vicinity of my notion of group agency, but weaker notions as well, even beyond the case we considered earlier. One way to see this is to consider packs of wild dogs that engage in cooperative and mutually responsive activity that isn't stabilized by anything closely resembling accepted reasons. That may seem to be group action in some recognizable sense. But it seems a form that is uncommon in humans when accepted reasons pull in another direction, and accepted reasons with us always seem to pull somewhere. And when it does exist in humans, its obvious contrast with more robust and ordinary forms shows that it isn't really group action at all. While even humans can engage in some recognizable group activities – for instance, certain sorts of crowd response at concerts, boat races, or jousts – that are not stabilized by accepted reasons and are even indeed such that all accepted reasons pull in another direction, they are then no more intentional actions by the group than an individual's trembling or fainting is intentional. They do not literally involve intentional action or trying.

That is also the cut between group acts in my sense and other weaker forms of collective activity that involve humans. For instance, Jackson and Tännsjö have proposed that there are group or collective actions that are conjunctions of individual actions independent of any sort of shared

41

coordination or goal.[34] The intention behind the collective action is perhaps merely the conjunction of all the individual intentions behind the individual actions that make it up. But this does not suffice for there to be a unified trying of the whole collective, with a unitary content. We might insist on further restrictions on the individual intentions that can sum to form a collective intention. But even shared goals do not suffice for intuitive unitary trying, since we can share a goal but be indisposed to cooperate together in pursuit of that goal. For instance, we can hate one another sufficiently that although we share a goal, we refuse to work together to accomplish it. We are specifically averse to trying to do anything together.

Group action in my sense is a fact. We have now located this phenomenon by reference to four richer and three weaker phenomena, and seen that it plausibly captures the minimum conditions required for literal trying and intentional action by a group. You may have questions about some details of this proposal – for instance, what it is to accept a reason – but we will return to such details in section V, after the preliminary sketch of MAC is complete.

III

The second key fact that undergirds MAC is that there is an overlapping multiplicity of agents and acts. Let me stress sequentially the multiplicity and the overlapping whose conjunction constitutes this key fact.

Multiplicity of agency is immediately evident from the nature of group agency: There are atomic agents, but they are not the only kind. Some acts are parts of other acts, and not necessarily acts of the same agent. Some agents are parts of other agents. This means that there is a multiplicity not only of numbers but also of types of agents. Some agents – indeed, the most intuitive – persist longer than atomic agents. There are various temporal scales of agents in the world – individuals in moments of their lives, during longer periods of their lives, or over whole lives. These are perhaps only somewhat unintuitively (though accurately) considered group agents. But some agents are intuitive group agents, and of various types and scales. There are group acts of families, friendships, corporations, departments, and universities. All of these types of agents are real, and all perform real actions from among real sets of optional alternatives.

34 Jackson (1987); Tännsjö (1989).

42

But this multiplicity is overlapping. Atomic agents in some sense constitute all agents. And particular atomic agents constitute at once parts of more than one group agent. You at this moment are at once part of a continuing person, and also of various organizations, families, and friendships. Indeed, even at a single moment you may be acting in some way that is relevant either by omission or commission to the group acts of all these groups. What you say now may at once support your career and an important family project but undercut your department and the crucial goal of your friendship with Y. In that way, it may at once violate your momentary role in certain group acts and fulfill your momentary role in others.

All the multiple agents of which you are now part overlap in the atomic agent that you are at this moment. And atomic agents characteristically form parts of overlapping but real agents of different types. This overlapping multiplicity is reflected in the reasons accepted by atomic agents, which help constitute them as parts of more than one group agent all at once. You accept at this moment some reasons that help constitute the you of the moment to be part of a persisting agent with persisting activities and plans, but also some reasons that help constitute you to be part of a cooperating department, and others that help constitute you to be part of a cooperating family. But we will come back to that complexity.

The key non-normative facts that support MAC are now before us. We will also presume that there is one basic normative fact, the truth of a consequentialist normative principle that stipulates an ordering of possible options from worst to best. It might be HMP or a classical utilitarian principle, but it need not be. This provides the basic normative information that consequentialist evaluation requires, and also the familiar normative rationale for direct consequentialist evaluation. I will argue in this and the following section that these two classes of facts together require Multiple-Act Consequentialism. I will begin by sketching the principal rationale for the two key tenets of MAC. In the next section, I will discuss pressing questions about the probity of this rationale.

The characteristic normative tenets of MAC are principles governing defection from group action and for balancing conflicting forms of group action. Identifying and motivating these tenets is our immediate goal. MAC specifies right acts for atomic agents, among other things. These acts are constituted as right by direct consequentialist evaluation – in other words, by the application of our basic normative principle for the specification of acts as best among available options. But this direct evaluation must be performed all at once on the options of the multiple genuine agents who overlap in a given atomic agent. This creates the possibility of conflicts, and so we must work toward some mechanism to adjudicate those conflicts. A form of consequentialism that does not provide some mechanism to resolve these conflicts does not provide a coherent criterion of right action. And such a mechanism is what the characteristic normative tenets of MAC provide.

MAC is a form of consequentialism. So its basic principles for adjudicating conflicting forms of agency that overlap in a given atomic agent should be closely rooted in our basic consequentialist normative principle. That is the method or class of methods with a straightforward consequentialist rationale. The two crucial normative tenets of MAC rest on this fact.

One key and characteristic situation is this. Imagine that an atomic agent may, as an individual, defect from a group agent with a good end, a group project that will not be undercut by that single defection. And imagine that in defecting, that atomic agent can grab some extra positive consequences on the side. We are all trying to save the passengers of a sinking ship, but I notice that the rest of you don't really need my help to do it. And I can defect to do some relatively minor positive good instead – say, polish the treasure box. This is a case of surplus cooperation.

There are a variety of possible consequentialist responses to this sort of case. One response is that of the traditional act consequentialist: The atomic agent should defect. Another is that of a rigid group consequentialist: The atomic agent should not defect.

Those are perhaps the natural responses, respectively, of someone who thinks that only actions, options, and agents at the scale of atomic agency are real, and of someone who thinks that only actions, options, or agents at the scale of groups of atomic agents (say, those constituting intuitively persisting individual agents with fixed intentions) are real. But the position of MAC is that all these acts are real and overlapping. Neither defecting nor cooperating has a more direct consequentialist rationale, because neither the group act nor the defecting individual act has a more direct rationale. So we have a real conflict here.

Still, it might be thought that the conflict is to be automatically resolved in cases of this sort in one way or the other. Perhaps the possible defecting act always dominates, or perhaps the group act always dominates, irrespective of the relative normative weight of their consequences. Of course, it wouldn't be appropriate simply to ignore either the group act or the individual defecting act, since both sorts of acts are real. The cases in which an atomic agent should defect from beneficent group acts and the cases in which it should not defect ought to reflect in some way the relative normative weight of the independent atomic agent and project, on the one hand, and the group agent and project, on the other, as assessed by our basic normative principle. But the question is, how should it reflect that relative weight? If the background of cooperative activity is preserved when figuring the options relevant to assessing defection, then that defection gains a little on the side and loses nothing. And so it seems that consequences are served if we defect. But if instead the action of the atomic agent is taken as fixed, with the cooperative activity of the group as the only variable item with normative weight, we get a predictably different answer.

The crucial question is what to properly leave fixed and what to take as properly variable when assessing the situation. The truth is that we must properly let both relevant factors vary, the group act and the individual act. It is those two alternatives that the atomic agent will pursue or shun by its choice, since to pursue a group act is to perform one's role in that act and to defect from a group act is to fail to perform it. And it is only by letting both acts vary that we can assess their relative normative weights. Properly motivated direct consequentialism requires that both acts be ceded relevant weight.

Here is a first pass at how to do that: Compare two situations. In the first situation, the form of cooperative agency in question does not exist, but the atomic agent pursues its alternative defecting project. In the second, the form of cooperative agency exists, but the atomic agent does not defect. The basic consequentialist normative principle will tell us which is better. If it is the first, then MAC says to defect. If it is the second, then MAC says not to defect.

That is approximately right, but it must be only a first pass, because there is too much indeterminacy about what would be the case if the form of cooperative agency in question did not exist. Should we consider the possibility that none of the other atomic agents that constitute the group exist, or that they exist but fail to constitute a group agent, or that they constitute a group agent but adopt some alternative cooperative activity, and, if so, which alternative cooperative activity? A second natural pass is the suggestion that all of the possibilities matter in which either the atomic agents exist but fail to constitute a group agent, or alternatively in which they constitute a group agent but perform some alternative project. A defector is in essence defecting from two group actions, that which constitutes the group agent, and also the particular action of the group. To the first defection, the existence of the group agent is the relevant alternative; to the second, the options of the group agent are relevant. But this second pass is unworkable. There are a number of alternative options that the group agent might have taken, with different values. And at least many of the options that the group agent would not have plausibly taken seem irrelevant to any balancing judgment. And there may not be a fact about which particular option it would have taken if it hadn't taken the one that it did, nor even determinate probabilities that it would have variously taken various alternatives. And, in any case, the complexity of the suggested comparisons is quite daunting, and indeed apparently beyond the capacity of familiar consequentialist valuation principles, including HMP.

So we need a third pass, which heeds the ambiguities of the first pass but avoids the unworkable complexity of the second. We need a single situation that can stand in for defection. Since in a case of genuine normative conflict between defection and adherence, the group agent in question can be presumed to have a properly beneficent project, and since the only group project with special salience is the one actually adopted, the situation relevant to defection is either that in which the group agent doesn't exist, though the atomic agents that make it up do of course exist, or that in which it exists but does nothing. But as far as I can see, these are equivalent. So here is a third and final pass:

To properly assess the conflict presented earlier, we should compare a first situation in which the atomic agent achieves what it can by defection but in which the various other atomic agents that in fact constitute the group agent do not constitute such an agent, to a second situation in which the group agent acts as it does and the atomic agent does not defect. If the first situation is better, then MAC says to defect. If the second situation is better, MAC says not to defect. And our basic consequentialist principle will determine which situations are better than which. I will call this conception of how to handle these conflicts the principle of Very Little Defection, or VLD. As I put it earlier, *one should defect from a group act with good consequences only if one can achieve better consequences by the defecting act alone than the entire group act achieves.* That is the first characteristic normative tenet of MAC.[35]

---

35 There may still be indeterminacies about what would be true on each of the counterfactual conditions deployed in the test. These will create genuine normative indeterminacies according to MAC.

Some indirect forms of consequentialism violate the natural normative rationale of consequentialism because they appeal to the merely hypothetical consequences of other people doing what in fact they will not do. But all consequentialist assessment depends on hypothetical claims of some sort – for instance, regarding what would or would not ensue if a particular act were performed or not performed. According to VLD, we assess the weight of both the group and the individual act in question by reference to the effects of its particular presence and absence, in the traditional direct way. Greater normative weight of that straightforward, well-motivated sort determines which act is properly dominant according to MAC.

In the case under consideration, defection will not disable the group project, and will yield extra positive consequences. So it is natural to worry that defection has a more direct consequentialist rationale, that properly motivated direct consequentialism does not require that we assess the relative weights of the group act and the defection in the way I have claimed.

But recall that individual acts that require a series of temporal steps are group acts in my sense. And remember Castañeda's "paradox" of act consequentialism. The temporal conjunction of two acts of one individual can have excellent consequences even when each conjunct performed alone would have horrible consequences. But commitment to direct consequentialist rationales surely does not forbid beneficent individual acts that are temporal conjunctions of acts that are not individually beneficent; and in fact, one popular response to Castañeda's point has been to conclude that such conjunctive acts are the only proper locus of direct consequentialist evaluation. Likewise, commitment to direct consequentialist rationales does not forbid participation in larger-scale group acts in which one's particular role is not individually beneficent. Of course, our case involves what Gibbard calls surplus cooperation, in which the group act will not be disabled by one's individual defection. But that may be true for all individual participants in a very weighty group act. The very existence of many important group acts, including temporally extended acts of persisting individual agents, requires that atomic agents not defect in cases of the sort under consideration.

The smallest agent is surely not always the dominant locus of direct consequentialist evaluation. You can try to do distinct things with various limbs and fingers. Perhaps, at least with practice, you might become capable of enough dexterity that we could literally speak of your various limbs and fingers trying to do various things. But it would not be appropriate to require that each of your limbs and fingers act individually, as much as possible, in direct accord with the basic consequentialist normative principle, so that you become incapable of unified action even in a moment. Direct consequentialist evaluation of all our actions of various types instead plausibly requires the sort of balancing that I have proposed. It is just that we aren't used to seeing that this rationale extends beyond cases of intuitively individual action such as those invoked by Castañeda's paradox, that it also encompasses group actions incorporating many people.

There is another characteristic normative tenet of MAC. We also need to balance conflicting forms of cooperative agency. And here the considerations we have already surveyed support the following proposal. We can assess the relative importance of two forms of group agency by ranking two situations: In the first situation, the first group agent doesn't exist because the atomic agents in question fail to properly constitute such an agent, but the second group agent has its actual form. In the second situation, the second group agent doesn't exist, but the first has its actual form. *If the first situation is better according to our basic consequentialist principle, then the second form of agency is more normatively significant, and MAC tells us not to defect from that group agent.* I will call this the principle of Defect to the Dominant, or DD. It is the second characteristic normative tenet of MAC.

IV

The last section sketched the main rationale for the key normative tenets of MAC. It rests on the facts of overlapping multiplicity of group agency and the presumed truth of some basic consequentialist normative principle. But those facts may seem to provide even better rationales for various alternatives. So, to buttress my argument, let me consider a few key contrasts and objections.

I've mentioned two already. One way of responding to the kinds of conflict cases presented in the last section is to claim that the conflicting acts of both agents are to be evaluated in regard to their own consequences. So an atomic agent acts rightly if it produces the most good it can as an atomic agent, and a group agent acts rightly if it produces the most good it can as a group agent. This means that there are situations in which not all agents can act rightly, in which if an atomic agent is to produce the most good it can, then the group agents of which it is part

48

cannot.[36] But that, it may seem, is just the way it is sometimes. The situation may seem analogous to a moral dilemma.

But, I reply, any practical ethics must resolve these conflicts in one way or another, whether they count as moral dilemmas or not. So we are forced to some other treatment of these cases.

Another key contrast bears repeating. All agents overlap in atomic agents. So, in a sense, consequentialism addresses its demands to atomic agents in particular. Hence it may seem that in the conflicts I have presented, atomic agents should be concerned first and foremost with the good that they can individually produce. In the first conflict case I presented, they should always defect, contrary to VLD. And there is another natural motivation for this alternative. That first conflict is one of surplus cooperation. There is extra good on the side that defection will achieve, and the group act will still achieve its goal. So consequences overall will be better served by defection.

But, I again reply, it is important to remember that you and I aren't single atomic agents. Since continuing individuals are sequences of atomic agents, and constitute group agents in my sense, and since there are conflict cases of the sort in question in which each atomic agent that makes up a continuing person with a continuing project might have equally beneficent motives to defect while presuming on the continued pursuit by the other atomic agents of the continuing goal, this proposal undercuts the conditions required for the very possibility of effective individual action over time. Since you and I are not single atomic agents, to free atomic agents for individual maximization of the good in the way this alternative suggests is to make our intuitive continuing individual pursuit of the good often impossible. This is not merely an argument from analogy. The conditions required for pursuit of individual projects over time that are normatively protected by MAC and that rationalize that protection are the same as those conditions that protect group acts that involve more than one person.

Still, we should consider other ways to resolve the conflicts in question. It may seem that MAC provides the dominant group act with too much protection. Consider not just VLD but DD. It may be that one's choice is between defections from two group acts. Imagine that the first group act has better consequences, but that those consequences will also be

---

36   Postow (1977) takes this line.

achieved if I defect. But the second act also has good consequences, and those consequences will not be achieved if I defect. And since MAC tells me to defect from the second group, that may sometimes seem inappropriate.[37] Consider this particular case:[38] Two disasters threaten humanity, Big Disaster, which is that we will all be boiled in oil for the rest of our lives, and Small Disaster, a small but nasty war. If a certain group agent in which I participate takes action, Big Disaster will be averted, though in the normal course of things Small Disaster will occur. But if I secretly defect from my role in that group, I can see to it that Small Disaster is avoided, through an individual project that takes time and hence is a smallish group act, and the big group will go ahead and achieve its goal without me. At least in some cases of surplus cooperation, it seems, we should defect from the weightiest group act.

MAC deploys different replies for different cases of this general sort. In the main and simple case, where what is achieved by defection is minimal and clearly forbidden by conditions required for being a nondefecting participant in the big group act, the motivational and other psychological conditions required for being a participant in the group action will generate criticism and acceptance of criticism of such defections. And then MAC will demand nondefection. Since consequentialist assessment of actions requires actions, this is not sufficient grounds for complaint against MAC. But there are other cases of the general sort under consideration in which defection clearly seems appropriate. And I think that those are cases, like that of the two disasters, in which we cannot imagine anyone even remotely like us who participates in the big group agent complaining about the alleged failure of reciprocity, or even having the suppressed disposition to do so. The participants in such a group agent are not disposed either to provide or to accept criticism for that sort of so-called defection. So it isn't really defection at all. The project of the group involves an at least implicit exception for the prevention of unnecessary disasters.[39] Actual group agents involve plentiful implicit exceptions of this sort, I think.

That in turn may generate another worry. Why can't we say in any case of beneficent defection that the group is operating to take advantage of unexpected opportunities, so that in fact the group action is preserved and generates better consequences than would otherwise be available?

37 Tom Carson first brought these cases to my attention.
38 I owe this case to Torbjörn Tännsjö.
39 Hooker (2000) develops this Brandtian move in a rule utilitarian context.

Again, the test is the nature of the criticism that the participants are disposed to give and accept, which helps determine the exact nature of the group action involved. When apparent defections are criticized, then there is no implicit exception.

It may seem troubling that MAC makes issues of right action for an individual turn not only on the consequences of their individual actions but also on the group acts that they are inside, and hence on the details of their motives and the reasons they accept. That delving into motives may seem hard to square with any straightforward consequentialist rationale. MAC treats the following two cases asymmetrically. In the first case, defection from a beneficent group agent will yield some extra benefit on the side. In the second case, defection from a merely beneficent group practice, which does not meet the motivational and other psychological tests I have proposed for group action, will yield some extra benefit on the side. Even if the consequences at stake are the same, in the first case MAC will forbid defection, and in the second it will require it. And the difference turns on the reasons accepted by the individuals in question and their motives. It seems not to turn on consequences.

But, I again reply, direct consequentialist assessment of actions requires that actions exist. And group actions require the extra conditions in question. So the difference in question is normatively relevant.

It may also seem troubling that MAC makes issues of right action for an individual turn on details of what other people do or don't do, and even on details of their motivations and accepted reasons. But the point is that you and I are literally part of group agents that include other people. Just as there are group agents that consist of many temporal periods of one person's life, so too there are group agents that consist of many people. So agents are not as separate as this worry presumes.

MAC, as so far characterized, requires significant respect for the demands of beneficent group actions of which one is already part. How does it tell us to determine which group acts to join? By straightforward consequentialist assessment of the effects of joining, as opposed to available alternatives, constrained of course in the usual way by the tenets of MAC. So MAC treats group acts of which we are already part and other group acts, which are merely possible or which actually exist but of which we are not part, in an asymmetrical way. And this may seem grounds for complaint.

The exact nature of this asymmetry according to MAC can be misunderstood, since future cooperators can be relevant parts of existing group agents according to MAC, as for instance the treatment of continuing individual projects that I have proposed requires. "Existing" is to be read timelessly.[40] But still there is an asymmetry. If A and B are engaging in a group action that produces a good result that would also be produced if C joined, but C can produce a little benefit instead of joining, MAC tells C not to join. But if C joins, then MAC will tell C not to defect, even if C can defect in time to produce that little benefit on the side.

But again, the integrity of the actions in question is what requires this. And it seems that the particular psychological conditions that group actions in my sense require allow MAC to track our intuitive reactions to such cases quite well. We react somewhat differently to defectors from ongoing beneficent group acts than to people who never join. There are different sorts of failures of reciprocity involved. But to see this properly, we will need to consider further details of MAC and its ethical applications. And we will need to turn more explicitly to issues about intuition.

V

The most characteristic features of MAC are now in place. You should defect from beneficent group acts only when you can create more value by the defection alone than the entire group act creates, and when such group acts conflict you should defect from the act that creates less value. And group action exists when there is common action by a number of agents rooted in common true belief that there is a shared goal, and in acceptance by all the members of the group that there is a reason to continue to coordinate activity until the goal is adequately accomplished, or indefinitely if it is not the sort of goal that will be finitely and definitely accomplished, a reason whose acceptance we can expect to occasion criticism and the acceptance of criticism for failure to continue coordination until the point (if any) at which the goal is accomplished or mutually abandoned, and which is supported by entwined motives of beneficence and reciprocity.

That is the minimum mechanism that is necessary to understand the main thrust of my application of MAC in the next chapter. But certain details of those applications, and some of our later discussions, will turn

---

40   The fact that future atomic agents who are a part of your future are inside a group act does not imply that you at this moment are already inside it. It does not imply this even if you at this moment and those future atomic agents are in fact parts of other group acts.

on two details of MAC that are the focus of this section. And you may have some questions about those details anyway.

First detail: Group action in my sense is rooted in common true belief about shared goals and also in shared accepted reasons, and that common true belief is also at least largely about accepted reasons. So you may wonder what it is to accept a reason. The answer is that it is something very like Allan Gibbard's conception of what it is to accept a norm, developed in Chapter 4 of *Wise Choices, Apt Feelings*.[41] But not quite.

Gibbard distinguishes three notions, those of accepting a norm, internalizing a norm, and being in the grip of a norm. While none of these three is exactly what we need, all are close. Consider two cases of motivational conflict that involve different forms of weakness of will. In the first, you think you ought to stop eating nuts at a banquet, but go on eating them. The reasons and norms you accept are in conflict with an appetite for nuts. In the second, in a Milgram-type obedience experiment, you administer the lash to someone at the direction of some suitably impressive authority though you feel some conflict about that, and yet outside of such an experimental situation you would readily assent to norms that forbid you to do such a thing.[42] In the first case, there is a conflict between reasons or norms you accept and other motivations. Gibbard suggests that in the second case, there is conflict between the norms you *accept* and the norms of politeness and submission to impressive authority that you are *in the grip of* during the experiment, and that both norms that you accept and norms that you are in the grip of count as *internalized norms*. But he also says that nonlinguistic animals like dogs can *internalize* norms, and that *accepting* a norm involves paradigmatically human linguistic phenomena, that it is a kind of governance by norms that one would express in spontaneous and sincere normative discussion and that would then be subject to conversational demands for consistency and agreement.

My notion of an accepted reason is the notion of something that is linguistically mediated like Gibbard's accepted norms, and yet something that you can be merely in the grip of in something like his sense. Distinguish two sorts of reaction in a Milgram situation. In the first case, you obey the authority just as a dog would obey. In that case, you accept no reasons supporting obedience in my sense. But in the second and more realistic case, various linguistic pronouncements involving the need

41   Gibbard (1990b: 55–82).
42   Ibid., 56–61; Milgram (1974).

to obey authority and to be polite bubble through your sensibility or unconscious in causally important ways, and you obey, even though you would not reflectively endorse those reasons in ordinary circumstances. In that case, you accept reasons supporting obedience in my sense, but do not accept corresponding norms in Gibbard's sense.

These minor analytical differences answer to the different demands of our theoretical projects. Gibbard is after an analysis of what it is to call or believe something rational. That is a rather stately and all-in notion. But here we need to identify various forms of perhaps conflicting group agency in which an atomic agent can participate, and which may have different degrees of motivational efficacy even in a single person at a single moment. Hence Gibbard's notion of accepting a norm ought to be more stately and all-in than my notion of accepting a reason.

There is another contrast worth noting. Reasons that are accepted needn't even be held as prima facie reasons in any very robust motivational sense. We have some tendency to act on reasons that are accepted, but it may not be a very strong tendency. It may be easily swamped by other motivations.

There are various ways in which the acceptance of reasons mediates our acts, and indeed in some sense it mediates all our acts. First, when human action is psychologically subject to guidance by normative principles in any full and familiar sense, it is governed not just by external sanctions but also by accepted reasons, and adult human action almost always is subject to normative principles in this way. Second, acceptance of certain sorts of reasons helps to constitute group activity of various sorts, as we have seen. Third, even in the absence of group action or obviously normative governance, accepted reasons play a role in our action, as deontologists in the tradition of Kant have long recognized. A human action in any full sense, an action that is intuitively fair game (unlike tics or reflexes) for normative evaluation, is governed by the reasons accepted by the subject, which help to constitute the action as intentional.

This is not to say that there are no limits to the efficacy of accepted reasons in us. There can be conflict in the reasons we accept, and different degrees to which we accept certain reasons. And sometimes we are torn by non-normative passions like hunger, and behave in a way contrary to all the reasons we accept. And sometimes we act out of habit or reflex and not intention. Indeed, it may be that it is only after a certain degree of relatively contingent training and maturity that we come to accept reasons at all. But accepted reasons are important in our actual lives as human agents.

And this is not to say that hungry fish or sharks, who accept no reasons, do not act. I think that wherever there is desire, there is action, and that sharks often have desires. But when animals capable of language accept reasons, then I claim that their agency is centrally and dominantly constituted by that "higher" capacity (which of course in turn plausibly depends on the existence of the capacity for mere animal desire). Our human intentions can be betrayed by our fear or hunger. Not so the attempts of a shark or a goldfish, I think. And even if you think that a long pursuit undertaken by a shark can be betrayed by a momentary passion without being abandoned, still the way in which that shark project is betrayed is not the same as the way in which the continuing individual project of a reason-accepting animal can be betrayed. At the moment the shark defects, it isn't obvious which is the dominant project. And while there are even forms of roughly intuitive group action that do not involve accepted reasons — which, for instance, dogs and some fish exhibit — still for animals who accept reasons, that "higher" capacity is where genuine group trying is crucially rooted.

And in any case, ethics can be practically relevant to action only when that action is either directly or indirectly governed by the acceptance of reasons. That is where ethical discussion can bring pressure to bear.

The second detail of the mechanism of MAC that we need to consider is related to the first. There are different roles in MAC for the reasons that agents accept. Some of the reasons that atomic agents accept help to constitute the existence of effective group agents with one specific project or another. I will call these "agent-constituting" reasons. Other reasons that they accept specify abstract forms of normative governance to which they assent. These are "agent-governing" reasons. Clearly also they must accept reasons (or have some other method) to resolve the conflicting demands of the various agents of which they are part, conflicting demands that are reflected in the conflicts of their agent-constituting reasons. These are "agent-balancing" reasons when suitably specific. Note that there are plausible agent-governing reasons that specify proper forms for both agent-balancing reasons and agent-constituting reasons. They are higher-order reasons. And note also that agent-governing reasons must provide some direction about what group acts to join.

MAC specifies all of these kinds of reasons at once in their proper form by direct application of a basic consequentialist valuation principle, and in a manner reflecting the two characteristic normative tenets of MAC. But let me say a little more about the three kinds that will be relevant to some details of our following discussions.

The principal role of agent-constituting reasons in MAC is the constitution of agents and actions. It is largely in the accepted reasons of atomic agents that group agency is rooted in the world. An atomic agent must not act merely from among its momentary options on the basis of the basic consequentialist normative principle. MAC will demand that it also act on the basis of various principles that constitute appropriate forms of group agency. Direct consequentialist choice by a group agent involves its atomic agents in acceptance of agent-constituting reasons that are different than the basic consequentialist normative principle. As we will eventually see, agent-constituting reasons correspond quite closely to familiar and intuitive individual virtues and also to familiar and intuitive deontological restrictions on action. They are a way in which MAC allows a role for recognizably Kantian respect among cooperators.

There are, at least in the case of some group agents, two kinds of agent-constituting reasons. In these agents, the existence of a particular group agent – say, a corporation – is distinct from its possessing at least certain group projects. Acceptance of reasons that give such a group a particular project will constitute a more refined and specific sort of group agent, so they are still agent-constituting. But I will call them in particular "project-constituting" reasons.

There are limits to the appropriate role of agent-constituting reasons according to MAC. Not all of the group actions and group agents of which an atomic agent is part represent genuine normative demands on that atomic agent according to MAC. That depends on the propriety and weight of the projects of those group agents. Agent-constituting reasons characteristically demand a kind of Kantian respect for fellow cooperators. But Kantian respect even for cooperators is limited according to MAC. For instance, horrific group projects of which we are part should not engage our Kantian respect. And various beneficent group projects of which we are part should engage more of our Kantian respect than others. The core of an account of proper projects and their weight is provided by the basic consequentialist valuation principle that we now assume and by our two key normative tenets, VLD and DD. Those principles are reflected in certain proper agent-governing reasons. But, as we will see, these are not the only appropriate agent-governing reasons.

Agent-governing reasons specify proper choices in a suitably abstract way. They govern appropriate agent-constituting reasons from above, and specify from above proper mechanisms for balancing forms of agency.

There are complexities involving proper projects of agents. For one thing, very good choice from among a set of options may not be choice of the best of those options. Not all options other than the best have the same evaluative status. Some are intuitively close enough to being best to count as pretty fine. In general, we need a rule that tells us when a choice or project is "proper" from among its options, proper in whatever normatively salient ways there are that can be rooted in our general normative principle. But we already have enough complexity regarding proper projects for our purposes, because of a detail I will note in the next section.

Another important complication is that agent-governing reasons must provide some direction about what group acts to join. But I've already noted that atomic agents (among others) should join group acts on direct consequentialist grounds, just as a direct consequentialist rationale would suggest. An atomic agent should join a group act when its individual contribution to the group act will generate the best consequences available to that atomic agent from among its various individual options, presuming that it has no countermanding obligations according to MAC.

The third kind of reasons deployed by MAC are agent-balancing reasons. The actual behavior of atomic agents who accept reasons that constitute conflicting and overlapping group agents will depend in part on the degree to which they accept the various reasons involved, and in part on the degree to which those reasons engage their motivation. But MAC must provide normative guidance regarding the proper way to resolve conflicts among conflicting agent-constituting reasons. These are agent-governing reasons when suitably abstract and higher-order. But when the acceptance of reasons constitutes an actual balancing by an atomic agent of specific forms of group action in which it partakes, the higher-order agent-governing reasons that prescribe a certain abstract form for appropriate balancing have a first-order echo in accepted action-balancing reasons.

VI

There is one remaining crucial detail before we turn to the application of MAC. As we will see in the next chapter, the actual existence of certain sorts of group agents is the key to MAC's response to standing objections to act consequentialism. It is uncontroversial that there are normatively weighty forms of cooperative practice with the nature I will deploy. For instance, the general practice of most people is to refrain from murder, and that serves a mutually beneficial goal. But the crucial fact for MAC is that there be corresponding group acts in my sense.

There are. For instance, refraining from murder is a *negative* group act. And yet it is an act, which we can try together to do. Such group cooperation is also what I will call a "one-off group act". The particular form of cooperation adopted by just those atomic agents simply exists or it doesn't; it involves only those two relevant options. And it is suitably good-producing, since if it does exist, that is better than if it doesn't. While at least some armies have some recognizable existence as group agents independent of shared commitment to at least some particular campaigns they are undertaking, the crucial group agent that refrains from murder is constituted by commitment to that specific project. There is no distinction between project-constituting and other sorts of agent-constituting reasons for such a group. For cases like these, as long as it is clear that the existence of such a group agent is better than its nonexistence, we needn't worry about the fine details of proper projects according to MAC.

I believe that many cooperative moral practices are one-off group acts that are in fact beneficent, which in fact have good consequences. These general normative practices are analogous to Aristotelian processes, and have no finitely achievable and distinct goals. But they have goals, and indeed normative goals, though they are sometimes negative goals. They have goals in a more robust sense than coordinated dog activity, since like all full-blooded human actions they are modulated by the acceptance of reasons. But they are also undergirded by motives of beneficence and reciprocity.

If I am right that these normative practices are group acts, then we will have two sorts of motivational involvement in such practices, modulated by and supporting accepted reasons, and this will be mutually recognized in certain at least hypothetical ways. And indeed, those two sorts of involvement will be entwined. Such a particular group act, a group act that is a kind of normative practice, will have in particular a normative goal, an even more obviously normative goal than other group acts that aren't normative practices, which will occasion one sort of involvement. And it is a cooperative group act, which all by itself will occasion another sort. And indeed, in group acts these two sorts of involvement are entwined. We should expect criticism of defections from such group acts of two different but entwined sorts, supported by motives of beneficence and reciprocity.

As I suggested in Chapter 1, benevolence and reciprocity are both basic moral motives. And benevolence is a certain sort of beneficence. In our broadly beneficent standing moral practices, benevolence and reciprocity are entwined in the way characteristic of group action. Many weighty normative practices meet the motivational conditions required to constitute group acts.

A case may make my meaning clearer. A murderer kills people, and that is a very bad result, which violates our sense of what proper benevolence, or at least beneficent nonmalevolence, requires – a proper goal that we all ought to share, and that at least most murderers often share. The murderer fails to properly acknowledge how bad it is for someone to meet a violent death. But the murderer also defaults from our important general cooperative practice of not murdering innocent people in peacetime, and to do that seems unjust and unfair. It violates our sense of proper reciprocity, and even makes some think he deserves himself to be killed. He defaults from his fair and ordinary role in a group agent. And if he is never inside that group practice – well, then he is merely a vicious animal, some feel. We will return to that point in a minute.

Notice that our motive of reciprocity is entwined with our motive of nonmalevolence. In such a case, we will criticize the defecting murderer out of both sentiments, which are entangled and mutually reinforcing. This case also reveals the mutual recognition of cooperation that group action requires. Our murderer knew that people don't go around killing people, at least outside of situations like war, and that we all aim at the good of avoiding the violent death of humans. It would be absurd for the murderer to deny knowledge of this cooperative practice.

The normative practices that I will deploy in the next chapter to dispose of intuitive objections to act consequentialism are plausibly all of this sort. Moral motivation, or at least our moral motivation, is generally rooted in entwined reciprocity and benevolence, or at least nonmalevolence. And there is the necessary mutual recognition of these forms of cooperation, supported by criticism of defectors and acceptance of criticism. So the common moral practices that I will deploy in the next chapter are in fact group agents in my sense, and indeed usually one-off group agents.

But consider this objection: It may seem that our moral practice of refraining from murder involves no mutual responsiveness. Each thinks that they have reason not to murder no matter what others do, and will continue not to murder even if others do murder. So, it seems, the non-murderers aren't a group agent.

But, I reply, there is some ambiguity in what it is to think one has a reason not to murder no matter what others do. Surely if some people murder, and even fall outside of the group act of refraining from murder, we do not conclude that we have no reason not to murder. But that is not contrary to MAC. Surely there is reason not to murder in most particular cases even independent of the existence of a group act of refraining from murder, since murder characteristically is not productive of the good. But the key question is whether or not there is a cooperative action of not murdering that involves a sentiment of reciprocity, so that we would be somewhat less motivated to refrain from murder if no one else in the world so refrained. And so we would. Another possible test, depending on the details of our project of nonmurdering and whom it is intended to protect, is whether we are somewhat less motivated to refrain from killing those who are outside of that very beneficent cooperative practice. And so, it seems, we are.

There is another worry about this treatment of our moral practices as group agents. In a one-off group agent, there is no difference between the existence of the agent and the pursuit of a particular project. But then it is hard to see how a particular atomic agent could be criticized, on grounds of the kind of reciprocity I am invoking, for failing to hold up their end of a group practice. If they murder, then they are outside of the group act of refraining from murder. Certainly a different past period of your life might be inside the relevant group agent, but if you at the moment are not, then you at the moment do not seem subject to criticism of that sort. While it is possible to be part of a team while not furthering a particular contingent goal of the team, it seems impossible to be part of the group practice of not murdering and yet murder. And indeed, even in the case of the team, you could not properly be criticized for defecting from the team itself simply because you defect from a particular project of the team.

My reply has three parts, and will involve a little more precision about the nature of defection from group acts, and hence about reciprocity. There are at least two relevant kinds of defection from group acts that involve different sorts of failures of reciprocity, and there is a third kind of failure of reciprocity that doesn't involve defection.

In the first case, you retain all the motivational and psychological conditions characteristic of participation in the group act, but you defect for the moment from the common action of the group – say, because of a conflict. When there is no conflict or analogous problem, you return to common action. And if there had been no such conflict, you would have acted in concert with the group. In this case, there is defection that yet leaves you inside the group agent at least to a degree, and criticism and acceptance of criticism on grounds of that sort of reciprocity seems appropriate. Humans are capable of the degree of motivational complexity such that some murderers are yet obviously involved in the one-off group act of refraining from murder, are trying not to murder in some recognizable sense, even as they murder. This is reflected in some complexity in our response to such murderers, so that in one sense they are still inside the reciprocal practice even when they violate it. And even when we are not quite prepared to say that they were trying not to murder even as they murdered, they can still retain a standing affinity to the group practice that generates criticism and acceptance of criticism on grounds of this first sort of reciprocity.

But there are other sorts of defection. Sometimes defection from a group act will put one outside of the motivational and psychological conditions characteristic of that act. One leaves the group. Even in these cases, one is likely to be criticized on grounds of reciprocity. But one will no longer accept that criticism as appropriate when it presumes continued membership in the group. The atomic agent that one now is is outside the group. But still, the agents who participate in the group act of not murdering are not merely atomic agents in realistic cases. They include intuitive continuing individuals who are sufficiently unified to have at least some persisting project. And they too are not only subject to but sensitive to criticism of at least a closely related sort, involving a somewhat different sort of failure of reciprocity. A continuing individual unified by one practice can be inside a second practice at one time and yet violate it at another.

There is yet a third kind of failure of reciprocity that we are inclined to criticize, one that would apply to those humans, if any, who are always completely outside the group act of refraining from murder. They fail to join this group act that they are characteristically obligated to join on strict consequentialist grounds, even though they benefit from it. And in the case at hand, this failure is so severe that they may seem more like sharks than like ordinary humans.

Consider one last objection. Because I will regard our common moral practices, such as telling the truth, or refraining from murder, as a series of one-off group agents, it is plausible to wonder why we shouldn't regard all our everyday moral practices taken together as constituting another one-off group agent. Given the plausibly massively beneficent effects of this agent, MAC would then almost never countenance defection from common moral practices, and so would be more conservative than seems desirable.

There are two replies to this objection, so to speak from above and from below. First from above: "Our common moral practices" may be taken widely, to cover the consensus of all reasonable people over all times and places, or more narrowly – say, merely to cover our particular society with its idiosyncratic current commitments. The dangers of conservatism flow mostly from parochial commitments. But MAC will customarily cede dominance to the broader and hence weightier group agent. Note also that the timeless conception of group agency that MAC deploys means that we may need to consider competing moral practices that span all time, so that the sorts of conservatism in question must be understood in the properly nontemporal sense.

But there is also a second reply, from below: In the case where some component norm of our common moral practice has bad effects, and there is a group agent that encompasses the full practice, still there is another group agent that includes the same atomic agents but eschews that component in its project and has relevantly better consequences on its own. There are two concentric one-off agents, such that the inner one with the less determinate project would have better consequences alone. So the inner agent is dominant according to MAC. Notice that this agent involves the same atomic agents, so this isn't a case in which some individual is defecting in order to gain some more positive consequences on the side. Rather, the same atomic agents participate in two one-off group agents, one nested in the other because its project is nested in that of the other. On the other hand, where each component of commonsense morality has positive effects in the relevant sense, this reply is not available. So MAC is basically conservative regarding elements of our common moral practice that have good effects, whose presence in the common practice is better than their absence would be.

This reply relies on a distinction between individual defection from a group agent in pursuit of surplus good, and reforming defection from harmful elements of a group project. And it may seem that such a distinction cannot be drawn. Reforming defection involves conflicting group acts, but so too would individual defection that takes some time. A reformer may be criticized on grounds of reciprocity by the unreformed. And individual defection in pursuit of surplus good may be rationalized by a suitable adjustment in the general project of a group. The project of the group can be modified to allow an exception.

But still, there is a relevant difference. There are constraints on what can plausibly be considered a concentric group agent that are set by constraints on what can plausibly be considered a component norm of the larger group project in question, which rest in turn on what can plausibly be considered the nature of that larger group project. Extensionally equivalent group projects are not always the same. Tryings involve intensionality and not just intentionality. So not all beneficent reforms in the project of a group agent can be achieved by movement to a concentric group agent, which simply eschews component norms in the project of the first. Individual exceptions are a frequent case in point. And there is a second relevant consideration. The propriety of the elimination of a component norm, its being consequentially helpful, will characteristically depend on the cooperative and to some degree general effects of the group action in question. But an individual pursues surplus good by a relevantly particular and individual defection, though it may involve a different sort of group action that constitutes an intuitive individual agent pursuing an individual project over time. To summarize, there is a difference between a rule change and an exception for an individual participant, and not all rule changes are simply the elimination of a component rule. And so the case of concentric group agents is a rather special case.

With the necessary mechanism in place, and with various immediate worries defused, we can now return to the three standard objections to act consequentialism and to a more concrete discussion of how MAC works.

3

Three Objections

I have given a more or less direct argument for the truth of MAC, which depends on the presumption that some basic consequentialist normative principle for ranking outcomes is true. But we must also see if MAC can evade the three standard intuitive objections to familiar forms of act consequentialism. And we need a better and more concrete sense of how it works.

I

One characteristic objection to act consequentialism is that it is too permissive. It sometimes allows or even requires the violation of very intuitive general moral prohibitions against killing, injuring, lying, and the like. There are two different aspects of this objection. First, it underlines the moral significance of certain sorts of goods – for instance, life, health, and true belief – that may be treated as basic by conceivable consequentialist normative principles but that characteristically aren't so treated. Second, it suggests that the maximization even of such goods as life and health by murder and injury – indeed, even of such goods as the relative absence of murders and injuries – is often immoral.

The gilded city is a gaudy reef of predators and pain. A wave of your wand, and it would disappear. Many lives would be lost today. But the world would be a happier place. Indeed, over time it would suffer fewer murders, and include more people, since innocent visitors would not be killed. Still, you should not wave your wand, even though it would maximize earthy goods like pleasure, happiness, and desire satisfaction to do so, even though it would maximize the number of lives and minimize the number of murders.

MAC provides the resources for an appropriate response to both aspects of this objection. We will begin with the first aspect – the moral significance of life, health, and the like – though our discussion will inevitably creep toward the second. And we will begin abstractly, but move toward a relatively concrete treatment of two cases: our duty not to lie and our duty not to murder.

The three main points I will make are simply stated. First, the relevant intuitive goods are indirectly supported by MAC as necessary preconditions for normatively proper actions. One's role in certain weighty group acts, and indeed the very existence of such acts, will sometimes require respect for these goods – for instance, informed belief – even if the basic normative principle conjoined with MAC is hedonistic in the manner of HMP or classical utilitarianism. MAC will deliver intuitive goods of these sorts even if the only basic normative good is pleasure. Second, MAC can deliver an appropriate account of intuitive normative distinctions between harming and not aiding, which underlie some standard deontological restrictions on action. Third, there are certain normative practices that are weighty group acts in my sense and that forbid certain sorts of activity by participating atomic agents, and these support intuitive deontological constraints. For instance, our normative practice of generally not lying is a group act that is quite valuable, and so VLD and DD will seldom countenance defecting lies.

This and the following two sections will elaborate these three points sequentially, and work toward a relatively detailed treatment of our duties not to lie and murder. In Chapter 8, this general conception will be elaborated in a code that delivers all standard deontic duties.

First point: Standard forms of consequentialism do not assure in the proper way the basic normative significance of certain sorts of goods. Life, true belief or knowledge, ordinary physical and mental abilities, freedom from injury, and freedom from manipulation and imprisonment seem normatively significant in a very deep way. Indeed, they seem very significant even if someone's happiness is served by their own death, false belief, injury, disability, imprisonment, or manipulation. But Multiple-Act Consequentialism helps in this regard, even when conjoined with a classical hedonistic or desire-satisfaction value theory.

Notice that true beliefs, life, physical and mental abilities, freedom from injury, and freedom from imprisonment and manipulation are standardly prerequisite for successful agency. Hence, as a mnemonic and abbreviation, we may call these goods "agency goods". Notice also that among the reasons whose acceptance MAC suggests are some that support or constitute various sorts of agency goods.

The first class of these are among the agent-constituting reasons that constitute conditions for group agency, and hence foster life, freedom from injury and imprisonment, and true belief, both for one's future selves and for other people within group agents in which one partakes. The dead, severely injured, imprisoned, and misled cannot effectively cooperate toward group goals. Agent-constituting reasons that foster agency goods within group agents can be of two sorts. Some support intuitively positive action in support of the goods. But some are negative restrictions against murder, lying, and injuring within the group.

And notice that there are general group actions on the part of at least most humans – or, at the very least, most human noncombatants – that are forms of one-off cooperation specifically eschewing murder, injury, and the like, at least in many circumstances, and that have positive consequences in even a classically utilitarian or otherwise hedonist sense. Most of us are parts of one-off group agents in my sense with such appropriate normative projects. That is a very big fact for MAC, to which we will return shortly.

This general cooperative activity reinforces a second class of relevant reasons that MAC supports. *Other* agents can effectively act toward goals only when their agency goods are respected by us, from the outside. So we can expect that MAC will stipulate that other agents with appropriate projects also involve agency goods that require our support. But even other agents without appropriate projects will in some degree reap the benefits of our own general group acts of refraining from murder and the like.

Indeed, MAC supports agency goods in so many ways that it may seem to threaten double- or triple-counting of such goods. But the weight of agency goods in MAC is felt only indirectly through the mechanism of VLD and DD. Agency goods do not feed directly into assessment of consequences, excepting some complications to which Chapter 8 will return, nor are we to engage in any summation of their value as delivered by various group practices.

MAC also suggests other characteristic complications. For one thing, the projects of agents must be appropriate if their agency is properly to command moral respect in some of the ways I have noted. They must be proper projects in the sense introduced in the last chapter. In general, agency goods are only *genuine* agency goods when they support appropriately beneficent projects. This may seem to provide intuitive but "nongenuine" agency goods with insufficient protection. For instance, while the dead can't act, they of course can't do wrong either. Still, mutual restraint from mutual murder is one very weighty form of group action according to MAC, and it seems a quite minimal level of cooperation required for any effective human group action. And by the strictures of that group act, we restrain ourselves at least to some degree from murdering even those humans who are outside the group act or who defect from its requirements.

Other agency goods, beyond life, require somewhat different and more complicated treatments, both intuitively and according to MAC. True belief is perhaps a paradigmatic case. Let me merely list some of the complications: (i) Those with false beliefs cannot characteristically act effectively. (ii) And there is a one-off cooperative practice of not telling at least explicit lies in many circumstances that has significant normative weight, and is a group agent. (iii) But the way in which circumstances are relevant according to that cooperative practice is complicated and indeed somewhat indeterminate. Our practice clearly allows us to lie sometimes, and sometimes does not determinately either forbid or allow lying. (iv) There is also a finite limit to the normative weight of that practice according to MAC. (v) Independent of that particular general group act forbidding lying, MAC suggests that true belief will have special normative significance only when it somehow supports the effective pursuit of proper goals. (vi) MAC also recommends lying within a group agent with a consequentially harmful project, if that harmful project overbalances the normative weight of our general group act eschewing lying or if that general act doesn't forbid that particular sort of lie. (vii) False belief only *characteristically* undercuts effective action. Sometimes group activity toward a proper project will be furthered by lying of some sorts within the group. (viii) And our one-off group act eschewing explicit lying is not the only general form of cooperative practice regarding truth telling that is possible. Perhaps a general group act that required positive truth telling in support of proper projects, and also forbade misleading in similar circumstances, would be better, and it may also be a form of group action of at least limited extent that one can foster by more or less prospective cooperation. (ix) And prospective cooperation may be very weighty on the timeless conception of relevant group agents implied by the treatment of continuing agency as group agency. (x) Another complexity is that, even independent of the proper forms of our one-off general group acts regarding lying and truth telling, the positive demands of true belief go beyond an absence of lies, especially within certain forms of small-scale group agent with weighty proper projects and in support of the proper projects of other agents.

This is a complex set of analytical factors. We will return in section III to a more concrete discussion of our obligations regarding lying according to MAC. But the immediate point is that MAC requires a relatively complicated story about when apparent agency goods like life and true belief require moral respect. They are genuine agency goods when in support of appropriate projects, at least when the proper projects in question are not outweighed by other projects. And they also properly command moral respect when they are otherwise protected by general group acts with proper projects. And agency goods can be fostered by accepted reasons recommended by MAC in a variety of different ways – for instance, by negative restrictions on action as well as by positive exhortations. And there are also the various complications I have just noted for the case of true belief.

This general picture is in accord with any determinate strictures of our reflective common sense, I believe. MAC grants truth and life and other agency goods a more or less fundamental normative status, but a more complex and nuanced status than some traditional theories allow. And these complexities are intuitive, as we will shortly see in suitable detail.

Another relevant intuitive complexity of MAC is this: MAC suggests a two-tiered account of what I will call *fundamental* normative goods. At the first and most basic level is whatever value is recognized in the basic consequentialist principle with which it is allied. It might be pleasure or desire satisfaction. But there is no action in accord with a basic principle unless there are agents. And effective agency in accord with a basic normative principle requires agency goods. Genuine agency goods are fundamental according to MAC, even if not quite basic. So too are other agency goods protected by beneficent one-off moral practices that are group agents. Some think that we ought first to maximize agency goods and only then turn to a secondary maximization of familiar consequentialist goods like pleasure and pain. Something like this has been suggested, for instance, by David Cummiskey.[1] But MAC instead grants a kind of deontological status to respect for certain agency goods within group agents and even among distinct agents, at least when the agency goods are in the proper

---

1 Cummiskey (1996).

service of basic value, and also grants other forms of nearly deontic respect to fundamental agency goods protected by weighty group acts that we are inside. It organizes two intuitive types of goods in a somewhat different but still plausibly intuitive way.

Another way to look at this structure of fundamental goods is by comparison to both standard utilitarian and Kantian treatments of nonhuman animals. Nonhuman animals can feel pain, but for the most part cooperation with nonhuman animals is impossible. So standard utilitarianism suggests that the standing of nonhuman animals as moral patients is basically the same as that of humans. But standard Kantian or contractarian views suggest that they have no normative standing. MAC allows something more complex, and indeed more intuitive, at least when allied with a classical value theory. Nonhuman animals have moral standing of indeed the primary and basic sort. Depending on the details of the beneficent group acts of humans, they may even have a further derived status as moral patients that should engage nearly deontic respect from those humans. But humans who engage in proper group action, or indeed individual activity, have a second sort of fundamental but not basic normative status, which indeed makes them moral patients in another but more exalted sense. They can lose some of this status by the viciousness of their projects. They can lose the respect due to proper cooperators and beneficent agents. That respect is not unconditional respect. Still, no matter how vicious they are, they retain the basic normative status of any sentient animal, and that is a real normative status, which enjoins a real though different form of unconditional respect. The picture of fundamental normative goods suggested by MAC is somewhat complicated, but it is complicated in an intuitive way.

In sketching the forms of respect that agency goods deserve according to MAC, we have edged toward an answer to the second aspect of our objection. MAC suggests a nearly deontological respect for agency goods within forms of group agents with appropriate projects, and also among distinct agents with proper projects. It may even suggest a nearly deontological respect by us for these goods wherever they are found, depending on the details of our own general moral practices that are group acts. Indeed, there is a degree to which it is arbitrary whether we complicate the account of agency goods, or instead complicate the account of roughly deontological respect that putative agency goods deserve. But let me now focus our discussion more closely and directly on that second aspect of our standing objection.

II

The second and perhaps most characteristic aspect of our first standard objection to act consequentialism reflects the inclination of common-sense morality toward what Samuel Scheffler has called "agent-centered restrictions".[2] Agent-centered restrictions forbid particular agents from doing certain things, even if the cost of their failure to do such a thing is that many other acts of exactly the same sort will be performed instead by others. For instance, an act that tortures the innocent may seem intuitively forbidden. It may seem intuitively forbidden even if the certain cost of refraining from that act of torture will be that many other people commit many such tortures.

Some may object that such situations are not coherently described, because to fail to perform the first act of torture is in fact to commit the others. But common sense incorporates a series of normative distinctions between acting and refraining, doing and allowing, harming and letting be harmed, which may be deployed to defend this aspect of the objection against that resistance, and which play other crucial roles in our commonsense morality. They are our focus in this section. We will complete our discussion of agent-centered restrictions only in the next section.

My argumentative situation is delicate at this point. In the end, as will be seen in Chapter 7, I will not admit that there is a deep distinction between acting and refraining, nor between omitting and committing. Consequentialism, in all its direct forms, inevitably avoids such a deep distinction. And yet I must deliver some normative differences between these things if consequentialism is to be suitably intuitive. MAC can deliver what is required, not too much and not too little, though it will take a little time to see this properly.

One way we can study the interaction of MAC and these distinctions is to grab a ride on the Trolley Problem. And so into the belly of the deontological beast we go.

The fashion for philosophy rooted in intuitions about concrete cases has characteristic dangers. To focus on a few cases can mislead, since other cases may push in different directions. And the absence of a systematic account can hide crucial difficulties. Nevertheless, it is such cases that will be our immediate concern.

2 Scheffler (1982).

To get a sense of how MAC can help with the Trolley Problem, we will begin with a quick review of what it ideally should deliver. The literature on trolleys began with Philippa Foot's classic "The Problem of Abortion and the Doctrine of Double Effect."[3] But I will emphasize the also classic development of Foot's cases by Judith Jarvis Thomson in "Killing, Letting Die, and the Trolley Problem" and "The Trolley Problem."[4] There are a number of concrete examples to which we will need to attend in order to collect a set of relevant intuitions. The puzzles of the trolley literature arise from clanging together the diverse intuitions generated by these various cases.

First, there is the case of Alfred and Bert. It is the standard assumption within the trolley literature that there isn't *always* a morally relevant difference between otherwise identical cases of killing and letting die, and that this case shows that.

[I]magine that

(1) Alfred hates his wife and wants her dead. He puts cleaning fluid in her coffee, thereby killing her, and that

(2) Bert hates his wife and wants her dead. She puts cleaning fluid in her coffee (being muddled, thinking it's cream). Bert happens to have the antidote to cleaning fluid, but he does not give it to her; he lets her die.[5]

Since these actions seem equally abhorrent, it seems that we should conclude with Thomson that the difference between killing and letting die isn't always morally significant, which is of course not at all to conclude that it isn't sometimes quite significant.

Second, there is Foot's original Trolley case, and its slight but significant modification in Thomson's Bystander case. Here is Thomson's statement of the original Trolley:

Suppose you are the driver of a trolley. The trolley rounds a bend, and there come into view ahead five track workmen, who have been repairing the track. . . . [Y]ou must stop the trolley if you are to avoid running the men down. . . . [T]he breaks don't work. . . . Now you suddenly see a spur of track leading off to the right. You can turn the trolley onto it, and thus save the five men. . . . Unfortunately, . . . there is one track workman on that spur of track. He can no more get off the track in

---

3 Foot (1967). This is reprinted in Foot (1978).
4 Thomson (1976, 1985). Both articles, as well as Foot (1967), are reprinted in Fischer and Ravizza (1992).
5 Thomson (1976), in Fischer and Ravizza (1992: 69).

time than the five can, so you will kill him if you turn the trolley onto him. Is it morally permissible for you to turn the trolley?[6]

With the majority, I intuit that this is morally permissible. Some think that this is a matter of choice between killing one and killing five, since as the driver of the trolley you are in charge of a hurtling object that will certainly kill someone. Some disagree. So, for clarity, let's introduce the slight modifications that give us the Bystander case:

[Y]ou have been strolling by the trolley track, and you can see the situation at a glance: The driver saw the five on the track ahead, he stamped on the brakes, the brakes failed, so he fainted. What do you do? Well, here is the switch, which you can throw, thereby turning the trolley yourself. Of course you will kill one if you do.[7]

With Thomson and the majority, I intuit that it is morally permissible for you to turn the trolley. Hence sometimes it is morally permissible to kill one to save five. Indeed, though this is apparently not the consensus view, it seems to me to be morally mandatory in this case, though I would hesitate to blame someone who failed to turn the trolley, because of the moral difficulty of the situation.

But compare our third case, Transplant:

[Y]ou transplant organs, and you are such a great surgeon that the organs you transplant always take. At the moment you have five patients who need organs. . . . If they do not get those organs today, they will all die; if you find organs for them today, they will all live. . . . [A] young man who has just come into your clinic for his yearly check-up has exactly the right blood-type. . . . Lo, you have a possible donor. All you need do is cut him up and distribute his parts among the five who need them. You ask, but he says . . . no. Would it be morally permissible for you to operate anyway?[8]

With the majority, I intuit that this would be morally impermissible. It is not always morally permissible to kill one even to save five.

To underline this fact, consider a fourth case, Fat Man:

[Y]ou are standing on a footbridge over the trolley track. You can see a trolley hurtling down the track, out of control. . . . [T]here are five workmen on the track. . . . [Y]ou know of one certain way to stop an out-of-control trolley: Drop a really heavy weight in its path. . . . It just so happens that standing next to you

---

6 Thomson (1985), in Fischer and Ravizza (1992: 280).
7 Ibid., 281.
8 Ibid., 280–281.

on the footbridge is a fat man, a really fat man.... [A]ll you need to do is give him a little shove.[9]

Here again I have the intuition, shared by almost all, that this would be wrong.

So we have one case, Albert and Bert, which shows that sometimes there is no morally significant difference between killing and letting die, and a second case, Bystander, in which it seems at least permissible to kill one to save five. But we have two other cases, Transplant and Fat Man, in which it seems impermissible to kill one even to save five.

Consider two more cases, which introduce other factors to which we will return. In reaction to the first new case, which I will call Bombing, many intuit that it is morally permissible to bomb an enemy factory while foreseeing but not intending that noncombatants will die, as a matter of collateral damage. But then consider Hospital Gas: "Suppose . . . that there are five patients in a hospital whose lives could be saved by the manufacture of a certain gas, but that this inevitably releases lethal fumes into the room of another patient whom for some reason we are unable to move."[10] In this case, with the majority, I intuit that this action would be wrong, despite its abstract similarity to Bombing.

There is a large literature that attempts to develop general explanations that support our intuitive normative reactions to this range of cases. But none of the obvious explanations generates intuitive results across the board. If negative rights are sometimes intuitively stronger than positive rights, still that difference doesn't seem relevant in the Bert and Albert case, and it apparently doesn't differentiate Bombing from Hospital Gas. If sometimes omissions that fail to save lives seem preferable to commissions that take lives, still one properly acts in the Bystander case to kill one, and that also doesn't explain the moral symmetry of Bert and Albert. If sometimes we have limited responsibility for foreseen but unintended consequences of our actions, that doesn't explain our reaction to Hospital Gas. If sometimes the temporal order of a harm and a causally connected good matters, that doesn't explain our differential reactions to Hospital Gas and Bombing.

Multiple-Act Consequentialism provides a new kind of general explanation of our various responses to these various cases. It is what might be called a framework explanation, which suggests the normative relevance

---

9 Ibid., 288.
10 Foot (1967), in Fischer and Ravizza (1992: 65).

73

of a variety of different factors in different cases. I believe it is in a sense a deeper level of explanation than those we have just canvassed, which explains why considerations such as those are important in some cases but not in others.

Still, it would be wrong to claim too much for MAC in this context. It is to a weak degree revisionary. It requires that not all our normative intuitions about cases be probative, though we will see that it does allow for the intuitive normative differences introduced through our survey of famous concrete cases. This slightly revisionary nature seems unobjectionable, since we *cannot* provide a coherent account that requires no revision at all in our intuitions about all trolley cases.

Why is this? For one thing, the order in which people are presented with concrete cases can affect the moral intuitions that the cases generate. People seem to remember their initial response, and to try to preserve consistency in their responses.[11] Second, Unger has shown that cases that involve four options can yield an intuitive response that is plausibly inconsistent with the intuitive response to analogous two-option cases that involve merely the deletion of two options from the first.[12] Third, there are also other groups of cases that show together that sometimes something is wrong with our intuitions. Let me explain this third point. Imagine a case like Fat Man, but in which the trolley is merely slowed after running him over, and hence slowly comes to a stop before the five workmen stuck on the tracks. Still, we retain our intuition that pushing him onto the tracks to save the five is wrong. Now imagine instead that the fat man is tied to a side track, which runs back onto the main line before the point at which the five are stuck on the main track. Our choice as a bystander is between letting the trolley run on straight to kill the five, or turning it onto the side track, which will slow it down sufficiently when it runs over the fat man to save the five, even though the trolley will come back onto the main track and stop just before them. At least if that case is presented after the original modification of Fat Man, most intuit that this is also wrong. Because we will run into this case again, I will give it a name, Sidetrack. Now imagine a third case, Loop. This is a lot like Sidetrack. The track that is off to the side, with the fat man tied down, continues on beyond where he is tied to the tracks. But rather

---

11 Unger (1996: 92).
12 Ibid., 88–94. Perhaps this is due to the fact that cognitive processing of complex cases involves a certain sort of abstraction and simplification, at least when that effect isn't swamped by the order of presentation of cases.

than coming back onto the main line immediately, as in Sidetrack, it instead loops around and comes back to the main line behind our five workmen.[13] If we do nothing, the five will be run over directly. If we turn the trolley, it will be slowed by running over the fat man before it gets back to our five, though it will come at them from behind, and would have run them over from that direction if it hadn't run him over. At least if presented this case after the preceding cases, most people intuit that it is wrong to turn the trolley onto the sidetrack, because the difference in the way in which the track is arranged in Sidetrack and Loop seems trivial and irrelevant. But notice that Loop is quite like Bystander, at least if there is a fat man on the sidetrack in that case, but with the slight addition in Loop of some unused track connecting the track running beyond the fat man back to the main line. It is hard to believe that unused track could be of grave moral significance, but in Bystander most intuit that it is permissible to turn the trolley. These cases together suggest that we cannot coherently treat all our intuitions about trolley cases as probative and stable.

Despite the fact that some revision of our intuitions about cases is inevitable and desirable, still Multiple-Act Consequentialism provides a mechanism to explain the intuitive differences among the various standard cases with which we began this section. In essence, MAC suggests a range of small factors that are sometimes relevant, and may sum together between various cases in various ways to deliver intuitive results. To develop this conception, first let me note some kinds of factors that MAC suggests may be relevant. Then I will go on to apply this analytical framework to deliver some of the more difficult intuitive differences among the standard cases with which we began.

Possible factors: First, when there is a particular group agent present in a case, that may cause a difference in the proper normative assessment of such a case according to MAC. For instance, it might allow us to deflect a risk within a cooperating group agent but not onto an outsider. Or, alternatively, it might be specially important to deflect the risk outside the group in order to defend group cooperation. Notice that people tied together on tracks might come for that very reason to share accepted reasons that constitute them as a group agent of some sort, for though their group attempts might be ineffectual, still they might be disposed to cooperative activity. Or, alternatively, it might be that because they are tied down, the individuals are in some ways not cooperating agents and

---

13   Loops like this were introduced by Thomson (1985). See Fischer and Ravizza (1992: 285).

hence not subject to the customary level of normative protection that that provides.

Second, it might be that the exact form of proper treatment of the deflection of risks and the like depends on a general cooperative practice about such things that is itself a group agent, a group agent that constitutes a general manner of handling the deflection of risks. If we all agree that people shouldn't be thrown onto the tracks when in the position of the fat man in the original Fat Man case, if we have a one-off cooperative practice that forbids that, that will be normatively relevant according to MAC when the practice meets the conditions, noted in the last chapter, required for group agency, and when it is a proper project.[14] Deontologists may not be happy that the propriety of such constraints is dependent on our actual practices. But deontological intuitions formed within contrary practices that were also suitably beneficent would plausibly be contrary to intuitions formed within our own.

Third, temporal order is tied up with the existence of group agents in interesting ways. Perhaps only those who precede an event can cooperate to prevent it.

Fourth, there are obvious differences between the forms of group agency that link people who share a hospital as doctors and patients and those that link or fail to link different populations at war.

While, as I've said, MAC provides a mere framework explanation of trolley cases, in which specific group acts suggest the importance of different sorts of factors in different cases, it certainly suggests the general overall importance of groups. That in itself may seem like another general explanation of our intuitions, on a par with the distinction between commission and omission or the Doctrine of Double Effect. And indeed, both Robert Hanna and Peter Unger have suggested that at least many of our different intuitions about these concrete cases can be generally explained by reference to our treating various groupings of people as normatively salient. We intuitively distinguish between innocent bystanders – like the fat man on the footbridge – and those already at risk in a situation – say, those tied to the tracks in the same area. Unger thinks that this is a cognitive distortion.[15] But Hanna thinks that it is appropriate.[16] MAC suggests a kind of middle course. Certain groups – namely, those constituting group agents or recognized as

14 Harris (1975) introduced the possibility of alternative risk-sharing practices.
15 Unger (1996: 96–101).
16 Hanna (1992: 320–336).

salient by specific group practices constituting group acts – are quite normatively salient, and may in different cases contribute different sorts of normatively relevant factors. But other intuitive groups may introduce cognitive distortions.

By way of contrast, consider Hanna's general account: There are moral situations to which some people are bystanders and in which some people are participants. It is impermissible for anyone to force a bystander to become a participant victim in a trolley case, but it is permissible for a participant to harm other participants in order to establish a better outcome.[17] The fat man on the footbridge is a bystander, but anyone already tied to the relevant tracks is a participant. So it is okay to turn the trolley and save five at the cost of one, but not to push the fat man onto the tracks.

I think that this is more or less right. Hanna's account of moral situations is expressed in a way that suggests rich, and I think implausible, metaphysical presumptions.[18] But I believe this to be an avoidable aspect of his presentation of the view. Still, while he provides hints about the distinction between bystanders and participants,[19] he does not provide an account of that distinction that would allow some independent rationale for our intuitive normative judgments about the cases. He instead suggests that we should work backward from our intuitive normative judgments about cases to the distinction.[20] This is problematic, because sometimes our intuitive judgments are affected by cognitive distortions. Remember the importance of the order of presentation of cases, and the other forms of incoherence in our judgments about cases noted earlier, which sometimes seem to be due to distortions introduced by grouping. What's more, we need an account that rationalizes our probative intuitive judgments about such cases, not an account that merely summarizes our intuitive judgments.

MAC provides a criterion for the distinction between properly relevant participants and bystanders that yields a rationale for our probative intuitive reactions to cases, and which suggests that while certain intuitive groupings introduce cognitive distortions in the way that Unger claims, many do not. It provides a kind of refinement of Hanna's general proposal, but one that also invokes specific distinct factors of the sorts noted

17 Ibid., 330.
18 Ibid., 329.
19 Ibid., 329–330.
20 Ibid., 333.

earlier, and that provides a reductive criterion for the bystander-participant distinction yielding a suitable rationale for a coherent and properly intuitive response to all trolley cases.

Still, so far I have only made rough suggestions about a kind of mechanism that MAC can apply to trolley cases. What may be more telling is an application of MAC to deliver some particular commonsense intuitions about differences between particular cases. As I've said, unlike standard attempts at unified explanations of all our intuitions in trolley cases, MAC suggests that a variety of small factors that involve group action in different specific ways can work together to generate significant differences in the moral status of different actions. But we need to see how this works in more detail.

Let's begin with cases that are intuitively far apart. Foot's original Trolley case and Transplant certainly occasion different intuitions. But notice that a trolley driver is a professional who is plausibly specially responsible for the trajectory of the trolley by virtue of a specific cooperative practice. This may constitute a group action, underwriting a special professional obligation to turn the trolley in the direction in which it will do least harm. If that isn't evident, we will discuss the interaction of MAC with special obligations in section IV. Notice also, coming from the other direction, that the doctor in Transplant is also a professional member of a cooperative practice providing health care – indeed, of a number of overlapping cooperative practices of that sort constituting various group agents – who has special obligations to patients in the hospital, and in general not to cause death.

But those are not the only relevant moral differences between these two cases. To the end of identifying some of the other factors, consider intuitively intervening cases – for instance, Bystander and Fat Man. It seems morally permissible, or even perhaps required, to turn the trolley in Bystander, but morally impermissible to push the fat man onto the tracks. How can MAC deliver this difference?

We have, I think, a real intuition that supports the Pauline Principle, the principle that you should not do evil (like pushing the fat man in front of the trolley to his certain death) even if a greater good would come of it (the life of the five), while on the other hand it is sometimes appropriate to do some great good while foreseeing that a smaller evil will come of it (like turning the trolley in Bystander). We also have, I believe, a real intuition that you shouldn't drag an innocent person like the fat man into a situation like the one in question against their will. We need to be a little careful, however, in how we handle these intuitions. For one thing, in real-life situations, when you do evil as a means to the good, the temporal priority of the evil makes it more certain than it would be if the temporal order of the good and evil were reversed. It is hard to control for the effects of this fact when considering hypothetical cases. Second, I have already noted that not all our intuitions about cases like these can be treated as probative. Still, there is something behind our intuitions that suggest some normative weight for the Pauline Principle and for the distinction between doing evil and refraining from doing good. But MAC can deliver that weight.

Recall, in this order, Fat Man, Sidetrack, Loop, and Bystander. We start with a case in which action to save the five seems intuitively quite wrong, and then end up with a case in which it seems permissible and even maybe required. Here is an analysis of this phenomenon according to MAC:

Between Fat Man and Sidetrack, these factors are relevant: (a) There is a basic scheme of group action of which almost all of us are participants, which is a kind of cooperative agreement not to draw uninvolved outsiders into such a situation against their will. If our generally accepted background practice were different – if, for instance, we had all agreed to share risks in some more rational but still intuitively very scary way – that would make this factor irrelevant. But under actual conditions it is relevant. And it is apparently very weighty by the basic normative tenets of MAC. (b) There may also be a second set of factors that MAC can deliver in at least some cases that meet the general description we are considering, though I am less confident of this. The fat man in Fat Man is outside the originally affected group. But at least if the people on the tracks are conscious, they may share acceptance of reasons supporting group action to get at least some of them to safety. They may be a group agent of one kind. Of course, on the other hand, the practical salience of this project may be minimized if they are tied down, and a person tied to a sidetrack will only plausibly share a relatively abstract group project and accepted reason with those on the main track. But there may also be another intuitively salient group that includes those who are stuck on the track and the choosing agent. And it is plausible that the fat man will not share acceptance of the relevant reasons with that group. He would then be in a recognizable sense outside of the relevant group that includes all of those on the tracks, and the other relevant group that includes those on the tracks and the choosing agent. And these groups correspond to certain group agents in my sense, which it is reasonable to think have proper projects. Notice how the normative details according to MAC will turn on subtleties about the reasons accepted by the various individuals present in such a case, as well as other psychological conditions, their attempts, and the normative weight of their group projects. But these complexities do not seem obviously unintuitive.

These two factors, or at least the first, introduce some weak normative differences according to MAC. But weak differences are the most that commonsense intuition finds between these cases anyway. As we move from Sidetrack to Loop, all those on the track seem even more closely linked by these weak factors.

Between Loop and Bystander, there are various factors that interfere with the probity of our intuition – for instance, the unreality of the very clear risks in trolley cases and also temporal prejudice. But at least the temporal factors might introduce a genuine difference accommodated by MAC, since almost all of us plausibly share a general scheme of group cooperation in accord with something like the Pauline Principle that plausibly constitutes a form of group action. We have a practice in which it is one thing to deflect a harm so that it kills someone else and quite a different thing to deflect the harm by killing that someone. And that practice is a normatively weighty group act we share, with a plausibly proper project.

I have been exploiting intuitive advantages that accrue to MAC because of our standing cooperative practices for distributing risks and harms. Alternatives are scary and unfamiliar. Still, these actual practices have costs also, and possible alternative practices might conceivably have better consequences. It is relevant according to MAC which cooperative practices of this sort we actually have, as long as they are group agents, but they must also have proper projects, must have basically beneficent results, in order to carry normative weight according to MAC. And it is also relevant that there may be prospective and alternative forms of cooperation that would have better results. Of course, our practices for distributing risks and harms are plausibly one-off group agents. And then the question is merely whether they are better than their absence. But even so, I believe that the background practices that give priority to leaving the fat man undisturbed are at least of questionable propriety according to MAC when it is allied with some plausible basic consequentialist principles, including HMP. But if they are properly beneficent – which, after all, common sense does presume – then MAC can deliver the intuitive differences in our reactions to Fat Man and Bystander. And if they are improper, then commonsense intuitions on this topic are suspect.

There is no deep difference between killing and letting die introduced by the mechanism of MAC, but rather a series of small differences that are indeed dependent in certain ways on our contingent practices and their results. We have seen a variety of small phenomena that intervene between Transplant and Bombing and between the other four cases that are in some intuitive sense between them. They create normative differences according to MAC, which track intuitive differences between the cases.

There are other, similar factors that MAC suggests may be relevant in other cases. For instance, we intuit that the presence of other human agents in a causal chain breaks to a degree our responsibility for the outcome of that chain, at least if they are not turned into mere instruments or means by threats or the like. But MAC might cede those other human agents a special normative role of that sort if there is a form of general group agency that makes it especially those others' business to interrupt such a chain. This might be assured by a general cooperative scheme, analogous to those for distributing risks and harms, which is a group agent with a proper project, or by the structure of a more particular and local group agent. To the degree that someone in the intervening chain fails to be a relevantly cooperating agent, this might undercut, according to MAC, the significance of their presence in the chain for the commutation of our responsibility for the relevant outcome, though that would depend on the details of the project of that group agent.

III

We have seen that MAC can deliver agency goods like true belief, and that it underwrites to some degree intuitive commonsense distinctions between killing and letting die and the like. But there is one last and key aspect of the standard deontological objection to act consequentialism under consideration. I will focus in this section on this aspect, on the agent-centered, deontological restrictions themselves. And I will treat in some detail the particular cases of lying and murdering.

MAC delivers agent-centered restrictions that are yet supported by direct consequentialist evaluation of options. Begin with this case: Nearly all of us participate in a group act of refraining from torture, which has significant normative weight even according to a classical utilitarian valuation principle or HMP. So VLD and DD will seldom countenance defections from that group act when conjoined with such a basic normative principle, even if a particular act of torture would serve the good – indeed, even if it would prevent several other tortures.

And this point can be extended. Group acts of refraining from violation of various intuitive deontic duties that directly protect agency goods like health and knowledge will yet characteristically have weighty overall positive consequences even according to plausible forms of hedonism. And remember that for one-off group acts this is all that is required to invoke the protection of VLD and DD. And we saw in section I that MAC generates various other kinds of respect for "genuine" agency goods, which support proper projects.

Crucial instances of agency goods are specially constituted or protected by familiar deontological restrictions on action that are delivered by the mechanism of MAC in these general ways. Some of the negative restrictions that we previously noted as crucially helping to constitute and foster these agency goods are quite often at least very close to full-blown agent-centered restrictions. Violation of standard deontological prescriptions is in fact often defection from standing group acts with quite weighty projects that we are almost all inside, and hence often a violation of DD or VLD. In actual fact, we accept agent-constituting and indeed higher-order agent-governing reasons of significant consequentialist weight, even as assessed by plausible hedonistic valuation principles, that reflect deontological restrictions, and MAC will endorse such agent-constituting and agent-governing reasons that enjoin deontological restrictions on action when one is inside groups with proper projects unless violations are sanctioned by DD or VLD. While this requires that the groups in question have appropriate projects, there are many forms of one-off group action that are forms of moral cooperation with good effects, the cooperative creation of spheres in which the standard deontological prescriptions are properly observed. Some are informal and local – say, when you and I have a special practice of not lying about certain things to each other. This may be local enough to constitute a special obligation, and we will turn to such cases in the next section. But some are almost universal, regarding both those who cooperate and those to whom the relevant respect is due according to the project of the group. They reflect contingent but relatively broad social conventions. These help constitute general obligations that are yet dependent on the existence of specific group acts. These are the key group acts for handling deontological objections to MAC.

What if you are outside the relevant groups? What if you are a congenital liar? I think that in fact almost no one is outside the relevant groups, because almost everyone accepts the relevant reasons to one limited degree or another. But, as I noted in the last chapter, MAC suggests not only that you should cooperate with the weighty group agents that you are inside, but also that you should join the weighty ones that you aren't inside if that is suggested by the true consequentialist valuation principle – in other words, if you can provide more additional value by joining than you might alternatively produce – as long as that doesn't violate other strictures of MAC. Once you are inside, you will then be tied in with something like deontological force. That is what you should *do* if you are outside the relevant groups, but what are you *owed*? Though there are no doubt differences in the treatment of liars and nonlying cooperators enjoined by our standing group act of refraining from lies, still you deserve at least some truthful dealing.

Let me treat a specific case in at least a little detail to show how this mechanism can work. In particular, let's continue with the case of lying. There are four key facts: (i) We are inside a variety of small-scale group agents with properly beneficent projects and such that to lie within the group is in fact to defect from the group project, as well as other small-scale agents in which it is somewhat indeterminate or vague whether an internal lie involves a defection. (ii) The proper projects of other beneficent agents should be supported by truth telling. (iii) But most important is that almost everyone is part of a very weighty group agent that is a one-off practice forbidding lies, except under various somewhat vaguely specified excusing conditions. And defection from that practice is often all too determinate. (iv) What's more, those few outside the practice will generally have a reason to join, on straightforward act consequentialist grounds. And if they join, then they will be bound inside.

There are subtleties that attend the last point: It is not, I think, that an atomic agent that is some reformed moment in the life of a former liar is specifically bound by the reforming choices of their past selves, but rather that to join a group agent is to come to accept relevant reasons, and in a reformed moment the agent finds itself inside the relevant group, by the natural temporal inertia of accepted reasons. And of course if some pill for changing the reasons we accept becomes available, it will still characteristically constitute defection from a group act to try to put your future selves outside it. And, as I noted in the last chapter, it is not merely atomic agents who join moral practices. But let's concentrate on the crucial normative implications of my four key points.

These four general considerations suggest the following four relatively concrete tenets as directives of MAC, which in the context of our actual practices are quite significant: (1) Do not lie, and more generally, do not create false expectations or fail to deliver relevant information, within a group agent with a properly beneficent goal that lies outside of the practice of cooperation itself,[21] unless a violation of that duty is sanctioned by VLD or DD, or the lie serves the project of the group, or the lie is acceptable in the practice. (2) If other things are equal, do not lie, and more generally, do not create false expectations or fail to deliver relevant information, to another agent or group agent with a properly beneficent project. (3) Do not lie, and more generally, do not create false expectations or fail to deliver relevant information, whenever you are within a one-off group action creating a sphere of truth telling of some sort that is itself a proper project, unless a violation of that duty is sanctioned by VLD or DD, or unless the lie is acceptable in that practice. (4) Join such groups whenever that is required on direct consequentialist grounds, except when that is forbidden by MAC.

Focus on the third directive. You and I are in fact within such a widespread one-off group agent, which is quite weighty according to most plausible consequentialist normative principles, and so VLD and DD will very seldom sanction exceptions from that practice. The practice itself, of course, specifies some appropriate exceptions from rigorous truth telling, though often only vaguely.

It is normatively quite significant according to MAC that we have a general cooperative practice that is a group agent generally forbidding lies though with various exceptions, and that does allow a certain amount of misleading speech. Roughly speaking, you should lie in a way forbidden by that practice only when you can gain as much value by that defection from our general group act as that whole vast cooperative practice creates.

Still, there are possibly more weighty practices in which one could engage in a way that contributes value by more strenuous truth telling, and strenuous truth telling will very rarely require defection from a less strenuous cooperative practice of truth telling. Independent of the actual details of our group practices and the contingencies of consequences, the difference between explicit and implicit lies and the difference between lying and withholding information are irrelevant according to MAC. MAC suggests that beneficent projects of any agent should characteristically be supported by truth telling.

Yet there are limits to the kinds of strenuous truth telling required by MAC. Perhaps it will seem that MAC cannot endorse enough lies. We do

---

21 This phrase distinguishes this obligation from that expressed by (3).

not plausibly gain more by lying to a murderer searching for an innocent victim than an entire practice of not lying gains the world. But still, our actual practice about lying endorses such exceptions, and indeed has better consequences than alternatives that are more rigid in the notorious Kantian way. So go ahead and lie to the murderer.

There is another sort of balance between lying and murder that we should consider, and along the way we can treat a second relatively concrete intuitive deontological restriction. It will take us a moment to get back to the issue of balance.

A precept forbidding killing is found in all standard intuitionist accounts of commonsense morality, but there are differences about killing animals. Traditional consequentialist hedonism in conjunction with MAC suggests that animal pain is normatively significant, but that killing nonhuman animals isn't especially important except in the unusual case in which it violates some form of mutual cooperation that is group action, which would be possible with other animals capable of speech and hence of accepting reasons in my sense, or in case it is specifically prohibited by beneficent elements of the project of a beneficent group act. Killing humans is another matter. Killing others with whom one is engaged in group activity of course eliminates the possibility of cooperative activity. Even in the unlikely event that the project of the group is favored by the murder of a single member, still this involves a violation of cooperative activity in pursuit of that goal, unless that possibility is specifically endorsed by the whole group and in particular the member murdered. And of course there is a general cooperative practice among humans of not murdering one another, which is a one-off group agent with a very weighty proper project, though it seems to allow – or at least it seems not determinately not to allow – certain exceptions for wartime, self-defense, and the like. It is also relevant that participation in this general form of cooperation is a likely precondition for admission into most forms of other cooperative activity, and that killing others will undercut their individual proper projects and those of the group agents of which they are part.

With those factors noted, we can see that the following analogues of our earlier precepts governing lying will be endorsed by MAC as weighty reasons: (1) Do not kill human or nonhuman cooperators within a group agent with any properly beneficent project having a goal that lies outside of that practice, unless a violation of that duty is sanctioned by VLD or DD. (2) If other things are equal, do not kill humans or other agents who have (or are parts of group agents that have) proper projects. (3) Do not kill whenever you are within a one-off group agent creating a sphere of nonmurder that is a proper project, unless a violation of that duty is sanctioned by VLD or DD, or is sanctioned by that practice as an appropriate exception. (4) Join such groups whenever that is required on direct consequentialist grounds, unless that is forbidden by MAC.

You and I are within such a practice as the third precept invokes. Since we have a general cooperative practice forbidding the murder of humans under most conditions, and which is a group act that is quite normatively significant by the tenets of MAC, MAC largely forbids such murder outright. You may murder to save the entire world from certain destruction, though probably you cannot murder an innocent even to stop a small war.

A characteristic sore spot for MAC is that when normative practices that are group acts conflict for an agent, it may be that the practice that has the weightiest consequences is a practice from which individual defection will be less weighty. And even individual defection may often achieve weighty goods. For instance, it may stop a war. Other possible examples of this general sort involve the interaction of lying and murder. And so we return to our question of balance.

You may of course lie to save a life, because that exception is clearly built into our truth-telling practice. And a more rigorous practice of truth telling would not have better consequences. Surely our practice also allows you to lie to avoid committing a murder, if there can be any such case. But if we were inside a group agent with a proper project that did not allow for these exceptions, then MAC also would not allow them, unless through defection you could help to create a weightier group act that incorporates the exceptions, or unless the group act of refraining from murder is weightier than the group act of refraining from lies. I believe that it is weightier in fact, so that there are two sorts of protection from murder by truth telling according to MAC, even beyond the unreality of a case in which our forced choice is to lie or to murder. But imagine that there are in fact situations in which the choice is between lying and murdering and must involve defection from some deontic practice, and that while to defect into murder individually is very weighty in a negative way, still the general group act of not lying is weightier than the general group act of not murdering, perhaps because we are not much inclined to murder even independent of that moral practice. Then MAC would tell you to murder rather than to lie. And, of course, that would be wrong. MAC characteristically decides between conflicting deontic duties by appeal to DD, by ceding priority to the duty that is part of the consequentially weightiest group act; and while that is at least generally intuitive, it is reasonable to worry that there may be exceptions.

Or consider again this abstract possibility: Perhaps you are part of two conflicting group acts that in particular constitute two deontic practices, and perhaps the first is somewhat weightier but would survive your defection, while the second would not. Yet DD prescribes that you stick with the first. That seems to me wrong also.

Still, I know no realistic and intuitively debilitating examples of these two sorts involving the conflict of two general deontic obligations, in part because intuitive deontological restrictions are characteristically negative, and in part because weighty normative practices would characteristically survive individual defection. Nor would participation in a weighty but still not nearly universal beneficent group act – say, a political party in pursuit of world peace – trump such deontic restrictions according to MAC, unless it could (implausibly) generate more weighty results than the entire deontic practice in question. And remember what I said in the last chapter about implicit exceptions and the Big and Small Disasters. Nevertheless, we will return again to difficult cases with this general structure during our discussion of special obligations.

IV

We have seen that MAC can evade one standard objection to act consequentialism. But a second standard objection to act consequentialism is its apparent failure, in Thomas Nagel's words, to respect the special obligations "we have toward those to whom we are closely related: parents, children, spouses, siblings, fellow members of a community or even a nation. Most people would acknowledge a noncontractual obligation to show special concern for some of these others – though there would be disagreement about the strength of the reasons and the width of the net."[22] There are also intuitive special obligations due to our specific past acts – for instance, duties to keep promises and to obey contracts, and duties of reparation and gratitude.

There are differences of opinion about the force and nature of these obligations, and indeed some internal confusion within most individuals about them. How much should we favor those to whom we intuitively owe gratitude? And there are a number of quite relevant traditional

---

22   Nagel (1986: 165).

87

consequentialist observations, deployed in traditional consequentialist responses to this objection. For instance, we have special ability to favor the interests of those we know well and to whom special affection ties us, as indeed to harm them by neglect. And of course consequentialists should consider the actual background for any action, in which in fact most act mostly to favor their own.

But Multiple-Act Consequentialism suggests the relevance of another class of factors that are very helpful in response to this second objection. Many intuitive special obligations parallel plausibly proper reasons according to MAC. There are different ways in which this is so. But the main point is that special obligations are often within relatively small group agents, and often help to constitute effective and appropriately valuable group agents. In fact, some of the explanations for intuitively general agent-centered restrictions that we surveyed in the last section are also explanations of special obligations dependent on the existence of particular, though sometimes very large, group agents. We probably have a somewhat special obligation not to murder other cooperating nonmurderers according to MAC, though that depends on the details of our group project of refraining from murder. Narrower and more intuitively special obligations are created by participation in smaller beneficent group agents in exactly the same way.

Acceptance of particular special obligations may be acceptance of agent-constituting reasons that help to constitute the existence of particular group agents – for instance, a particular cooperating family, or a group act of two bound by a promise and by whatever reciprocal conditions elicited the promise. Of course, the normative details turn, according to MAC, on details of the psychologies of the parties involved, as well as on the normative weight of these group agents. So no special group agent is created when a lying promise is made. But the general deontic practice of refraining from false promises and other lies is of course itself a very weighty group agent in which nearly everyone takes part and that others have direct consequentialist reason to join.

Acceptance of special obligations may also be, more narrowly, acceptance of agent-constituting reasons that help give a family a certain appropriate project. Or, more broadly, it may be the general acceptance of agent-governing reasons of the appropriate sort, at least given plausible contingent but general conditions that imply our special ability to harm or help those to whom we are closely tied. Given the general recognition of a general obligation to support effective social practices of child care, those contingent conditions may imply the need to accept a special obligation. And acceptance of general forms of special obligation – say, general obligations of gratitude – may constitute someone as an effective candidate for many forms of group action. What's more, standard forms of social arrangement often involve generalized group action that supports particular sorts of smaller group agents, or that singles out the normative relevance of certain factors to their proper functioning.

One quite characteristic and at least generally intuitive feature of MAC's treatment of special obligations follows from the fact that small group agents – say, particular friendships – ordinarily have less weighty consequences than massive group agents, such as the general practice of refraining from murder. So, by the principle DD, MAC will seldom allow special obligations to trump the deontological restrictions we discussed in the last section.

But this structural feature of MAC may seem to raise an intuitive difficulty in some cases that are analogous to the conflict cases we discussed at the end of the last section and in the last chapter, but in which the conflict of special obligations and weighty beneficent group practices is at stake. Imagine that someone's role in a group agent requires that he or she work on Wednesday afternoons toward a charitable goal, and that the group agent does massive amounts of good, but that any Wednesday's contribution from that individual is relatively trivial. Now imagine that on a Wednesday there is a choice for that individual between saving their own son from drowning and performing their role in the charity. It may seem that MAC requires that the parent let the son drown, and that of course would be wrong. But, as I noted, special obligations according to MAC involve not only small-scale group agents that constitute particular special groups, particular families, but also larger and hence plausibly weightier group agents that are social practices supporting and governing such particular group agents. And our very widespread practices of that sort are weightily beneficent group agents that mandate an intuitive treatment of the conflict in question, and that plausibly trump the effects of any specific charity. And there is also plausibly a general obligation to rescue in emergencies that reflects a group agent that also trumps the weight of the charity according to MAC. What's more, recall that in cases where we have no tendency to criticize defections from a group act in favor of a pressing alternative, there is an implicit exception within the project of that group act.

Despite these various analytical complexities, special obligations, on the conception suggested here, are primarily proper agent-constituting reasons that create certain forms of relatively local group agents.

Consider a social arrangement with many families. Each family may be a group agent. In a typical case, it may be a family crucially and centrally engaged in a project of mutual care extending especially to the young and the old. When engaging in that project involves the acceptance of supporting reasons, which seems the common case, they are agent-constituting reasons. Of course, the family may also have other group projects, which involve acceptance of project-constituting reasons. Or it may be that even in the absence of such a locally beneficent central project, some family still cedes special normative authority to the decisions of some elder; it accepts them as reasons, as agent-constituting reasons. Either family suggested is a group agent. And a supporting social arrangement may itself be the group action of a larger group agent, cooperation by all on a form of child raising.

Partly because of the nature of standard background arrangements, which require that families care for their own children and elderly members in order to assure good care, partly because of the natural effects of propinquity and natural sentiments on the effectiveness of this general strategy, but mostly because the care of the young and the old is an important project by the direct light of standard consequentialist basic principles and because the effective creation and education of moral agents is a crucial moral task, the central project of the first family noted in the last paragraph is characteristically in proper accord with standard basic consequentialist principles. The project of that first family is a proper project.

It may seem that we have special obligations to help family members even in activities that aren't essential to the family or part of any of its group projects – say, to help them pursue a sport on their own that has nothing to do with any project of the family, or to help them make a good career move to another city. And such obligations may seem unavailable to MAC. But notice that these obligations are often folded into the general standard central project of caring for and nurturing the young and the old, and that when they are not so folded, they seem intuitively less pressing.

MAC also suggests characteristic complications involving proper projects. If the central project of a family, perhaps because of its political or economic power, or because of its cruelty to its members, is not in general accord with the basic consequentialist normative principle, then MAC would suggest that the special obligations in question would be attenuated or overridden. There might be agent-constituting reasons accepted that make such a family exist as a group agent, but they would be improper. And the initial asymmetry in power of parents and children suggests that vicious parents can easily assure this. Still, it may also

90

be that each individual family has a central project that plays a role in some higher-order group agent, a project for each family that is not itself in direct accord with the basic consequentialist normative principle, but such that the project of the higher-order group agent is proper. And there may be several different group agents with different central projects that overlap in the same intuitive family, and some of them may be proper while others are not.

As we have already noted for some difficult cases, a second characteristic complication of MAC is that it suggests that we must properly balance this form of group agency, even when it has a proper project, against others. Indeed, there is more than one form of group agency automatically in play even in the case of a family with a proper project. There is a particular cooperative project of some family, and then the existence of that group agent, and then the larger group agent cooperating on a social form. MAC balances forms of agency by favoring the normatively weightiest form, and hence will in some instances – say, where the very existence of a family is more significant than some small failing even in its central project – cede that greater significance. Need it characteristically cede greater dominance to the larger social project, the cooperative form of families? That is in one sense a characteristic suggestion of MAC, but the issue introduces many complexities. There may be many competing forms of possible family structure, with some more entrenched but others more beneficent. And the kinds of group agents that MAC deploys are timeless, so that relevant cooperative practices can be prospective. And the actual form of a family may put it outside of some larger social form without involving a conflict within atomic agents of the sort that engages the characteristic tenets of MAC. And of course the larger social form may not, on balance, represent a group agent with a proper project, or even any sort of group agent. MAC's analysis of special obligations is complicated in what seems to me a suggestive and properly intuitive way, and provides a plausible framework for further normative exploration.

MAC naturally treats many familiar institutions as group agents, which hence invoke this general analysis of allied special obligations. Indeed, it may be worth noting that there is a natural analysis of all institutions that is suggested by MAC, one that itself suggests that they are often group agents in my sense.[23] Let me approach it by way of a contrast. Rawls suggested that an institution is a "public system of rules which

---

23   This is developed at greater length in Mendola (1988).

91

defines offices and positions... [and specifies] certain forms of action as permissible, others as forbidden.... An institution exists at a certain time and place when the actions specified by it are regularly carried out in accordance with a public understanding that the system of rules defining the institution is to be followed."[24] But there are two problems with this account as it stands, which seem to demand some generalization. First, it concerns only systems of rules that define specific offices and positions, such as judge, senator, batter, or umpire. But not all social communities have such a form. Consider a group of agents who accept rules about general courtesy. We can imagine less institutionalized forms of society than our own, where there are many fewer rules about the privileges and duties of particular offices, less division of labor. Second, Rawls's rules specify certain forms of actions as permissible and forbidden, rather than, say, as better or worse. They are supported by penalties and defenses rather than, say, by a sense of excellence. But we can certainly imagine forms of society in which a conception of what is good, as opposed to what is permissible or wrong, plays a dominant organizing role. If we stretch Rawls's notion of an institution to include shared conceptions of the good as well as of the right, and if we don't require a division of labor, we should perhaps cease to speak of rules. The general phenomenon of which rule following and talk of the good are parts seems to be normative evaluation, citing and accepting reasons for and against things. So here is my proposal: A social community, any social community, is a group of agents who accept the same reasons. It is not that agents must share acceptance of all reasons in order to form a community, but that there corresponds, to any set of reasons accepted by an intuitive group, a particular community. This is a weaker condition than is required for group action, but it would seem that in humans accepted reasons naturally assume that other, richer form. The accepted reasons naturally engage our sentiments of reciprocity and benevolence. So many communities are not just groups of agents, but also group agents in the sense specified in the last chapter, and they are of greater normative weight according to MAC than other forms of community, at least when those other forms of community are not recognized as significant in the content of a group act.

The general pattern of analysis of special obligations I have suggested here also provides MAC with an intuitive conception of proper punishment, which in turn underlies its conception of obligations of gratitude

24   Rawls (1971: 55).

92

and reparation. We are enjoined by MAC to cooperate in a variety of normatively weighty one-off schemes like that of not murdering other humans. But if someone violates such a cooperative practice, MAC implies a change in their normative status. Depending on the existence of other weighty group actions in which the perpetrator continues to engage, and depending on whether the one-off group agent of refraining from murder involves a directive to refrain from the murder of even noncooperators, the propriety of the individual punishment of perpetrators may then even turn directly on the consequences of such punishment as evaluated by the basic consequentialist principle. In effect, under realistic conditions, given the kinds of general group acts in which we engage, MAC implies a kind of automatic normative punishment for those who violate certain forms of normatively weighty cooperation that are group acts, which is a change in normative status. This may in turn defeat a normative presumption against a more concrete form of punishment.

This sort of normative punishment applies also in less weighty cases than those that would properly occasion significant institutional punishment such as imprisonment. And this in turn suggests a natural analysis of duties of reparation and gratitude. Duties of reparation are at least sometimes duties to restore forms of group action that one has violated, or, more specifically, to make it be that in fact one hasn't in the end really violated a reciprocal obligation in the manner that one's past activity alone would suggest. Duties of reparation can be in this way a present shadow cast by the combination of one's former cooperative obligations within a group agent and one's past action in apparent violation of those obligations. And duties of gratitude may sometimes be duties to avoid the failures that occasion duties of reparation, the shadows of shadows, as well as straightforward cooperative obligations that root later duties of reparation.

There are many details that require further exploration. But special obligations and analogous phenomena do not provide an evident difficulty for MAC, no more than deontological restrictions. They just involve smaller group agents.

V

The final objection we must consider is that act consequentialism seems too demanding. Indeed, it may even seem so demanding as to undermine individual integrity. Bernard Williams persuasively reminded us that a person

is identified with his actions as flowing from projects and attitudes which in some cases he takes seriously at the deepest level, as what his life is about. . . . It is absurd to demand . . . that he should just step aside from his own project and decision and acknowledge the decision which utilitarian calculation requires. It is to alienate him in a real sense from his actions and the source of his action in his own convictions. . . . It is thus, in the most literal sense, an attack on his integrity.[25]

But there are two crucial things to notice about this class of objections. First, it is a class, and has different forms with more or less unequivocal support from reflective common sense. Second, the unequivocal forms can be evaded by Multiple-Act Consequentialism. If consequentialism literally undermined one's individual integrity as an agent, that would indeed be deeply counterintuitive. But if consequentialism just erects a few barriers to the unbridled pursuit of the most trivial sorts of self-interest, that is a different matter. If a moral theory implies that we must spend a bit more on famine relief than the ordinary person spends, when that has a trivial effect on their self-interest and well-being, then we do not immediately know on intuitive grounds that that moral theory is hence false. Any intuition to the contrary is so obviously self-serving as to be immediately suspect. Still, there are more intense demands that a moral theory might make, and that are intuitively disturbing demands of some forms of consequentialism. But MAC does not underwrite those demands.

First case: Familiar act consequentialism may allow or require that in pursuit of famine relief we routinely violate intuitive special obligations to our children and general deontological obligations not to steal or to deceive others. But as we saw earlier, MAC delivers intuitive special obligations and deontological constraints, though with various characteristic complications.

Second case: It may well be that familiar act consequentialism requires so much of us that it is sometimes in the most literal sense an attack on our integrity, as Williams suggested. But Multiple-Act Consequentialism does not require that much.

There is some ambiguity regarding what Williams meant, and we should consider more than one reading. We might read him as complaining that consequentialism literally demands of act consequentialists

25   Williams (1973: 116–117).

94

the cessation of their own moral agency. But anything literally required by one's continuing moral agency, or indeed by one's continuing effective moral agency, at least when that agency is in the service of appropriately beneficent projects, is characteristically protected by MAC.

According to MAC, one must characteristically treat one's future selves with sufficient respect so as to constitute oneself as an effective cooperative group agent over time. Agent-constituting reasons that help root that unified continuing agency often trump direct consequentialist action by an atomic agent. Of course, there are complexities that attend the balancing of agents required to underwrite respect for one's future selves. First, there seems to be a weighty group agent in which we nearly all participate that enjoins at least minimal concern for one's future selves, whatever their projects. But second, if one's obligations to one's future selves are not rooted merely in such a general group agent, such additional respect characteristically depends on one's acceptance of a temporally persisting, effective, and proper project. It also depends on the demands of proper agent-balancing reasons. Sometimes the project of the moment may be more normatively weighty than a long-term consequentialist project. There may even be times when one's continuing agency must properly be sacrificed. If one reliably pursues bad consequences, that may often be so. But we have no intuitive consensus that there aren't any times when morality is demanding in this way. Whatever Kant would say, it is not unintuitive that morality demands that the autonomy of the immoral sometimes be undercut. If I am so deeply and ineluctably immoral that I cannot at will become a properly moral agent, then I should do what is necessary to tie myself to the mast. Despite these various complexities, as I said, MAC characteristically requires that one treat one's future selves with the respect due to cooperating agents sharing a beneficent group project. MAC requires an asymmetrical treatment of existing group agents of which one is part and merely possible agents. But existing agents in the relevant timeless sense include cooperators in the future, and so your future selves.

MAC provides in these ways a general framework to underwrite the intuitive plausibility of some moral duties to oneself, including one's future selves, and also the intuitive significance of many individual virtues, including many that root standard virtue-based objections to consequentialism. The two basic points are simple. Such duties to self and virtues can be enjoined by beneficent one-off general group agents, general practices that meet the strictures of MAC. And one's own continuing, effective, and proper moral agency is something that MAC will directly underwrite with a variety of agent-constituting reasons shared over a continuing life. This is because one's continuing agency is a kind of group agent, constituted in part by these accepted reasons. There are agent-governing reasons that suggest duties to develop one's stable and properly effective moral character. But there are also agent-constituting reasons that suggest this. And there are other agent-constituting reasons that indeed help constitute, when stably accepted, at least some part of that stable character, at least some part of the requisite stable dispositions to behavior and feeling that constitute such a character. Individual virtues are, on the conception developed here, naturally entwined with a certain crucial form of group action that you undertake all by yourself. Traditional individual virtues exhibit the characteristic entwining of reciprocity and benevolence that we should expect of genuine group action. We want to be fair to ourselves, and to take care of ourselves, and those motives entwine.

So MAC does not undermine one's integrity insofar as one's integrity is protected by duties to self and often quite self-serving traditional virtues. But my discussion may seem to ignore what Williams really meant. More plausibly, he just meant that consequentialism is way too demanding, that it leaves insufficient room for normal human life outside the main consequentialist project, even if it can allow room for individual virtues, duties to self, and general and special deontic obligations. MAC will endorse a variety of projects of weighty group agents outside the general consequentialist project of individual good-doing by atomic agents, and indeed characteristically cedes them greater weight. But that still may seem to duck the major issue. While MAC won't characteristically require any literal sacrifice of one's personhood or of traditional individual virtues and duties or of all alternative projects, and while it is appropriately consistent with common sense if MAC is slightly more demanding than our usual grossly selfish practice, still direct consequentialism may seem way more demanding than is appropriate.

Just how demanding is MAC? What exactly does it require of the well-off in a world full of human suffering? What specifically are our obligations to the starving according to MAC? That depends in part on the general consequentialist normative principle with which it is conjoined. But it is possible to say something general.

According to MAC, our obligations to the poor or starving characteristically depend on the group acts that already exist and their normative weight. We can explore this characteristic feature of MAC by contrast with Liam Murphy's recent alternative proposal, the collective principle of beneficence: "The collective principle of beneficence . . . requires agents to promote the well-being of others up to the level of sacrifice that would be optimal under full compliance" with that principle by others from this point forward in time.[26] In other words, you should do this: Figure out the size that your sacrifice would have to be if everyone contributed properly from now on to the relief of poverty. But given that they won't, efficiently allocate your individual sacrifice to yield the best consequences. It seems unfair to require more sacrifice of you than that, and yet your sacrifice should be efficiently distributed in light of the fact that others didn't and won't comply. It also isn't just to diminish the size of the contribution required of you by considering the mass of people who have failed to contribute in the past, and who got us into this unfortunate state.

If you are a member of the sole small rich society in the world, this may put enormous demands on you. But if you are a member of many rich societies in which most in fact are very selfish, it will put limited demands on you.

This proposal attractively focuses on the cooperative acts of others. But MAC and the familiar rationale of direct consequentialism suggest that we should specifically focus not, as Murphy does, on hypothetical cooperation, but rather on actual cooperation, on actual group acts of aiding the poor and starving. MAC and intuition suggest that forms of real past and present cooperation matter more than Murphy suggests.[27]

There are various asymmetries in Murphy's story that are neither intuitively appropriate nor appropriately motivated according to MAC. If you are in the sole rich country in the world because some people in the past have been grievously unjust inside various poor countries, Murphy suggests that there are enormous demands on you. But if you are the only less-than-selfish person in the whole pretty rich world now and henceforth, and if you know for a fact that everyone else will neglect their duty, still what they very hypothetically would do if they weren't so selfish gets you off easy. This asymmetry seems morally arbitrary.

But my main worry about Murphy's proposal is this: What if everyone in the past has worked with might and main to alleviate suffering in the world, and only the current and immediately succeeding generations, raised in debilitating luxury, are and will be largely very selfish? And what if some recent natural disaster somewhere were exacerbated by this general selfishness? You know your peers won't contribute as your ancestors did,

---

26 Murphy (2000: 7). For a fuller statement of the principle, see pp. 117–118.
27 Hooker (2000: 164) makes a similar complaint.

and your ancestors would have mitigated the disaster anyway. But Murphy suggests that you still should figure out what you ought to do on the basis of what *would happen* if your peers and future generations all became selfless, even if that is much less demanding, because of current wealth, than what your ancestors *in fact* did, or indeed even if it is much less than the few relatively selfless people in the world are *now* doing. Indeed, you only have to do your part of that highly hypothetical sort even if everyone else in the generation to come will have to do much more, and you know they will, because your selfish generation is really going to mess things up.

MAC suggests, rather, that you look to actual group agents, which may include past and foreseen atomic agents, for guidance. The temporal position of the other cooperators is irrelevant to MAC, since, for instance, cooperation with your past and future selves is a relevant group act. While group action requires a kind of mutual recognition, your ancestors can recognize you in much the same relatively abstract way that the you of this moment can recognize your future selves. MAC suggests that you should cooperate with the weighty group agents that you are inside, and join the weighty ones that you aren't inside if that is suggested by the true consequentialist valuation principle, in other words, if you can provide more additional value by joining than you would hence give up. Once you are inside, you will be tied in with something like deontological force. You should defect only if you can create as much value by your individual defection as the entire group act achieves.

There seem to be at least three real group acts that are quite relevant to the issue we face. First, Thomas Pogge has plausibly argued that we support our governments when they engage in vigorous activity – for instance, bargaining activity – in support of optional details of the international global economic order that kill millions every year.[28] While we haven't considered how MAC would specify evil acts, still if that governmental activity or that international global economic order constitutes a group act in which we participate, then it is plausible that our individual participation is genuinely evil according to MAC. We must desist and consider the demands of proper reparation. But I will focus here on positive and general moral obligations to the poor and starving, which the mechanism I have already developed can treat.

---

28 Pogge (2002).

The second relevant group act reflects the fact that, throughout history, many of the rich have accepted the idea that they have a special obligation to charity. This acceptance plausibly helps constitute a weighty group agent in my sense. And you and I are arguably rich enough to qualify. But I will focus yet more narrowly, on a third and probably more important group agent that we are more certainly eligible to join.

There has been and continues to be a large normative practice in which many merely reasonably well-off people accept that they must contribute a certain fixed percentage of wealth or income to the relief of the poor and starving. This seems to be a weighty group act in my sense, supported by entwined benevolence and reciprocity that will occasion criticism of known defectors. MAC is not so much an easy guide to action as a criterion of right and wrong action, and this case reveals that our duties according to MAC turn on facts about real group actions that may be hard to discover. And of course I am no historian. But here is my best shot: There has at least sometimes been a traditional Jewish and Christian practice of dedicating between one-quarter and one-third of the traditional tithe to support for the poor and starving.[29] Over time, there seems to have been variation regarding whether the tithe applied to particular agricultural and animal products or to general income, with ancient temporal movement toward the more expansive conception. And participation was generally conceived as obligatory. Furthermore, the Islamic practice of *zakāt* prescribes the contribution of at least 2.5 percent of *wealth* each year by those meeting certain minimal standards, primarily for the alleviation of poverty.[30] Indeed, this obligation is one of the five pillars of Islam. In light of these details of history, we might presume a relatively conservative understanding of what participation in the relevant group act requires, which would also encompass the largest group. So I claim that there has been and is a weighty group agent that contributes at least 2.5 percent of income to the poor and starving. There are complications – for instance, the fact that such obligations have often been focused within local communities or religious groups. But contemporary means of communication and travel broaden possible communities in such a way, and there are enough starving people of various religious affiliations, that

29 Wigoder (2002: 776); Vischer (1966: 4, 9); Clarke (1894: 85). Singer (1993: 246) suggests tithing as a morally obligatory contribution to the poor, though he claims it would be arbitrary. On medieval support of the poor in Europe, see Gilchrist (1969).
30 Al-Shiekh (1995); Weiss (2002).

these are arguably details that can be enfolded into a division of labor within a single group agent.

These historical facts imply that even a tithe, and certainly one-quarter of that, would not be so demanding of us as to undercut our individual autonomy in any realistic sense. Most of us are richer than most members of traditional societies. And they suggest there is a real group agent of significant normative weight that donates 2.5 percent of gross income to relief of the poor and starving. Whatever religious reasons people have had for accepting the reasons that constitute this group agent are largely irrelevant according to MAC. The group agent exists, and atheists can join. You may accept reasons, at least in a tenuous way, that put you already inside such a group agent to one degree or another, and that hence require your participation with something like deontological force according to MAC. It would be appropriate to defect only if you can achieve as much good by that defection as the entire group act will achieve over time. And even if you are not already inside such an agent, it is likely that the diversion of this trivial amount of your income to famine relief will generate weightier effects by the tenets of MAC than its present use, and also that the other costs and benefits of joining the group act – due, for instance, to the psychological conditions on participation – will not forbid joining. So you are obligated to join up and do your part, and then you will become bound inside.

Real cooperative practices are naturally salient moral coordination points according to MAC. You should join the two relevant group agents if you are not inside them already, and you should cooperate if you are. You should give at least 2.5 percent if you are relatively poor for a reader of this book, and you should give more lavishly if you are relatively rich. The poor and starving have a natural moral claim on us, and so do those who give. Only that level of individual sacrifice would be suitably fair to those real people out there, in the past and present and in the future, who have tried, are trying, and will try to hold their end up. This proposal is not very demanding, but it isn't trivial. Shifting 1.25 percent of the aggregate income enjoyed by the 903 million people like you and me who live in high-income economies would plausibly eradicate serious poverty worldwide.[31] We are not awash in endless human misery. We are miserly and self-indulgent. We need only do as much to alleviate poverty

---

31 Pogge (2002: 2).

100

in our contemporary global community as our ancestors did within their local communities. But we don't do it.

Do you have a direct individual obligation to do even more in our largely selfish world, on direct act consequentialist grounds, according to MAC? Or do you have an obligation to join more rigorously charitable group activities? That will depend on the normative weight of the generally beneficent group acts from which you must hence defect – say, by failing to educate your children or yourself to the fullest extent, by straining your future selves and friendships, by eschewing good clothes and housing. There is not only your individual project to educate your own children, but also the general project of educating children. And the second has great weight according to MAC. Even group acts supporting hobbies may conceivably have relevant weight, since lots of small satisfactions may trump food benefits for individual starving people according to some traditional consequentialist valuation principles. And more serious general projects like that of education and good housing will certainly provide suitable moral cover.

What MAC will not characteristically protect is costly individual idiosyncracies, either in the way roles in large group projects are fulfilled – for instance, inefficiently and at great expense – or involving commitment to activities that do not fulfill roles in weighty group projects. MAC will not protect individual whims that deflect large amounts of money to selfish pursuits that are not themselves suitably weighty and that are not protected by their role in weighty group acts. Expensive hobbies and quirky, costly desires do not receive much protection. It is of course possible for a continuing individual project to be a group act with weighty consequences. So if you are Gauguin, MAC may also provide some further moral cover.

But think of a person who is not yet a part of any collective group act, or who has left all such projects behind. There may be enormous demands placed by MAC on that person. It may seem unfair that there is this asymmetry in demands on those not inculcated into familiar moral commitments.

However, as we noted in the last chapter, and will discuss again in Chapter 8, the conditions required for being inside familiar group acts are not very robust. You need merely to accept the reasons in question and grant them a limited sort of motivational and practical weight. I think very few of us are genuinely outside most of the demands of commonsense morality, except for the very young, who are incapable of accepting reasons and hence incapable of genuine morally governed action, and the decrepit, who are incapable of significant action.

Still, there may be supermen or sociopaths who have genuinely thrown off conventional morality and other sorts of customary group action in the full light of some blinding day. But let such supermen or sociopaths be governed by act consequentialist demands, I say, in their lonely strength and pride. If they are beyond the customary robust restrictions on murder, then they shouldn't complain if they are beyond any customary limitations on the demands of proper benevolence also.

But what if you are a member of two charity groups, and while the second is more beneficent, your contribution to the first is much more crucial to the success of its project? It may seem that MAC suggests that the less a charity needs you, the greater is your obligation to give. And that seems wrong.

But as we saw in the last chapter for structurally similar cases, what is crucial is whether you would be criticized for defecting from the weightier group agent in order to contribute your more significant share to the less weighty agent. In cases in which it seems clear that you should defect from the weightier group, you would not be. And so the group act in question incorporates a relevant exception into its project. You would not in fact be defecting when you contribute in an effective way to the less weighty group.

MAC is a little demanding, but not terribly so. Normal human lives are certainly possible within its strictures.

Commonsense morality is a very weighty one-off group agent in my sense. Aside from the refinements required if we properly eschew counter-productive individual elements of the project of commonsense morality in favor of a more beneficent concentric group agent – counterproductive elements that include its recent excessive selfishness – the demands of commonsense morality are largely endorsed by MAC. If commonsense morality delivers an intuitive set of obligations, exceptions, and resolutions of moral conflicts, then so will MAC.

We will return in Part Four to the specific injunctions of MAC when conjoined with HMP in particular. But we have already seen that it can evade the three standard intuitive objections to act consequentialism when conjoined with plausible basic consequentialist normative principles. It is not too demanding; it is not too permissive; and it implies intuitive special obligations.

Part Two

Hedonism

4

Intuitive Hedonism

Multiple-Act Consequentialism must be accompanied by a basic normative principle, and the basic normative principle proposed here is the Hedonic Maximin Principle. HMP has two elements, which are developed in this and the following part. The next part concerns its maximin structure. This part concerns its hedonism.

Hedonism is the view that pleasure is the basic ethical or normative value, and pain the basic disvalue. Chapter 5 will argue that hedonism is true, whether we like it or not and whatever our normative intuitions. But this chapter argues that it is appropriately intuitive.

The hoary philosophical tradition of hedonism suggests that it is at least reasonably and roughly intuitive. But philosophers no longer treat it that way. For the most part, they think that they know it to be obviously false on intuitive grounds, much more obviously false on such grounds than familiar competitors. I will argue that this consensus is wrong. I will defend the intuitive cogency of hedonism relative to the now dominant desire-based and objectivist conceptions of well-being and the good. I will argue that hedonism is still a contender, and indeed that our current understanding of commonsense intuition on balance supports it.

It may seem quite unlikely that such an argument will succeed. For instance, here is Sumner's relatively sympathetic evaluation of hedonism's prospects:

Time and philosophical fashion have not been kind to hedonism. Although hedonistic theories of various sorts flourished for three centuries or so in their congenial empiricist habitat, they have all but disappeared from the scene. Do they now merit even passing attention, for other than nostalgic purposes?

Like endangered species, discredited ideas do sometimes manage to make a comeback.[1]

Of course, always at issue is who has the intuitions that count. Is it Spenser's Una, Sojourner Truth, or Simone de Beauvoir? The fact that hedonism was a serious contender within philosophy for much longer than even the three centuries Sumner notes suggests that it might still have a life outside of the trained intuitions of contemporary analytic moral philosophers. Nevertheless, it is those intuitions that I will address. Some of my strategy will be to delimit the kind of hedonism that I will defend, which will soften its conflict with our trained intuition. But most of my strategy will be to undercut or adjust the intuitions that seem to discredit hedonism, by appeal to other intuitions that are more favorable and forceful.

Section I distinguishes the form of hedonism that I will defend from others in its near vicinity. Sections II, III, and IV argue that hedonism is suitably intuitive, despite recent fashion.

I

The hedonism I will defend is at once very crude, which may make it seem especially hard to defend on intuitive grounds, and yet deployed in a specific way that somewhat eases that task. Let's begin with the crudity. Focus on the pleasantness of physical pleasures and the painfulness of physical pains. On my view, the pleasantness of physical pleasure *is* a kind of hedonic value; it is a single homogenous sensory property, varying merely in intensity as well as in extent and duration, which is yet a kind of goodness. Likewise for pain and hedonic disvalue. We will get to the details of this conception in the next chapter. Alternatively, and less idiosyncratically, one might claim that the sensory pleasantness of physical pains *has* a value that would be in that sense hedonic. This difference won't matter for our present purposes.

While physical pains and crude physical pleasures provide the paradigmatic examples of the hedonic value and disvalue that I will deploy, other "higher" pleasures and pains may involve attenuated experience of the same kind. But that may not seem to help much. Such a view is reminiscent of the classical hedonism of Bentham, which is the sort now most widely ridiculed. Most of the few contemporary hedonists deploy

1 Sumner (1996: 83).

106

more sophisticated conceptions of pleasure or enjoyment,[2] and even these more sophisticated forms of hedonism are widely thought untenable. At least since Sidgwick, it has been perhaps the dominant view even among hedonists that there isn't a single homogeneous quality of sensation characteristic of all pleasures or of all pains. I believe that some real phenomenal differences between pains and pleasures can be delivered by felt elements other than hedonic value, and I do not insist that hedonic value or disvalue provide a phenomenal reduction of, or a necessary condition for, all pains and pleasures. Still, there is no questioning the relatively simple crudity of the basic phenomenal properties that I will defend as the basic normative properties. Contemporary defenders of hedonism usually adopt what Sumner has called an externalist conception of pain and pleasure, in which pain is characterized as involving a certain sort of aversion to a wide range of phenomenal experiences.[3] But hedonic value is internalist in this sense and also phenomenally homogeneous.

Still, even my crude hedonism does not identify pleasure itself with positive value, but rather merely considers the positive hedonic tone characteristic of physical pleasures to be the sole irreducible kind of positive value. And simple internalist conceptions of pleasure and pain do have certain intuitive advantages, well summarized by Sumner:

The attitude model [of pain, which identifies it with all aversive phenomenal states,] can make no sense at all of the testimony of lobotomized subjects who say that they continue to feel pain but are no longer averse to it. More seriously, it also runs foul of the perfectly obvious fact that pain is not the only physical feeling to which we are (normally) averse. Think for a moment of the many physical symptoms which, when persistent, can make our lives miserable: nausea, hiccups, sneezing, dizziness, disorientation, loss of balance, itching, 'pins and needles', 'restless legs', tics, twitching, fatigue, difficulty in breathing, and so on. While none of these is quite the same as physical pain, we experience each as intrinsically disagreeable. The attitude model simply obliterates these categorial boundaries by treating all these states indifferently as pain.[4]

But my crude conception has exactly corresponding disadvantages. It deploys phenomenal hedonic disvalue and disvalue of a simple sort even

---

2 Sidgwick (1907); Edwards (1979); Sumner (1996). It is a stretch to call Sumner a hedonist, but we will return to his view shortly. Feldman (2004) is the best-developed recent hedonist proposal, and deploys a highly sophisticated conception. Tännsjö (1998) is closer to my own proposal, and I will discuss crucial elements of his account in Chapter 5.
3 See, for instance, Edwards (1979) and Sidgwick (1907).
4 Sumner (1996: 102–103).

to characterize the phenomenal value component of itching or pins and needles. And the fact that we sometimes do not mind hedonic disvalue and sometimes do mind other phenomenological states is not obviously an intuitive advantage for my account. Let me put it this way: Perhaps it is reasonable to follow Casell and distinguish between pleasure and pain on the one hand and enjoyment and suffering on the other, where pain and pleasure are mere sensations but enjoyment and suffering involve, perhaps only, the attitudes that externalism customarily deploys.[5] But then pain that isn't suffering and pleasure that isn't enjoyment may seem intuitively irrelevant to our well-being or good. And hence a plausible hedonism may seem of necessity to be a hedonism of enjoyment and suffering, and not of pleasure and pain, let alone of the homogeneous and crude hedonic tone that I deploy.

Nevertheless, I will defend my crude hedonism as suitably intuitive. One thing that helps is the relative specificity of the role in which I will defend it. First, my hedonism is in no interesting sense psychological hedonism. I make no claim that hedonic value is our ultimate goal or desire, and indeed no claim that it plays any specific motivational or psychological role at all. And even within normative hedonism, we must heed some distinctions.

First, I deploy hedonic value and disvalue, and not pain and pleasure or suffering and enjoyment *strictu sensu*, as we will see in full detail in the next chapter. As I suggested earlier, hedonic value is a single sort of phenomenal quality that is a component of paradigmatic physical pleasures, but it is found outside of states we call "pleasure", and it is not a part of many states we do. So my view is hedonism in, though a recognizable, still an extended sense.

Second, there is a variety of different normative roles in which pleasure or hedonic value may be deployed. It might be thought to be the only thing that is good, or the only thing that is intrinsically or non-instrumentally good. Or it might be thought that one's own pleasure is all that is ultimately good for one or all that can constitute one's well-being. Indeed, there may be more than one notion of well-being to which pleasure contributes in different ways, since, as a number of authors have noted, different notions of individual well-being may be differentially appropriate for different normative purposes – say, for the distribution of certain government services or the retrospective evaluation of one's own

5 Casell (1982: 11); Sumner (1996: 103).

108

life.[6] But in fact I will not deploy hedonic value in any of these exact normative roles. I will defend hedonic value and disvalue only as providing what one might call *basic* value, which must be augmented, for instance, by a plausible consequentialist account of other sorts of value, such as that delivered by MAC, and also by the distribution sensitivity delivered by the maximin structure of HMP.

But still my view is recognizably within the classical utilitarian tradition. There is a recognizable sense in which I hold that the overall normative status of things rests on what we might call the basic well-being and good of sentient beings, and not on their overall or final well-being or good, which includes all those complications. And there is also a recognizable sense in which I hold that this basic well-being and good is constituted by their pleasure and pain, or, more precisely, by the crude hedonic value that is a component of their paradigmatic and hence physical pains and pleasures. So, despite the complications I have noted, the best way to engage the hedonism I will defend and contemporary intuition is by regard to current discussions of well-being and the good.

Perhaps it will seem that some other form of normative hedonism is more intuitive than my own – for instance, a more complicated internalist model that recognizes more sorts of experienced value, or a sophisticated externalist model like Feldman's recent proposal.[7] In light of the general disrepute of hedonism, I will not focus here on trying to win these relatively internecine battles. My primary goal is to convince you not to dismiss hedonism, any form of hedonism, out of hand. But sophisticated hedonisms such as these are made so by the complications they introduce in concession to intuitive objections made by the opponents of hedonism to crude forms like my own. And so in defending my proposal against the dominant alternatives to hedonism, I will also present the materials for further argument against closer competitors.

The following sections probe successively into what I take to be sequentially deeper strata of intuitive objections to normative hedonism. Sections II and III introduce alternative accounts of well-being, and prominent intuitive concrete cases that seem to undercut hedonism and support the alternatives. Section IV, by reference to W. D. Ross's discussion in *The Right and the Good*,[8] addresses in a general way the intuitions that lie behind these specific cases.

6   One well-developed example is Scanlon (1998: Chapter 3).
7   Feldman (2004).
8   Ross (1930).

Parfit provides the following typography of theories of what is good for one: "On the *Hedonistic Theory*, what would be best for someone is what would give him most happiness. . . . On the *Desire-Fulfilment Theory*, what would be best for someone is what would best fulfill his desires throughout his life. . . . On the *Objective List Theory*, certain things are good or bad for us, even if we would not want to have the good things or avoid the bad things."[9] Griffin adopts a similar organization of extant competitive accounts of well-being in his well-known treatment of that issue.[10] To save words and letters, I will speak simply of "hedonism", "desire-based theories", and "objectivism".

It is important to notice that there is more than one possible form of each type of account. As I said, since hedonism is so widely disparaged, my primary concern throughout this chapter will be to defend the intuitive cogency of my crude hedonism relative to dominant desire-based and objectivist accounts of well-being and the good.[11] And I cannot hope in the short space of a chapter to conclusively refute all alternatives to hedonism. My smaller aim, rather, is to defend the overall relative intuitive plausibility of hedonism. I hope to establish definitively that hedonism is at least an intuitive competitor, that it cannot properly be summarily dismissed as radically counterintuitive. It isn't trendy, but it deserves respect. I also, more ambitiously, hope to convince you that on balance our current understanding of commonsense intuition suggests that hedonism is the most intuitive account overall.

As I've noted, this is not a popular view. Contemporary arguments against hedonism and for alternative conceptions of well-being and the good rest heavily on certain concrete cases, which are deployed to engage our commonsense intuition against hedonism or in favor of its competitors. They have seemed quite convincing.

Concrete cases can be vivid and forceful, and they are a typical methodology used throughout contemporary analytic philosophy. Nevertheless, they should be handled with some care. First, it is hard in a very concrete case to avoid elements that distract intuition from the crucial features that it is supposed to test. The very concreteness of cases can make them impure. Second, overall judgments about normative and other

---

9 Parfit (1984: 4).
10 Griffin (1986). He distinguishes between objective accounts and perfectionist accounts, which I will treat together.
11 For an effective defense of a considerably less crude form, see Feldman (2004).

philosophical matters may be complex, and may require that we balance competing intuitive inclinations in a complex way. So it is important to consider a suitably wide range of different concrete cases that may pull in different directions, if we are to come to a plausible overall understanding of our intuitive judgments. We must be wary of hasty overgeneralization from single cases. Third, the intuitions of sober and relevant judges may differ. And so not all individual intuitions can be taken as decisive.

Unfortunately, perhaps just because hedonism no longer seems like a serious contender, the discussions of hedonism even by very able, conscientious, and relatively sympathetic authors are now less than ideal in these ways. I will begin with the standard cases that seem to undercut hedonism. I will focus our discussion on the negative treatment of views like my own by Griffin and by Sumner, who propose instead recognizably desire-based accounts.[12] Part of my point will be that their accounts of well-being are unusually able and conscientious, relatively sympathetic to hedonism, and standard. They are a best case. The likely explanation for the problems that we will uncover in their discussions is that crude hedonism like my own no longer seems worth real attention. That is also part of my point.

Sumner says of hedonism that the "two strongest objections to an account of this sort have been nicely summarized by James Griffin."[13] But it is striking that Griffin is effectively done with hedonism by the fourth page of his first chapter.[14] His two objections are two sorts of concrete counterexample. The first objection is deployed against simple, homogeneous hedonic tone accounts such as mine and Bentham's, while the second objection is deployed against more complex hedonisms that identify well-being with "states of mind" of a broader sort. Since my hedonism is so crude, and since the second objection would count against crude as well as more complex hedonisms, we can safely ignore that detail.

First, there is Freud in pain. Here is the entire relevant passage from Griffin:

At the very end of his life, Freud, ill and in pain, refused drugs except aspirin. 'I prefer', he said, 'to think in torment than not to be able to think clearly'. But can we find a single feeling or mental state present in both of Freud's options in virtue of which he ranked them as he did? The truth seems, rather, that often we

---

12   Carson (2000) also provides an excellent discussion of desire-based theories. It suggests that hedonism may be defensible on moral realist grounds such as I deploy in the next chapter.
13   Sumner (1996: 92).
14   Griffin (1986).

just rank options, period. Some preferences – Freud's seems to be one – are basic. That is, preferences do not always rest upon our judgments about the quantity of some homogeneous mental state found in, or produced by, each option.[15]

First point: A normative hedonist need not deny that we prefer other things than pleasure. I certainly do not deny that we have nonhedonic preferences, even if we ignore complexities like the instrumentality of some desires. I just claim that such preferences can be mistaken. And notice that this paragraph mostly just reminds us that Freud had a nonhedonic preference. Griffin presents this as an objection to a certain conception of utility in particular, which might perhaps plausibly be defined by reference to individual preference. But the problem is that this paragraph constitutes Griffin's entire attack on a simple hedonist notion of well-being, with which utility has been linked on his preceding page.

And there is a second point: While Griffin is a desire-based theorist, he is an *informed* desire-based theorist. He thinks that desires must be corrected by full information if they are to have normative weight. Two pages after the paragraph I have quoted, he rejects the "actual-desire" account in this way:

[N]otoriously, we mistake our own interests. It is depressingly common that even when some of our strongest and most central desires are fulfilled, we are no better, even worse, off. Since the notion we are after is the ordinary notion of 'well-being', what must matter for utility will have to be, not persons' actual desires, but their desires in some way improved. The objection to the actual-desire account is overwhelming.[16]

But if the actual-desire account is false, then a simple appeal to contrary preference cannot establish the falsity of hedonism.

Perhaps my reading of Griffin's case is unsympathetic. Perhaps his central thought was not that Freud simply had these preferences, but that he "ranked" the states in question, in some way expressing what we are to take to be an intuitive normative judgment about his well-being. Sumner stresses this alternative way of reading Griffin's case as an argument against simple hedonism: "On Bentham's version of the classical view, Freud seems plainly to have chosen the option which was worse for him. But that is a judgment few of us would join in making, and one which he himself would presumably have rejected."[17]

15 Ibid., 8.
16 Ibid., 10.
17 Sumner (1996: 92).

112

But remember the first characteristic danger of concrete cases that I noted earlier. The Freud case is complex, and its very impurity makes it hard to isolate those of our reactions that reflect intuitive judgments about individual well-being. Freud was surely moved by considerations other than his own well-being, given the grand nature of his intellectual ambition and self-conception and the therapeutic nature of his overall project. He may legitimately have preferred clear thinking, but on grounds other than a mere selfish concern with his own well-being. So this concrete case is inconclusive.

Considerations of the general sorts that are in play in this first case arise again in Griffin's more extended second objection, where Griffin and Sumner focus most of their discussion. So let's turn there. Here again is the entire relevant passage from Griffin:

The trouble with [the hedonist] account is that we do seem to desire things other than states of mind, even independently of the states of mind they produce. This is the point that Robert Nozick has forcefully made with some science fiction. Imagine an experience machine programmed to give you any experience you want; it will stimulate your brain so that you think you are living the most ideal life, while all the while you float in a tank with electrodes in your brain. Would you plug in? 'What else can matter to us', Nozick asks, 'other than how our lives feel from the inside?' And he replies, surely rightly, that we also want to do certain things, to be certain things, and to be receptive to what there is in life beyond what humans make. The point does not need science fiction; there are plenty of examples in ordinary life. I certainly want control over my own fate. Even if you convince me that, as my personal despot, you would produce more desirable consciousness for me than I do for myself, I shall want to go on being my own master, at least as long as your record would not be much better than mine. I prefer, in important areas of my life, bitter truth to comfortable delusion. Even if I were surrounded by consummate actors able to give me sweet simulacra of love and affection, I should prefer the relatively bitter diet of their authentic reactions. And I should prefer it not because it would be morally better, or aesthetically better, or more noble, but because it would make for a better life for me to live. Perhaps some such preferences, looked at with a cold eye, will turn out to be of dubious rationality, but not all will. This fact presents a serious challenge to [the hedonist account.][18]

First point: Notice that for the most part this passage also simply observes that we desire, want, or prefer things other than our own hedonic

18   Griffin (1986: 9).

113

tone. And still, by now on the next page, what we prefer is rejected by Griffin as a criterion for our well-being on "overwhelming" grounds.

There are, though, other elements in this passage. The third-to-the-last sentence claims that interfering factors – factors other than intuitive judgments about individual well-being – do not play a role in our reaction to the cases, or at least no ineliminable role, that the cases are suitably pure. The second-to-the-last sentence approaches the claim that some of the preferences in question are correct, though perhaps it doesn't quite get there, since the claim that something is not of dubious rationality may be merely the claim that it isn't mad or incoherent and not quite the claim that it is correct in the relevant sense. And it is striking that though Griffin says that some of the preferences he's noted are not of dubious rationality, he doesn't tell us which ones. But my main point is that the claims in the second- and third-last sentences are controversial and in part normative claims about the concrete cases, and not parts of those cases.

There are many elements in these concrete cases that disturb our ability to factor out confounding elements. The experience machine is unfamiliar gadgetry that invokes our fear of the unfamiliar. It certainly is wildly unrealistic.[19] It involves a troubling irrevocability.[20] And it seems to at least threaten risks of even hedonic harm that the corresponding actual life would not present.[21] Griffin deploys other concrete cases, from "ordinary life" and not from science fiction: the personal despot and the consummate actors. But of course these are not all that realistic. Consummate actors would not realistically devote their lives to the project suggested. And even if they did, there would always be the realistic possibility that things might go radically amiss, in a way that wouldn't threaten an ordinary life such as the actors were only simulating.

A second important cluster of confounding factors that influences our reaction to all these cases is that things other than our own well-being are in play in all of them, and matter to us. For instance, our lives have effects on other people that are quite significant, and that we care about, and that the judgments Griffin favors apparently ignore.[22] It is hard to suspend consideration of those effects. It is hard to forget that one's loved ones would be hurt in Nozick's scenario, and that one might blunder badly,

---

19   Haslett (1990).
20   Goldsworthy (1992: 18–20).
21   Sumner (1996: 94–95).
22   Haslett (1990).

through the ministrations of the consummate actors, in any attempt to help those one cares about.[23]

Mill's satisfied pig – who, you will recall, it is supposed to be worse to be than Socrates dissatisfied – is one ancestor of these cases.[24] Plato's happy "creatures who live in shells in the sea" are more distant ancestors.[25] But of course serious contemplation of becoming a pig or a mollusk invokes interfering factors of all the kinds we have traced, with a little species pride thrown in.

There is indeed yet another cluster of considerations that interfere with our ability to draw clean judgments from these cases, but it is perhaps best to consider these in light of another general set of worries about the use of concrete cases that I noted earlier. As I said, it is important to consider a range of concrete cases all at once in order to form a properly balanced judgment about our complex normative intuitions.

Let me focus specifically on the intuitive significance of living in the truth. Griffin's cases do reveal a certain revulsion we feel not merely to being deceived, but also to false experience itself. The personal despot may more manipulate than deceive, and it is interesting that there Griffin retreats to a relatively weak claim about control over one's own fate, that he'd prefer to be his own master as long as the benevolent personal despot didn't have a much better record. Still, even just the truth of an experience involves more complexities than a single case or a few cases can easily reveal.

We all grant that truth is the characteristic epistemic value of beliefs. So when other things are equal, of course true beliefs are better in some sense, though not necessarily a morally relevant sense partly constituting individual well-being. And of course true beliefs allow more certain action toward one's goals, whatever they are. But the crucial question is whether living in the truth is of significance to well-being in itself and not for its various effects – for instance, whether there are decisive commonsense intuitions that show that someone would be intuitively better off if less happy but more in the truth. There is some suggestion of this in Griffin's claim about bitter truth. But our intuitions on these matters are complex and delicate, and not adequately revealed by our reaction to a single case.

---

23 I presume that some of these might not be among the consummate actors, or that one might even care about some of the consummate actors regardless of their lies.
24 Mill (1979: 7–9).
25 Plato (1975: 21d).

Sumner's discussion uncovers some of the relevant complexities. To understand this discussion, it is useful to know that *his* view is that welfare consists of authentic happiness.[26] Happiness is supposed to be life satisfaction, which has an affective component that involves experiencing the condition of your life as fulfilling or rewarding, and a cognitive component, which involves judging that your life is going well. Such happiness is supposed to be authentic when it is informed, and autonomous. But of course the crucial question is how to balance off authenticity and happiness. And Sumner has interesting things to say on this topic, our current concern.

Sumner suggests, plausibly, that Griffin's cases alone may suggest too rigid a view. Virtual reality machines might be something that we would enjoy in limited ways. Here it seems perhaps that individual preferences should guide us in judgments about well-being. Some people may like experience machines for some purposes, and some may not. But there are even more difficult cases. Sumner considers a mother asking a sergeant whether or not her soldier son died in agony, saying that she'd rather be so unhappy that she'd want to die than to delude herself. But then, after having been informed of her son's agonized death, she writes, "I wanted to know and got what I thought I wanted."[27]

In the end, in light of the various complexities he considers, Sumner proposes an account of the relevance of falsehood to well-being that rests on individual retrospective judgments. Consider

the case of a woman who, for a while, lives in ignorant bliss with a faithless partner. Her endorsement of her life lacks information about his character and intentions. Is this information relevant? It is if her possessing it would undermine that endorsement. There are, therefore, two possibilities, which open up once she has been undeceived. One is that she re-evaluates how well her life was going . . . during the period of deception: 'I thought everything was going well, but now I can see that it was all a farce.' In that case, the discount rate she now imposes on her earlier assessment of her well-being determines how relevant the information was. The other possibility is that she does not care: 'C'est la vie; at least he was charming and we had a lot of fun.' Here the information turns out to have zero relevance, since that is the status she confers on it.[28]

One sort of objectivist account would hold that the truth of an experience matters to its contribution to well-being, period, whatever our

26 Sumner (1996: 138–183).
27 Ibid., 97.
28 Ibid., 160–161.

individual beliefs and preferences on the matter. That still leaves the problem of determining how much it counts, how much happiness is worth how much truth. But the main problem with such an account is that it is unintuitive to insist on the significance of truth despite individual preference to the contrary. Sumner's is a kind of desire-based account,[29] and appropriately and attractively rests the issue on individual preference. The relevant preferences can't be revealed during the deception, but they can be afterward, retrospectively.

Sumner goes on to require that the revealed preferences be informed and authentic, and we might wonder about whether there is a determinate fact of the matter about what we would desire if fully informed. And there are other worries also. We can so assess the state of those *terminally* duped only by reference to counterfactual retrospective enlightenment, and there are a range of different possible counterfactual enlightenments that might lead to different judgments.

But what's worse, and in the end decisive against Sumner's account, is that it is implausible to assume that actual (or hypothetical) retrospective judgments will be stable over time. On good days our now undeceived woman may be glad she was deceived and had a good time, and on bad days she may not be. And both attitudes may survive confrontation with full information. Even when such a judgment is stable, it may be an irrelevant accident that it is so. Sumner's retrospective account hence fails, at least in some cases.

Nor are there obvious desire-based alternatives to Sumner's proposal. It will not be sufficient to appeal to actual preferences about hypothetical scenarios rather than to retrospective preferences. Remember the mother and the sergeant. And it won't be sufficient to consider what one hypothetically would prefer if one in fact knew about the deception, since then one wouldn't be blissfully ignorant. And in any case there may be an indeterminacy about what one would prefer in that hypothetical condition, as there is about what one would prefer if fully informed.

Obvious objectivist accounts of well-being that invoke the significance of the truth of an experience fail intuitively, because they fail to take individual differences seriously. But obvious desire-based accounts that invoke truth also fail for the reasons just noted. Since there is no extant account that handles all extant cases relevant to assessing the relationship of truth to well-being in an obviously intuitive way, these cases hardly

---

29 Though closer to classical hedonism than most.

constitute decisive objections to hedonism that adequately support competitive accounts against it. Since we do not know that all our intuitions in this arena can be made coherent, we do not know that hedonism is false.

And notice that desire-based accounts such as Sumner's fail in this context in a revealing way, a way that reflects a general difficulty for some of the apparent concrete counterexamples to hedonism that we have been discussing. There is more than one perspective invoked by these examples, and it is not always obvious that one particular perspective is intuitively dominant, at least when a full range of cases is considered. The experience machine, the consummate actors, Socrates and the pig, and the deceived woman all involve a dual or multiple perspective on things that makes them unrealistic or unusual, and that hence perhaps directly undercuts the probity of the intuitions that they generate. But it also creates the important issue of whose perspective takes precedence, even whose corrected perspective. In the experience machine case, one makes a judgment regarding one's later state from an original perspective in which one feels discomfort about the possibility of deception, but such that one will not feel that deception later because in fact one will be deceived. It isn't obvious that the first perspective has automatic normative authority over the second, and indeed it isn't obvious that the view from the first perspective isn't distorted by irrational discomforts. We can see this more clearly in the case of the soldier's mother. Or consider this case: You are amputating Ahab's leg without anesthetic, and he is screaming that he'd rather die. Then he wakes up the next morning and thanks you. You feel better, of course. But why think that Ahab in the morning is the better authority on what the pain was worth? After all, he isn't feeling it anymore, and it is safely in the past.[30]

We can evade differing temporal perspectives in these cases only by considering counterfactual judgments or actual judgments about hypothetical cases. But as I've already noted, people's actual judgments about hypothetical cases may not reflect their judgments should things like that in fact become actual. When we ask real deceived people whether they'd always like to know the truth, we can reasonably suspect their positive answer is a hope that they will find out that their illusory beliefs are true. The relevance of that attitude is undercut if they turn out later to be miserable in light of the truth. And I also noted that there are

---

30 I owe this case to a public lecture by Thomas Schelling.

sometimes indeterminacies regarding the judgment that a hypothetically fully informed person would make, and that such indeterminacies also infect what someone would judge under other hypothetical conditions. And in addition, judgments under hypothetical enlightenment cannot reveal the relevant preferences of the ignorant. It is not relevant to know that I would prefer fine claret if suitably educated, when what I really want is a beer. What's more, we have noted that even fully informed judgments may not be temporally stable.

We have seen that the standard concrete cases that apparently undercut hedonism are not sufficient, for a variety of reasons, to dismiss hedonism as an uncompetitive relic. And in fact the issue of the relation of true beliefs to well-being does on balance suggest some intuitive grounds to prefer hedonism. Let me turn now to that positive case.

Clearly, another important and relevant set of concrete cases probing the relationship between truth and well-being stems from the observation that, depending on how we factor out effects on other people from the concrete cases we have been considering, we may be left with cases that are oddly reminiscent of some familiar metaphysical views that don't intuitively threaten well-being.[31] Presume that Berkeley is right about the world. It would seem intuitively that your well-being is as great as it would be if, for instance, Cartesian dualism were true, if all other relevant facts were unchanged. Presume that you feel good about your life because you have climbed a large mountain in Berkeley's world. Now ask what the relevant difference is between being in Berkeley's world and in Nozick's machine. Perhaps it is normatively relevant that other people experience things as you do in Berkeley's world but not in Nozick's. Still, to cleanly assure ourselves that we aren't influenced by considerations of other people's well-being in making our judgments about such a case, we'd have to put everybody affected relevantly by your life – say, your whole family – into a similar machine. Now what's the difference? Perhaps you'd still worry that some people, or God, would see that the whole family was being manipulated, and indeed that some were engaged in that manipulation. But consider the coordinating role that God plays even on Berkeley's conception. Why is that any better? Or for that matter, consider the coordinating role of the Galilean colorless world on some physicalist conceptions of our color experience. These things seem analogous to the manipulation you would undergo in the experience machine, at least if

---

31 Carson (2000: 51–53).

enough people were placed along with you in coordinated experience machines. And it should be that, if anything, actual manipulation and not merely people's perception of it is what matters, since those perceptions might be false, and we wouldn't want to quickly grant that other people's false perceptions make us worse off in some intrinsic way. If people think you are deceived but in fact you are not, probably that shouldn't matter *directly* to your well-being, independent of its effects. Of course, philosophers often have cherished metaphysical views. Perhaps it is deeply significant to you whether idealism or physicalism is true, and perhaps if Berkeley's world were true you would judge your life to be much worse. But then that fact will distort the relevance of your judgment about this case as a clue to the general significance of truth to individual well-being. We should consider rather the judgment of the nonphilosopher who has no idiosyncratic commitments at risk in just this area.

The obvious parallels between these metaphysical cases and more ordinary deception cases suggest some support for the hedonist treatment of deception. And there are less metaphysically extravagant scenarios that can make something like the same point. Assume that you want to be loved, and that your family acts throughout your life in some behaviorally loving way. But now presume both that our ordinary conceptions of love, shared by you and your family, are naive, and that the complex facts of human psychology are very dark, so that in fact no one is loved in the way in which our folk theory suggests that people would love people if they behaved as your family behaves toward you. Does that mean you are worse off than you believe yourself to be? Not, I think, in any clear way supported by commonsense intuition. This case may occasion worries in those with significant and hence idiosyncratic theoretical commitments about the truth of behaviorism or of some psychological theory of love, but those idiosyncratic commitments seem an element of distortion.

And my positive case has another component. There is yet another set of related cases that we need to bear in mind if we are to judge adequately the intuitive significance of the truth of experience for well-being. These, like the metaphysical cases, are related to cases we have reviewed that apparently tell against hedonism, yet they intuitively tell, on balance, against at least the dominant desire-based accounts and for something like hedonism. These cases indeed invoke a characteristic difficulty for desire-based accounts.[32]

32 Overvold (1980, 1982).

120

The true satisfaction of desires may make no difference in one's experience, and in a way that hence has no obvious intuitive relevance to one's well-being. One may have desires for something to happen much later to a stranger one meets momentarily on a ferry and will never see again, and the fulfillment of those desires has nothing intuitive to do with one's well-being.[33] And many object to the thought that one's well-being can be affected by things that happen after one's death, even if some informed desire is fulfilled after death. The obvious way to modify desire-based accounts to evade these difficulties is to build in an experience requirement, that one experience the satisfaction of the relevant desire. But of course that doesn't allow desire-based accounts to deploy some of their alleged intuitive advantages over hedonism in dealing with the truth of experience.[34]

Griffin, for reasons like this, doesn't build an experience requirement into his characteristic desire-based account, and grants that it is in some sense initially intuitive to insist that the satisfaction of a desire after death is irrelevant to well-being. But he argues that there is a slide between cases that are intuitively better for his view and these after-death cases, which should adjust our intuitions about the latter:

Some of our aims are not fulfilled until we are dead; some, indeed, being desires for then, could not be. But is this so embarrassing after all? You might have a desire – it could be an informed one, I think – to have your achievements recognized and acknowledged. An enemy of yours might go around slandering you behind your back, successfully persuading everyone that you stole all your ideas, and they, to avoid unpleasantness, pretend in your presence to believe you. If that could make your life less good, then why could it not be made less good by his slandering you with the extra distance behind your back that death brings? You might well be willing to exert yourself, at risk of your life, to prevent these slanders being disseminated after your death. You might, with full eyes open, prefer that course to longer life with a ruined reputation after it. There seems nothing irrational in attaching this value to posthumous reputation. And the value being attached to it doesn't seem to be moral or aesthetic or any kind other than the value to be attached to the life as a life to be lived.[35]

33 Parfit (1984: 494).
34 It also requires that we develop some way of balancing experienced satisfaction of a desire accompanied by unknown frustration, which, if it is not to collapse into hedonism, requires adjudication of some of the balancing difficulties that Sumner faces.
35 Griffin (1986: 23).

121

There are various things to note about this paragraph that are related to problems with Griffin's cases against hedonism that we've already discussed. Again, his appeal is largely to our actual preferences, and once again there is a pretty weak claim to nonirrationality playing a crucial role. What's more, value attached to a life as a life to be lived is not obviously the same as well-being. It is also hard to control in our reactions to this case for the real risks of real unhappiness that such slander during your life would imply. But my main point is that a slippery slope argument can be run in two directions. If we are confident that the satisfaction of desires after death does not matter to well-being, as many are, then Griffin's argument should convince us that slandering us behind our backs doesn't in itself affect our well-being during life. What makes us first and misleadingly think there is a difference in the cases is simply their impurity, the fact that slander while we are alive creates all sorts of risks that we will suffer experienced effects even if, in lucky fact, we don't ever suffer those effects.

This is not to say that there are no currents in our common sense that suggest the significance of what happens after death to well-being. But they are hardly decisive. The majority of philosophers who are not theologically inclined should be especially wary of distortions that have been introduced by the long historical focus on salvation. Aristotle perhaps introduced this topic into philosophy,[36] and even his own conclusion on the topic does not support a strong significance for what happens after death, but merely a "weak and negligible" one. And it is probably also relevant that some of his wording suggests literal causal effects on the dead that we should not take seriously.

Certainly, there is plenty in our tradition to suggest that what happens after death does not matter. If there is any text which can claim to be central to our tradition, Sophocles' *Oedipus the King* is such a text.[37] It's final line is "[C]ount no man happy till he dies, free of pain at last."[38] It is also interesting that the final speech of the chorus, which concludes with that line, in fact suggests a link between the issue of effects on the dead and the general importance of deception and truth to well-being. The overall suggestion of the play, perhaps the most important and dramatic example in our literature of a life lived, for a while, in serious falsehood, is in accord with the suggestions of hedonism. Oedipus falls

36 Aristotle (1980: Book I, Chapters 9–11).
37 Sophocles (1984).
38 Ibid., 251.

122

calamitously into a bad life, the play suggests, when he finds out the truth about himself. It contrasts his former greatness with the black sea of terror which has *now* overwhelmed him.[39] Immediately following the main revelation to Oedipus, the chorus says that the joy of his life is ground down to nothing.[40] The messenger who reports Jocasta's death and Oedipus's self-blinding in the next scene says of the pair:

> The joy they had so lately,
> the fortune of their old ancestral house
> was deep joy indeed. Now, in this one day,
> wailing, madness and doom, death, disgrace,
> all the griefs in the world that you can name,
> all are theirs forever.[41]

Don't we really agree that he was better off not knowing? Of course, this does not imply that Oedipus would not have been better off than he actually was even before finding out the horrible truth if his then false beliefs had been true. But the dominant suggestion of the play is certainly that living in falsehood — living in falsehood in perhaps the grandest and most terrible manner in our literature — is of quite limited significance to well-being. Otherwise there would be no calamitous fall for Oedipus upon his discovery of the truth.

At the very least, the relationship between truth and well-being is too intuitively complex for the concrete cases of deception we have surveyed to firmly establish that desire-based accounts or objectivist accounts are superior to hedonism. And indeed, the great difficulties and complexities that they introduce into these accounts suggest some argumentative advantage for hedonism, which at least gives a simple and definite answer that isn't obviously false for all the cases, and is supported by some intuitions. Still, this is not to deny that the concrete cases that are customarily deployed against hedonism reflect deep and general intuitive currents that are worthy of respect and further consideration, and that a deeper consideration of trade-offs between happiness and truth is required. We will return to these issues in a more general and abstract way in section IV. While the concrete cases that are customarily deployed against hedonism are not alone adequate to privilege competitors over it, we will later try to probe the deeper and more important general currents beneath them.

39 Ibid., 251.
40 Ibid., 234.
41 Ibid., 237.

III

While our discussion has already involved some concrete cases that concern objectivist theorists, our primary focus so far has been largely on the dominant desire-based accounts. Contemporary arguments for objectivist accounts of well-being over hedonism, at least to the degree that they are distinct from the alleged counterexamples that we have already discussed, seem to rest less on particular concrete cases, and perhaps more on the general intuitive considerations that we will discuss in the next section. Still, let me say a little about some relevant and relatively concrete cases that may seem to specially favor objectivism.

Objectivist accounts have a variety of forms, but all specify individual well-being or good without regard to individual psychological attitudes. Perhaps there is a set of basic and objective human needs – say, paradigmatically, food or health – which we all have independent of any of our subjective desires or pleasures. These needs may define our well-being. Or perhaps there is an objective form of human flourishing of a more traditional Aristotelian and perfectionist sort. Or perhaps, as Rawls suggests in *A Theory of Justice*, we should compare the well-being of individual lives by comparing amounts of "primary goods" possessed by the individuals in question, where primary goods are, more or less, universal instrumental goods, goods that one wants as a means of pursuing one's projects whatever those subjective projects turn out to be.[42]

Consider the first and second forms of objectivism, needs-based and perfectionist accounts. There are such accounts that make room for the significance of truth. The most obvious forms have intuitive difficulties we've already noted, in failing to allow for the proper treatment of cases in which individuals fail to care about the truth of their experience. But the health of those who don't care about it and receive no pain from ill health is another reasonably concrete case that may intuitively support objectivism of these sorts against hedonism or desire-based accounts.

But such a case is double-edged, since there are also related intuitive difficulties for objectivist accounts of well-being that, unlike hedonist or desire-based accounts, are not rooted in individual psychological states. While it is clear that health has intuitive relevance to well-being, that is most obvious when we care about it, and hence when its value is recognized by desire-based accounts or other mental-state accounts like hedonism. Objectivist accounts, to the degree that they do invoke features

---

42   Rawls (1971).

of people's lives that they do not care about, are not particularly intuitive. Unlike both hedonist and desire-satisfaction accounts of well-being, they can be criticized as intuitively insufficiently subjectivist, as paying too little attention to relevant features of individual psychology.[43]

Another relevant point about health is this: Many things have intuitively healthy states – for instance, coral reefs and corporations, and even cancers and viruses. But it is probably the dominant intuition that it is things with psychologies, in particular, that are of genuine normative significance. If life matters for its own sake, it is hard to see why all life doesn't matter for its own sake.[44] And it is certainly hard to balance the health of different organisms.

But the main point is that it is not obvious to common sense that health is important to an individual's well-being when at least their rational individual preference suggests otherwise. Other things may matter more, even selfishly. Imagine spending some health on salvation or on artistic, athletic, or intellectual achievement. Of course, preferences aren't pleasure, even though frustrated preferences are characteristically unpleasant. But I am in the process of arguing that rational preferences for one's well-being will track hedonic tone. And one's health that is not ever reflected in hedonic tone does not seem properly to matter much. Ill health is characteristically eventually painful. But if we know that some form of ill health will never cause us any pain – say, because we will certainly die first – then it seems insignificant to our well-being. Death is perhaps an extreme form of ill health, but of course it removes all possibility of pleasure.

Similar intuitive difficulties trouble the third type of objectivist account. Universal means, of the type of Rawls's primary goods, involve elements that because of individual peculiarities of projects or motivation may bear insufficient relation to the things someone cares about, and hence are not intuitively relevant to their well-being. What's more, some individuals – for instance, those with certain sorts of handicaps – are not able to transform such objective "goods" into intuitive well-being as efficiently as others. They hence seem subject to discrimination by such accounts, and indeed in a way that suggests that there must be some deeper phenomenon against which we intuitively assess individual well-being and hence their relative discrimination. This is not to deny that institutions of certain particular kinds should distribute some generally helpful good that it is their special concern to distribute – for instance, money or food or medical

---

43   Sumner (1996: 45–80).
44   Sumner (1996) makes similar points.

treatment – without regard to individual peculiarities. But, as Griffin has argued, there is plausibly a rationale explaining why these generally helpful goods are good that lies in their aiding some human well-being of a deeper sort.[45] It is by reference to that deeper well-being that we can see that wealth is a good. But it is also by reference to that deeper sort of well-being that we can argue – as, for instance, Plato argues in the *Laws* – that too much wealth is destructive of well-being, or that certain individuals for special reasons should receive less or more of some particular generally helpful good, or instead some alternative good that is especially helpful to them. Levels of generally helpful goods are not intuitively sensitive enough to determine the well-being of those who are unusual in various ways.

One complication: Hedonism itself is in a recognizable sense an objectivist view. But still, our pain and pleasure that we don't care much about in the specific sense involving desire are yet at least recognizably relevant to our own selfish good.

We have so far identified no clear intuitive support for objectivism over hedonism. Indeed, the reverse may be true. There are two final classes of relatively concrete intuitive objections to hedonism that we have yet to consider, which are not specifically identified with either objectivist or desire-based accounts. Perhaps they simply suggest a hedonism more sophisticated and qualified than my own, but in any case we should consider them.

First, it has long been held that certain pleasures or desires shouldn't count normatively because of their sources. Foolish happiness, which we've already discussed, may be an instance of this, but there are others that are more characteristic of this set of objections. It may seem intuitive to claim that the pleasures of sadism or successful murder have no positive normative significance at all. And if the oppressed feel no pain about something, that may be just a sign of their deeper and more insidious psychological oppression.[46] Second, it may seem that the pain of the evil is a good thing, and the happiness of the evil is a bad thing, even independent of its particular source for them. Kant famously says at the beginning of the first section of the *Groundwork*: "[A]n impartial rational spectator can take no delight in seeing the uninterrupted prosperity of a being graced with no feature of a pure and good will, so that a good will

---

45   Griffin (1986: 40–55).
46   Sen (1987: 45–46).

seems to constitute the indispensable condition even of worthiness to be happy."[47]

My first point in response is that such cases are not all on balance intuitively troubling against simple hedonist conceptions, nor against contrary simple desire-based conceptions, of *individual well-being*. Even intuitive retributionist conceptions of punishment must suppose that bad things happen to the evildoer who is punished, that the punishment is bad for them.[48] Otherwise it wouldn't be a punishment. And the sadist is, after all, intuitively one who finds their own good in the suffering of another. That is part of what makes sadism so troubling and abhorrent. Note also, in the quote from Kant, that his point is that prosperity and happiness themselves are what those without pure will don't deserve. Pain is bad for the evil as for the good, and pleasure is good for them equally. If not, these things would not intuitively constitute punishments and rewards that might be justly or unjustly distributed.

Still, it might be that nonautonomous pleasures, in the sense we've already noted in our discussion of Sumner, provide decent concrete cases that tell intuitively against hedonic conceptions of well-being. But note also that these cases provide intuitive difficulties for any familiar account. Desire-based accounts obviously suffer analogous difficulties, and no intuitively plausible objectivist account can simply ignore the intuitive relevance of happiness to the well-being even of the deeply psychologically oppressed. Oppressed as they are, would they be better off being miserable also?

And yet, there is a sense in which the oppression of someone may play an intuitively negative role in their well-being that isn't easily captured by hedonist accounts, analogous to the intuitively negative role of false experience that Sumner and Griffin do succeed in invoking. And there is, in any case, a recognizable intuitive pull to the claim that the pleasure of the evil shouldn't count normatively as good even if it does count intuitively toward their own abhorrent well-being. There is, we should admit, some contrast between one's well-being and goodness *tout court*. Perhaps the pleasures of the guilty or sadistic ought to count against the overall value of a state of affairs, and not for it at all. The pains of a guilty person may not be bad from the point of view of the universe even if they are bad for the evildoer.

47 Kant (1996a: 49).
48 Carson (2000: 70–71).

To address these matters properly, we will need to turn now from a piecemeal consideration of concrete cases relevant to individual well-being to a more general consideration of intuitive features of competing conceptions of the good. The hedonic tradition is one version of a plausible insistence that overall good must ultimately be rooted in the well-being and good of the sentient. But issues about punishment and reward remind us of the possible difference between conceptions of individual well-being, which have been our main concern so far, and conceptions of the good. The latter will be our primary focus in the next section. And of course we have also seen throughout this and the preceding section that single concrete cases are indecisive even for issues about intuitive individual well-being. We must, it seems, consider things more generally and abstractly if we are to make adequate progress in developing our understanding of commonsense commitments about well-being or the good.

IV

The methodological difficulties presented by reliance on concrete intuitive cases suggest that it would be better to deploy abstract cases. This can assure at once that impurities are minimized and that a relatively wide range of particular concrete instances are considered simultaneously, at least by implication. The best discussion of well-being or the good with this form that I know, which in fact incorporates most of the various important general factors suggested by the concrete cases we have surveyed in the last two sections but in a purer and more systematic way, is eight pages of W. D. Ross's *The Right and the Good*.[49] This discussion is reminiscent of, and probably modeled on, Plato's excellent discussion in the *Philebus*, but applied to a wider range of goods.[50]

Ross argues that four things are intrinsically good: pleasure, virtuous disposition and action, knowledge, and the proper apportionment of pleasure and pain to the virtuous and vicious.[51] He does so by deploying a characteristic pattern of argument to each of the relevant cases. Here's

49 Ross (1930: "V: What Things are Good?," 134–141).
50 It is also reminiscent of Moore (1903: 84). For effective criticism of Moore's argument, see Feldman (2004: 191–192.)
51 There are certain qualifications of his claims about pleasure and pain, to which we will return.

the case against mere hedonism and for the intrinsic good of virtuous disposition and action:

> And if any one is inclined... to think that, say, pleasure alone is intrinsically good, it seems to me enough to ask the question whether, of two states of the universe holding equal amounts of pleasure, we should really think no better of one in which the actions and dispositions of all the persons in it were thoroughly virtuous than of one in which they were highly vicious. Most hedonists would shrink from giving the plainly false answer which their theory clearly requires.[52]

As honest hedonists we should admit that, if the profiles of hedonic tone present in two situations are identical, and if the probabilities of future profiles of hedonic tone associated with those situations are likewise identical, and if in one situation all actions and dispositions are vicious and in the other virtuous, then we are committed to the answer Ross thinks plainly false. Nevertheless, we have a reasonable response to his objection. Arguments with this general pattern, which may seem to support against mere hedonism the basic normative significance of virtue or knowledge or of the retributory distribution of pleasure and pain, are misleading. The paired cases under consideration involve equalized basic value of the kind introduced in section I, I claim. Therefore, they magnify the intuitive significance of any other sorts of value that they contain. But of course this need not be basic value.

Indeed, Ross misses some kinds of value that are delivered by his test but that have little plausible moral weight. There are intuitive characteristic excellences with a certain rough degree of specificity for all sorts of human projects, activities, artifacts, and institutions, and also for entities and organs created by mechanisms of natural selection or that mimic natural selection. Equalized cases such as Ross deploys can magnify the intuitive significance of such intuitive excellences and goods until they seem to be of basic normative significance. But they aren't. Or at the very least, not all of them are.

Some instances of this phenomenon are the goods beyond pleasure that Ross suggests are also intrinsic: (i) As we saw in the last part, consequentialism can indirectly deliver the derived normative significance of virtues and the right. And considerations of equitable distribution, and not merely the amount of basic value contained, may plausibly constrain our sense of the relative value of overall states of affairs. (ii) The truth

---

52   Ross (1930: 134).

of beliefs is an obvious epistemic value, and there is perhaps a further epistemic value of knowledge beyond mere true belief.

And there are other cases that Ross's method shows to be significant in some sense, which he ignores, and which cannot plausibly be incorporated into any overall account of basic normative value in all of their instances. They include (i) the health of all organisms and even of organs and cells,[53] (ii) the satisfaction of at least most desires or whims, (iii) the excellence of forms of practice of almost any sort, and (iv) the significance of works of art according to any set of coherent standards. All these things, all members of each class, can be made to seem significant using Ross's method. If other sorts of value are otherwise equal, why wouldn't it be better for there to be a healthy rhododendron, a satisfied whim, a flourishing corporation, or better intonation in the woodwinds? Of course, these new sorts of value will conflict in real cases, which set the health of one organ or the success of one institution against another. But equalized cases of the sort that Ross deploys suggest that they have some sort of value nonetheless. However, my point is that it need not be basic normative value, or even value of any ethical or political significance.

We cannot tell using the method of equalized cases the nature of the value in question – whether, for instance, the value has basic significance for ethics, or whether indeed it reflects forms of assessment that can be justified at all. And yet we saw that concrete cases alone are deceptive. So what are we to do? We might retreat to the claim that commonsense intuition can tell us nothing of significance. But I believe that we can do somewhat better. We did somewhat better even in the last two sections – for instance, in our treatment of truth and unrecognized satisfactions, where we saw enough pattern in our intuitions about relatively concrete cases to suggest some intuitive advantage for hedonism. But clearly some further development of the method of abstract cases is desirable.

As a first step, we should develop Ross's abstract intuition tests so that they treat a wider range of cases than merely simple equalized pairs. If we consider abstract trade-off cases, in which we force our intuition to balance the significance of more of one good and less of another, we may still be unable to fully assess the intuitive nature of the values involved, but we can get a better sense of their intuitive significance and depth, of their overall importance when the chips are down. Important and dominant good at least points in the direction of the sort of basic value that we seek.

---

53 Indeed, he seems to explicitly discount the significance of disease on page 134.

Ross himself takes some steps in this direction.[54] But, since his treatment is the best intuitionist treatment of these issues that we possess, it is unfortunate that his development of the topic is incomplete and in some particulars not very convincing. It would indeed be a very large task to treat abstract trade-off cases properly. Still, we can gain some insight from Ross's attempt.

What I am calling trade-off cases are pairs of situations in which it is specified that, holding all other sorts of value constant (and all attendant counterfactuals and probabilities relevantly identical, and hence their contribution to intuitive value identical), one situation is clearly worse in respect to one sort of value but better in respect to a second, while the second situation is clearly better in respect to the first sort of value and worse in respect to the second. To prevent various concrete irrelevancies from influencing our intuition, and so that these pairs capture at once a range of instances, we should at least as a first stab articulate the pairs in something like the pure and abstract manner that Ross deploys. We should develop abstract trade-off cases.

While it is important that the cases we consider be abstract and pure, it may be that there are some additional concrete conditions that are useful in avoiding obviously misleading currents in our intuition when dealing with the significance of certain goods like pleasure. For instance, perhaps it is important that the pleasure in question not be our own, because our normative intuitions are not cleanly engaged in cases where our own pleasure is at issue, in part because of natural selfishness and in part because of the desire to avoid obvious selfishness. But such concrete additions may themselves be dangerous and misleading, and perhaps sufficient abstraction can also guard against most misleading elements in our responses. So let's attempt this method.

To narrow our treatment to the cases that seem most significant for our purposes, I will consider trade-off cases that range across the goods deployed in the alleged counterexamples to hedonism discussed in the last two sections and also the goods that Ross's own discussion suggests are intrinsic goods. Ross fails to isolate the intuitive intrinsic value of health that some objectivists may favor, and also that of unrecognized desire satisfaction. But, as I said, he does isolate virtuous action, knowledge (implying true belief), and the concordance of pleasure and virtue. He also suggests, in a manner apparently supported by his test, that pleasure is

54   Ross (1930: "VI: Degrees of Goodness," 142–154).

an intrinsic good somewhat unlike the others. It is an intrinsic good only when it has appropriate causes, when it isn't vicious pleasure. We should consider this qualification on hedonism as well.

There are two relevant kinds of trade-off cases, those that compare goods within the abstract categories just noted and those that make cross-category comparisons. Consideration of the first sort of pairs may sometimes help put the second sort in the proper light. Consider health. Any genuine foundational role for health requires some account of how the health of one cell or organism or organ or ecosystem trades against another. Nevertheless, let me focus on the crucial cross-category comparisons – in the first instance, the trading of pleasure for health.

Here we can be guided by our discussion in the last section, which was at least implicitly abstract. Imagine the relevantly abstract pair of situations. The kind of health that isn't eventually positively reflected in the hedonic tone of the creatures involved, the kind our pair introduces, seems for that very reason of lesser significance. Intuitively, the health of the sentient is the health that intuitively matters, and its worth is at least reflected in its effects on that sentience, mediated perhaps by preference. Intuition cedes, it seems, the dominance of pleasure over health in this abstract trade-off case. So Ross was right to ignore these trade-offs. The method we are attempting works for these cases, but doesn't reveal an interesting new basic good.

What of unrecognized desire satisfaction? Here, as we saw at least implicitly in section II, there are no firm commonsense intuitions that resolve these issues abstractly and at once in favor of competitors to hedonism. Rather, there are conflicting intuitions, which, for instance, can slide up or down the slippery slope between unrecognized satisfactions received after death and those received during life. There isn't a uniform intuition abstractly rooted. Concrete details matter in conflicting ways. I believe that we also saw on balance in section II that cases of this general sort, indeed of a more general sort that includes the significance of true belief to well-being, favor hedonism. But the methodology of abstract cases itself apparently fails to achieve adequate resolution in this application.

So far, abstract trade-off cases have yielded little. But there is a still more refined version of the method that we might attempt. It might be that relatively general factors found in the concrete cases that favor hedonism regarding the significance of true belief and unrecognized satisfaction in the preceding sections can somehow be parlayed into specially relevant general conditions, which allow us to specify extra but still fairly general constraints on what we might call "relatively abstract" trade-off cases. The conditions might allow our intuition some determinate purchase, yet be conditions that we can see to be appropriately revealing and not inappropriately misleading.

Still, we shouldn't be confident of that possibility for trade-offs involving unrecognized satisfaction, since the factors to which I appealed in section II don't seem to be of the proper form to allow it. We instead relied, for instance, on the firmness of intuitions about well-being after death and on abstract similarities with other cases where intuitions were less firm. So again, the fact that Ross ignored these sorts of cases may seem hence reasonable. They don't seem good instances for his method or anything in its rough vicinity.

Yet the issue of unrecognized satisfaction is closely related to that of true belief, and this we can treat by reference to Ross's explicit discussion of that issue. So perhaps this provides an opening for something like Ross's method. Consider knowledge.

Here the first sort of abstract trade-off tests, which probe trade-offs within a single category of good, are quite interesting. Ross attempts to develop an account of how various forms of knowledge and true belief are properly to be traded against other forms, and while it is perhaps not convincing, we should be sensitive to the obvious difficulties that he faced. To work things out properly we would need, for instance, to consider the relative weight of truth as opposed to the third condition beyond belief required for knowledge. I find it hard to believe that the presence or absence of false barns in one's vicinity, which consensus now holds relevant to the third condition, could plausibly be held relevant to one's well-being, but still perhaps something beyond the truth of one's belief might intuitively be so relevant. Ross considers such factors as the degree of match of conviction and evidence and also the generality of the content of the beliefs in question. Issues about content are especially complex. It may seem that deception on some matters is more intuitively harmful to individual well-being than deception on other matters, whether an individual cares about that difference or not. But yet it also seems unsupportably paternalistic to ignore individual tastes and preferences about the relative seriousness of different forms of deception. There are many difficulties, and I commend Ross's discussion to your attention, though it clearly requires further development.

But, however that development goes, the crucial cases for our purposes are relatively abstract trade-offs across categories of goods: of pleasure, on the one hand, and life in the truth on the other. How much suffering is more true belief worth? My own even fully abstract intuition is that true belief bought for suffering is of no deep and intrinsic worth to well-being, and is only good in an obvious epistemic sense that is of no intrinsic moral significance. I have a firm intuitive reaction to even a fully abstract trade-off case of this sort. But perhaps that is idiosyncratic. Still, clearly the fully abstract trade-off does not count against hedonism in any definite way. We saw at least that in section II. Ross himself finds this general issue too difficult, and so retreats to the claim that the desire for knowledge is a virtue and that is hence why knowledge is of real, but hence somewhat indirect, significance.[55] Our central immediate concern is whether *relatively* abstract trade-off cases can be developed in a manner that provides intuitive resolution of this trade-off across categories. Still, the situation of that test regarding true belief seems no better than that regarding unrecognized satisfaction. It isn't obvious that the concrete cases that on balance support hedonism over competitors in this trade-off, as we saw section II, have general features that can appropriately be imported into relatively abstract trade-off cases. We seem left in this case with the piecemeal method of the preceding sections.

Perhaps the crucial and most troubling cases for hedonism involve the foundational significance of virtuous action, the just commensuration of pleasure to virtue, and the related concern that vicious pleasures shouldn't count normatively. Some concerns about a foundational significance for these things are in effect objections to consequentialism. Some are concerns about the value of overall states of affairs that include pleasures and pains as parts. They hence do not seem to be concerns about what I have called the basic normative value of pleasure itself. Nevertheless, we can get some grip on the intuitive relevance of these things to basic value by a consideration of abstract trade-off cases, or at least by a consideration of relatively abstract trade-off cases. It is less than first may meet the eye.

If we consider a pair of situations, with the attendant counterfactuals and probabilities specified as relevantly identical, such that the first clearly involves more suffering and less pleasure but also more virtuous action (and perhaps knowledge) and also more intuitively commensurate suffering for the intuitively guilty, my own honest but not firm intuition is that the first is worse overall than the second. Still, it does seem plausible to insist that some of the relatively concrete details will matter if we are to establish any firm and clear intuitive reaction. If we specify that it is the vicious only

---

55 Ibid., 151–152.

who suffer more, or that the suffering replaces a vicious pleasure, then my hedonist reaction is undercut. But if, on the other hand, we specify that it is the innocent who suffer more, my hedonist intuition is stronger still. The intuition in question is even stronger if the sufferer is one of the worst-off. And indeed, if the "guilty" or "vicious" person is the worst off, this undercuts even my weak intuition that perhaps the guilty or vicious should suffer more, since it seems that in the scenario in question they've already suffered enough to count as appropriately innocent and should properly grab for what they can get.

Without some relatively concrete specificity, fully abstract trade-off cases are apparently indecisive in this instance. But in this situation I claim that at least a relatively abstract trade-off case is available and effective. There are relatively abstract features that seem relevant and can resolve our intuition. What's relevant is whether the extra suffering is for the relatively worse off.

But not everyone will agree. The issue really becomes whether this is the proper relatively concrete specificity to introduce into these trade-offs. This focus on the suffering of the worst-off may seem to some an arbitrary and misleading concretizing of the pairs, because if we focus on extra suffering for the well-off and especially the well-off guilty or vicious, then we'd have other intuitions. I will argue in the next part that a focus on the suffering of the worst-off is not arbitrary here. I will argue, following Rawls and Scanlon, that it is the appropriate way to consider complex trade-offs of well-being and reflects the proper means of summing value into the overall value of states of affairs. When we cannot form an overall intuitive judgment about such a trade-off pair described with full abstraction, then consideration of the worst-off is the appropriate relative concretization to make. In this case, though not in the case of life in the truth, an effective and appropriate relatively abstract trade-off case is available, and it supports hedonism. That is because the vicious and the worst-off may not be the same individual, so methods of balancing the interests of the worst-off versus other moral interests become most clearly relevant. A relative concretization of this sort may also allow us some purchase even on the relative general importance of truth and suffering, but not in the most characteristic and telling location to resolve that particular issue, where the suffering and the deceived are the same person. So in that case we are forced back to the intuitional method of the last two sections.

My argument that the kind of relative concretization that supports hedonism is appropriate is yet to come. But there are also other grounds to believe that any relatively abstract trade-off case that introduces greater suffering or less happiness for the vicious will be misleading, that there cannot be a proper relatively abstract trade-off case that supports the view that the pain of the vicious has positive value or that their pleasure should be discounted. Any case that would properly suggest this would have to be suitably pure. And that is certainly hard to assure when such intuitive punishment for the guilty is involved, and indeed is probably impossible. That is because the phenomenon of punishment introduces all sorts of complications. For instance, in any relevant trade-off case, the extra pain of the vicious could have no positive deterrent effect. So it would be crucial that all the facts other than the extra pain be preserved in the two situations that are compared, including all the hypothetical truth about what would concretely occur if the vicious person did not suffer at all. The extra pain would have to be in that way gratuitous. But even that would not be enough to assure proper purity in the case. Remember that MAC implies a conception of the duties of reparation and of proper punishment that introduces a kind of derived normative value for punishment of the guilty even in the absence of deterrence. It would be important for any relatively abstract trade-off case that is not misleading to assure that only comparisons of basic value are in question. And when intuitive punishment is involved, that seems impossible.

But independent of my argument in the next part that proper concretization involves a focus on the worst-off, and independent of the argument that greater suffering for the vicious is a misleading concretization, there is also the following general and methodological point: The proper development of the abstract method of this section requires an understanding of the general and intuitive theoretical rationales for intuitive responses, and not just those particular intuitions themselves.

In the case at hand, as I've said, I believe that such a rationale is available to us. Kant says that "one has never heard of anyone who was sentenced to death for murder complaining that he was dealt with too severely and therefore wronged; everyone would laugh in his face if he said this."[56] But let me vary the figure. We might address a relatively badly off suffering person and suggest that they might have been better off, but then the world would have needed to include more lying or ignorance or a more striking mismatch between virtue and happiness, even though for some reason all that wouldn't in fact have made anyone else suffer more. If we

---

56   Kant (1996b: 475).

136

concluded, "Things really are better this way, though you must, regrettably, suffer more," then I think we should reasonably and intuitively feel very uncomfortable about that. Frankly, it would seem appropriate if they did worse than chuckle. The next part will explain why this point isn't merely rhetorical, why it is appropriate to require that relatively abstract trade-off cases assume this particular form.

Absent a consensus on such a rationale, intuitions will differ and cannot resolve the issue. That is the most crucial point of this section. But I also think a comparison to what Ross says puts my own intuitions, supported by a rationale or not, in at least a relatively good light:

I think... that pleasure is definitely inferior in value to virtue and knowledge.... Most people are convinced that human life is in itself something more valuable than animal life, though it seems highly probable that the lives of many animals contain a greater balance of pleasure over pain than the lives of many human beings. Most people would accept Mill's dictum that 'it is better to be a human being dissatisfied than a pig satisfied'.... Many people whose opinion deserves the greatest respect have undoubtedly thought that the promotion of the general happiness was the highest possible ideal. But the happy state of the human race which they aimed at producing was such a state as the progress of civilization naturally leads us to look forward to, a state much of whose pleasantness would spring from such things as the practice of virtue.... [I]f they thought the state of maximum happiness would be one whose happiness sprang from such things as the indulgence of cruelty, the light-hearted adoption of ill-grounded opinions, and enjoyment of the ugly, they would immediately reject such an ideal.... [What] amount of pleasure is precisely equal in value to a given amount of virtue?... [I]t seems to me much more likely that *no* amount of pleasure is equal to any amount of virtue.[57]

Some analytical remarks about this paragraph. From Ross's sensitive general method, we first get a retreat to the single and misleading concrete case of the contented pig, which is not supported (like relative concretization involving the worst-off) by a suitable rationale. It *is* so supported in Aristotle, but Ross lacks his account of a species-specific human *telos*. Then we get an implausible prediction about the opinions of others, citing grounds for their rejection of pleasures that are to the contrary embraced by many contemporary fans of *jouissance*. And we end, worst of all, with a wildly counterintuitive and even offensive general claim.[58]

---

57 Ross (1930: 149–150).
58 This is the guts of Ross's discussion of these trade-offs. But he makes some other arguments, and I commend his overall discussion to your attention. Ross (1939: 252–310) revisits the

How *dare* we say to the suffering that no amount of their suffering would make the world worse when traded for a little more virtue somewhere, or a bit more general knowledge, or a bit more suffering for the intuitively guilty?

But, as I said, Ross does provide the best and most thoughtful anti-hedonist discussion of the good I know that is rooted in intuition and couched at the proper level of generality and purity. It just isn't good enough.

We can properly conclude three things, in decreasing order of certainty. First, there are no extant competitive conceptions of the good or well-being that possess a definite overall intuitive advantage over hedonism. This is not grounds, of course, to stop trying for something better than all current competitors. But the competitors span the three types deployed in standard characterizations of possible conceptions of the good or well-being. And until we have a coherent account of all our intuitions, we have no reason to believe it to be possible. Hence we come to my second conclusion. Many ethicists believe that they *know*, on grounds of intuition, that hedonism is false. But they know no such thing. Third, at least if the rationale for a specific appropriate concretization of relatively abstract trade-off cases that I have promised in this section is available, but to a large degree even if it is not, hedonism is better supported by our overall intuition than its competitors.

good. But the overall thrust of his remarks is defensive elaboration, rather than the development of a systematic alternative to the account in the earlier book. One relevant detail is on page 275, where he suggests that his earlier claim that any amount of virtue trumps any amount of pleasure is not mistaken, but that he should have concluded from it that pleasure and virtue are different sorts of value.

5

Natural Good

Hedonism is in adequate accord with our normative intuitions. But I have also promised a direct argument, independent of appeals to normative intuition, for the truth of that element of the Hedonic Maximin Principle. That is the task of this chapter.

Here is the short version: Ethical discourse is justificatory reason giving. And this requires hedonism, in the world we inhabit, whether we like it or not and whatever our normative intuitions. That is because pain and pleasure involve the only unconstituted natural normative properties found in the world.

This is a new metaethical alternative, within the cracks between familiar views. Justificatory reason giving has a metaphysical cost, but because there is this new metaethical alternative, we can pay it.

You may reasonably worry that hedonism is antecedently more plausible than any of the controversial metaphysical and metaethical claims that I will make here in support of it. But the nature of ethical discourse as justificatory reason giving requires an objective and asymmetrical vindication of its key normative claims over possible competitors. Normative intuitions alone are not enough. We must develop some understanding of what conditions might make our intuitions suitably true or otherwise asymmetrically appropriate, and see that those conditions are in fact plausible. And the only obvious thing that could provide such a vindication of a specific conception of the sole basic normative value is the existence in our world and all relevant alternatives of merely that type of basic value. While the story I will tell here is inevitably controversial, it is a plausible story that would deliver the truth of hedonism. And I will argue that there is no other suitably plausible story that can deliver the truth of hedonism or any competitor.

Section I sketches background for my metaethical proposal. Section II presents hedonic value as unconstituted natural good. Sections III through V develop crucial details that matter later on, including the interpersonally comparable ordinality of that value.

I

Cognitivism holds that normative sentences can be true or false of the world in the manner of ordinary declarative sentences about ice cubes in a glass of lemonade. My hedonism involves a form of cognitivism, but not a familiar form. It is not a kind of non-naturalism, nor is it a kind of what I will call "constitutive naturalism". And yet it bears certain affinities with both. It holds that there are *basic* properties – by which I mean properties not constituted by others – that are at once natural and normative. It is, in particular, the view that physical pain and pleasure often involve such properties.

Before I sketch this view, it is helpful to consider the range of currently dominant metaethical alternatives. Each of those alternatives falls prey to a variant of the same abstract argument. None can reconcile a plausible and widely shared conception of the world, on the one hand, and the demands of justificatory reason giving, on the other. This provides motivation to pursue my metaethical proposal, even beyond its truth. Of course, I cannot hope to disprove all standing metaethical views within a single section. But it will be worth articulating a general worry about these familiar views in order to provide necessary contrast and motivation for my positive proposal.

There are two key presumptions of my abstract negative argument. First, normative practice, by which I mean our practice of ethical and political evaluation, has as a central and indefeasible commitment something I have called "justificatory reason giving". Justificatory reason giving crucially involves (a) normative claims that express justificatory reasons for or against things, which reasons are (b) governed by consistency and other logical constraints, and are also (c) capable of something we might call "deep justification". To give a deep justification of a normative claim is to show that no conflicting claim is appropriate, that there is an objective asymmetry that vindicates a practice of reason giving deploying the first against a practice deploying the second.

Let me explain some of this jargon. The peculiarly *normative* feature of normative discourse, of ethical and political discourse, is its capacity to provide an articulation of reasons as justifications. This is a relatively complex feature of that discourse, and it is related closely to, but yet distinct from, other aspects.

Reasons as justifications are *not* simply reasons as motives. We should grant that normative utterance expressing ethical or political evaluation has a peculiar capacity to motivate people. Coming to believe that someone has done *wrong* can invoke complicated and potentially powerful emotions, which some have thought that all normative utterance expresses. And normative utterance can be used to command people, to push them around, because it not only expresses emotion, but also engages it. And not only emotion but also wants and desires seem closely connected to normative utterance or judgment. It seems at least unusual to judge something wrong and have no motivation at all to avoid it. Also, I have noted ways in which benevolence and reciprocity are key moral motives. But there is no simple connection between motivation and the normative. It is possible to judge something wrong and yet do it, and indeed want to do it. It is possible to feel very guilty about something and yet know that it is right. And so the crucial normativity of moral utterance reflects its connection not to reasons as *motives* to act, but to reasons as *justifications* of acts. If such things as reasons as justifications can be made sense of independent of motivation, and we will see that they can, then the motivational force of normative claims might be a rather contingent matter, not essential to their meaning in any strong sense. But in any case, we must distinguish between justificatory reason giving and providing reasons as motives. We may not want to do what we ought to do.

Ethical theories should not rest on bad puns. Words are ambiguous, and sometimes we fail to note the ambiguities. "Reason" and "rational" are a crucial case in point. Some theorists simply conflate reasons as motivations with reasons as justifications. But there are other, subtler conflations of which we should also be wary. Some say that we must attribute thoughts to persons and interpret their utterances under a constraint of "rationality", that we must assume that thinkers and speakers will rationally infer, say, P *and* Q from P and from Q, and also move in a rational way from wanting P and believing that Q is a means to P to doing Q.[1] But rationality seems to involve reasons, and reasons to introduce normativity of some sort. Still, it is important to see that this sort of rationality, which may be crucial to interpretation, isn't "normative" in anything like the

---

1 Since people sometimes fail to make obvious inferences, perhaps we should ascribe thoughts and interpretations that make them seem as rational as possible. Only if they fail to be minimally rational will they lack thoughts and meaningful speech.

141

traditional sense appropriate to the good and right. If I think that it would have been rational, in the sense relevant to interpretation, for Hitler to invade England before he invaded the Soviet Union, I am not normatively endorsing his invading England in any sense. I am not claiming that he had any justification for that. Rather than infer from his premises or act on his desire, I think he should have shot himself sooner or gone back to painting. The "normativity" of the right and the good, which some people think cannot be constituted out of mundane concrete things, has nothing obvious to do with the rationality that allegedly constrains interpretation. Reasons even as *coherent* motivations are not obviously reasons as justifications.

Both reasons as motivations and rationality as coherence are different phenomena than reasons as justifications. They may be entwined with reasons as justifications, and they may overlap, but they are at least somewhat different. It is reasons as justifications that are our concern here, the feature of our normative practice on which my argument rests.

Justificatory reason giving in this sense is a deep feature of our normative practice. As I said in Chapter 1, it is deep enough that skepticism about its possibility can generate a corrosive skepticism about ethics and the normative in general. It is indeed arguably the *most* central and crucial feature of our normative practice. But whether it is most central or not, it is surely central enough that at least many of us would conclude, if this commitment of ethics cannot be vindicated, that ethics is a kind of scam, just a lot of hot air. This is in fact what many philosophers and nonphilosophers believe, and for something recognizably like this reason. We can see in this way that justificatory reason giving is quite central to our practice of normative evaluation, that its loss would be enormous and shattering.

And in proper justificatory reason giving, any legitimate normative claim must be capable of asymmetrical vindication relative to possible competitors. Justificatory reasons are reasons for and against things that themselves can be vindicated. Normative evaluation is a process of evaluation that yet can itself withstand reflective evaluation and demands for legitimation. Those who come to think justificatory reason giving impossible or nonsensical often become skeptical about the entire normative enterprise, and people become skeptical about justificatory reason giving because it comes to seem arbitrary that certain things are counted as reasons for and certain things as reasons against, because it comes to seem impossible to provide the kind of deep reflective legitimation of our first-order standards of right and wrong that is characteristic of at least our form of justificatory reason giving. I grant that there might be creatures who pursue something we might appropriately, if loosely, call "justificatory reason giving" that does not demand the sort of deep reflective justification specially characteristic of our form. Indeed, our own normative practice seems to include certain people whose spade is turned fairly early, who can rest content with the assurance that something is required by our moral point of view, by our first-order practice of calling things good and bad, without requiring any deeper legitimation of that point of view. But if we are unable to make sense of some kind of legitimation of our particular first-order normative practices that drives quite deep, that rests on no starting points about which a certain arbitrariness can be suspected, on no starting points that have genuinely credible competitors, then the corrosive skepticism about the normative that many reasonable and reflective people feel seems to me quite appropriate.

This first key presumption of our argument comes down to the claim that proper normative principles must be capable of being supported by what I have been calling a direct argument. A mere appeal to normative intuitions that have obvious possible competitors is not enough.

But there is also a second key presumption of our argument here. I will presume, with the consensus of current philosophers, that it is, at least at base, a concrete world, made up of the down-to-earth and familiar things that appear in our ordinary sensory experience, or at least via the various sorts of experimental apparatus with which we now extend our experience. These are familiar things that we can taste, see, smell, measure, kick, and manipulate with instruments. I presume that there are concrete trees, tables, rocks, and humans, with spatio-temporal locations and relations, perhaps colors and other sensory properties, and maybe causal powers. And these, I presume, are in turn made up of concrete spatio-temporal bits. For instance, humans are made up of complex but concrete living cells, and these in turn perhaps of little concrete particles with causal tendencies to deflect one another and move oil drops. Even some dualist and idealist conceptions, which deploy ghostly but quasi-physical substances and powers, or sense data with concrete sensory properties, are consistent with this concrete notion of the world, but physicalist conceptions are perhaps the paradigmatic such conceptions.

Somehow everything, even complex political, social, and economic phenomena, is constituted out of relatively concrete and familiar things and their machinations and relations. Or at least that is so to this degree: Any two complete situations of the sort with which our analysis need concern itself, any two "metaphysically possible worlds", are such that if they are qualitatively identical in all their concrete micro-detail (say, the way in which the particles that make them up are arranged and ruled by basic physical laws), then they are qualitatively identical in all other ways, or at the very least in all other ways relevant to ethics. Among metaphysically possible worlds, any two that are identical in all concrete micro-detail are identical in all details. While there *are* competing conceptions of the world, they involve quite controversial, non-commonsensical, and at least prima facie implausible resources, strange abstracta like irreducible numbers or propositions, or strange non-natural properties that we can only access by bizarre faculties of Platonic intuition, strange properties that can vary while all the spatio-temporal concrete structure and detail of the world yet remains unchanged. That is why this second presumption, which we might put as the claim that everything is constituted out of the natural and hence concrete, is in accord with the rough consensus of current analytic philosophers.

My general argument in this section is that if we survey the usual metaethical suspects in light of the dual requirements set by justificatory reason giving and our concrete world, we are quickly forced to the novel metaethical position that supports my variant of hedonism, whether we like hedonism or not. The ordinary alternatives cannot deliver the necessary direct vindication of normative claims about basic value given the concrete nature of our world. But to see this, we will need to consider each class of familiar alternatives.

First candidate: non-naturalism.[2] This is the view that there are normative properties of things that yet are not constituted by the basic natural properties and relations of things in the world.[3] Non-natural properties of this type might provide a direct vindication of normative claims, but they are of course excluded by our presumption that the world is concrete. Any two relevant possible worlds that are qualitatively identical in regard to natural properties are qualitatively identical *tout court*. A robustly concrete sense of reality demands no less.

But it is also instructive to consider a second negative point, which is more closely analogous to forms of our abstract negative argument that will be deployed in the rest of this section. Despite his paradigmatic non-naturalism, G. E. Moore believed that the moral *supervened* on the natural,[4] that two things could not differ in goodness unless they differed in natural

2 Moore (1903).
3 If we include as a "thing in the world" the world itself.
4 Though he didn't use the term.

properties. And this is important if non-naturalism is to seem at all plausible. Certainly our normative practice presumes that there are criteria for goodness in natural properties. Any practice that lacked this feature would seem terribly arbitrary in its normative deliverances, probably even to those who accept that we have a bizarre and implausible faculty of discerning bizarre and unnatural moral goodness. Under such conditions, someone could do concretely exactly what someone acting rightly did, and yet be correctly discerned by the moral faculty to be doing wrong. Supervenience of the normative on the natural is a deeply indefeasible aspect of our normative practice. A moral practice without it is too radically unlike our own to be justificatory reason giving in anything like the full sense. Without supervenience, non-naturalism is absurd. But my point is that if non-naturalism is true, supervenience is not plausibly explicable. When constitution links properties – for instance, when being H-O-H constitutes being water – then it is plausible that being water supervenes on being H-O-H. But non-naturalism denies the constitution of the normative by the natural. Nor can causation plausibly link the natural and the normative properties of things, given our successful consensus view about the kinds of causal laws that govern our world. Non-naturalists may propose sui generis synthetic a priori and necessary connections between properties not linked by causation or constitution, but no one believes these at all plausible but themselves. If we exclude causation and constitution (and presume that identity is a degenerate form of constitution), then the supervenience of non-natural normative on natural properties is not plausibly explicable. And it is required for any justificatory reason giving worthy of the name. Even Moore and other non-naturalists, by their insistence on the supervenience of the normative on the natural, in fact admit this. The truly *characteristic* form of non-naturalism, which denies that supervenience, is too bizarre to take seriously. But such a bizarre and implausible situation is what we should expect if normative properties are in fact distinct in the manner that non-naturalists propose.

Second candidate: noncognitivism. Noncognitivism holds, roughly, that normative sentences do not function in the manner of ordinary declarative sentences, to assert facts about the world, but rather to express attitudes or prescribe actions. Noncognitivism is largely motivated by a robust sense of concrete reality, so it has no problem with our second presumption. But such views also have a notorious difficulty that is immediately relevant to our concerns about justificatory reason giving.

For instance, according to both Ayer and Stevenson, even when all disagreements in genuine belief about the world are removed, there may

well remain significant disagreements in attitude or emotion that underlie the acceptance of apparently contradictory normative utterances and
principles, and such that one such utterance or principle will be no more
justified or justifiable than the other.[5] Hence these paradigmatic noncog-
nitivisms cannot underwrite the central nature of our normative discourse
as justificatory reason giving. No deep and asymmetrical legitimation
of basic normative principles is possible according to these views. Later
noncognitivists work hard to develop other resources to better capture the
role of reason giving in our normative discussion.[6] But even those later
and more sophisticated forms suffer analogous problems. For instance, on
Gibbard's view, as on any reasonably plausible noncognitivist view, we are
left with the possibility of alternative practices of norm acceptance different from our own, the practices of mythical coherent anorexics or Nazis
or actual religious fanatics, which have a sort of normative symmetry with
our own, to which ours is not objectively superior. We may choose to
shield ourselves from normative interaction with such people, to eschew
normative discussion with them so as to prevent them from influencing
us, and to emote in various sophisticated ways against them, but there
is no fact that constitutes them as being in error. These people are not
subject to evaluation as irrational in some *asymmetrical* way, in some way
they cannot with equal and symmetric right apply against us.[7] Hence the
essential justificatory reason giving nature of our normative discussion is
once again lost.

There are other sorts of metaethical projects that, while not classically
noncognitivist, bear crucial similarities to noncognitivism, and that suffer
what are from our perspective similar problems. For instance, Bernard
Williams held that we cannot hope to address a justification of an intuitively ethical life something like our own to those who do not share
more or less our dispositions and desires, to those outside our own tradition.[8] But this metaethical view is problematic for the reasons we have
just traced.[9] It cannot provide the necessary asymmetrical vindication
required for the existence of genuine justificatory reason giving. There are
also "practical-reasoning theories" and "constructivist" accounts, which

5 Ayer (1936: Chapter 6); Stevenson (1937, 1944).
6 Hare (1952, 1963); Blackburn (1971, 1984, 1985, 1988); Gibbard (1990b, 1992). But see
   also Geach (1958, 1965) and van Roojen (1996).
7 Hare (1952, 1963) does not constitute an exception to this claim, because he admits the
   possibility of fanatics, though his later work improbably denies this.
8 Williams (1985). Alasdair MacIntyre is also in this tradition.
9 For elaboration of this point, see Mendola (1990a).

are popular competitors of traditional metaethical cognitivism.[10] Such accounts hold that proper normative judgments are those that are the result of proper practical reasoning,[11] or of some sort of proper construction process analogous to Rawls's use of the Original Position as a choice procedure for principles of social justice.[12] Such accounts can take two possible forms, one in which the constraints on proper reasoning or construction are capable of asymmetrical and direct vindication, and another in which they are not. I have nothing to say against the first, though the vindication of the various constraints evidently then collapses into the other metaethical alternatives. Indeed, I will deploy a variant of this form in the next chapter. But famous extant forms deploy constraints that are not capable of asymmetrical and direct vindication. This explains, for instance, Rawls's famous retreat in the Dewey Lectures and in *Political Liberalism* from any real attempt to provide one.[13] These forms fall prey to our now-familiar argument against views analogous to noncognitivism.

Since noncognitivism and its analogues and also non-naturalism are inadequate, we seem forced to naturalist cognitivism. But there is a variety of relevant types. First, there are relativist forms.[14] But naturalist relativisms either fail to capture the conflict among apparently contradictory normative practices that must be preserved as a precondition of the legitimation of one rather than another, or, even if they can preserve such conflicts of truth, fail to provide the resources for an adequate legitimation of just one of the alternative practices. In either case, naturalist relativism does not provide what the crucial justificatory reason-giving nature of our normative practice requires, the necessary objective asymmetry. So we must turn to substantially nonrelativist versions of cognitivism.[15] There are three relevant forms. Two are familiar, but fail. The third is the new alternative sketched in section II.

First, there is the traditional form of naturalist cognitivism that involves analytic reductions of normative properties to non-normative concrete base properties. Possession of particular non-normative concrete base properties is supposed to entail possession of particular normative

---

10 Darwall, Gibbard, and Railton (1992).
11 Baier (1978a, 1978b); Parfit (1984: 1–114); Gauthier (1986). But see Mendola (1986).
12 Rawls (1971, 1980, 1985).
13 Rawls (1980, 1993).
14 Harman (1975).
15 Most normative theories imply a limited kind of relativism. But what is crucial is that there be some basic level of (nonrelative) normative property that supervenes (in some nonrelative way) on some particular natural (and presumably general) properties.

properties. But it would seem that Moore's familiar open-question argument disables such accounts. Any non-normative base properties that analytically entailed the presence of a normative property could not coherently be said not to involve such a property, and yet it seems that there are equally coherent and yet distinct normative practices that differ regarding what non-normative base is sufficient for the good or the right. So the first form of naturalist cognitivism seems inadequate, and for reasons that reflect our abstract negative argument.

The second familiar form holds that while normative properties aren't themselves basic natural properties or relations, they are constituted by them, and yet in a way that doesn't require analytic reductions. This form is perhaps paradigmatically represented by Sturgeon, Brink, and Boyd.[16] Discussion of this "constitutive naturalism" requires some background.

Traditional analytic reductive naturalism presumed a traditional identification of the analytic and a priori and necessary. It is this that makes it apparently vulnerable to the open-question argument. But we have learned a new orthodoxy. Kripke has convinced us that the identity of water and H-O-H is necessary but a posteriori.[17] It is now generally believed that theoretical identities are necessary and yet cannot be evaluated on a priori grounds. This seems to undercut the Moorean worry that if normative property X is to be identical to or constituted by non-normative properties Y, then that can be evaluated on a priori grounds such as those deployed in the open-question argument. It is this space opened by our recent orthodoxy that is occupied by constitutive naturalism.

But even if we accept this general picture, it is important that the constituted normative property be at once recognizably natural and recognizably normative, that we capture the crucial normativity of the moral in a way that can properly underwrite objective asymmetries between different practices of normative evaluation. The constituted properties must be recognizably *justificatory*, and not merely motivational or merely such as to perform the causal work of the normative. The detailed constitutive naturalist proposals seem to me insufficiently convincing in this respect.[18] Hence the clearly normative and natural properties on which I will shortly

---

16 Sturgeon (1985); Boyd (1988); Brink (1989).
17 Kripke (1980).
18 The charge about normativity can be found in Sayre-McCord (1988). For apparent asymmetries between standard theoretical identities and the case at hand, rooted in normativity, see Horgan and Timmons (1990–91, 1992).

focus would serve, I believe, as the best candidates for such a treatment even if the semantic and metaphysical conception that undergirds constitutive naturalism were true.

But the central motivation for my proposal lies elsewhere. The situation is more difficult for naturalist cognitivism than these elements of recent orthodoxy suggest. The semantic and metaphysical conception that undergirds constitutive naturalism is false, and hence so is the view itself. Or at the very least that orthodoxy, rooted in a particular and controversial interpretation of Kripke, is breaking down. I believe justly so. There is wide interest in the development of what has been called "two-dimensionalism" as an alternative to the formerly standard treatment of Kripke-style cases.[19] This view,[20] which has developed a gathering confluence of support that is almost a trend, underlies the new metaethical alternative I will propose, though I believe that the objective hedonism proposed in the next section is also the most attractive way to deliver natural normativity even if constitutive naturalism is true.

Two-dimensionalism in its paradigmatic forms suggests that statements like "water is identical to H-O-H" express something that can be factored into two parts, an a posteriori and contingent claim like "H-O-H is the locally dominant watery stuff" and an a priori claim like "Water is the locally dominant watery stuff." In the strict sense, there are no necessary a posteriori propositions involved.[21] Water, if it exists, fills the watery role in our world, and that is a truth of armchair analysis, perhaps contingent but still a priori. But it is contingent and a posteriori that H-O-H, in particular, happens to fill that role.

Nevertheless, at least according to some partisans of two-dimensionalism, including David Lewis, Frank Jackson, and David Chalmers, if H-O-H were present in a possible world then it would of necessity be suitably watery, and this can be known a priori.[22] It is this point that is of greatest significance for us. For the effect of this semantical and metaphysical conception is to undergird the open-question argument against constitutive naturalism. If non-normative natural properties can suffice

---

19 Stalnaker (1978); Davies and Humberstone (1980); Horgan (1984); D. Lewis (1994); Chalmers (1996); Mendola (1997: 108–113); Jackson (1998).
20 Or rather something closely analogous that is sketched in Mendola (1997: 108–113).
21 If "water" is a rigid designator, that is only because it means something like the rigidified description "the actual locally dominant watery stuff", or more precisely *dthat* [locally dominant watery stuff], where *dthat* [x] is read so as to incorporate the description in brackets in its semantic value.
22 For critical discussion, see Byrne (1999) and Block and Stalnaker (1999).

to constitute a normative property, than that must be analytic, more or less. In light of the asymmetrical vindication of normative claims that justificatory reason giving requires, basic natural properties must imply analytically the crucial normativity of the ethical. But if all basic natural properties are non-normative, then they do not.

Ironically, the two applications of two-dimensionalism to ethics that have been developed by well-known partisans, by Jackson and Lewis, are reminiscent in various ways of proposals by constitutive naturalists and even old analytic naturalists, and hence apparently fail in familiar ways.[23] It seems to me that we are instead forced by two-dimensionalism and its ilk to a treatment of the ethical case that is analogous to Chalmer's dualist treatment of phenomenal experience – of qualia – in light of two-dimensionalism. The normativity of the ethical is such a strange feature of things that it is reminiscent of the oddity of physically unconstituted phenomenal qualia. The normativity of concrete properties can be delivered consistently with the strictures of two-dimensionalism and naturalism only if there are unconstituted natural properties that are themselves yet normative.

That indeed is my position.[24] It is a form of non-constitutive naturalist cognitivism, which identifies some normative properties with some basic natural properties. Such a position has no more problem with the open-question argument than non-naturalism, and it likewise delivers the necessary asymmetrical vindication of normative claims. And yet it assures the (degenerate) supervenience of the normative on the natural, and avoids non-natural metaphysical extravagance. And it doesn't rest on shaky and controversial necessary a posteriori propositions. And I stress again that it helpfully delivers the essential normativity of normative properties even if two-dimensionalism is a confusion and constitutive naturalism is indeed true.

Before I sketch this view, there is another class of current metaethical competitors that are worth mentioning by way of contrast, and that

---

23 D. Lewis (1989). Jackson (1998: 113–162) develops one possible strategy against the open-question argument.

24 I sometimes think that there is a complication: While two-dimensionalism or something closely analogous provides the correct analysis of the identity of water and H-O-H, still it may be that there are genuine a posteriori necessities linking our physical states to our phenomenal experience. Since the natural normative properties that I will eventually note here involve our experience of pain, that may seem to provide room for the truth of constitutive naturalism. But it is the experience of pain and not painfulness itself that might be reasonably thought to be constituted by the physical. And this would not be sufficient to deliver natural goodness. We will return to this point in section V.

also fall into the crack between traditional cognitivist and noncognitivist accounts.[25] These accounts are the so-called sensibility theories, predominantly those of Wiggins and McDowell.[26] Such accounts hold that normative properties are akin to secondary properties like color as conceived by Boyle, properties that are present in our experience of things only because of our peculiar sensibilities. And yet, these accounts continue, such properties are not for that reason seriously defective. Perhaps the property of being funny is an even more revealing analogy than color. Those who find things funny are motivated to laugh, and hence normative properties might on this model provide reasons as motivations. Maybe X is funny iff X is such as to appropriately cause the comic sentiment. It is not that all people find truly funny things humorous, since not all have a sense of humor. Nor will anything that anyone finds funny be so, since not all humor is appropriate. But people with the right comic sensibilities will find the funny so. The humor of something will be a matter of its noncomic properties, which engage the comic sensibilities of those with a good sense of humor, and yet there are unlikely to be precise noncomic criteria for being funny. The true humor of things will be present in the experience of those with the appropriate comic sensibilities, and their sense of humor will allow us to figure out to a very rough degree what in the world constitutes humorous things. Some sorts of humor will be merely in the eye of those who have poor comic sensibilities, and humor will be absent in the experience of those with no comic sensibility at all, and yet humor might be an objective and genuine property of things. Perhaps this is because, with McDowell, we've softened up our sense of the mind-independence and objectivity of everything else, or perhaps it is because there is a specific set of natural properties in the world that engage proper humor.

It is important, in order to understand the contrast between such views and my proposal, to remember that there are other traditions of thought about, for instance, phenomenal color than those on which McDowell and Wiggins rely. Since at least Galileo, some have held that color statements are flatly false – for instance, because colors lack the kind of mind-independence and objectivity that they seem to have in our experience. These are views analogous to my proposal, though inverted into skepticism. On my account, normative properties are like colors as conceived by Aristotle, like concrete colors of a kind that Galileo denied.

---

25   Blackburn's noncognitivist view is closely allied to these quasi-cognitivist alternatives.
26   McDowell (1978, 1979, 1981, 1985); Wiggins (1987a, 1987b, 1987c).

It is important to distinguish two theses: that while objects out in the world lack colors, still sense data have them, and that while we have experience of things with color, literally there is nothing, not even a part of the mind, that has color. Even sense-data theorists agree with Aristotelians in the relevant sense. But sensibility theorists are in a tradition that holds a third thing, that there is in the material world itself color, as a reflection of our sensibility (and also perhaps because that experience is ultimately responsive to some genuine and mind-independent features of the world).[27]

A form of our abstract negative argument tells against sensibility theories. Even if we grant the conception of color on which McDowell and Wiggins rely, it is undeniable that different animals and people have different sorts of color experience. Think of the color-blind. And of course at least true humor is there only in the experience of those with the appropriate humor sensibility. But this invokes our familiar problem about vindication. Clearly there can be those who lack the sentiments that constitute our particular moral responses. There may be those who have a kind of overarching aesthetic or religious sentiment that allows them to see the sacred or beautiful where those with our moral sensibility see merely great injustice, and this may seem to them to trump our evanescent moral concerns, just as we see our moral concerns to trump theirs. They of course lack a sensibility. But so do we. We are back to a situation much like that which the noncognitivists and Williams faced. There are alternative sensibilities than our own, just as there are alternative practices of normative evaluation, and no means to privilege one as correct or appropriate. But then, if the sensibility theorists are correct, we cannot provide the ultimate legitimation that justificatory reason-giving practice demands.

Nevertheless, the sensibility theories seem in one way close to the truth. What is required if we are to make sense of the reason-giving nature of our normative practice is something like color, but color as it was conceived not by Boyle, but rather by his Aristotelian opponents, or even by sense data theorists, a property really there in our experience and in the world itself, mind-independent at least in the way that the color of sense data would be mind-independent, a truly and fully objective component of the world, there for all (at least on some people's sense data) even if not all see it, a property not dependent on variable sensibility in the way that humorousness is. That more or less Aristotelian property would be at once

---

27 McDowell would probably not like the last bit.

a natural and a normative property. It would be a normative property that was unconstituted by other natural properties, as the non-naturalists held, while yet being itself a natural concrete property of the sort favored by naturalist cognitivists.

In the cracks between previous cognitivist theories we can glimpse the possibility of nonconstitutive naturalist cognitivism. It deploys no suspect non-natural properties whose supervenience on the natural cannot be plausibly explained, and yet it deploys natural properties that are in fact normative, properties that don't merely constitute the normative in the controversial, and I believe ultimately implausible, manner proposed by contemporary constitutive naturalists. Indeed, such properties are like colors, though not quite as the sensibility theorists conceive them.

Nice work if you can get it, some may say. But in fact such unconstituted normative and yet natural properties are plausibly involved in our concrete experience of pain and pleasure. That is the position that I will occupy over the rest of this chapter. Because this cognitivism fits into the cracks between the various views that we have surveyed, it avoids their characteristic failures to provide a proper account of justificatory reason giving in our concrete world.

II

Justificatory reason giving apparently requires objective normative properties and facts, which are there in the world for all.[28] And such properties in our concrete world must plausibly be unconstituted concrete properties, or at the very least must be constituted by other natural properties and yet still be obviously normative. Are there any such properties?

There plausibly are. Consider intense physical pain. And consider it in this light: Assume that there are phenomenal states or qualia or sense data or raw feels that are a part of it. And further assume, in accord with one controversial but live current contender, that someone's phenomenal experience is not constituted solely by the physical facts about them, by the machinations of their molecules or those of their environment.[29] The phenomenal nastiness of pain is still a natural property. But, I claim, it is a normative property.

Let me go slowly at this crucial point. Consider violent murder – say, of the red knight by the gold knight, on the point of a lance in

---

28 This section and parts of the next are based on Mendola (1990b).
29 See, for instance, Chalmers (1996).

his golden arms. Perhaps some murders are, in all their context and with all their consequences, for the best. Perhaps in this case the gold knight was not unreasonable. But most ethicists would like to believe that there is something about at least most violent murders, considered at least in isolation from their context and consequences, that is bad. Is there any suitably objective intrinsic disvalue present in such cases? Since it seems likely that the worst part of murder is that it hurts the murdered, focus attention on intrinsically bad things that might be thought to happen to the victim of such a violent murder. And put it this way: Is there anything in what happened to the red knight that cannot be adequately and completely described without admitting its disvalue? I believe there is.

Ignore for a moment the knight's psychological states, his pain and dismay. Consider the nonpsychological side of what happened to him. Some sharp metal cut some live human flesh, some blood surged out of its customary place and, we shall assume, choked the organism. Respiration ceased, and then the red knight died. This is something that we are likely to feel squeamish about, that we may regret, but is there anything in the machination of molecules that we believe this piercing and surging and choking to be that involves disvalue? I think not. One can certainly imagine this fleshy part of the murder described quite completely and adequately by Martians, with the detachment of a biologist studying yeast metabolism. The Martians might provide a complete and adequate description of the phenomenon that admitted no normative properties at all. Perhaps the red knight was too proud or surprised to scream, but even had he thrashed and screamed, limbs scrambling and the emission of screaming sounds can be adequately described in a way colorless of value. If there is more to screaming and thrashing than this sort of movement, it should be found in the victim's psychology.

Let us widen our consideration of the murder to include the red knight's psychological states. First, he no doubt wanted not to be murdered and, more generally, not to be cut or pierced. No doubt he thought such things were bad. But propositional attitudes like beliefs and desires seem, at least on the surface, not generally to require commitment to normative properties in their adequate and complete descriptions.[30] Martians could

---

30 Not all agree. Some hold that there are normative properties involved whenever there is a state with meaning or content, because such states are constrained by principles of rationality or are governed by standards of correctness. But this rests on the conflation of two senses of "rationality" or of "correctness" noted earlier.

describe the knight's wanting not to be murdered, as we might describe an amoeba's fleeing our pipette, without talking about disvalue at all. And since they can describe his belief in witches without committing themselves to the existence of witches, or describe his disbelief in microbes without denying that there are microbes, it seems they can also adequately characterize his belief in disvalue without committing themselves to the existence of disvalue. Our Martians are describing, not evaluating, the red knight's desires. And in the concrete world we presume, there is nothing more to his wanting and believing than the concrete – for instance, behavior and neural machinations and maybe qualia. At least there are no irreducible psychological relations to irreducible Platonic forms of evil. That the red knight did not value the murder and that the gold knight did implies nothing about its having objective value or disvalue.

Are there other of the red knight's psychological states whose description might require commitment to disvalue? Since he died, his consciousness ceased, though this too seems characterizable without commitment to disvalue. But now consider what he experienced, what he sensed and felt. Assume that there were phenomenal states, sense data or raw feels, that he experienced in being murdered. Assume that, in Nagel's phrase, it was like something to be him then.[31] And further assume, in accord with one controversial but live current contender, that his phenomenal experience is not constituted by the physical facts about him, by the machinations of his molecules or those of his environment.

Is the red knight's phenomenal experience in being murdered characterizable by the Martians without commitment to value or disvalue?

No doubt we have already considered a part of his agony, his flinching or running or screaming behavior and his negative conative attitude toward being stuck and killed. Such things can, it seems, be described without commitment to disvalue. But such things are not all there is to at least some pain. Consider the phenomenal component of agony, the sensations and feelings and raw experience that accompany being stabbed. No one, not even a Martian, I claim, could give a complete and adequate description of the red knight's psychological states without characterizing those raw feels, which we are presuming for the moment to be physically unconstituted and hence to involve the presentation to him of characteristic natural phenomenal properties not constituted by other natural properties.

31   Nagel (1979).

155

We may be able to imagine a very strange man who, when in a phenomenal state like that of the red knight, whistled and snapped his fingers and did math sums.[32] Perhaps we can imagine someone being stabbed and writhing like him while having a phenomenal state like that of intense sexual pleasure centered on the wound. But neither of these are our protagonist. There are phenomenal and not merely behavioral differences, differences in raw experience and not merely in propositional attitudes, between those in bliss and those in agony. Any complete and adequate characterization of the red knight's murder must do these justice.

Some will hold that complete and adequate descriptions of situations involving phenomenal experience do not necessarily involve commitment to phenomenal properties. Perhaps phenomenal states are constituted in such a way that someone's physical characterization entails the presence of the relevant phenomenal states – for instance, the experiencing of the phenomenal properties – without anything in fact having those phenomenal properties. Perhaps feeling a phenomenal property is like believing in witches. Or perhaps phenomenal properties are real, but constituted by other natural properties. Still, one live contemporary alternative, consistent with our metaphysical presumptions so far, is that adequate characterizations of situations involving phenomenal states must involve commitment to various irreducible and otherwise unconstituted phenomenal properties.

It is not implausible to claim that unconstituted phenomenal properties must be captured by any complete and adequate description of the red knight's murder. And indeed, the case for concrete pleasure and pain involving certain concrete phenomenal properties is strong even if the metaphysical picture that undergirds constitutive naturalism is correct and such properties are constituted by physical properties. But let me be very clear about the asymmetry I am claiming here. We can desire to be a witch when there are no witches, but if we have phenomenal experience of yellow, then something is yellow. In fact, I also claim, there is something irreducibly and unconstitutedly yellow, either something really out in the world, or at least a sense datum under our hats.[33]

While this view is of course controversial in our historical situation, in which many hold that sensory experience is as of yellow though there is nothing in the world that is so, not even a sense datum, or at the very

32 D. Lewis (1980).
33 If yellow is out in the world, then perhaps a hallucination of yellow, like one of pain, requires no such postulation. We will return to this.

least that the yellow we experience is a natural property constituted by physical properties like a certain range of surface spectral reflectance, still the view in question is, as I've said, one live competitor. Indeed, it is often motivated by arguments that are structurally similar to the open-question argument: You look at a gold bar and have a certain sort of phenomenal experience. But it seems to some that it might well be an open question whether your physical twin in a physically identical environment has the same phenomenal experience, or any at all. He might be a zombie or a qualia invert. And the openness of that question suggests to some that the physical cannot constitute your phenomenal experience.

At least such qualia dualism is relatively concrete and robust. Even though it involves physically unconstituted qualia, it involves nothing that is non-natural in Moore's sense. It is at least concretely comprehensible. And that gives it a great advantage over alternative forms of normative realism.

That is my main point, that this so far familiar qualia dualism unexpectedly but very plausibly implies a form of *normative* realism. Painfulness – or, more accurately, the phenomenal property present in certain sorts of extreme and paradigmatic physical pain – is a kind of *disvalue*. That is my new idea.[34] The phenomenal difference between those in bliss and those in agony includes a difference in a sort of felt phenomenal value. The phenomenal difference between pain and pleasure seems (at least in part and sometimes) to be that the phenomenal component of the former is nastier, intrinsically worse than that of the second.

The red knight was stabbed to death. Just as no one can adequately describe what it was like to be him without capturing his sensation of his red and flowing blood and hence the property of phenomenal redness, so no one can describe what it was like to be him without capturing the nasty sensations he felt and hence the property of phenomenal nastiness or disvalue. And no one can understand what his phenomenal state was without knowing that it was intrinsically bad, worse than pleasure. No one, not even a Martian, can give a complete and adequate characterization of the red knight's murder while ignoring the phenomenal state that was a part of that situation. And no one, not even a Martian, can give a complete and adequate characterization of that phenomenal state without capturing its nastiness, its intrinsic disvalue. The red knight's murder possessed what we might call objective intrinsic disvalue.

---

34 Not very new. See the discussion of antecedents in Mendola (1990b), and especially Lewis (1946).

If someone feels bad, then there is something bad, at least in cases of extreme physical pain. My further claim, to which constitutive naturalists dissent, is that this involves unconstituted but natural disvalue. Like other phenomenal properties, the disvalue present in agony is unconstituted by physical properties, though it is itself concrete and natural. It is just like phenomenal yellow. The objective but unconstituted phenomenal component of agony involves a correspondingly objective and unconstituted phenomenal property that is usually present in cases of at least extreme physical pain, a painfulness or "unpleasant hedonic tone", as it was once called.[35] And such objective phenomenal properties are, at least in part, a sort of intrinsic disvalue or badness. Something analogous is true of certain paradigmatic physical pleasures. They involve objective intrinsic value.

All of my claims here are controversial. Some deny that there are phenomenal experiences. Some deny that phenomenal experience cannot be constituted solely out of other natural properties. That the experience of pain at least often involves a phenomenal "hedonic tone" was classically held by Broad, Duncker, and Edwards.[36] But there were also classic objections to pleasure's being like a sensation or feeling.[37] And I suspect that the claim that vivid physical painfulness is a normative property will not be attractive even to some who accept unconstituted hedonic tone.

But while all of these claims are somewhat controversial, they all have at least some plausibility. Together, these claims represent a plausible concrete case for an objective and suitably normative fact, which is something we have regrettably lacked. If the most plausible forms of two-dimensionalism[38] are correct, then there is little hope for another. And the phenomenal disvalue of agony is a lonely plausible case for a normative but natural fact even if constitutive naturalism is true, and the phenomenal and normative are constituted by the physical.

While it turns out that the kind of unconstituted natural normative property in our world is a certain kind of value and disvalue, which I call objective intrinsic value or goodness, this claim should not be misunderstood. I don't think this exhausts the meaning of "good" in English, nor even any intuitive notion of intrinsic good. It is not possible, I think, to

---

35 Broad (1930: 229–233).
36 Duncker (1940–41); Edwards (1979: 46–47).
37 Ryle (1954: 54–67); Broad (1930: 231); Perry (1967).
38 Or analogous views like my own.

158

"meaningfully" question whether it *is* good, but it is possible to question whether it is *all* the good. In fact, it isn't. Nor do I think that some sort of dominance of value words over other normative terms — say, those that deontologists prefer — is available by meaning analysis. It is just that the kind of normative property that there happens to be in our world fits certain value terms. Perhaps it fits certain deontic terms also.

Still, even if you grant the general plausibility of my key metaphysical presumptions here, there remain natural objections to the view I have sketched.

Objection One: Pain is supposed here to be bad *tout court*, from the point of view of the universe. But isn't my experience of my pain bad for me in particular?

Reply: Just as in the case of phenomenal yellow, such an analysis is too complex for the content of a simple phenomenal state. My physical pain presents itself as bad, not specifically as bad for me or bad for all people, but bad. Perhaps one way to see this is to consider on the alternative supposition exactly to whom my pain presents itself as bad. To me at this moment, to me as a continuing entity, or to my genetic line?

Objection Two: But if the disvalue we find in pain is disvalue from the point of view of the universe in this way, in what sense does this support a hedonistic conception of our well-being? How is our pain bad for us?

Reply: The value I am speaking of need not be something that specifically constitutes individual well-being. So I am defending hedonism in what is perhaps only an unusual and attenuated sense. Recall the first section of the last chapter.

Objection Three: It is implausible that all pains involve this sort of objective nastiness. Consider painful anxiety. It has little in common phenomenally with the physical pain of being stabbed.

Reply: I do not claim that all pains involve this negative hedonic tone. I have only so far claimed that a few paradigmatic and vivid concrete physical pains involve it.

Objection Four: If the painfulness of paradigmatic physical pains is a kind of badness, if to judge that a pain of that sort is getting worse is to make a value judgment, then hedonism is in fact endangered. We cannot then argue that such a change should be avoided *because* it involves more pain. There isn't the space between the painfulness and the to-be-avoidedness that that "because" invokes.

Reply: We can argue that such a change should be, in itself and irrespective of context, avoided because it would involve more painful hedonic tone. But the "because" links two properties that are not as firmly distinct

159

as in some more familiar cases. There are other cases like this. There is water in the lake because it is filled with H-O-H.

Objection Five: It is a central claim here that some natural facts about pain are irreducibly normative, in that they provide justifying reasons without being anything other than natural facts themselves. This view is contrasted with the view of non-naturalists, on the one hand, who hold that there are normative facts that cannot be reduced to natural facts, and the view of noncognitivists, on the other hand, who hold that there are no normative facts because the only facts are natural ones. But the view that there is a middle position is problematic. Let us grant that natural facts, such facts as that someone is in pain, often function as reasons, and so have normative force. No non-naturalist need deny this. What he or she denies is that the true proposition that a natural fact is a reason is itself a natural fact. And noncognitivists agree with the non-naturalist about that. This is because Moore's open-question argument is taken by both to show that it is a mistake to think that the proposition that something is a reason is itself a natural fact, or that the predicate "is a reason" refers to a natural property of natural objects. If this is correct, however, it seems to leave only two positions possible. The first is non-naturalism, according to which, while the predicate "is a reason" does not refer to a natural property, it can still be predicated truly or falsely of natural facts. The second is noncognitivism, according to which, since the predicate "is a reason" does not refer to any natural property, it cannot, strictly, be predicated truly or falsely of anything at all. There is no middle ground to occupy, unless, contrary to what Moore's argument suggests, "is a reason" does refer to a particular natural property. In light of this, the claim that there are irreducibly normative natural facts is either trivial or obscure. Either it means only that some natural facts, such as facts about pain, are reasons, which no one denies. Or it means that some natural facts are themselves facts about what natural facts are reasons, which has not been shown.

Reply: My claim is that there is in fact a third position that we have generally overlooked, that there are properties that are at once paradigmatically natural and paradigmatically normative, as those words are customarily used. And this possibility cannot be undercut by Moore's open-question argument, even though the two-dimensionalist analysis of the identity of water and H-O-H is correct.

To see this properly, it is important to first recall that I do not claim of our word "value", no more than of our word "reason", that its meaning is such that it applies by definition to just and only the objective value discerned here. Rather, whatever determinate meanings such words have specifies conditions that are met by the objective property I've noted. The property I've suggested is, as it were, one kind of possible value or reason, the objective and unconstituted kind there happens to be in the world. So I agree in a sense that "is a reason" does not refer to a natural property, or indeed to any single basic property, non-natural or natural. My argument for the existence of the objective value we have noted isn't really a semantic argument at all.

Can Moore's argument show that there isn't this sort of objective value? Of course it can in some weak sense be meaningfully asked whether hedonic value of the sort I note is bad, just as it can in the same sense be meaningfully asked if bachelors are unmarried. But that is presumably not the kind of meaningfulness that Moore's question properly isolates. My central claim is that to fail to note the badness of phenomenal painfulness is to miss something that is necessary to a complete description of what some pains involve. So in the relevant sense I claim to have shown that Moore's question is not open for this one sort of case. Still, there might be other kinds of things properly called value for which the question is open.

The objection is phrased in terms of a paradigmatically deontological property rather than in terms of value. We will turn to the issue of the exact nature of phenomenal value and disvalue in the next section, but it is, I think, of a nature that might also be captured by talk of reasons in a suitably broad sense rather than of value. The central point for now is the general nature of the phenomenal property itself and its normativity. The detailed nature of the property will dictate how it is best characterized in detail, and indeed it may have more than one proper normative characterization, drawn from different traditions of normative vocabulary. Perhaps we might call the natural normative property of pain "to-be-eliminatedness".

Now focus on the contrast between my view and non-naturalism and noncognitivism. For a non-naturalist or noncognitivist, the claim that the natural phenomenal painfulness we have discerned is intrinsically bad would have to be open in the Moorean sense. That is the difference between my view and an analogous sort of non-naturalism or noncognitivism. It is, I claim, a difference that is to my advantage.

Let me put the elements of this long reply together explicitly: In fact there is middle ground, which closes Moore's open question for hedonic value despite the fact that "is a reason" is not itself a single natural property.

Objection Six: The suggestion is that negative hedonic tone is disvalue, even though "disvalue" doesn't mean the same as "negative hedonic tone". Why isn't this proposal vulnerable to the two-dimensionalist objection that was proposed against constitutive naturalism in section I? That objection denies the possibility of genuine necessary a posteriori propositions – for instance, property identities.

Reply: Because there is an a priori entailment linking negative hedonic tone with disvalue. But notice that the entailment runs only in one direction. No identity of meaning is required.

Objection Seven: There are various rival accounts of pain. For instance, there is the view that there is no phenomenal experience characteristic of pain, but merely that aversion is. Second, there is the view that there is something phenomenal characteristic of pain but that it is not badness. Third, there is the view that there are different kinds of phenomenal badness. Why is the view suggested here, that there is one kind of phenomenal painfulness which is badness, to be preferred?

Reply: Aversion alone cannot constitute painfulness, since even pleasure of some sorts is something to which someone might have an aversion. But nonetheless there are a variety of things that might properly be called "pain" in English, some perhaps constituted merely by aversion at least to a large degree. And there are a variety of phenomenal properties in which distinct pains do differ. Indeed, there are rubbing feelings or the like that are *characteristic* parts of the phenomenal component of certain sorts of pains. So my claim is limited: that the basic phenomenal component of the paradigmatic physical pains – as colors of particular sorts are the basic phenomenal components of visual experiences – is the phenomenal badness I've noted. Aversion plus other phenomenal properties cannot fully capture paradigmatic pains. There is a variety of things that might properly be called pains, given the various meanings of the term, but my claim is not primarily a claim about the meaning of "pain", nor even about its essential properties, but rather about the nature of a certain phenomenal property that we in fact experience in paradigmatic instances of physical pain.

Objection Eight: Under the influence of certain drugs, we can experience pain without minding it or finding disvalue in it. So even paradigmatic physical pain doesn't have to include disvalue, and it is only when we mind pain and want to be free of it that we find comparative disvalue in the experience. But why then say that disvalue is an additional element in the experience of having a pain and being bothered by it? Why not say that all that distinguishes pain we mind from pain we don't is the fact of minding or not minding it?

Reply: But it is not the minding of even disliked physical pain that constitutes its phenomenal component to involve disvalue of the appropriately objective sort we are discussing. Badness in my sense needn't be minded, and indeed that is part of the evidence that it is objective badness in the relevant sense.

Objection Nine: We cannot understand the anguish of the red knight without realizing that he is disposed to avoid it, and we cannot understand it without ourselves being disposed to avoid such a thing. This provides grounds for the objective vindication of a desire-based conception of the good.

Reply: We cannot understand bloodthirstiness without realizing that it involves a positive preference for horrible things. But that does not provide a direct vindication of the value of such horrible things. What's more, we can in fact understand the preference of the red knight without sharing it, and even understand his painful hedonic tone without caring about it. As the previous objection noted, we can even feel our *own* painful hedonic tone, and hence suitably understand it, without minding it. Still, it is of such a nature that we ought to care about it.

Objection Ten: There are some philosophical circles in which any appeal to phenomenal properties is immediately suspect. Some object that Wittgenstein's private language argument has *shown* that there are no such things as phenomenal properties.[39]

Reply: But we should not be so easily intimidated. Aristotelian colors, the most familiar analogs of phenomenal value, are not necessarily private in any sense. And whatever the notoriously evasive private language argument is, it is controversial. Qualia, phenomenal properties by another name, are a central topic in contemporary philosophy of mind, and hence no established orthodoxy within the philosophical discipline that centrally concerns them now rules them out of consideration. So it certainly isn't appropriate for ethicists to rule them out of consideration by dropping a name.

Nevertheless, the private language argument does point to an important practical difficulty. If I am right so far, then it is crucial to develop a more specific characterization of the general sort of normative properties under consideration. And it is clear that introspection, or at least observation that is not measurement of ordinary kinds, must play a crucial role in this. Of course, it might be introspection by more than one individual, and hence might involve the standard empirical studies of quality spaces that play an important role even in some parts of chemistry and psychology. But introspection is quite fallible, and we must proceed with caution and modesty.

---

39   One place this objection is made is Korsgaard (1996a: 131–166).

I have claimed that there is a type of phenomenal and hence unconstituted natural property that is present, though not in all forms of suffering or even in all cases that we call "pain", at least in paradigmatic sorts of physical pain. This is a type of normative property. In particular, it is a kind of disvalue or badness, though not by any means the only form of disvalue or badness. It is objective disvalue, which is bad from the point of view of the universe, in Sidgwick's inevitable phrase.

We have focused so far primarily on pain and hence phenomenal badness, but there is obviously another type of phenomenal property present in some cases of physical pleasure that is likewise a type of normative property, a form of positive value or goodness. This claim may be slightly more controversial than my claims about pain. Some hold that only pain is a sensation, that only pain involves a special kind of sensory experience, while pleasure does not. But this is wrong. A special sort of sensory experience also in part constitutes pleasure, at least in a range of central cases. In at least some cases we call pleasure, which include some of the very down-to-earth pleasures of eating, scratching, defecating, and sex, there is an experience of localized pleasantness that is closely analogous to the experience of localized painfulness characteristic of physical pain. This is a kind of objective goodness. Lots of things we call pleasures are not robustly physical and localizable in this way. Some involve no special phenomenal properties at all. Some things we call pains are also not robustly physical. But there are at least the clear and vivid cases of some physical pains and pleasures, which involve positive and negative hedonic value.

Classical hedonists conceived pleasures and pains to differ as do positive and negative value, and also always to be comparable in value despite being felt by different persons. But they further conceived the value of pleasures and pain to have an arithmetical or cardinal structure, to involve quantities that one might add and subtract or even multiply in familiar ways. Pains were supposed to differ in amount, but in several different ways that were implicitly reconciled in that cardinal structure. Bentham held that pains differed in intensity and duration.[40] But we might also reasonably consider spatial differences – between, say, a pain in my whole arm and one just in my elbow. And perhaps there is another

---

40 Bentham (1970: Chapter IV, 38). In this passage, Bentham also mentions the certainty and propinquity of a pleasure as relevant to its value. But this is because of his psychological hedonism coupled with his recognition that the certainty and temporal rapidity of a punishment or reward are relevant to its motivational effect. See, for instance, pp. 170–171.

sort of phenomenal difference in quantity, between the vividness of actual pains and the faintness of remembered or anticipated physical pains. Perhaps those are all instances of one type of quantity.

But it seems to me that the truth about hedonic value is slightly more complex, and it will take a while to explain it.[41]

First, there is one dimension of value and disvalue levels, with three subdivisions: positive value, disvalue, and the null state in between.

Second, both positive value and disvalue come in greater and lesser degrees.

Third, each discriminable momentary bit of phenomenal experience has either a particular degree of value, a particular degree of disvalue, or a null valence. The null valence is had by many discriminable bits. But there are also many bits with value or disvalue, which sum to provide pleasures and pains that are temporally or spatially extended.

Fourth, these degrees of value are "interpersonally comparable". It makes sense to say that two persons experience bits with the same level of value, though of course we may lack conclusive evidence that they do.

A fifth and crucial point is more debatable: While a pleasantness can present itself as better than a lesser pleasantness, it does not present itself, as the classical utilitarian requires, as twice or three times better. In this respect, phenomenal value is analogous to phenomenal color. It makes sense to say that something is bluer than something else, but not that it is two or three times so without reference to some arbitrary scale. Intrinsic phenomenal value comes, as economists and mathematicians say, ordinally.

Let me explain. I claim that phenomenal value is ordinal. Consider four levels of phenomenal value. Call them A, B, C, and D. Sometimes it will make sense to say that the difference in intrinsic value between A and D is greater than that between B and C. For instance, it might be that A is better than B, which is better than C, which is better than D. B and C might be in between. But when one difference is not enclosed in another in this manner, it is senseless to say that one is a greater difference than the other. There is nothing in the phenomenal facts to ground that comparison. Intrinsic phenomenal value comes ordinally. It makes sense to speak of inter- and intrapersonal comparisons of value levels, hence to ascribe numbers for ease of reference in this way: to the indifferent level of phenomenal value a 0, to each level of positive value some arbitrary positive rational number with greater numbers assigned to better levels,

---

41 This discussion is an improvement over the less adequate treatment in Mendola (1997: Chapter 6).

and to each level of disvalue some arbitrary negative rational with lesser numbers assigned to worse levels. It will not make sense to take these representatives in other than an ordinal sense, as bearing information about the relative size of value differences. Any assignment of rationals meeting the stipulations noted will be as good as any other.

Let me stress the two crucial and controversial features of this initial characterization of hedonic value, both of which will matter in the next chapter. First, I am claiming that there are objective facts not only about intrapersonal but also about interpersonal comparisons of phenomenal value levels. The nature of phenomenal value is very simple. The value I experience presents itself not as value for me but as value *simpliciter*. And there is an objective fact whether or not a person experiences phenomenal value of level X, and whether or not another experiences value of the same level, just as there is an objective fact whether those two persons experience the same shade of phenomenal blue. Of course it may be hard or impossible to figure out exactly what shade of phenomenal color or level of hedonic value someone else is experiencing, and hence whether two people are experiencing the same shade or level. But still, I presume, there are objective facts in the relevant sense about those things, true for all whether or not anyone has epistemic access to such facts.

Second, I am claiming that phenomenal intrinsic value comes ordinally. Even if you come with me most of the way, you may balk at ordinality. You may agree that objective phenomenal value exists, but believe that it comes cardinally, so that it makes sense to speak of an experience being exactly twice better than another of the same spatial extent and duration. I can find little phenomenal grounds for this position, and believe it due to a confusion of our ordinary judgments about the value of phenomenal states with their phenomenal value itself, but still it is an obvious alternative possibility. Or you may hold an intermediate position on the ordinality-cardinality controversy, that an ordinal comparison of some happiness differences is rooted in phenomenal value.[42] Consider, for instance, comparisons between an intuitively huge increase in pleasure and a nearly imperceptible increase in pain. Also, it might be that pain presents itself – as, for instance, negative utilitarians believed – as more significant than pleasure, as we will consider again in the next part.

Still, it is massively implausible that the property of being exactly twice as good as something else could present itself in experience. That is

---

42   If all differences are comparable in that manner it will yield standard cardinal assessments.

not only because that is an implausibly exact feature to be present there, but also because it seems too relational and complex a feature even if it were made suitably vague. It is normatively relevant, for instance, only to the evaluation of wholes and risks containing such a cardinal value. Nor was it, I believe, the explicit contention of any classical utilitarian that that kind of phenomenal specificity is in fact present in our experience, despite the fact that they sometimes concluded as if it were. It is more as if, in their rush to moral arithmetic, they didn't consider plausible alternatives. There is no obvious analogue of this alleged phenomenon in other forms of sensory experience. Could something present itself as exactly twice as blue as another, without regard to some arbitrary scale? Nor do things even present themselves as twice as loud as another, or twice as bright. Phenomenal spatial and temporal intervals may present themselves with such a structure, but we aren't considering at the moment spatial and temporal features of phenomenal value. Phenomenal value and disvalue are of the same general type as the intrinsic phenomenal properties that are characteristic of particular senses and sense fields, like felt pressure or color. And in those cases, cardinal metrics seem out of place.

Nevertheless, there are forms of this general type of objection to my simple ordinal scheme that I believe to possess significant force. It is not just that some phenomenal loudnesses seem greater than others, but that some *differences* in phenomenal loudness seem greater than other *differences*. A difference in loudness may be nearly imperceptible, or intuitively large, even if one difference isn't enclosed in another, even if there are four levels of loudness involved and we are comparing differences between levels such that those differences do not overlap. Analogously, it is not implausible to insist that at least *some* such differences in value level present themselves as greater than some other such differences even when my ordinalism of value levels cannot underwrite it.

My response to this important objection is merely this: The relatively simple ordinalism of value levels that I have so far presumed is apparently consistent with my own introspection, and hence I will continue to pursue it as our primary conception as we proceed. But I will also try to explore the implications of alternative plausible conceptions.[43] For one thing, I will keep the traditional cardinal conception in play.

43 Indeed, one instance of the final suggestion incorporated in the objection may indeed be useful in the next part, because that minor level of additional structure may help underwrite one key feature of our construction.

But even if the phenomenal facts are exactly as I have claimed them to be, there may still seem to be a way to, more or less indirectly, deliver cardinality, and hence to undercut the mere ordinality of basic value on which I rely in the next chapter. In fact, there may seem to be two ways.

Von Neumann and Morgenstern suggested that we derive cardinality from rational behavior under risks.[44] Presume that a person experiences successively more positive levels of hedonic tone, from the null valence to some positive level N. We stipulate that the value of the null valence is 0 and the value of N is 1. Now we expose them to a choice of lotteries over possible outcomes. They are given, for instance, the choice between the certainty of some intermediate level of hedonic tone, on one hand, and a lottery with a 40 percent chance of the null valence and a 60 percent chance of N, on the other. Von Neumann and Morgenstern showed that if the individual's choices between lotteries exhibit certain intuitively rational patterns, we can assign cardinal values to the levels for that individual. And remember that I am already presuming interpersonal comparability.

But, I reply, real people do not uniformly or even usually exhibit those particular allegedly "rational" patterns for choices over lotteries. You may be unwilling to risk any chance of torture, no matter how small, in a lottery that will very likely generate a big increase in your hedonic value. And that will violate the conditions of "rationality" in question. And of course there is nothing normatively inappropriate about that. At stake here are ultimately the proper standards for behavior under risks. The conditions of "rationality" that von Neumann and Morgenstern presume are not realistic, and are themselves in need of direct vindication if they are to root appropriate normative judgments. In Chapter 6, we will return to the issue of the proper treatment of risks if ordinal hedonic value is as I have claimed it to be. And it will not deliver cardinality for levels of hedonic tone.[45]

But there is also a second possible route to cardinality. Edgeworth developed Bentham's proposal that we focus on just perceivable increments in levels of value.[46] We might count the number of just perceivable increments between levels to generate comparisons of differences in value levels that will yield cardinal comparisons of a sort. If level X is four discriminable levels below level Y, and Y is eight discriminable levels below Z, we can claim that the difference between X and Y is half the difference

44 von Neumann and Morgenstern (1944).
45 It may also be that the kinds of interpersonal comparisons I presume will not mesh with the cardinality that von Neumann and Morgenstern can deliver.
46 Edgeworth (1881: 7); Baumgardt (1952: 555).

between Y and Z. But phenomenal differences can be indiscernible in some comparisons and discernible through others. Two shades of color may each appear phenomenally identical to a third and intervening shade, but not to each other. So it may be that different ways of moving from one level of value to another will yield different numbers of just perceivable increments between them. Tännsjö has proposed that the relevant number of increments between two levels for an individual is the maximum number it is possible for that individual to discern between the two.[47] But he does not deploy objective hedonic value with interpersonal comparisons of the sort I have suggested, and so evades a problem of coherence created by the interaction of his mechanism and objective hedonic value. It is this: Two different individuals may be capable of different numbers of level discriminations between the same two levels of objective ordinal hedonic value. So we cannot develop a coherent set of interpersonal cardinal comparisons for the particular sort of hedonic value that I am proposing in this way. For the same reason, if phenomenal value in fact comes cardinally, that might yield a different and conflicting sort of cardinality than Tännsjö's mechanism. Since single individuals can plausibly differ in their discriminatory capacities over time and with education, this problem also probably undercuts the use of this mechanism to deliver cardinal comparisons of phenomenal value within a life. We might alternatively fix the absolute number of increments between value levels by the maximum number of differences that anyone can perceive between them. But that leads to the following difficulty: Under that conception, we might increase the hedonic tone of all the less than fully discriminating individuals in the world by a single increment that they cannot even perceive, and hence create a huge number of positive level differences unnoticeable by those who experience them that yet normatively trump the relatively fewer but very noticeable negative increments involved in the torture of a single individual. Tännsjö endorses something analogous to this.[48] But it is hard to see how such a judgment might be objectively required. That seems to me the greatest difficulty with this general mechanism when deployed in our current argumentative context. The cardinal judgments rooted in these various sorts of discriminable and indiscriminable differences do not seem subject to suitable and objective asymmetric vindication relative to possible competitors. It is not only that there are different possible detailed mechanisms of the general sort in question,

47   Tännsjö (1998: 68).
48   Ibid., 72–75.

169

but also that it is not obvious why appeals to numbers of discriminable and subdiscriminable increments suffice to provide a direct argument for cardinal judgments that trade off greater pains for some to gain greater pleasures for others – for instance, in the torture case I just mentioned.

But let me be clear. I don't claim to know with any certainty that hedonic value itself is not cardinal even in intrinsic phenomenal nature. And I certainly don't claim to know with any certainty that it is fully ordinal, that there are no objective facts about differences in value levels that go beyond ordinality. So while I will continue to develop the implications of the simple ordinal conception, I will also try to track the implications for my central claims if a more traditional cardinal conception is correct. I will also attend as well as I can, which isn't very well, to the complications that ensue if some intermediate conception is correct.

IV

Even if you grant ordinality and my other presumptions about phenomenal value so far, you may wonder whether we need to introduce some other sort of structure into phenomenal value. In particular, are there different sorts of phenomenal value of the general sort I have suggested, and are they perhaps not fully comparable? Are there different "qualities" of phenomenal value and disvalue – for instance, those associated with pushpin and poetry, or satisfied pigs and discontented philosophers?

Let me begin my response to this crucial cluster of questions by admitting one small complication into our model of value. If you can see a color, then, at least if you are among the majority, you can see something at least roughly like it in your mind's eye, in memory or imagination. Call this "quasi-experience" of the color. Likewise, if you can feel pain, in memory or imagination you can feel a kind of quasi-pain. If we call the phenomenal difference between felt and remembered pains a difference in vividness, then we might ask if vividness is another sort of "quantity" possessed by phenomenal value, other than ordinal intensity and spatial and temporal extent.

I think it would not be completely implausible to presume that phenomenal painfulness or pleasantness is instantiated in the world only in cases where there is fully vivid experience of it, of the sort involved in our ordinary sensory experience. My own memories, imaginings, and dreams do not obviously involve experienced badness, though perhaps they more plausibly involve experienced goodness. But perhaps this is an individual idiosyncrasy or just dumb luck. And in any case, my best overall guess is that phenomenal badness can be present in certain experiences that are not in fact physical pains, and yet be of the same phenomenal type as that present in physical pains, just of minimal intensity. So I will presume here that phenomenal value and disvalue can be present in these less than fully vivid ways, in experience or quasi-experience, but will also presume that these differences in vividness are in fact differences in intensity of the sort we have already discussed. This might not seem to be a terribly plausible response if we first consider analogs like the intensity of a blue, but it seems more plausible if we think about felt pressure. So while I admit that there are phenomenal value properties beyond the central cases of paradigmatic sensory pains and pleasures we have so far considered, I believe that they in fact require no modification of our general characterization of phenomenal value properties. They just involve less intense versions of phenomenal painfulness and pleasantness.

There are other possible complications in this general vicinity that might be relevant. One might presume, for instance, that hallucinatory pains involve the presence of genuine objective painfulness, but that the imagination of past pain does not.[49] But in any case, let me turn to the general issue of whether there are different sorts of phenomenal value beyond those I have sketched, whether in the case of the imagination or more generally. Even if my general model of objective value and disvalue as present within phenomenal experience is accepted, and even my treatment of the quasi-experience of pain and pleasure, still to maintain that a single continuum of painfulness and pleasantness is the only sort of normative property present within our phenomenal experience may seem grossly oversimplified. An objector may plausibly postulate a range of different normative or quasi-normative properties in a variety of different classes:

(a) Even by ancient writers like Plato, the bodily pleasures and pains were augmented with mental pleasures – for instance, the pleasures of anticipation and memory.[50] These may involve a different kind of pleasure than physical pleasure, and not just a fainter or less intense pleasure of the same kind. And it may involve different phenomenal value properties.

---

49 In any case, it seems implausible that the memory or imagination of a pain really is itself a very significant pain, though of course imagination and memory of all sorts of situations can be accompanied by present uncomfortable feelings that are present pains of some significance. On the ethical view developed here, whether or not hallucinatory pains and dream pains count normatively in the same manner as ordinary pains comes down to whether they involve the presence in the world of objective painfulness, at least on sense data, and in exactly what form. That is the natural implication of normative realism.
50 See, for instance, the *Philebus*.

(b) The previous distinction may or may not be identical to the distinction that some authors have drawn between localized pains and pleasures of paradigmatically physical sorts, and nonlocalized pleasures such as that of reading a good book.[51]

(c) There is a long utilitarian tradition that suggests that there are differences in *quality* among phenomenal pleasures that affect their phenomenal nature, so that the pleasures of pushpin and poetry are not commensurable in the way I have presumed.[52]

(d) There is neurophysiological evidence for specific itch receptors, which when stimulated may present a sensory experience demanding itching in particular, while, one might argue, ordinary painfulness demands succor instead.

(e) There is a very wide range of emotional states, including anger, joy, depression, guilt, shame, and anxiety. These arguably involve complex phenomenal presentations that may involve subtly different sorts of phenomenal normative properties. To focus on a specific vivid case, think about grief. This is a highly negative state that involves a distinctive phenomenal component of emotional pain, but doesn't seem to involve the same sort of phenomenal badness as physical pain.

(f) A number of sensibility theorists, such as Wiggins and McDowell, have held that properties like humorousness may be present in our experience, properties presenting things as properly laughable. This may involve yet other sorts of phenomenal normative properties, of very complex varieties.

(g) One may read the continental phenomenological tradition, leading down through Heidegger and Sartre, as proposing a yet more expansive conception of phenomenal experience that provides grounds for yet subtler forms of normativity.[53] According to Heidegger, perhaps even the basic sort of experience of things is emotional, so that the anxiety of our situation is presented to us but our knowledge is mostly know-how. But more to the immediate point, perhaps tools present themselves as at hand in their full teleological nature, or other people present themselves in experience as radically different from the inanimate and as deserving relevant care. In general, tools or other *Dasein* may present themselves in our phenomenal experience as demanding care of some specific sort, and not merely avoidance or pursuit in the manner of pleasantness and painfulness. According to Sartre, there are specific negativities present in our experience,

---

51 Hospers (1961); Edwards (1979: 35–45).
52 Mill's *Utilitarianism* is one obvious source. It may well be that quality in his sense is defined by our tendency to choose certain pleasures over others when we've had experience of both, so that it isn't a phenomenal feature of pleasures at all. But presumably there are phenomenal differences among pleasures to which the differential judgments that constitute quality are partially sensitive. See also Hutcheson (1968: vol. I, 117–119) and Edwards (1979).
53 Heidegger (1996: Division One); Sartre (1953: Part One).

such as Simone's not being as expected in the *Flore*, and such absences may present themselves as normative lacks to be filled in quite specific ways.

I grant the intuitive force of some of these cases, and admit that this is a point that requires considerable attention if the general conception I have sketched is roughly correct. Nevertheless, let me defend my simple conception of phenomenal value as more than just a first and oversimple model. There is an understanding of the nature of our phenomenal experience that is plausibly adequate to all of these complex phenomena, and that yet involves the postulation of no additional and complex normative properties. It deploys the following elements:

(a) There is our ordinary sensory experience of material entities – for instance, tools and other people's behaving bodies.
(b) There is our complex and subtle sensory experience of our own bodily states.
(c) Either (a) or (b) may include the experience of localized pleasantness and painfulness of various degrees and spatial distributions.
(d) We can have a kind of quasi-experience of all these concrete sorts, in the mind's eye (or the mind's throat or body), in imagination or in memory. In some cases, this will be quasi-pain and hence involve a low intensity of phenomenal disvalue.[54] But there are other important phenomena of this general sort. For instance, we can experience in imagination the picking up of a tool or a laugh, an action that we are disposed to perform but aren't performing.

This is a complex set of resources, and it provides, I believe, enough to account for all the complex phenomena noted in the objection, at least when these experiences and quasi-experiences are linked up in the appropriate way – say, by neural mechanisms underwriting what we would once have called "association". This is, roughly, how: The pleasures of anticipation and memory may often include the quasi-experience, in imagination, of bodily pleasures and pains, but only vaguely localized. A lot of the complex phenomenal differences between what are alleged to be different qualities of pleasure, or that are involved in different emotional states, may be, as James famously suggested, differences in the experience of one's associated bodily states,[55] or perhaps differences in quasi-experience of analogous sorts. For instance, there may be special, even evolutionarily

---

54 This quasi-experience may involve a certain degree of phenomenal vagueness – say, regarding the location of a pleasure.
55 James (1950: Chapter 25).

fixed, bodily responses triggered by whatever emotional stimulus also generates whatever pleasure or pain happens to be a component of an emotion. And so one's special phenomenal experience of an emotion may include not merely an experience of that pleasure or pain but the experience of one's bodily response. And indeed, there may be a kind of association between analogous sorts of quasi-experience as well. Also, one's dispositions to pick up what is present at hand and use it in some way, or to laugh at the humorous, or to act toward something or someone in a caring way, can be present in one's faint quasi-experience of what one might do but isn't doing, when the activated disposition for such an act moves one to a degree but isn't sufficiently powerful to actually generate the act.

What supports this model over more expansive alternatives? I adopt it largely because it is a relatively simple model that is not obviously false, and that seems adequate to at least my own introspection. But there are other reasons to prefer it. Painfulness and pleasantness of the sort I have presumed are quite familiar and concrete properties, quite analogous to traditional sensory properties. And other candidate phenomenal normative properties seem quite different. It seems that our experience is experience of the concrete, even if sometimes in faint imagination, that the concrete indeed exhausts what we seem capable even of introspecting. For instance, our genuine introspection of what we can think seems to involve merely the faint presence to us of words that we hear in our mind's ear or speak in our mind's throat, and perhaps concrete elements of their meaning. If the content of an experience were concretely identical to mine, it would plausibly be at least qualitatively identical in content. But it is plausible that most of the other candidate normative properties proposed as phenomenal additions either supervene on the more ordinary sensory presentations of experience, or are clearly due to additional and idiosyncratic associations brought to that experience that our model can capture in exactly that manner. But in either case, our simple model is preferable as a model of the phenomenal content of experience.

Compare, for instance, humorousness and painfulness: One can imagine two otherwise concretely identical experiences of things, one that is painful, and one that is not (perhaps because of some drug one has taken). Painfulness varies independent of other phenomenal properties in our experience, so we can understand what it is for objective painfulness to be suitably independent of other sensory properties in the world. We can understand the possibility of two otherwise concretely identical flowers, one that is painful to touch and one that is not. But humorousness seems to be a different sort of case. Either it is the case that two otherwise

174

concretely identical situations can fail to be equally humorous, as they can fail to be equally painful, or it is not. But the first half of the fork, which supports the view that there are additional phenomenal normative properties, is implausible. It is clear that two otherwise concretely identical situations must be equivalent in humorousness, and that the supervenience of any allegedly distinct humorousness that can be squared with this fact could not be plausibly explained. Other than causation, there are plausibly no necessary connections between distinct existences. So if humorousness supervenes on the ordinary concrete features of things, which it plausibly must, it cannot really be a distinct phenomenal property. Perhaps Heidegger held that in a situation otherwise concretely identical to this one, objective anxiety could fail to be present, or that an animal concretely identical to you or me could fail to present that *je ne se quai* characteristic of full humanity. But we shouldn't take such possibilities seriously. Of course, different people's experience of the same situation can be distinct. Perhaps a café concretely identical to Les Deux Maggots on a certain day could fail to present to Sartre the absence of Pierre. But that isn't really the first half of the fork. Whatever anxiety or absence is present in experience in such cases clearly involves idiosyncratic reactions to identical concrete presentations. Our model can explain these by deploying concrete quasi-experience of idiosyncratic actions we are inclined to perform or of idiosyncratic fantasies we undergo in such situations. If, for instance, an irreducible *telos* can be present in our phenomenal experience of things, then it should be possible that an exact concrete duplicate of my tool yet not be ready to hand in the same manner, and not merely that I take one to be ready to hand and not the other. Don't believe it.

None of this is conclusive. If the picture I have presented here is even roughly correct, then this is one place where further work would be most useful. But let me give a little more attention to what I take to be the most troubling specific cases. There are in effect three sorts of phenomenal complications that seem most plausibly to require revisions and complications in my model.

First, there may be types of phenomenal value that are not fully comparable – for instance, those associated with sex and poetry. But, as indeed Mill's classic discussion suggests, differences in "quality" of pleasures may be differences in the degree to which we prefer them, rather than phenomenal differences. Of course, it may be objected, these differences in judgments might reflect some difference in phenomenal quality. But it need not be a difference in a value property.

Second, different acts may seem to be the appropriate result of distinct sorts of phenomenal value. Consider the phenomenal experience of an itch. Here we have something very like other sorts of sensory experience, which is, for instance, obviously spatial, and which in fact involves a distinct set of sensory receptors. And it seems to specify a certain sort of appropriate response beyond the general to-be-eliminatedness that pain presents. But, I reply, the way in which scratching seems appropriate to an itch, if not simply a matter of our dispositions in response to the phenomenal experience, seems to reflect some sort of quasi-experience of the scratching, and that seems something that is the presentation not of another value property but of an imagined response to a value property. There is, apparently, something phenomenally special about itches, but not something that involves a different sort of phenomenal value.

Third, there are some emotional states that apparently involve distinct value phenomenologies very different from localized physical pains and pleasures. Consider, for instance, depression or grief. But some of the most characteristic elements of these emotions are behavioral, or at least involve dispositions to behave. They involve distinctive phenomenologies only in the sense that the appropriate range of bodily responses is felt, at least in quasi-experience. This may sometimes involve no phenomenal value at all. Or it may involve what Edwards called a "universally localized feeling" that is felt all over, as in the pains of fatigue and chill. But I think it paradigmatically involves a somewhat vaguely localized pain, of the sort characteristic of quasi-experience, and in a way that is not constant, at least across individuals. Someone has a vague sinking feeling in their stomach, someone else a gnawing in their chest, and that may involve quasi-experience of painfulness.[56]

V

Our consideration of the structural details of the natural normative properties is now concluded. But we still have a little way to go in sketching this conception. A second important set of complications involves how these objective phenomenal unconstituted normative properties might fit into the world.

There are two ways. According to the first, sensory properties just as we experience them to be – for instance, the irreducible and unconstituted

---

56 Edwards (1979: 41).

phenomenal yellow of a certain flower or taxi, or of the wrapping on a package – are right there on the surfaces of the ordinary material objects that we experience to have such properties. The yellow is on the surface of the flower itself.

But what objects do we experience to be painful in the relevant way? What plays the role in the case of phenomenal disvalue that the flower plays in the case of yellow, according to this first way of discharging our metaphysical presumption? Two possibilities: When we experience a throbbing pain in our arm, it might be that the nasty painfulness or disvalue is right in there, a property of the flesh inside our arm, or perhaps of some ghostly (and ghastly) object that comes and goes in our arm as the pain throbs. Another possibility: Sometimes we experience physical pain as if it is on the surface of an ordinary external concrete object that is hurting us, the hot stove burner or the sharp edge of a Cuisinart blade or the leaves of plants that burn everyone who touches them. And it might be, on this conception, that these experiences are veridical, that hedonic disvalue is on the objects.

This first way (or pair of ways) in which phenomenal properties generally and hence phenomenal value and disvalue in particular may be present in the world is reflected in the natural and naive human conception of things. This is what we fall into believing when we are least philosophically reflective, and it probably underlies ordinary talk that there is a pain in my arm, right there where it hurts. Notice the exact symmetry on this conception between ordinary sensory properties like phenomenal yellow, on the one hand, and physical painfulness and pleasantness, on the other. We can coherently conceive that a schoolbus remains yellow even in the dark or when there is no one around to see it. Likewise, on this conception, in some broad sense of possibility, phenomenal disvalue *could* exist – say, on the surface of a plant or the edge of a Cuisinart blade – when no one was around to experience it. The analogy with yellow also suggests that there may be cases of the mere imagination of pain or the nonveridical perception of it, as of golden skyscrapers. In such cases, it may be, on this conception, that nothing really has phenomenal disvalue. Or it may be that there is something suitably painful, but merely the kind of thing deployed by the second manner of discharging our metaphysical presumption that there is hedonic value, which we are about to consider.

Despite the fact that this first way to fit objective hedonic value into the world is the most naive and straightforward, it will no doubt seem objectionable to many analytic ethicists. It suggests that sensory experience in general involves the presence of irreducible and unconstituted phenomenal properties on external objects, which may seem unscientific and implausible, and certainly unfashionable and out of date. And it presumes a kind of symmetry between the case of ordinary sensory experience and the experience of pain that some may find misleading. So some may prefer the second conception of how phenomenal value or disvalue fits into the concrete world, which, while more baroque and less natural to humans, as are all alternatives to the naive conception, yet probably has more living partisans among analytic philosophers.

On that second conception, phenomenal properties, the properties that appear in our immediate experience, are not out there in the external world of ordinary material objects. Or at least such properties that are traditional "secondary" properties are not out there. There are no irreducible phenomenal colors splashed on trees and tables. Such properties are, rather, had by odd corners of dualist substance, or at least by sense data. In idealist variants of this view, such sense data or immaterial minds constitute everything there is. But in what is probably the paradigmatic such conception, sense data or internally colored dualist substances are somehow causally secreted by physical brains that have the right level of active complexity.

On this second way of discharging our key metaphysical presumption, hedonic value and disvalue are really in the world, but are lodged in rather unusual regions of it, on the physically unconstituted entities that, according to such conceptions, help to make up creatures with complicated psychologies. On such a view, it may well be that the imagination or imaginative recollection of pain involves some genuine disvalue – say, on the surface of the sense data involved in that quasi-experience – and such a model of quasi-experience may be favored even by those who favor our first manner of discharging our metaphysical presumption for the case of ordinary sensory experience.

According to either of these two conceptions, there are unconstituted but natural phenomenal properties of physical painfulness and pleasantness and hence badness and goodness instantiated in the world. To feel paradigmatic physical pain is literally to feel bad. To feel such pleasure is literally to feel good. When you have a throbbing pain in your arm you literally have a throbbing badness in your arm, or at least on the surface of your sense data.

There is an obvious pressing objection, which goes like this: Such painfulness and pleasantness are not plausible properties of real objective things. Certainly there are states of people's experiencing pain. But there are no genuine things *pains* in the world, with genuine, full-fledged, and unconstituted concrete properties of painfulness – for instance, located in our arms. Nor do ordinary concrete objects like Cuisinart blades really have painfulness on their surfaces. Nor is it at all plausible to think that there are sense data under our hats with properties of painfulness either, nor other dualist claptrap. Physicalism is the correct conception of the world. Everything is constituted out of the little particles and universal forces that physics has discovered or will discover. Such resources certainly underwrite no properties of unconstituted painfulness, nor even of irreducible phenomenal yellowness. Either yellow is constituted somehow out of the physical properties of ordinary things – for instance, by their surface spectral reflectances – or there is no yellow in the world at all but merely the experience of yellow, which is itself somehow constituted out of the machinations of the microphysical. Ever since Galileo, it has seemed radically implausible to suppose that color just as we experience it to be, color unreduced, phenomenal color – in which, for example, reddish purple is very similar to bluish purple even though they correspond to wildly different wavelengths of light – is really out there on the surfaces of things. What's more, even if there were phenomenal properties like that out in the world, still there is a crucial disanalogy between yellow and the case of hedonic value. Perhaps yellow presents itself as a property of external objects in our experience in a way that may mislead the unwary and unreflective, but painfulness is a very different sort of thing. Painfulness isn't on the edge of sharp blades, nor even literally inside of our hurt arms, and this was evident even to prescientific common sense. Pain is much too subjective a thing for that. No one feels the pain in someone else's leg, even if their hand is nearby, even if they are touching the leg, indeed even if their hand is inside the leg. Far from being included in the very naive and pre-theoretical view of the world, hedonic value is really at home only in massively implausible dualist, idealist, or sense data conceptions of the world.

Reply: Not everyone, even among analytic philosophers, is a physicalist. Dualists and others who believe in unconstituted qualia may plausibly incorporate hedonic value and disvalue and hence objective normative properties into their conceptions of the world. Indeed, qualia are generally accepted to be one of the greatest difficulties facing physicalism. It is certainly not inconsistent with any current consensus to hold that qualia are unconstituted by the physical and that qualitative experience cannot be constituted by the physical. That is, it is not inconsistent with any current consensus to hold that dualism, or neutral monism, or even idealism of appropriate sorts involving unconstituted qualia, is correct. You can call this merely "property dualism", if *that* makes you feel better. A number of current authors even endorse a more or less naive direct realism, with unconstituted qualitative properties on objects, and though this is probably not within the central consensus of analytic philosophers, it is at least the standard unreflective view. And it certainly avoids the baroque machinery of idealism and dualism. If unconstituted qualia exist in any of these ways, then there is no barrier to the model presumed here. What's more, physicalists who accept that phenomenal experiences can be constituted by the physical often do so because they reject two-dimensionalism in its paradigmatic forms, and embrace necessary a posteriori propositions, which link certain physical states to qualitative experiences of certain kinds, but not via meaning links assessable a priori. There are two ways in which they might think this works. It might be that the mere experience of certain phenomenal properties is constituted by the physical, as thought of unicorns is constituted by conditions that include no unicorns, or it might be that phenomenal properties are themselves constituted by the physical. In the second case, on something like the model suggested by constitutive naturalism, they can accept that the natural normative phenomenon that I have identified exists, and insist only that it is constituted out of the physical in a way forbidden by paradigmatic forms of two-dimensionalism. It would still remain the only at once plausibly natural and normative phenomenon.

But my general point is that the hedonic value and disvalue I am suggesting should be treated just as any other qualia are treated. There are physicalist accounts of qualitative experience that reject the conditions necessary for the plausibility of my proposal, but they are far from a consensus view. What's more, I repeat, the most naive and natural human conception of the world, to which even Galileo would have reverted when hauled into court to testify, is not only one in which phenomenal color, color just as we experience it to be and not as constituted by a tendency to reflect certain wavelengths of light, is found on the surfaces of ordinary material things, but also one in which physical pain, a really bad object, can literally be found in hurting legs and broken fingers and drilled teeth.[57] Perhaps, at least before we think about it reflectively, we think things that imply that anything else inside a hurting finger or tooth *would* confront the pain, that it is not really a subjective entity. Or perhaps we pre-reflectively believe in subjective objects, which only single

---

57   In Mendola (1997), I called this the "forensic truth".

individuals can experience. Berkeley not implausibly pointed out that the sensory experience of intense heat or cold seems to be an experience of painfulness, so perhaps, before we think reflectively about it, we presume not only that phenomenal heat is to be found on activated stove burners but also that intense painfulness is there, which everyone would feel if only they touched the burners. And naive conceptions like this may have a certain sort of natural and appropriate epistemic weight, however far behind we've left them in our more philosophically reflective moments.

What do I think? That probably isn't relevant, but in any case there is more than one answer. I once was a dualist, and once a naive realist. But sometimes now I am a physicalist who thinks that experience of qualia is like belief in unicorns, which is a problem. Still, in *Human Thought* I argue in this way:[58] Neither dualism, idealism, neutral monism, nor naive realism is adequately plausible, but many contemporary physicalist philosophers are wrong to think that their particular view of the world is any more plausible. No positive and coherent conception of the world of which humans are capable can be privileged over those that deploy unconstituted qualia, and hence hedonic value and disvalue. The central normative claims made in this chapter have as good an epistemic status as any other positive claims about the world that we humans can coherently conceive; they are equally reflective of the shared, though perhaps hallucinatory, conception of the world that our shared human experience underwrites. And indeed, hedonic value and disvalue are the only sort of unconstituted normative phenomena that are coherently conceivable by human beings. That is one sort of vindication of the normative in general and of my proposal in particular, at least relative to anything else we might plan to privilege over them. Of course that may be less vindication than seems desirable, but perhaps it is the best we can get.

The conception proposed in this chapter is reminiscent of the sensibility views rejected in section I. But I claim that we can conceive of hedonic value and disvalue as fully objective properties, and that they are part of a natural human conception of things that would vindicate our normative practice if only that natural human conception turned out to be right. The sensibility theorists do not and, I believe, cannot plausibly make such a claim about the normative properties they favor. What's more, no human, nor for that matter any rational shark or pain-feeling dragon or Martian, is beyond the range of the particular "sensibility"

58   Ibid.

181

I deploy, beyond pain and pleasure, which is not the case of the more socially idiosyncratic normative sensibilities proposed by contemporary sensibility theorists. Consider the analogy of humorousness. This is whatever it is that the suitably refined find humorous, according to sensibility theories. But the relationship alleged to exist between the feeling or sensory experience involved in humor and objective humorousness is not the same as that between the experience of pain and hedonic disvalue. Even the unrefined can feel genuine pain. What's more, people differ not only in what things they find humorous, but also in having much of a sense of humor at all. While not everybody feels physical pain from the same causes, everybody knows what it's like.[59] There is no need for a direct vindication of pain sensibility over others available to humans, for in the suitable sense there are no alternative sensibilities available to humans. These are crucial differences between my proposal and the view of the sensibility theorists.

Mackie's famous queerness objection seems to this degree correct: No ordinary machinations of the physical stuff of which we believe at least most of the world to consist can generate normative properties. Something as strange and as plausibly nonphysical as the phenomenal must be considered before objective value becomes plausible. But that is not so strange as the nonconcrete non-natural properties of Moore. We are stuck with the problem of qualia in any case, and so we can have objective hedonic value for free. Well, maybe not quite for free. The crucial normativity of value may seem queerer still than ordinary phenomenal properties. But if I am right that the characteristic phenomenal property involved in paradigmatic physical pains is in fact a kind of nastiness, that when we feel bad we literally feel one fundamental sort of badness, then we can plausibly explain the crucial supervenience of the normative on the natural in a way in which those who favor Moorean non-natural normative properties cannot, and we can form some genuine understanding of what such otherwise spooky unconstituted normative properties might be.

Where are we? We have isolated the sole type of unconstituted natural normative property, ordinal hedonic value or disvalue, though I have also promised to consider plausible close variants, which deploy cardinal structure or something intermediate. Instances of such a property must support proper justificatory reason giving in our world, probably even if two-dimensionalism is false and constitutive naturalism is true, but

---

59   Or rather, while some very unfortunate and often short-lived humans don't feel pain, they agree that this is a defect.

almost certainly if two-dimensionalism[60] is true. The only other reasonably live competitors are outright skepticism about justificatory reasons, and some complicated phenomenologically based extension of my proposal. Whether we like or not, some kind of hedonism is the sole theory of basic value plausibly consistent with the facts, and my specific ordinal variant seems the most plausible and simplest form. We also saw in the last chapter that hedonism is in proper accord with our normative intuitions of the same level of generality and abstraction. So the first element of the Hedonic Maximin Principle is suitably secure.

60 Or a close analogue like my own view.

183

Part Three

Maximin

6

Just Construction

The second element of the Hedonic Maximin Principle – its maximin structure – is the central subject of this part. Chapter 7 will argue that it is suitably intuitive. This chapter develops a direct argument for HMP on the basis of the ordinal hedonic value discerned in the last chapter. We will also consider the implications of other conceptions of hedonic value – for instance, a cardinal conception.

"Possible worlds" are fully detailed ways the universe might be. If there are other sorts of basic value than ordinal hedonic value found in other wildly possible worlds, still I will presume, for most of our discussion here, that such worlds are too unrealistic to be of concern to ethics. Call the worlds that are in question for us, which have merely ordinal hedonic value, "feasible worlds".

The Hedonic Maximin Principle specifies the proper ordering, from worst to best, allowing for ties, of lotteries over feasible worlds.

That this is an *ordering* of things from worst to best means that (a) each member of the set of those things is either better, worse, or as good as any other specific member; (b) the "better than", "worse than", and "as good as" relations are transitive; and (c) nothing in the set holds more than one of the "worse than", "better than", or "as good as" relations to any other specific member.

Lotteries over feasible worlds are simply collections of the worlds, each world with a probability attached, and such that the sum of the probabilities in each collection is one. We face risky alternatives, and lotteries over worlds are a way to model risky alternatives. The point is that we must assess actions, and actions result in lotteries over outcomes and not merely in particular outcomes.

The question of the proper ordering of lotteries over feasible worlds is only one normative question. I begin with this question because it is the one question that I know how to answer directly on the basis of ordinal hedonic value that yet can plausibly root ethics, through the mechanism of Multiple-Act Consequentialism.

As we will see, the ordinality of hedonic value has significant implications regarding this question. That is not a surprise. There are developed literatures on the implications of analogous sorts of ordinality involving preferences for the summary evaluation of states of affairs, which make the principal conclusions of this chapter quite expectable.[1] Ordinality, we know, in the context of other plausible constraints, leads quite naturally to maximin. Indeed, it is only peculiar details of our construction – in particular, the differences among null, positive, and negative hedonic value – that require that I develop my own treatment.

That maximin is an obvious implication of ordinality is intuitively advantageous at least in some ways. One standard objection to classical utilitarianism can be evaded by HMP through its maximin structure. The sum of individual pleasures, which classical utilitarianism aims to maximize – and, more generally, the summation of value in states of affairs to determine their overall value – seems intuitively objectionable. Here is Samuel Scheffler:

[U]tilitarianism gives no direct weight to considerations of justice or fairness in the distribution of goods. Provided that net aggregate satisfaction is maximized, in other words, utilitarianism is indifferent as to how satisfactions and dissatisfactions are distributed among distinct individuals. So if overall satisfaction will be maximized under an arrangement in which goods and resources are channeled to people whose circumstances are already comfortable, while other people are allowed to languish in abject poverty, then that arrangement is precisely the one that utilitarianism will recommend. . . . [Since utilitarianism] makes the importance of distributive considerations entirely dependent on their efficacy in promoting maximum satisfaction, it both denies their intrinsic moral significance and requires them to be set aside if ever and whenever their efficacy lapses.[2]

This intuitive worry supports the modification of classical utilitarianism that we adopt in this part.

---

1 D'Aspremont and Gevers (1971); Hammond (1976); Strasnick (1975).
2 Scheffler (1988: 2–3).

Nevertheless, our concern in this chapter will not be normative intuitions. Indeed, despite the general intuitive structural advantage that the distributionally sensitive form of HMP provides, some of its particular structural details may initially seem quite counterintuitive. We will see in the next chapter that such a structure is in fact intuitively defensible, at least when allied with hedonism. And we will see in Chapter 8 that, in conjunction with MAC, it delivers a properly intuitive detailed moral code. So I request your patience on this crucial point. But our immediate concern is to provide a direct vindication of the maximin structure of HMP, independent of moral intuitions.

I must also request your patience in a second way. My argument here will be a dry thicket, and I lack the art to sugarcoat it. But there is a positive and somewhat intuitive thread through this labyrinth. Marx, Gandhi, De Beauvoir, and King each reminded us of obvious inequalities. And in a world where it makes no sense to add and subtract value in the manner of classical utilitarians, where it makes no sense to claim that transferring resources from the well-off to the badly-off could entail that the well-off would lose more than the badly-off would gain, this is perhaps especially inexcusable. But again, our focus here is not on normative intuitions.

This chapter develops an ordering of lotteries over feasible worlds by deploying construction principles that, in conjunction with ordinal hedonic value, imply it. These construction principles, which are capable of asymmetrical vindication relative to competitors, give my metaethical view some affinities with practical reasoning and constructivist views. They also assure that HMP reflects basic distributional justice of at least one kind, that it is in one sense a *just* good that we specify here.

The three immediately succeeding sections focus specifically on the proper principle for ordering feasible worlds, which I will hereafter call "worlds", from worst to best. Section I articulates certain constraints on the proper ordering of feasible worlds. Section II shows that they are capable of a properly deep legitimation in the world we inhabit. Section III argues that the constraints, which reflect the nature of ordinal hedonic value as well as the relevant construction principles, entail a specific ordering of feasible worlds.[3] Section IV examines the dependent question of the proper ordering of lotteries over feasible worlds. Section V

3 This central argument of the chapter is adapted with many modifications from Mendola (1990c).

189

considers the effects of relaxing some of the constraints, and also considers what follows if hedonic value is cardinal or has some intermediate sort of structure.

I

I will argue in this and the following two sections that the proper ordering of feasible worlds follows a maximin rule with the following form: Given two worlds that contain the same number of momentary bits of phenomenal experience, which I will call "flecks" of phenomenal experience, the better world is the one that has the better (namely, more hedonically valuable or least disvaluable) worst (namely, most hedonically disvaluable or least valuable) fleck of phenomenal experience, or, in case of a tie, the better second-worst fleck, or, in case of a further tie, the better third-worst fleck, and so on. This is a *lexical* maximin rule: We maximize the state of the worst-off, and in case of ties move on to the second-worst-off, and so on. I will argue that, since there is a null level of hedonic value, any world is equal in value to any other world that has the same number of flecks of phenomenal experience as the first at each level of hedonic value and disvalue plus any number of null-valenced flecks. So if we can rank feasible worlds containing the same number of flecks of experience, then we can also rank those that do not.

I will close the gap between the ordinal hedonic value found in feasible worlds and the proper ordering of those worlds by deploying various construction principles, principles that constrain the way in which the relative value of a whole feasible world is a function of the value contained within it. The next section will legitimate the construction principles I deploy. This section merely articulates those principles, and also two further constraints that capture the nature of hedonic value and that of our question. I will provide in this section only the minimal motivation and discussion required to allow the constraints to be understood.

Review our situation. Feasible worlds contain only one sort of basic value and disvalue, we presume. Each fleck of experience in such a world exhibits a single level of positive hedonic value and hence goodness, or a single level of negative hedonic value and hence badness, or it exhibits no positive hedonic value or disvalue and hence a null value. All hedonic disvalue is worse than all hedonic value, and the null valence is in between. And hedonic value and disvalue come merely ordinally, though interpersonal comparisons are possible. There are various objective levels of ordinal hedonic value and disvalue. Hedonic value or disvalue with that general character is the first key element of our situation.

What's more, we face a certain question. We are attempting to determine the proper ordering of feasible worlds, on the way to answering a dependent question about the proper ordering of lotteries over worlds.

I will assume that nine constraints govern the construction of an ordering of feasible worlds containing merely the hedonic value and disvalue that I have noted.[4] These restrictions are:

Restriction 0 (Completeness): *There is a complete ordering from worst to best (allowing for ties) of feasible worlds.*

This restriction is set by our question, by the problem we address. It might seem quite optimistic, but it is a kind of practical necessity if full normative evaluation is to be possible, and we will see that this restriction can be met. Of course, lots of moral assessments might be possible without completeness, even if there is no complete moral ordering of worlds. But we will see that there is such an ordering.

Because this is an *ordering* from worst to best, it will have the following properties: If one world is better than (respectively worse than, equal in value to) another, and that world is better than (respectively worse than, equal in value to) still another, then the first is better than (respectively worse than, equal in value to) the third. If one world is better than another that is equal in value to a third, then the first is better than the third. I also presume that the relations of being better than, worse than, and equal in value to are transitive, and that no world bears more than one of those relations to any given other. Because our ordering is *complete*, any given feasible world is better than, worse than, or equal in value to any other.

But also note a limitation on the feasible worlds to be considered here, which qualifies this claim of completeness: I will restrict our consideration to feasible worlds each of which contains only a finite number of flecks of phenomenal experience. Hereafter by "feasible worlds" or "worlds" these are what I mean. The reason for this restriction is straightforward: Since infinite collections can be put in one-to-one correspondence with parts of themselves, any ordering of such collections based on purely ordinal information is a breeding ground for paradox. Infinite sums are subject to the same sorts of difficulties, so this isn't a *special* problem for the view to be developed here. One might object that even if there plausibly isn't an infinite number of creatures with experience in any feasible world, still a

---

4 As I've noted, this conception reflects developments in the social choice literature. See, for example, Sen (1986).

given individual may have an infinity of infinitesimal flecks of experience. I don't believe this, because experience has a finite grain and hence flecks are not infinitesimal. But in any case, by deploying temporal and spatial grains of some arbitrary but still finite size, we can model even a temporal and spatial continuum of infinitesimal flecks to whatever degree of precision is required.

The next constraint is Restriction A (Abstraction): *The information relevant to determining the relative value of a world is merely the number of flecks of phenomenal experience of each degree of objective hedonic value or disvalue (or null value) that it contains.*

Hedonic value is the only basic value that there is in feasible worlds. Worlds that contain the same numbers of flecks of experience at each level of value and disvalue are equivalent in value. How such moments are located in the world that contains them – for instance, how they are bundled together into individual lives – does not affect the relative value of the worlds. This assumption may seem problematic, and we will return to the issue of its legitimacy in the next section.

Restriction A raises the issue of how to represent the hedonic value of flecks of experience. Such value comes ordinally, but it also involves a three-way difference among null, positive, and negative hedonic value. We can properly speak of inter- and intrapersonal comparisons of value levels, hence properly ascribe numbers to those levels in this way: To the null level of value a 0, to each level of positive value some arbitrary positive rational number with greater numbers assigned to better levels, and to each level of negative hedonic value some arbitrary negative rational number with lower numbers assigned to worse levels. But we cannot properly take these representations in other than an ordinal sense, as bearing information about the relative size of value differences. Any assignment of rationals meeting the stipulations noted will be as good as any other.

By Restriction A, and given a particular assignment of rational numbers to levels, the information about a world relevant to the determination of its relative value is born by a set of rationals, which contains for each fleck of experience in the world an element representing its level of hedonic value or disvalue. Hence our problem of ordering worlds from worst to best reduces to that of ordering, in regard to the value of what they represent, sets of rationals. This will allow a second and quasi-formal expression of the constraints we have yet to consider, which will be useful in our quasi-formal proof in section III that they entail the ordering of worlds I have promised. Let such a set representing a world be said to be ">" (respectively =, <) another iff the world the first represents is better than (respectively equal in value to, worse than) that the second represents. I will consider the problem in the guise of ordering not sets but rather ordered n-tuples of rationals, one n-tuple generated from each set of rationals by arranging it from the least rational on the left to the greatest on the right, allowing of course for ties.

With this background in place, we can go on to the other constraints, in first an informal and then in a quasi-formal guise. The informal guise will be important when we legitimate the constraints in the next section, and the quasi-formal guise will be important when we trace their implications in section III.

Restriction B (Null Addition): *Adding to or deleting from a world a fleck of experience with null hedonic value yields a new world equal in value to the original.*

In other words, the null valence is just that, a valence of value that makes no difference to the value of the worlds in which it is contained. Adding or removing a fleck of phenomenal experience of null value to or from a world yields a new world equal in value to the first. There is nothing in the new state of affairs that makes it better or worse than the original. Here is the quasi-formal expression of this restriction: *Adding a zero or deleting one from an n-tuple yields a (n + 1)-tuple or (n − 1)-tuple that is equal to the original.*

Restriction C (Generality): *The proper principle for ordering worlds must be insensitive to the particular numbers of flecks of experience they contain,* in the sense that there isn't a distinct normative principle for ordering distinct groups of worlds where all members of a group are of the same size in this respect but where different groups have different sized members. In other words, we can't deploy different sorts of ordering principles for different sorts of cases, for different sized worlds. Note that this does not rule out averaging principles, since n would not vary if we were given a particular set of n-tuples of the same n to order. Why this constraint? We need a general principle, which isn't just a summary of different principles for each size n. Nothing else could have a plausible general rationale. And it is also plausible that the number of parts of a whole cannot influence the proper method of deriving the value of the whole from the value of those parts. Some fans of organic unity (in other words, some fans of the thesis that the value of the whole may depend crucially on the arrangement and relations of parts that in other contexts would not contribute any value, or at least not the same sort of value, to a whole) may find this questionable, but we will return to that point in the next section. Here is

193

the quasi-formal expression of this restriction: *The proper ordering of a set of n-tuples of equal n must not be sensitive to the value of n.*

Given that flecks of phenomenal experience are the only value-bearing elements of worlds, and given traditional conceptions of how the value of a whole is a function of the value of its parts, three more restrictions also seem obviously appropriate:

Restriction D (Value Responsiveness): *If one world is better than a second, then that is because some fleck of experience in the first is of greater hedonic value than some fleck (or some flecks) in the second.*

In other words, a positive difference in the value of two whole worlds must be a function of a positive difference in the hedonic value that is contained in them. If one world A is better than another B that contains the same number of flecks of experience, then there is some pairing of the flecks of experience in A to the flecks in B that meets two conditions: (i) In it, A contributes the better member of one or more pairs, and (ii) A is better because it contributes the better member or members of that pair or those pairs. I gloss (ii) as follows: "A is better because it contributes the better members of those pairs" means that if A had contributed the worse members of those pairs while B and everything else about A were unchanged, then A would have been worse than B. The reasons for this restriction are straightforward. Only the flecks of phenomenal experience in worlds determine the value of those worlds, but certainly a world does not get to be better than a second world because it has a less valuable element or only equally valuable elements. It might seem that there are other routes to being better, but we will return to that issue in section II. There is a slightly stronger constraint than D that would serve our purposes equally well and is easier to understand and motivate: For any two worlds, if one is better than the other, then some fleck in the first world is of greater hedonic value than some fleck in the second. But I will presume the weaker condition, since I can. Here is the alternative quasi-formal formulation of Restriction D: *If an n-tuple A is > an n-tuple B, then there is some pairing of elements of A and B such that (i) A contributes the greater member of one or more pairs and (ii) if A had contributed the lesser member of that pair or those pairs while B remained unchanged and A was otherwise unchanged, then A would be < B.*

Restriction E (Weak Pareto): *Making every fleck of experience better off in regard to the hedonic value it presents would yield a better world.* It would be better if every fleck of experience had a higher level of hedonic value. Making each and every fleck of experience in a world better would yield a better world. The stronger Pareto principle that if some flecks are better off and none are worse off then the world is better is also plausible, but we will see that it is implied by Restriction E in the context of our other restrictions. Alternative formulation: *For n-tuples A and B of equal n, if the ith member of A is greater than that of B for all i, then A > B.*

Restriction F (Separability): *Adding to a pair of worlds (or deleting from them) flecks of phenomenal experience with equal hedonic values doesn't affect the relative value of the resulting wholes.* An analogous condition in the economics literature is known as the irrelevance of unaffected individuals. In other words, if you remove from each of two worlds flecks of experience that are equal, then the ordering of the worlds that result preserves the order of their predecessors. In other words: *If A is > (respectively =, <) B, then for all pairs of n-tuples A*, B* formed from the originals by the addition to (or deletion from) each of a single element equal to that added to (or deleted from) the other, then A* is > (respectively =, <) B*.*

The next constraint is built into our characterization of the hedonic value found in the world, so it isn't really a new construction principle but rather a familiar constraint set by the world and by the nature of hedonic value.

Restriction G (Strong Ordinality): *A complete representation of hedonic value must respect merely the three-part organization provided by positive, negative, and null value, and its merely ordinal nature.* In other words, hedonic value is merely ordinal (beyond the difference between positive, null, and negative value), and any representation that captures that ordinal structure is as good as any other. No principle for ordering worlds that depends on privileging one such representation over another is legitimate. The social choice literature calls such a condition the irrelevance of cardinal information. This constraint constitutes the major difference between the view developed here and classical utilitarianism, but it is required by the kind of objective value found in feasible worlds. In our alternative style of expression it becomes this: *A correct principle for ordering worlds must yield the same ordering of the worlds for any possible assignment of rationals to hedonic value and disvalue levels meeting the restrictions on such assignments noted earlier.* The proper ordering principle must not be sensitive to differences in assignments that are, given the ordinality of hedonic value, arbitrary.

The previous restrictions underdetermine an ordering of worlds, but not by much. There is only one ordering that meets our former eight restrictions and also holds that it would be better if a relatively better fleck were worse off to the gain of a still worse fleck in at least one case of each of three sorts – involving all positively valued, all negatively valued, or

195

mixed flecks. I will assume, as the final constraint on our construction, the very weak equity assumption that picks out this ordering.

Restriction H (Weak Equity): Consider pairs of worlds that cannot be ordered given our previous constraints. *For at least one such pair of worlds that contain only flecks of experience with negative hedonic value, and for at least one such pair of worlds that contain only flecks of experience with positive hedonic value, and for at least one such pair of worlds each of which contains some flecks with negative value and some with positive value, the better world of the pair is the world whose worse fleck is better than the worse fleck in the other.* In other words, it would sometimes be better to make a worse fleck in a world better off at the expense of a relatively better-off fleck in at least one case of each of these three natural types. This constraint has an unintuitively complicated form, but that is because it is very weak and specifically addressed to our situation, which includes the differences among null, positive, and negative value. We will return to the legitimation of this constraint in the next section. In quasi-formal form for two-fleck worlds it is: *For some x, y, w, z such that $x < y < w < z < 0$, $<x,z> > <y,w>$, and for some x, y, w, z such that $0 < x < y < w < z$, $<x,z> > <y,w>$, and for some x, y, w, z such that $x < y < 0 < w < z$, $<x,z> > <y,w>$.*

II

This section legitimates the construction principles introduced in the last section. Normative evaluation is justificatory reason giving, so the normative principle to which the construction principles will lead in section III must be vindicated relative to possible competitors. This in turn requires a reasoned vindication of the construction principles that support it.

Restriction 0 (Completeness) is set by the question we seek to answer. If a complete ordering is unavailable, we might hope to act at least sometimes on the basis of a partial ordering of worlds. But the rest of our constraints do deliver a single complete ordering. And it is a practical desideratum that this constraint obtain.

Restriction A (Abstraction) allows us to characterize feasible worlds for purposes of basic normative evaluation simply by reference to the number of flecks of experience of each level of hedonic value and disvalue they contain, by their number of instances of each distinguishable basic normative property.

Hedonic value and disvalue are the only basic normative properties that are instanced in feasible worlds. So a characterization of a world by those instances is its characterization by all the elements in it that can plausibly be thought to constitute its basic normative status. So the legitimation of Restriction A is quite straightforward.

Given that the ordinal hedonic values of flecks of phenomenal experience are the only unconstituted normative elements in feasible worlds, they are the only things relevant to the normative value of those wholes. Or, to put it more precisely, they constitute everything about such worlds that can be so relevant. What else could be relevant to the value of a whole but all its basic value-bearing elements? To be still more precise, what else could be relevant to the value of a whole but all its basic value-bearing elements when there are no unconstituted normative elements of other sorts that might somehow help to constitute its overall value?

Any practice of justificatory reason giving must ultimately vindicate judgments about normative status by appeal to objective and basic normative phenomena, as we saw in Part Two. But we presume here that the ordinal hedonic values and disvalues of flecks of experience constitute all the objective and basic normative phenomena that there are. If anything else were treated as relevant to the value of a whole feasible world, then it would be a feature whose relevance could not be legitimated. A practice of so-called justificatory reason giving that treated as relevant to the value of a whole elements of *that* sort would not be similar enough to genuine and coherent justificatory reason giving to be properly worthy of that name. It would deploy as legitimations of certain evaluations phenomena that are, we know from the last part, inappropriate to ground such justifications. It would not *be* in the full sense evaluation as justificatory reason giving. It would suffer from a kind of incoherence, treating as relevant to value what at the same time it implied is not relevant.

Objections to this argument may seem pressing, and indeed it must be refined in certain ways.[5] First objection: Perhaps certain unconstituted normative elements *plus other non-normative elements* together constitute some sort of objective value in a world. Indeed, it may seem that this is

---

5 One objection is this: Perhaps the phrase "value-bearing elements" is ambiguous in a way that makes the simple argument for Restriction A seem more plausible than it is. If a whole has some sort of value, then that value can be ascribed in some sense to its elements, but that doesn't imply that the value accrues to the elements outside of that context. Broome (1991) develops a way to bundle value into elements that implies standard utilitarian summation procedures and yet can mimic a wide variety of apparently competing normative conceptions, though this procedure doesn't imply that the relevant sort of value accrues to the elements outside of their context. But I mean "value-bearing" in the second sense suggested by this objection, which presumes that the value accrues to the elements in themselves and independent of their context.

just what this chapter suggests, when it deploys principles of construction to help determine the value of worlds.

Reply: Our construction doesn't deploy any other *elements* of feasible worlds to constitute the value of wholes. The principles of construction aren't literally *elements* in the worlds, contingent bits that make them up, in the sense that the hedonic values of flecks of experience are elements of such worlds. And to the degree that some sort of fact is constituted by elements that are literally in worlds beyond the basic normative elements, those additional non-normative bits of that fact remain non-normative. Everything basic and normative about that fact is captured by its basic normative constituents.

Objection Two: We are trying to legitimate constraints that fix the value of a whole given the value of its parts, and it may intuitively seem that such constraints could deploy extra information about the world, beyond that expressing its basic normative elements, and suffer from no obvious incoherence in doing so. Consider three intuitive instances. First, the way in which flecks of experience are arranged into lives may well be thought intuitively relevant to any sort of appropriate distributive concerns that play into determining the proper overall evaluation of feasible worlds, distributive concerns that our Weak Equity restriction may seem to reflect in only an unintuitive form. Second, some favor principles of organic unity for determining the value of wholes, and they may believe that some sort of overall pattern or arrangement of basic value elements, which cannot be captured under the strictures of Restriction A, is relevant to determining the value of a whole. Third, many believe, Kant perhaps most notoriously, that happiness – or, more to the immediate point, positive hedonic tone – does not always provide impartial rational spectators with grounds for positive normative approbation, that it is good if the guilty get what they deserve, which is not to be happy but to suffer, and bad if someone receives pleasure from doing evil.[6] They believe that the positive hedonic tone of the evil is not good without qualification. While *desert* may well seem intuitively relevant to the value of wholes, Restriction A screens out facts relevant to determining desert. In at least these three ways, Restriction A may seem to rule out intuitive normative alternatives without any adequate legitimation.

Let me reply by saying something general, illustrate it by application to the organic unity case, and then go on to the other two cases. There

---

6 See the opening paragraph of Section I of Kant (1996a).

are two general points. The first is that we are not immediately concerned with normative intuitions, though intuitions about the maximin structure of HMP are our focus in the next chapter, and we have already discussed intuitions regarding guilty pleasures. The second point, however, admits a qualification or limitation of the positive argument I have just deployed.

Our world is one in which there is only one sort of unconstituted normative value, indeed only one sort of unconstituted normative property at all. And that property has a particular form that is immediately significant. The nature of the basic normative phenomena is what determines ultimately how they are relevant to the value of a whole containing them. If instances of phenomenal hedonic value were such as to present themselves as relevant to the value of a whole only in a certain kind of context, for instance, that might help to legitimate other sorts of normative principles than my own, and to undercut Restriction A. It is crucial that physical pleasures involve positive hedonic value that is just that, which presents itself as good or bad to a certain degree, and not as good-if-felt-by-the-innocent-or-in-certain-lives to a certain degree. The latter is much too complex a property to be plausibly present in phenomenal experience of the concrete sort we actually have. Like it or not, hedonic value comes unqualified and simple. But some intuitive forms of resistance to Restriction A must deny that.

There are other ways in which the exact nature of hedonic value serves to buttress Restriction A. For instance, the classic organic unity view holds that some organically unified arrangements of natural but non-normative entities somehow possess as wholes some sort of normative status. But, after the last part, we know that the normative cannot be constituted out of the non-normative, and that any probably inconceivable and certainly ghostly and implausible nonconstituted normative property of a whole, in effect a kind of non-natural normative property, would not plausibly supervene on its natural properties in the way classic organic unity views demand. It is our world that rules against such accounts, which deploy a kind of value element not found in feasible worlds. No organic unity account with which I am familiar really violates one general principle that underlies Restriction A, and that indeed implies it in our presumed situation, in which the simple ordinal value of moments of experience is the only unconstituted normative element in relevant worlds. That general principle is that the normative status of a whole is dependent on the basic normative properties that it instances, and whatever they invoke as relevant, and nothing else.

This general principle may be accepted by forms of the other two contrary views that we need to discuss, as indeed by certain forms of organic unity account. But that is only when the basic normative properties deployed to provide the requisite direct vindication of such accounts involve metaphysical complexities that are not found in the basic concrete properties of feasible worlds.

Turn, now for the second time, to the case of guilty pleasures. There are two sorts of metaphysical complications in basic normative properties that might legitimate our discounting such pleasures. First, Kant notoriously held that good will is the only thing that is good without qualification, and indeed his equally notorious claim that the happiness of the evil is not good is deployed as an intuitive argument for just that claim. Kant, with his fondness for transcendental arguments of his individual sort, probably did not think that there are objective normative properties of the kind that we have seen to be crucial to legitimate normative practice, but if he had, they would have to be nonconcrete and non-natural normative properties, somewhat analogous to those underwriting familiar forms of organic unity in the manner suggested earlier, which are forbidden in feasible worlds. Likewise, a conception that value accrues somehow to lives as a whole in the first instance, and not merely to their individual flecks of experience, might be underwritten by such an alternative metaphysics of value.

A second sort of metaphysical complication in basic normative properties might also deliver what is required, if basic hedonic value presented itself as merely good-when-caused-by-innocent-action, or good-when-in-a-certain-life. Then the basic normative properties themselves would specify that certain non-normative information about a world is relevant to valuation.

But these two metaphysical complications are ruled out by the nature of feasible worlds. The basic normative properties in feasible worlds have the simple concrete and nonrelational form that we discovered in Part Two. Hence no principle for the ordering of worlds that violates Restriction A can be asymmetrically vindicated in the appropriate way versus possible competitive violating principles, which, for instance, admit different conditions as relevant to the contributory value of guilty pleasures.

Quite generally, the value of a whole is captured by the instances of basic normative property that it contains in conjunction with the conditions, if any, that those properties specify as relevant to that value. Otherwise, the requirements of direct vindication are violated. But this implies Restriction A, given the nature of feasible worlds and the very simple value that they incorporate.

All this should not be taken to imply, of course, that information relevant to determining desert and distribution over lives is not relevant in any way to recognizably normative evaluation – for instance, to determining right action. It is merely that it is irrelevant in our circumstances to the basic normative ordering of worlds from worst to best. That is a cost of the kind of objective value that there is in fact, like it or not. Whatever our normative intuitions, the simple nature of hedonic value and the nature of direct vindication have tied our hands. Restriction A (Abstraction) governs the proper ordering of worlds.

We next will consider restrictions B, C, D, E, and F. We can do so all at once. But first let me remind you of these constraints.

Restriction B (Null Addition): *Adding to or deleting from a world a fleck of experience with null hedonic value yields a new world equal in value to the original.*

Restriction C (Generality): *The proper principle for ordering worlds must be insensitive to the particular numbers of flecks of experience they contain.*

Restriction D (Value Responsiveness): *If one world is better than a second, then that is because some fleck of experience in the first is of greater hedonic value than some fleck (or some flecks) in the second.*

Restriction E (Weak Pareto): *Making every fleck of experience better off in regard to the hedonic value it presents would yield a better world.*

Restriction F (Separability): *Adding to a pair of worlds (or deleting from them) flecks of phenomenal experience with equal hedonic values doesn't affect the relative value of the resulting wholes.*

Recall that the hedonic value of flecks of experience is the only basic value – that instances of such value are the only basic value-bearing elements – of feasible worlds. Recall also, as we recently reviewed, that this basic value is simple. It presents itself as value *simpliciter*, and not for instance as value-in-a-certain-context or value-when-caused-in-an-innocent-way. Those facts bridge these restrictions and more general constraints. Just substitute "basic value-bearing element" for "fleck of experience", and "simple value" for "hedonic value". Now ask what legitimates these more general restrictions.

Principles like many of these were held to be self-evident by, for instance, some Cambridge Platonists. But various things have appeared self-evident to various people that haven't turned out to be true, and in any case we presume a metaphysical framework that is not hospitable to the synthetic a priori. Generalizations of Restrictions B through F are, I think, arguably *analytically* rooted in our notion of the value of a whole. But then the question becomes why we should have a notion of the value of a whole like our own rather than a different one. I will instead legitimate our restrictions in two other ways, which I take to be two different ways of making the same point.

First of all, the nature of simple value, such as that found in feasible worlds, requires these constraints. What is it to be null simple value, for instance, but to be a property of something that when added to or deleted from a whole makes no difference, and hence no difference to the value of a whole? Hence Restriction B (Null Addition). This may seem too quick. If something is null value, that may imply it has no value on its own, but leave open whether it might contribute value to a larger whole. But remember that hedonic value is not relational in that way. It is null *simple* value, in the way we just noted.

What is it to be a positive element of simple value except to make a positive contribution, and what is it to be a greater positive simple value than to make a greater positive contribution? Hence Restrictions D (Value Responsiveness) and E (Weak Pareto). What is it to be of the same simple value as another element except to underwrite Restriction F (Separability)? And Restriction C (Generality) seems trivially true of any sort of unitary ordering procedure rooted in simple value.

One caveat is in order. There is a difficulty that has been created by my formulation of Restriction D. One might reasonably worry about this vindication of Restriction D because classical utilitarians have denied it while deploying more or less simple value. Those who hold that the utility of a whole is a sum of the values of basic value-bearing elements may hold that replacing one value-bearing element by two of lesser value may improve the value of a whole. And indeed, many may think that there are situations in which one ends up with a better world if certain value-bearing elements cease to exist and are replaced by others. But recall the context provided by Restriction A, which rules out information about the individual identity of flecks of experience across worlds, among other things, and also recall the gloss and explanation that was given for Restriction D when it was introduced, and that is reflected in the semiformal expression of D that will play a role in our later argument. Let me repeat this with italics in order to make the relevant point clear: A positive difference in the value of two whole worlds must be a function of a positive difference in the hedonic value that is contained in them. If one world A is better than another B *that contains the same number of flecks of experience*, then there is some pairing of the flecks of experience in A to the flecks in B that meets two conditions: (i) In it, A contributes the better member of one or more pairs, and (ii) A is better because it contributes the better member or members of that pair or those pairs. I glossed (ii) as follows: "A is better because it contributes the better members of those pairs" means that if A had contributed the worse members of those pairs while B and everything else about A were unchanged, then A would have been worse than B. The italicized phrase undercuts the objection.

Still, someone might continue to object, there might be simple ordinal value elements, relevant to the choice among those elements, and yet which would not make a contribution to the *value* of a whole of the sort that Restrictions B through F imply. The normative positivity of value might not be a positive contribution to the *value* of a whole. But emphasizing a second aspect of the considerations that we've just observed, looking at the same considerations from another direction, can help to show why this is a mistake.

Choice of something is always implicitly choice of something that is part of the whole containing it, and ultimately of the way the world is. Any practice of reason giving answering the question that is our concern in this part that violated constraints such as these would in fact be incoherent. It would not in fact be a coherent practice of all-told evaluation rooted in justificatory reason giving. If the positive value of an element is to be a positive reason, then it must be a positive reason for choice, and choice is always implicitly of wholes. To recognize the positive value of an element that does not make a positive contribution to a whole would be to recognize it as a reason for doing something "locally" that was inconsistent with what it required "globally", but the local and the global cannot come apart in a coherent practice of overall valuation of worlds in this way. This is sufficient legitimation for our purposes.

Such an argument may seem too strong, for it may seem that there have been obviously coherent views that have denied precisely such constraints. Perhaps the most pressing historical example of such a denial is once again the principle of organic unities. According to this principle, wholes have a value that is not the kind of function of the individual value of their parts that our principles of construction require. Another example is Kant's insistence that sometimes it is a better world if the guilty suffer, that not all additional good things that can happen to individuals increase the overall value of the world.[7]

But, I reply, it is important to consider once again the simple nature of the objective normative value we have uncovered, and the very different

---

7 For another set of relevant considerations, see Temkin (1993b).

nature of basic value according to traditional principles of organic unity or analogous Kantian conceptions, in which either only wholes or good wills have basic value, or alternatively in which the value of flecks of experience is not simple but rather relativized to contexts or sources. These normative alternatives are coherent, but only because they deploy a kind of basic value that is other than the simple value presumed by our constraints and delivered by the facts. Given that there is only simple ordinal hedonic value found in feasible worlds, Restrictions B through F must govern any evaluative practice that is justificatory reason giving at all worthy the name and that answers the question before us. They must govern any such practice that is at all recognizably similar to our own and fulfills its own central requirements.

We turn now to Restriction G (Strong Ordinality): *A complete representation of hedonic value must respect merely the three-part organization provided by positive, negative, and null value, and its merely ordinal nature.* The legitimation of this constraint rests straightforwardly on the nature of ordinal hedonic value, which it expresses.

Hedonic value is merely ordinal (beyond the three-part structure provided by positive, negative, and null value). So any representation that captures that ordinal structure is as good as any other. No principle for ordering worlds that depends on privileging one such representation over another is legitimate; the proper ordering principle must not be sensitive to differences in representations that are, given the ordinality of hedonic value, arbitrary. For instance, cardinal comparisons of value levels are ruled out by the very nature of the basic value found in feasible worlds.

But consider an objection. Strong Ordinality might be thought too strong to capture the kind of ordinality that basic value exhibits. Strong Ordinality assures that classical total utilitarianism is incorrect. But it may seem that the ordinal nature of basic value doesn't forbid such a classical ordering, even if the classical ordering involves cardinality. It may seem that it merely implies that such an ordering cannot be legitimated relative to alternatives.

The nature of ordinal basic value does in fact suffice against this objection. Hedonic value is ordinal and not cardinal, and that ordinality is expressed by Restriction G. But a further reply is also possible: There is no nonarbitrary way to justify any particular one of the alternative orderings of the sort invoked by the objection that do not meet the Strong Ordinality constraint. So to propose such an ordering is to fall afoul of the demand for asymmetrical legitimation that must be capable of being met by any sort of evaluation that is properly rooted in justificatory reason giving.

The orderings that meet Strong Ordinality do have the kind of objective asymmetry required relative to possible competitors that do not meet it.

Still, someone might say, the point of this objection is not to attempt to privilege a single alternative, but rather to argue that there is merely a partial ordering of worlds.

But, I reply, our constraints do go all the way to a single ordering. And so there is this counterargument: Remember Restriction 0 (Completeness). Now add an abstract principle of legitimation, a kind of Principle of Sufficient Reason. Contrary to Leibniz's suggestion, there are probably things that happen in the world without a reason. But at least within the sphere of a coherent practice of evaluation rooted in justificatory reason giving, there must be a reason to properly prefer one evaluation over another and competing one. Now put our two abstract principles together, Restriction 0 and this Principle of Sufficient Reason. There is a single correct ordering of worlds, we presume, and yet we cannot legitimate any of the alternative orderings proposed by the objection under discussion, relative to one another. So, by our two abstract principles together, none of them is correct. Consider orderings that meet all our other restrictions but G. Many remain. But it is not possible to pick out any orderings but those that meet Restriction G in other than an arbitrary way, given the nature of hedonic value that is found in feasible worlds.

We have only one more constraint to vindicate. But that will take a while. Restriction H (Weak Equity) concerns pairs of worlds that cannot be ordered by our previous constraints alone. The most relevant such pairs are "questionable cases". These are such pairs that contain the same number of flecks of experience. We know that each world can be represented by the levels of value of its flecks ordered from worst to best. The ranks of these two representations allow pairwise comparison of the values of paired flecks in the different worlds if the worlds contain the same number of flecks. In questionable cases, one world is better in one rank and the other world is better in another. That is what leaves them unordered by the other constraints alone. Restriction H is this: *For at least one such pair of worlds that contain only flecks of experience with negative hedonic value, and for at least one such pair of worlds that contain only flecks of experience with positive hedonic value, and for at least one such pair of worlds each of which contains some flecks with negative value and some with positive value, the better world of the pair is the world whose worse fleck is better than the worse fleck in the other.*[8]

---

8 My quasi-formal expression of this constraint will be, strictly speaking, for questionable cases where n = 2. This implies the existence of particular sorts of questionable cases, but as far

Note that this is, in one sense, a *very* weak constraint. Because of the cumulative force of the other constraints, as we will see in the next section, all we will need to show is that what are called maximax principles, which maximize the well-being of the best-off at the cost of the worst-off, are incorrect, in just *one* example of each of the natural cases noted in the constraint, to underwrite our general principle for ordering worlds. But there is unfortunately that slight complexity. We need to underwrite a maximin treatment for *three* separate cases, one for each of the three natural classes distinguished by the constraint.

Maximin principles like HMP are, certainly in contrast to maximax principles, egalitarian. One historically important class of arguments in favor of egalitarian normative principles is what we might call the class of "conceptual" arguments. These arguments, analogous to arguments from analyticity that one might deploy in an attempt to legitimate constraints like B through F, point to some concept of the moral as legitimating Weak Equity or its analogs. For instance, one might invoke the inherent, perhaps indeed the analytic, weak egalitarianism of "the moral point of view", which requires us to give everyone equal consideration. But of course what is at issue here is the legitimation of such a particularly *moral* point of view, why we need to have or use a concept like that one.

There is also a long tradition of holding various principles at least analogous to our Weak Equity constraint to be self-evident deliverances of "right reason". Of all the Cambridge Platonists, Henry More seems most detailed in his specification of such principles. And he held that there were two "axioms or intellectual principles", which were "immediately and irresistibly true" in the manner of mathematical axioms, and which seem relevant here. He noted one axiom of rational prudence, supposed to govern an individual's own life, which he called "Noema VII". It says: " 'Tis more eligible to want a good, which for weight and duration is very great, than to bear an evil of the same proportion. . . ."[9] This implies a kind of skewing of our interest toward the relief of evils in our own lives, reminiscent of some implications of our maximin principle. And More proposed another principle to govern our actions toward others that may be even more directly relevant. His Noema XIX is this: " 'Tis better that one man be disabled from living voluptuously, than that another

as I can see there are no grounds for objecting to this if the arguments of this section are successful.

9 More (1997: 23).

should live in want and calamity."[10] But, of course, our metaphysical presumptions here are not hospitable to Platonic faculties of intellectual intuition, and many people have had seemingly analogous intuitions of the false.

Nevertheless, egalitarian forms of the traditions of right reason and the moral point of view, as well as the long tradition of Golden Rule arguments, reflect an important and relevant truth. Justificatory reason giving requires that like be treated as like, that deviations from equal treatment demand special justification. This truism underwrites the second of the two arguments that in fact properly legitimate Weak Equity.

We might call the two arguments that properly support Weak Equity the Argument from Value and the Argument from Equity. As will soon be clear, I endorse the first argument only in a limited sense, as underwriting only one clause of Weak Equity. But there are also further possibilities for this form of argument that are at least worth discussing.

The Argument from Value appeals to the nature of basic hedonic value. That argument is, schematically, that the nature of basic value requires Weak Equity. Familiar egalitarian arguments of this general form are not useful to us, because they require a conception of objective value considerably different from our hedonistic conception. Brink and Cummiskey, for instance, recognize two very distinct classes of goods, with universal possession of certain basic goods alleged to take a kind of lexical priority over the maximization of other sorts of less basic goods.[11] Still, there are analogous arguments that might underwrite Weak Equity by legitimating the requisite treatment of at least one instance of each of the three types of cases we face.

Let's begin with the best case for this argument. Consider what I have called a *questionable* pair of worlds, each incorporating both positive and negative hedonic value. A questionable case like this one cannot be ordered by our other constraints alone. I believe that the nature of hedonic value supports the following claim about such a pair: Physical painfulness – negative hedonic tone – presents itself phenomenally as more important to choice than positive hedonic tone, as more urgent. Or, at the very least, *some* physical painfulness presents itself as more worthy of succor, as more urgently needing decrease than *some* physical pleasantness requires increase. This form of argument may have been what moved some to

10   Ibid., 26.
11   Brink (1989: 270–273); Cummiskey (1996).

adopt the negative utilitarianism of Popper, which is analogous in certain ways to my normative principle.[12]

Can we plausibly extend this argument to our unmixed questionable cases? It is at least arguable, on the basis of the nature of negative hedonic tone, that greater painfulness in at least one case demands succor prior to lesser. The case of unmixed pleasure seems somewhat more difficult. There is an asymmetry in our account of hedonic value that we shouldn't ignore, namely, that there is a floor for positive hedonic tone while there is a ceiling for negative hedonic tone. But it is also relevant that our very weak Weak Equity requires only one case of each type. There is, if I am lucky, at least one relevant case of even unmixed pleasures, which involves some level of physical pleasure that is vast enough to present itself as less important to be increased than is some lower.

But some care is in order here, even if my two questionably optimistic claims about the nature of the phenomenal properties in question, which can rest only on introspection, are correct. First of all, it is slightly misleading to speak of increasing the value of a particular fleck of experience or succoring a pain at all, when what is really at issue is the dominant member of a pair of flecks in a rank in a value profile of two feasible worlds. More importantly, Strong Ordinality implies that there are no differences among levels of hedonic disvalue, or among levels of hedonic value, other than those captured by their ordering. It implies, for instance, that there are no facts about the relative size of certain differences in value level, and that there are no structurally privileged levels of positive or negative value. So such arguments as I have just given cannot properly turn on intuitions that a certain size decrease in a particular level of physical pain is worth a certain size increase in another particular level, while another size decrease in another level would not be.[13] Or at least they cannot properly turn on these intuitions unless we modify Strong Ordinality.

It is consistent with Strong Ordinality that pains in general dominate pleasures, that elimination of a negative hedonic tone dominates an increase in a positive hedonic tone. But that is in part because Strong Ordinality allows an objective difference between positive and negative hedonic tone that is beyond mere ordinality.[14] An extension of this form of

---

12 Popper (1966: vol. 1, 235). But see also the objections in R. N. Smart (1958) and J. J. C. Smart (1973: 28–30).

13 Except in certain very unusual cases where those facts can be captured by representations consistent with Strong Ordinality, which are not the cases we need here.

14 Even in this case we need to be careful. It may be that the most intuitive form of the Argument from Value for even our most promising case, a form that doesn't treat *all* pains

argument to the two unmixed cases properly requires one of three things: First, it might require that the differences between different unmixed pairs is not relevant, that all the relevant cases of each of the two types present themselves in a way that underwrites Weak Equity. I believe this an implausibly strong claim. Second, somewhat more plausibly, Strong Ordinality might be slightly relaxed, to allow the introduction of further structure into hedonic value in order to underwrite Weak Equity in unmixed cases, without affecting the overall implications of our hence modified constraints. I believe this to be possible, but I can't prove it. Third, we might deploy a two-step argument in which the second step is analogous in certain ways to the Argument from Equity that we will shortly consider. Perhaps after justifying the clause of Weak Equity relevant to mixed cases by the nature of hedonic value and disvalue, we might go on to argue that there is a certain kind of like treatment of unmixed pairs that is required by coherent justificatory reason giving and that delivers the rest of Weak Equity.

I commend these alternatives to your attention. They may be viable. However, I cautiously adopt a fourth and more conservative possibility, that the Argument from Value can deliver only one of the three cases we require, that it can underwrite only that part of Weak Equity dealing with mixed cases. This rests on the relevant phenomenal claim about which I have most confidence, and it is consistent with unmodified Strong Ordinality.

So we must turn now to the Argument from Equity. As I've suggested, arguments of this general form are familiar, and may well underlie certain traditional appeals to the moral point of view or right reason. Practice rooted properly in justificatory reason giving treats like as like. And this is a kind of equity. Justificatory reason giving *directly* requires a kind of equity, not because of quite contingent aspects of our concept of reason giving, but because justificatory reason giving is indeed justificatory reason giving. Reason commands that we treat like as like, so to engage in a practice of evaluation as justificatory reason giving is to engage in a practice that requires like evaluation and treatment of like. In effect, there is no further

---

as more urgent than *all* pleasures, is not strictly consistent with Strong Ordinality. Perhaps it is merely some *differences* in pain, either anchored at particular beginning or ending points or involving particular intervals, that present themselves as more urgent, as relatively larger, than some opposing *differences* in pleasure. It may be only *intense* pain *seriously* assuaged that intuitively trumps some normal increases in pleasure, and it may be that intuition about these matters is guided by the nature of value itself. Intense pleasures, or at least intuitively huge increases in pleasure, may seem intuitively to trump mild relief of mild pain.

need to justify equality of treatment or of evaluation. It is deviations from equality that require special justification, that have a necessary burden of proof.[15]

But such generalities are not enough. We need a particular argument with this general form. We need to bridge the general conception that like should be treated as like and the particulars of our Weak Equity constraint. Familiar forms of equity focus on intuitively equal treatment of people. But our Weak Equity constraint has a rather odd and unfamiliar focus, on the ordinal hedonic value of flecks of experience, indeed on the profiles of instances of such value present in feasible worlds.

As we will see in the next chapter, there is in fact a conceptual bridge between, on one hand, abstract principles requiring equal respect for proper moral patients that underlie traditional concerns with equal respect for persons and, on the other hand, our particular Weak Equity constraint. Despite the presumption of many contemporary philosophers that individual lives are the appropriate focus of distributional concern, that lives are the appropriate unit of concern and respect, this is a mistake. Indeed, it is a mistake for two reasons. It is wrong in our world because of the actual nature of basic value, and whether we like it or not. But it is also wrong on grounds of properly reflective normative intuition, such as those invoked in the next chapter.

But for now our argument must be direct, with no detour through the notion of an intuitively proper moral patient. To accept reasons as governing proper evaluation, to accept that normative evaluation is justificatory reason giving, is to accept that like cases be treated alike. In the case of ordering feasible worlds including flecks of experience with ordinal hedonic value, and in the case of considering alternative such orderings, relevant likeness is governed by Restriction A and our other previous constraints. All we can properly do is compare worlds by reference to the patterns of levels of hedonic value that they incorporate. Like treatment involves, other things being equal, a preference for equal outcomes. And in this context, this requires Weak Equity. But why?

Presume that we are faced with certain questionable cases of the three sorts relevant to Weak Equity. In particular, consider three cases in which the paired worlds differ in only two ranks. In each case, we have a choice between a pair of worlds in which there is more, or alternatively less, spread between the values of two paired flecks of experience, holding

<hr />

15 This abstract form of argument is developed in another context by Barry (1989: Chapter VI).

everything else equal. We cannot order the pairs by reference to our other constraints alone. Such identity of flecks as we can trace between the worlds is constituted by their place in the patterns of value representing the worlds. What could a preference for equal outcomes be in such a situation, what could a concern with equity be, other than a preference for the world in which there is less spread between the relevant flecks?

In various questionable cases that we might consider, equal treatment supports Weak Equity in somewhat various ways. First, Weak Equity can be supported by a preference, if we choose our questionable cases cleverly, for genuinely equal outcomes over unequal outcomes in which some flecks of experience are at higher levels and some at lower.[16] But this preference is constitutive of the equal treatment required by justificatory reason giving. Recall that we need only one case of each of our three natural types to support Weak Equity, and this argument will deliver them. Second, equal treatment in a greater selection of questionable cases underwrites the truth of Weak Equity in another and more general way, by favoring a diminished spread between extremes. That is a movement in the direction of equity in one clear sense. Equal treatment requires in questionable cases a decrease of the spread between the well-being of the relatively well-off and badly-off. And recall again that we require only three cases of this sort to underwrite Weak Equity, which this argument can also deliver. Third, equal treatment also requires (and indeed perhaps more importantly requires, since the "direction" of equity invoked by my second point involves dragging down what's above) going in a direction that in the long run, after many transformations that would not necessarily occur even in an infinity of actual transformations, pulls every fleck up. Equal treatment requires that there be a limit to how far down other flecks of value can be dragged by allegedly overall positive transformations of the world, a floor beneath which no fleck falls on any bettering transformation. This third argument supports the treatment that Weak Equity requires of mixed and negative cases. Care is in order about this third point. We aren't in fact concerned here to legitimate principles for just the *transformation* of the *same* flecks of consciousness, let alone the same persons, to better states, but rather to rank outcomes in which the particular identity of persons or flecks of consciousness is not normatively relevant beyond whatever facts are fixed by the nature of the value profiles

---

16 This treatment of mixed cases presumes that the zero point counts as within both the painful and pleasant ranges.

of the worlds. Still, Restriction A leaves us only information about their place in patterns of hedonic value to constitute any relevant identity of flecks across worlds, so concerns for equal treatment of this third sort can be addressed only in this unusual way.

The orderings mandated by Weak Equity, at least in the context of the other constraints, give every fleck of experience three kinds of equal consideration, which reflect the three abstract differences between maximin and maximax principles that are available to us consistent with Strong Ordinality: Maximin provides a floor; it favors less spread between extremes in "questionable cases"; and it reflects a preference for literally equal worlds in some questionable cases. That is sufficient legitimation for Weak Equity.

To put this the other way around: As we will see, the alternative to Weak Equity is, given our other constraints, various maximax orderings – always looking to better still further the better-off at whatever cost to the worse-off, indeed to many worse-off elements. And that is contrary to the equal treatment that reason demands.

It may seem that I am equivocating between formal and substantive understandings of "equal treatment". Justificatory reason giving will involve general criteria, but general criteria are captured by even a maximax principle, so general criteria, it may seem, can't be enough to deliver substantively equal treatment. But in fact I am claiming that a restriction to relevant general criteria in our particular argumentative context does imply a substantive result, that there is a burden of proof for any substantively unequal treatment that is to be suitably justified. Notice that those who hold that substantively unequal treatment is justified customarily attempt to discharge that burden of proof, though in ways that are untenable in the world we actually inhabit.

The ideal form for our arguments in this section involves imagining practices of alleged justificatory reason giving that deploy or neglect the relevant constraints, and then asking ourselves whether they are at all recognizably justificatory reason giving. And certainly very inegalitarian forms of what is recognizably similar to justificatory reason giving are possible. But the most familiar rest on false beliefs – for instance, about what might properly justify unequal treatment – or they are subtly incoherent – in the manner of practices that violate the Principle of Sufficient Reason previously discussed. Indeed, that principle itself underwrites the basically egalitarian nature of justificatory reason giving. The form of egalitarian concern that is relevant in our unfamiliar argumentative context is unfamiliar. But egalitarian concern of the unfamiliar

212

form we have developed here is what falls out of a general concern with equity under our unfamiliar argumentative circumstances. And equity of that abstract sort is a commitment of coherent justificatory reason giving.

You may wonder how the arguments I have given here fit into the metaethical alternatives we discussed in the first section of the last chapter. The answer is that I have augmented the nonconstitutive naturalism of the last chapter with various constraints that are supposed to be analytically required by the notion of justificatory reason giving and the question we face. These underwrite the construction principles that link the basic natural normative properties to other normative properties. They do not link non-normative natural properties with normative properties in the manner of the traditional analytic naturalism that I criticized.

III

Our nine restrictions are now vindicated. But they imply the lexical maximin principle for ordering feasible worlds that I have promised, as this section will explain. Here is that principle: Of two worlds that contain the same (finite) number of flecks of phenomenal experience, the better world is the one that has the better (more physically pleasant or less painful) worst (most painful or least pleasant) fleck of experience, or in case of ties the better second-worst fleck, and so forth. Any world is equal in value to another that has the same number of flecks of experience as the first at each level of value and disvalue plus any number of null-valenced flecks. So, since we can order worlds containing the same number of flecks, we can also order those that do not.

As I've said, this implication isn't a surprise. There is a developed literature in decision theory tracing the implications of various sorts of ordinalism involving preferences, and analogous results in the formal literature on social choice rooted in Arrow's famous work. Ordinality of the sort that governs hedonic value is widely known to have something like the implications I will exploit here. Still, there are a few trivial differences between the case we face and more familiar ordinalisms. Since we are discussing ordinal *value* in particular, this involves a somewhat different series of constraints and a somewhat different sort of modeling of those constraints than is required for analogous cases involving preferences or votes. We face a difference between value, disvalue, and null value. And we need to rank alternatives that consist of different numbers of flecks

213

of experience. But those two differences cancel out. We can add null flecks to worlds to get worlds equal in value to the originals, and hence indirectly rank worlds containing different numbers of flecks.

While what I say in this section is no real surprise, nevertheless here is my argument that our restrictions require our ordering:

(1) By Restriction B (Null Addition), we can add zeros to (n-x)-tuples to create n-tuples equal to their successors. We just add the number of null elements we need or want. Hence we can order (n-x)-tuples relative to n-tuples if we can order n-tuples. This is as our maximin principle requires, and reduces our problem to showing that the restrictions require that the orderings of n-tuples for each arbitrary value of n are as our principle specifies.

(2) Restrictions E and F together imply something that in our context can do the work of a strong Pareto principle. Call it P: For n-tuples A and B of equal arbitrary n, A > B if for no i is the ith element of A < that of B, and for some k the kth element of A > the kth element of B. And clearly an n-tuple equals itself. All this too is as our principle demands. We need then merely determine that our restrictions require that the proper orderings of pairs of n-tuples of equal arbitrary n that are (i) not identical and (ii) such that one is not greater than the other according to this intermediate principle are as our maximin rule demands. The remainder of this section argues that this is so.

(3) First, some terminology: An ordering of two n-tuples is "questionable" iff it is of two n-tuples that are not identical and such that one is not better by P than the other. Let the "rank-i" of n-tuples A and B be the pair of elements consisting of the ith element of A and the ith element of B for some specific i. An ordering of A and B can be questionable iff there is some rank such that its element from A is greater than its element from B and another rank such that its element from B is greater than its element from A.

There are three types of questionable orderings: Type I are those in which the n-tuples consist wholly of rationals greater than or equal to zero. Type II are those in which the n-tuples consist wholly of rationals less than or equal to zero. And Type III are those that include among them both positive and negative rationals. I will argue in the several steps of (4) that the constraints require that Type I questionable cases be adjudicated in accord with our normative principle, before generalizing to the other types in (5).

(4) Step One: *Questionable cases of Type I cannot be equalities.* Here are the questionable cases of Type I where n = 2: $<x,y>$ and $<z,w>$ where

214

$0 \geq x < z < w < y$. If in some cases of this sort $<x,y> = <z,w>$, then by Restriction G in all cases of this sort $<x,y> = <z,w>$. Hence $<1,6> = <3,4>$, and $<2,7> = <3,4>$, and so $<1,6> = <2,7>$. But this violates Restrictions E and F. By Restriction C, this generalizes to cases where n does not equal two.

Some more terminology: Let a single rank or pair of elements from n-tuples A and B be said to "dominate" the ordering of A and B iff A is $>$ B whenever its member of that pair or rank is greater. The greater member of a dominating rank or pair "dominates" the lesser.

Step Two: *If questionable cases of Type I are not equalities, then there is a single dominating pair for each Type I case.* If they are not equalities, then in each case one n-tuple is greater than the other, by Restriction 0. But then by Restriction D, there is either some single pair of elements or some plural set of pairs that dominates the ordering of each case. In general, if plural sets dominate orderings, then it is possible for some of the dominating pairs to favor one n-tuple in a questionable case and some the other, and if a plural set dominates it must do so in a manner that is decisive under such conditions. There are only two sorts of procedures of plural domination that are so decisive, summation procedures sensitive to the size of the elements in the n-tuples, and majoritarian procedures sensitive to the number of pairs favoring one n-tuple over the other. But Restriction G rules out any summation procedure, and a majoritarian procedure violates the transitivity of our ordering and Restriction 0. For instance, a majoritarian procedure pairing by ranks, where the greater n-tuple contributes the greater members of a majority of ranks, requires that $<3,6,9> > <2,5,11>$, $<2,5,11> > <1,7,10>$, and $<1,7,10> > <3,6,9>$. So there must be a single dominating pair.

Step Three: *If there is a single dominating pair for Type I cases, then there is a dominating rank in those cases.* Consider B $= <2,8>$ and A $= <3,5>$. If A $>$ B and there is a single dominating pair, then Restriction D requires that either (i) 5 dominates 2 or (ii) 3 dominates 2. If B $>$ A, then either (iii) 8 dominates 5 or (iv) 8 dominates 3. Possibilities (ii) and (iii) are rank dominations, in which the dominating pairs are members of the same rank. Possibilities (i) and (iv) are "cross-dominations", where the dominating pairs are not members of the same rank. Possibilities (i) and (iv) are inconsistent, and there is no principled way to favor one over another that does not itself invoke rank domination. It will not always be the case that the extreme and intermediate elements of n-tuples of a questionable case will exhibit the order of this example, with both elements of one 2-tuple inside those of another, so a description of the

215

favored cross-domination making use of that order will not always be available. Possibilities (i) and (iv) cannot generalize into distinct principles that can determine all questionable cases. So we are left with rank dominations.

Step Four: *If a rank dominates in Type I cases, then Type I cases are adjudicated by our normative principle.* Consider the questionable cases of 2-tuples A = <1,5> and B = <3,4>. (a) If a rank dominates the pair of A and B, then either the rank consisting of (1,3) dominates or that consisting of (5,4) does. (b) By Restrictions G and H, (5,4) does not, hence if a rank dominates, (1,3) does. (c) But if (1,3) dominates, it does so under a characterization equivalent to "first rank from the left with unequal elements": (i) (1,3) in A and B is degenerately a rank that fits such a characterization. (ii) By Restriction F, we can add equal elements to A and B to yield successor n-tuples preserving their predecessors' order. When the added elements are less than or equal to one or greater than or equal to three, (1,3) will be in the successors the first rank with unequal elements. (iii) The only way we can add equal elements and create successor n-tuples both meeting Restriction F by preserving the order of their predecessors and such that their first rank that does not consist of equal elements does not consist of (1,3) is the following: The equal elements are less than three and greater than one. For example, two would create the successors <1,2,5> and <2,3,4>. But then the first unequal rank of the successors preserves the relative domination of the first rank of the predecessors, and domination by the first unequal rank would yield what Restriction F demands. (iv) By Restriction C, any ordering principle that applies to A and B must apply to their successors. Hence if (1,3) is dominant for A and B, it is under some characterization of that rank equivalent to "the first rank from the left with unequal elements". But by Restriction G, this generalizes to all Type I 2-tuples, and by Restriction C to Type I n-tuples of arbitrary n. Hence if a rank dominates in Type I cases, then the correct principle for Type I cases is our lexical maximin principle.

(5) By the four steps of (4), we know that Type I questionable cases are adjudicated by our principle. But the preceding argument generalizes to cases of Type II and Type III as well, utilizing the other clauses of Restriction H, and by (3) these are the only questionable cases. Hence the restrictions require that all questionable cases, and hence by (1) and (2) all orderings of worlds, be adjudicated by our lexical maximin principle.

We have come through a rather dense thicket, but we know now which feasible worlds are better than which others. Still, we don't yet have the answer that this chapter ultimately seeks. We don't yet know which chances or risks of which worlds, which lotteries over worlds, are better than which others, except of course in the degenerate case of lotteries that have only one possible outcome each. And to assess actions in our chancy world, it seems, we must assess lotteries. This section will close that gap.

Consider lotteries over feasible worlds. For a lottery over some set of feasible worlds to be the case is for there to be some nonzero probability that each member of the set is the case and a probability of one that some member of the set is the case. It is for there to be some chance that each of those worlds is actual and no chance that none of them are. A general theory of value should tell us, it seems, which lotteries over worlds are better than which others, and we will know this when we have an ordering of lotteries from worst to best, allowing of course for ties.

What is the proper ordering of lotteries over feasible worlds, given the ordering of worlds (and hence of degenerate lotteries having only one possible outcome each) that we discovered in the preceding sections of this chapter? We can answer this question by a construction reminiscent of our former construction of an ordering of worlds from their ordinal hedonic value. The questions are quite analogous.

I will assume that the relative value of lotteries is a function of the relative value of their outcomes. This is the intuitive view. Consider lotteries A and B. Assume that they have an equal number of equally probable outcomes such that all of the outcomes of A are better than any of the outcomes of B. Will it not follow that A is the better lottery? I can imagine someone who denied such a principle – for instance, evaluating lotteries by the relative equality of the probabilities of their outcomes. But no one could conceive of lotteries in such a way that some property of the lotteries legitimated this. How could an objective probability itself be a normative value? We seek a kind of objective value of lotteries. For a lottery to be the case is for its possible outcomes to be variously probably the case, so it seems that the intrinsic value of lotteries over worlds must be a function of the value of the worlds themselves. Such objective value as is to be found in a lottery seems to be found in its outcomes.

How then can we use our ordering of worlds to determine an ordering of lotteries over them? There are various ways to reduce the question we face. Consider lotteries over outcomes with rational probabilities. A lottery with a 60 percent chance of outcome A and a 40 percent chance of outcome B is the same as a lottery with two 20 percent chances of B and three 20 percent chances of A. We can always represent a lottery over outcomes with rational probabilities in this way, as a lottery over equally probable outcomes. Call a lottery over equally probable outcomes an "equiprobable" lottery. If there is any reason to consider irrational probabilities, which I doubt, then we can approximate a representation of them in this way as closely as we want. We can order lotteries over worlds if we can order equiprobable lotteries over worlds.

We will need to order equiprobable lotteries over different numbers of outcomes. But consider a pair of equiprobable lotteries A and B, such that the probability of each outcome of A is a and the probability of each outcome of B is b. The number of possible outcomes of A will be 1/a, that of B will be 1/b. We can form two new lotteries from our original pair, replacing each outcome of A with 1/b similar outcomes of a(b/1) probability, and each outcome of B with 1/a similar outcomes of b(a/1) probability. These new lotteries are equivalent to their predecessors. Hence we can order pairs of equiprobable lotteries if we can order equiprobable lotteries with the same number of possible outcomes. Hence our problem reduces to that of ordering equiprobable lotteries with the same number of outcomes.

Several restrictions on such an ordering are evident. The first three are beyond reasonable question, in the sense that any practice that violated those three would not recognizably be a practice of treatment of risks rooted in justificatory reason giving. The fourth, given our previous general principle that an objective ordering of lotteries over worlds must reflect the value of the worlds, follows from the merely ordinal valuation of worlds we have developed.

(i) If one of these lotteries is better than another, it is because there is some outcome or are some outcomes of the first that is or are better than some outcome or outcomes of the second.

(ii) If there is a one-to-one pairing of the outcomes of lottery A and lottery B such that no outcome of A is worse than and at least one is better than that of B with which it is paired, then A is better than B.

(iii) Consider lottery A, which is either better than, worse than, or equal in value to lottery B. If we form a new equiprobable lottery from A and another from B by eliminating (or adding) an equally valuable outcome from (or to) each, we form two new lotteries that preserve the relative value of their predecessors.

(iv) No ordering of lotteries that requires more than a merely ordinal valuation of worlds is admissible.

These constraints generate a problem that will look familiar. The problem of constructing an ordering of lotteries from ordinally valued worlds is quite similar to that of constructing an ordering of worlds from ordinally valued moments of experience. Our current problem, ordering equiprobable lotteries with the same numbers of possible outcomes, is as our previous problem about ordering worlds would have been had there been no zero point in value levels and had we needed only to order worlds that contain the same number of flecks of experience. Those differences cancel out; the lack of a zero world for lotteries is unimportant given the presence of the method already outlined for reducing the ordering of lotteries over different numbers of outcomes to the ordering of equiprobable lotteries over the same number.

Given our four constraints, the correct ordering of equiprobable lotteries over the same numbers of outcomes would follow a maximin rule or a maximax rule. That is because the second constraint reduces the problem to that of ordering pairs of lotteries that are closely analogous to the "questionable cases" of the previous section, in which appropriate pairwise comparisons of the outcomes of the two lotteries do not all favor one lottery. And the three other constraints require that we treat such cases uniformly in the maximin or the maximax way, as the analogous constraints we discussed in the last section require rankings resting on maximin or maximax. The maximin rule for risks holds that the better lottery is the one with the better worst-possible outcome, or, in case of ties, the better second-worst-possible outcome, and so on. The maximax rule holds that the better lottery is the one with the better best-possible outcome, or, in case of ties, the better second-best-possible outcome, and so on.

An additional restriction specifying a weak conservatism over risks would ensure that the maximin ordering is correct. In light of the other constraints governing an ordering of lotteries, it need only rule out the very risky maximax ordering in one relevant case, an ordering that tells us to order lotteries by their best possible outcomes no matter how improbable they are.

Why is this constraint legitimate? If someone takes a normative risk with someone else's fate, then intuitively a choice following the maximin principle would make it much easier to justify an unlucky outcome to its victim than would a choice following a maximax principle. Of course, there might be a very good chance that a maximin choice would end up with a worse outcome than some principle that worried a lot about serious bad risks and not only about the very worst possible outcome. But because of our other constraints, and particularly because we have only an ordinal valuation of outcomes, such intuitive middle routes are not available to us. All weak conservatism requires is that there be some very risky shot that is ruled out. And very risky shots are intuitively very difficult to justify, especially if they go wrong. It is our other constraints, and especially the ordinal valuation of feasible worlds, that yield a maximin principle in particular in this context.

But, of course, intuition is not our current concern. So we need another argument. There is an argument that justifies a maximin treatment of risks – or, more directly, weak conservatism about risks – by appeal to the nature of the objective value of lotteries and hence of worlds, which is analogous to our earlier Argument from Value for Weak Equity. It might seem that such an argument is more problematic in this instance, because the kind of objective value that worlds possess is only the constructed sort we developed earlier, and hence a bad world doesn't seem plausibly to incorporate some special urgency of the sort that the phenomenal disvalue of flecks of experience seems to possess. On the other hand, the very same disvalue of flecks of experience that makes up the disvalue of worlds plausibly has, at least in the single instance we require to underwrite weak conservatism over risks, the necessary stringency. Painfulness, or at the very least, painfulness of a certain level, demands not merely that it be assuaged, but that it not be idly risked, I believe.

There are also analogues of our Argument from Equity that are available. Like a maximin principle for evaluating outcomes, a maximin principle for risks is recognizably equitable – in the way in which it treats possible outcomes, in the way (if this is relevant) in which it treats possible or actual people in the situations that they would inhabit in each possible outcome, and even in the way it treats possible or actual flecks of experience or levels of value. I believe that because reason requires like treatment of like, a practice of evaluation rooted in justificatory reason giving needs on pain of incoherence to accept a principle equivalent to at least our very weak conservatism over risks. Perhaps it will be useful to recall again that this merely requires that there be *some* very risky shot at some good outcome that involves great risk of a very bad outcome that is forbidden. Our other constraints take up the rest of the argumentative slack and lead to an overall maximin treatment of risks.

So we have an ordering of lotteries over worlds that is analogous in some ways to our ordering of feasible worlds. Just as in ordering worlds we are to look to maximize the relative value of the worst-off fleck of experience, so in ordering lotteries we are to look to maximize the value of the worst possible outcome. As our principle for ordering worlds is quite distribution-sensitive, so too our principle for ordering lotteries is quite risk-sensitive.

My argument here may inspire objection that focuses on restriction (iv). If worlds can be assigned only ordinal value, it might be claimed, still that ordinality doesn't rule out lottery orderings that adopt different cardinal comparisons. It just prevents one ordering from being legitimated by the value of the objects ordered. If this objection were correct, then even given an ordering of worlds and all our other constraints, we would have only a partial ordering of lotteries: Two equiprobable lotteries A and B of the same number of outcomes are such that A is better than B iff there is a pairing of outcomes of A and B in which all outcomes of A are better than or as good as those of B to which they are paired, and at least one is better. It might also be, however, that other reasonable constraints on lotteries could provide still greater resolution. Alternatively, someone may object to weak conservatism over risks. If weak conservatism alone were relaxed, then both the maximin and maximax orderings of lotteries previously suggested would slip by. But I believe that these objections fail and my argument stands.

I have presumed that it is necessary for a basic normative principle to order lotteries, and that is not undeniable. We seek here not so much a decision procedure for actions as a factual criterion of rightness, which may be very difficult to apply in our epistemic ignorance. And so it may seem that one way to avoid the rigid risk aversion of my principle is to insist that one should always choose the lottery that will in fact have the best outcome. I believe that such a treatment of risks would provide insufficient normative information for ethics, because the alternatives open to agents will not characteristically involve this level of factual determinacy.[17] But that is a long story for another day. So while I will continue to pursue the implications of my own risk-averse principle, I also commend such an alternative treatment to your consideration.

V

We can now conclude the main argument of this chapter: A crucial feature of our evaluative practice is that it is rooted in justificatory reason

---

17 Mendola (1987) argues that our options are too indeterminate even to be captured by lotteries.

giving. So any proper evaluation must be capable of being legitimated by an appropriately objective and asymmetrical vindication. We have discovered two elements that allow us to discharge that obligation in answering the particular question we face. Those elements are the ordinal hedonic value found in flecks of experience and explored in Part Two, and the construction principles whose legitimation we explored in this chapter. But those elements together imply the Hedonic Maximin Principle, the basic normative principle of my proposal. HMP is this:

First, of two lotteries over feasible worlds that consist of the same number of equally probable outcomes, the better lottery is the one that has the better worst-possible outcome. If they have equally bad worst-possible outcomes, then the better lottery is the one that has the better second-worst-possible outcome, and so on. Given the method noted in the previous section for turning lotteries with different numbers of unequally probable outcomes into equiprobable lotteries with the same numbers of possible outcomes, this yields a complete ordering of lotteries over worlds, which implies that of any two lotteries over worlds, the better lottery is the one that has the better worst-possible outcome.

Second, of two feasible worlds that contain the same number of flecks of experience, the better world is the one that has the better worst fleck. If they have equally bad worst flecks, then the better world is the one that has the better second-worst fleck, and so on. And any world is equivalent in value to another that has the same number of flecks of experience at each level of positive or negative ordinal phenomenal value as the first plus any number of flecks of null value. So we have a complete ordering of feasible worlds.

It hasn't been pretty, but the battle is over. HMP is true, I have argued, whether we like it or not and whatever our normative intuitions. But Chapter 4 showed that its hedonism is properly intuitive. And the next chapter will show that its maximin structure is also properly intuitive. You may not think this can be done. Once I didn't either. But I was wrong. Part Four will further reveal that, in conjunction with MAC, HMP has appropriately intuitive normative implications about cases.

The argument of this chapter has turned crucially on the ordinal nature of hedonic value. Of course, I may be wrong about that. And, in the last chapter, I promised to track some of the complications that ensue if hedonic value is not as I have presumed it to be.

If there are various sorts of incomparable phenomenal ordinal value – say, those associated with pushpin and poetry – then each provides an independent ordering of worlds. Consider a case in which there are two sorts of incomparable value. Then the ordering by regard to one sort of value might distinguish among ties within an ordering by regard to the other, or vice versa. But we should not expect a single complete ordering of worlds. If one sort of phenomenal value is lexically dominant over a second, a complete ordering is possible in the obvious way. The subordinate ordering would serve only to distinguish ties according to the dominant ordering.

Restriction G (Strong Ordinality) captures the ordinality of intrinsic value by ruling out any principle of construction that is sensitive to supposed comparisons in value differences as well as levels. And there are various ways to object to Restriction G.

One might think that the proper response to the ordinality of value is not to rule out constructions that variously adopt different cardinal comparisons, but merely to realize that none can be asymmetrically justified by the value of the objects ordered. Restriction H in such an eventuality would have relatively trivial and implausibly isolated implications, which it would hence perhaps be best to abandon. If we relax Restrictions G and H, the other restrictions still rule out many candidate orderings. Any ordering slips through that obeys Restriction B and a sort of Pareto principle: If two worlds A and B contain an identical number of flecks of experience, and the flecks of the two can be paired such that (i) for each pair, the fleck in A is better than or equal in value to that in B and (ii) for at least one pair, the fleck in A is better than that in B, then A is better than B. In other words, this yields only a partial ordering of worlds.

But a more obvious and promising way that Restriction G might be wrong is that hedonic value might come cardinally, with interpersonal comparisons possible. Then various restrictions quite like those we have deployed, minus Weak Equity and Strong Ordinality, would yield a standard classical *total* utilitarian evaluation of worlds. We would sum the values in the world to get the overall value of the world. If hedonic value comes cardinally, it is also clear that a more standard utilitarian attitude toward risks – namely, the maximization of expected utility – would be justified by the kind of construction that we have been pursuing here.

Something resembling Weak Equity might be rendered consistent with such a largely classical utilitarian ordering of worlds by allowing that, in case of ties under the standard total utilitarian evaluation, equity sometimes matters. Something like that was indeed proposed by Sidgwick. But there are difficulties. Given that we seek a principle that has a direct vindication, it is worrisome whether there could be an appropriately privileged distributional locus on this conception, which would tell us to attend specifically to equal distributions among people, or moments of their lives, or even flecks. Perhaps any locus might be given appropriate consideration, other things being equal, but there might be no privileged way to adjudicate conflicts among the demands of different sorts of distributional loci. Or perhaps we are forced back to a concern, or at least a first concern, with distribution among flecks. Since, in any case, these sorts of equity could matter only in cases of ties in total utility, they probably wouldn't practically matter very much anyway. For all practical purposes, we might as well just stick with simple total utilitarianism. So I will not attempt to track the implications of this particular sort of complication.

Another class of alternative conceptions of hedonic value deploys various sorts of intermediate structure, somewhere between ordinality and cardinality. One interesting case deploys *ordinal* comparisons of *some* value *differences*. But this class implies a complex situation that I do not understand.

There are indeed various classes of alternatives that are in some sense between standard hedonic total utilitarianism and HMP. Some seem attractive. For instance, I would have antecedently preferred a principle whose locus of distributional concern wasn't flecks, but rather whole lives, or at least whole brief periods of lives. And I would have antecedently preferred a principle that was egalitarian, but not so ruthlessly egalitarian as maximin. For that matter, I would have liked a principle that, while somewhat risk-averse, was not so risk-averse as HMP. But it is hard to see how specific complicated structures of these sorts could be rooted in a plausibly simple form of phenomenal value. And otherwise it is hard to see rationales for particular such conceptions that are sufficiently robust to constitute direct vindications. For that matter, such conceptions may seem attractive only because they are vague and undeveloped. But still, it may be that hedonic value has some structure between ordinality and cardinality that delivers something that is in some way intermediate between HMP and total utilitarianism.

The price of ethics is direct vindication, the price of that is normative realism, and the price of normative realism is that you may not be able to get the ethical principles you like the best. I wouldn't be delighted if total utilitarianism were true, especially because it has no fully adequate response to the objection from distribution with which this chapter began. In fact, I would be appalled. But since in conjunction with MAC it delivers adequately intuitive normative implications, as we will see, ethics would not fail even if total utilitarianism were true. Or so I believe. One of the heads of one of our dragons would take a bite, but not a fatal bite. I will give the total utilitarian alternative to HMP some attention in Part Four, so that we can see that in conjunction with MAC it is, barely, enough.

But the most plausible alternative to ordinality is not cardinality. It is rather something intermediate. Because I don't understand these intermediate structures and their implications, I will presume simply that an intermediate structure would yield intermediate implications. I hope that someone else can see more clearly, and find something better. But I will presume here that by showing that the two extremes – HMP and total utilitarianism – are intuitively adequately acceptable, I will have shown that principles rooted in intermediate structure would be acceptable also.

In the end, it all turns on the nature of hedonic value. If there is none, then ethics fails because there are no genuine practical reasons. Or so I believe. If it is cardinal, then total utilitarianism is true. If it is ordinal, then HMP is true. And if it is in between, then we are in between. In Chapter 8, we will return to the detailed normative implications of both HMP and total utilitarianism in conjunction with MAC, and see that they are suitably intuitive. We probably know already that we can live, grumbling, with the abstract structure of total utilitarianism, though it isn't completely adequate. And in the next chapter I will argue that the abstract structure of HMP is suitably intuitive. As I've said, I think these various tests by intuition are important. But the immediately crucial point is that the true basic normative principle also turns crucially on the normative facts.

They are mostly contingent normative facts. I have deployed some analytic and necessary claims here. Consider, for instance, some of the abstract claims that root the Argument from Equity. But since ethical principles must have a direct vindication and hence depend on the world, and since the world is concrete and its elements are contingent, ethics turns on contingent normative facts. In particular, it turns on the contingent nature of phenomenal value. Ethics is not a purely a priori discipline, and yet it is a cognitive discipline. If the Hedonic Maximin Principle is false, it isn't because I've tried to square the circle, or because I've tried to drive a cart with square wheels, but because I've claimed that there are corners on the sun.

7

Maximin, Risks, and Flecks

The specific maximin structure of the Hedonic Maximin Principle is mandated by the direct argument of the last chapter. It may seem intuitively troubling in various respects. But this chapter argues that such a structure is in fact in appropriate concord with commonsense normative intuitions of the same level of generality and abstraction. You may be initially disinclined to believe this. So was I. But please bear with me, since I hope to surprise you. In the next chapter, we will consider the detailed normative implications of this structure in conjunction with hedonism and Multiple-Act Consequentialism, and see that they are also properly intuitive.

There are three controversial elements of this structure. First, it is a *maximin* structure, which gives special preference to the maximization of the well-being of the worst-off, regardless of the cost to others who will remain nevertheless relatively better-off. Second, it considers distribution not over individual lives but rather over individual *moments* of lives, and indeed, to be precise, over individual bits of individual moments of lives, over *flecks* of experience. Third, it incorporates a maximin treatment of *risks*, and hence is very risk-averse.

Sections I, II, and III concern the plausibility of flecks of moments of lives as the basic locus of moral concern. Section IV concerns maximin. Section V concerns risk aversion. Section VI traces relevant interactions of these three structural elements.

Entire lives are perhaps the customary basic locus of concern in moral theory. Our contrary road to flecks as the basic locus has two stages, from lives to short periods of lives, and from short periods to flecks. The long first stage will occupy two sections. Please forget about flecks for the moment. First, I will try to convince you that distribution within a life intuitively matters in only some of the ways that are ultimately relevant.

I

Prudence – the maximization of one's own welfare irrespective of temporal propinquity – seems to many obviously rational. Special, controversial, and often difficult argument seems necessary to show that an equivalent concern with the welfare of others is rational. But Henry Sidgwick asked an important question about this distribution of the burden of proof:

I do not see why the axiom of Prudence should not be questioned, when it conflicts with present inclination, on a ground similar to that on which Egoists refuse to admit the axiom of Rational Benevolence. If the Utilitarian has to answer the question, 'Why should I sacrifice my own happiness for the greater happiness of another?' it must surely be permissible to ask the Egoist, 'Why should I sacrifice a present pleasure for a greater one in the future? Why should I concern myself about my own future feelings any more than about the feelings of other persons?'[1]

Thomas Nagel and Derek Parfit have gone on to argue that the rationality of prudence may in fact require the rationality of the generalized benevolence favored by Sidgwick and other utilitarians.[2]

Sidgwick, Nagel, and Parfit are right to suggest that there is a close symmetry between the proper distribution and summation of good or well-being within individual lives and across distinct lives. But I think they are wrong to conclude on this basis that we should inflate prudential maximization within a life into utilitarian maximization that ignores the differences between lives. We should, rather, argue in the other direction. The kinds of distributional concerns that intuitively engage us when many lives are in question should also play a similar role within lives. Periods of individual lives – indeed, short periods of lives – should receive the same sort of distributional concern that lives receive in recent discussions. Temporal segments of all our lives are the central and proper focus of moral and rational concern, or at least close to it.

One prominent complaint against utilitarianism is that it attempts to extend principles of maximization of welfare traditionally thought appropriate within individual lives outward across people, and hence fails to

<hr/>

1   Sidgwick (1907: 418).
2   Nagel (1970); Parfit (1984: 115–347).

properly respect the real distinctions between persons.[3] But both traditional utilitarianism and its contemporary competitors often fail to properly respect the real differences between periods of people's lives.

Egalitarian principles are thought by many to properly govern distributions among equal people. The welfare of each should be of real and equal concern, it is generally thought, even if that will not in the end translate into equal welfare for all. And this equal concern, it is also generally thought, requires distributional sensitivity that is violated by maximizing utilitarianism. But I claim that such principles must be extended inward, to govern distribution within individual lives. We should extend to periods of lives the same rough kind of real and equal concern that general consensus now holds must be extended to individual lives. Call this an egalitarianism of periods.

An egalitarianism of periods may be the proper response to a variety of normative questions, and there are complex and controversial relations among those questions. There is a range of views about how the overall goodness of the world should affect moral decision making. And there is range of views about how the well-being of people, including malefactors, is relevant to the overall value of the world. There is also a range of views about the relation between the rational and the moral. But in the context of the rest of this book, the currently relevant question is this: How is the value of the whole world affected by the distribution of well-being *within* the lives of individuals? Still, it may also be revealing that we can answer another question at the same time. Presume a situation in which only one person's life is in question – say, your own. Then ask how one should rationally assess different distributions of well-being within that life. I will argue in section II that an egalitarianism of periods is the proper response to both these questions.

My argument there will traverse three steps. First, the temporal distribution of good or well-being within a life does matter in some ways and to some degree, as a matter of well-founded intuition. Second, there are various possible attempts to account for the normative importance of such distributions in a nonegalitarian way, notably by reference to the normative significance of temporal patterns of two sorts, objective and perspectival. Third, neither objective nor perspectival temporal patterns of these sorts are normatively significant, and hence neither can properly account for our well-founded intuitions about the significance of

---

3 Rawls (1971: 22–27).

the temporal distribution of good or well-being within lives. That will leave only an egalitarianism of periods to properly underwrite the real normative importance of distribution within a life.

But before we can take these three steps, some background will be necessary. It is the focus of the rest of this section.

Traditional prudence is familiar, and hence may seem for that very reason more antecedently plausible than an egalitarianism of periods. But the first piece of necessary background for our argument is that common sense itself is not as determinate on these questions as our tradition pretends. We can see this by considering five specific points.

First point: Our normative intuitions reflect our common practice, and our common practice is not necessarily in accord with traditional philosophers' conceptions of individual rationality. For instance, we don't really engage in much expected utility calculation about the satisfaction of our own preferences, even in our selfish evaluations of our own future lives. Rather, we think imaginatively about various possible future outcomes and give special attention to especially bad or painful or troubling outcomes that we act to avoid, or to especially tempting positive outcomes that we pursue. Damasio has argued that most of our practical reasoning takes something like this form.[4] And Fredrickson and Kahneman have found that there is a general tendency to evaluate aversive experiences by regard to their peaks and ends, and to relatively neglect the durations of aversive experiences.[5] It is also very clear that people do in fact at least sometimes act so as to discount the future and favor their immediate pleasures more than the traditional philosophers' conception of rationality allows. People certainly need to be trained into the kinds of long-term thinking that the supposedly intuitive traditional prudential evaluation of lives requires, and that training is far from completely successful despite its venerable pedigree.

The second point is that it is far from clear that our normative intuitions, even when we can see that they do diverge from common practice, support the sort of evaluation of lives that traditional prudence suggests. People in old age sometimes seem remarkably distant from those same people in youth, to the degree that intuitions that happiness at one age can make up for unhappiness at another become unclear. And many

4 Damasio (1994).
5 Fredrickson and Kahneman (1993); Kahneman et al. (1993). We will soon see reason to question the probity of the aspect of these intuitions that involve a differential treatment of ends and beginnings.

people even coolly and reflectively discount future suffering in favor of present gain.

The third point is that normative intuitions, and for that matter features of our actual practice, that do favor or reflect prudence are schooled and hence perhaps corrupted. They do not represent common sense in its pristine state. At least since Plato, philosophers have been engaged in an attempt to sell to recalcitrant and flighty common sense the thought that we should act prudently to maximize our happiness over our lives, and then should commit to moral treatment of others on the basis of that reformation of our naturally imprudent selves. Attempts to bribe us to morality by promises of salvation have reinforced this. Intuitions favoring traditional prudence certainly aren't natural and inevitable, but are the result of a long tradition of teaching and training which may of course be corrected.

The fourth point is that we should be wary of a tendency to discount the testimony of common sense in bad circumstances over its testimony in good circumstances, as we need to be wary of discounting the testimony of those who are badly off in general. Remember a case from Chapter 4. As Ahab has his gangrenous leg sawed off by the ship's surgeon, without anesthetic, he may cry out, "This is so painful that I'd rather die." As surgeons, you and I would likely ignore such cries as best we could, expecting that Ahab would thank us in the morning. And if he did, we might think that proved we did the right thing. But would it? Any judgment that, for instance, his later pleasure in life is or is not worth the pain of the surgery is essentially comparative, and neither Ahab during the operation nor Ahab on the morning after concurrently experiences both of the values that are being compared. It really isn't clear that Ahab on the morning after has greater comparative authority. For one thing, we are happily adept at forgetting the intensity of past pains. Maybe only Ahab as he is experiencing the pain really knows what it is worth.[6] His cries are, after all, commonsense testimony, and maybe the only such testimony that is suitably and fully confronted with the single most relevant fact.

All this is not meant to suggest that traditional prudence does not enjoy some apparent intuitive advantages over an egalitarianism of periods. But the fifth point is that some of these advantages do not lie at a helpful spot for opponents of that egalitarianism. Individual lives, as opposed to periods of lives, matter most to our normative intuitions when we consider

---

6 I owe this case to a public lecture by Thomas Schelling.

goods that are thought to be rewards for desert. And this isn't the kind of distribution of well-being or good with which we are immediately concerned here, the kind of distribution that we dominantly consider when we make judgments about how well lives go.

Still, there is some distance between real tendencies in our current normative intuition and an egalitarianism of periods. That is why my main argumentative strategy will be to put commonsense intuition under the pressure of confrontation with certain unacknowledged possibilities, and to argue that the properly reflective and revised common sense that results would support my view.

But there are two more pieces of background that are necessary before we can traverse that argument. The first can be quickly sketched. Our central argument will incorporate a foil, the Traditional View. That is one obvious expression of the traditional conception of prudence. It is the view that one's rational individual self-interest is served by the maximization of one's good or well-being over one's life, where that good is the additive sum of one's good during each period of one's life, irrespective of the temporal order of those periods or the distribution of that good among them.[7]

Our argument will evaluate the Traditional View relative to more plausible competitors by considering certain cases. Four assumptions must govern our treatment of these cases. These four assumptions are the last piece of necessary background.

First assumption: To engage the Traditional View and some alternative views, we will need sometimes to assume, for argument's sake, that we can speak meaningfully of the sum of the well-being or good in a life. This assumption is intuitively questionable, and indeed violates the ordinality of basic value. But it will allow proper interaction of our discussion with relevant extant literatures, and charitably allow for the coherence of some of the competitor positions that are in play.

Second assumption: To achieve proper understanding of the key issues involved here, we will need to presume that we can somehow control for the uncertainty of the future, and for secondary effects occasioned by the pains and pleasures of anticipation and memory. With the literature, we will presume that we can talk about certain choices between arbitrary patterns of the distribution of well-being or good among relevant

---

7 Whether one's well-being can be affected by things that happen after death will not be directly in play in our argument, but one might ascribe any such goods to the last period of life for bookkeeping purposes.

231

periods of a life. If the effects of anticipation and memory matter, they are somehow subsumed into that well-being. We will also presume with the literature that these very hypothetical features of our cases will not disable our intuition.

The third assumption is a related though somewhat subtler point, and will itself require some background. The issue ultimately in question for us is the traditional normative issue of how alternatives are to be properly and rationally assessed, in particular when the outcomes involve the distribution of well-being within lives. That means that what is in question here is the rationally proper way to distribute well-being or good in order to maximize the quality of a life.

But talk about the proper way to distribute well-being and to assess the weight of that distribution within a life may invite objections. Someone may worry that there are all sorts of preferences about the shape of one's life, about how well-being is best distributed in that life, that it isn't irrational to have. None of these preferences may seem rationally privileged over the others. For any given person, the distribution of good across their life is better, it may seem, if it more closely mirrors their preferences, whatever they are. Or, perhaps it may seem, while certain preferences for the shape of one's life seem irrational and hence should properly be ignored, not many are.[8]

The correct response to this objection involves two key aspects. The first aspect is precision about the questions at issue here. Our ultimate goal is to determine the proper and rational way in which the distribution of well-being determines the overall value of outcomes or single lives. But note that "rational" in one sense of the word, the sense mostly invoked by the objection, is weaker than "rational" in the sense invoked by our goal. "Rational" in one sense means simply not wildly irrational. If preferences are not wildly irrational, they may still be mistaken in the sense at issue here. And of course we are talking not about the distribution of ordinary goods like money and health but rather about the temporal distribution of well-being or basic normative good in lives.

The second aspect of the response is that the objection invokes preferences, but the relationship between preference satisfaction and the well-being and good that are our immediate concern is complex in relevant ways. One standard view of well-being identifies it with desire satisfaction. But after Chapter 4, we know that this is problematic. And in any case, it

8   Thanks to Mark van Roojen for this objection.

is widely recognized that only the satisfaction of informed and corrected desires can plausibly be identified with well-being. Perhaps the success of the Traditional View suggests that some actual preferences for the shape of a life do seem contrary to reason. And there is a special difficulty that would face any attempt to root judgments about the overall well-being of a life in individual preferences about the temporal shape of a life. According to the most straightforward desire-satisfaction accounts of individual well-being, a preference for the shape of a life would be a higher-order preference about the temporal order of the relative satisfaction of other, lower-order preferences. We are hence faced with the difficulty of balancing off the satisfaction of the higher-order and lower-order preferences. And even if we grant the higher-order preference complete dominance in determining well-being, or specify that lower-order well-being is not defined by reference to preference satisfaction, still it is important to see that not everyone has such a higher-order preference for the shape of their life, and that even when they do, it will very likely change over time. It will very likely do that even if it is corrected. So we *cannot* properly assess the overall well-being of many lives, on the way to making an overall normative assessment of outcomes, by a simple appeal to individual preferences about the shape of one's life.

More complex desire-based accounts are, of course, possible. For instance, we might consider each of the hypothetical fully informed preferences for distribution of goods within a life that an individual would have at each moment of that life if asked specifically about such distributions, and then maximize the sum of the satisfaction of those higher-order hypothetical momentary preferences.[9] But such preferences are too abstract and hypothetical, and their summation too unfamiliar, to give such a controversial normative alternative an obvious intuitive advantage over alternative views on the simple ground that we need to respect people's preferences. Such preferences are too far removed from actual people's actual preferences.

All this is not to suggest that individual preferences for the shape of a life should not matter at all in the evaluation of outcomes. And here we come back to the necessary third assumption of our central argument:

Just as we will presume that we can control for the effects of anticipation and memory by incorporating them into the well-being or good distributed within the life, so also the satisfaction or frustration of individual

---

9 For something like this proposal, see Carson (2000: 86–87).

preferences for the shape of a life should play exactly the same role in determining the well-being or good of a period that any satisfied or frustrated preference of that period appropriately plays. If a life with a certain shape is for someone the most important thing at any particular time, then that will show in their relevant frustration or satisfaction at that time and hence their good at that time, at least, that is, if the frustration or satisfaction of preferences is crucial to their well-being or good. And for those for whom such a shape isn't that important, frustration or satisfaction of such abstract temporal preferences won't significantly affect their well-being or good. *That* is proper respect for actual individual differences in preference.

We are of course ultimately concerned here with distribution within a life not of normative value *tout court*, but merely of basic value that is in fact intrinsic hedonic value. But since frustration or satisfaction often affects hedonic tone, my fourth and final presumption will be that this detail will not derail our argument. In any case, our present concern is not with hedonism, but merely with a certain abstract structural feature of HMP, independent of the specific conception of basic good that HMP also incorporates.

II

With the necessary preliminaries out of the way, we can now traverse our argument. It has three steps. The first step is the recognition that the Traditional View, concerned to maximize individual well-being irrespective of its temporal distribution, is intuitively wrong. Indeed, it is so obviously wrong that we can wonder if anyone ever really held it except on paper. Intuitively, the distribution of good within a life matters some to the overall quality of that life.

The most obvious cases that reveal this involve equalized sums of well-being in two possible lives of equal duration, and reveal that distribution matters, at least once the sum of well-being is fixed. For instance, it intuitively matters if two lives with equal sums of well-being involve respectively compensating moments of agony and bliss or simply an even keel. It matters if all the joy of a life is in youth or in some limited period of age, or spread about more evenly through the life.[10]

---

10 And even if it is not coherent to talk about equalized sums of well-being in two distinct lives, the temporal patterns noted remain intuitively salient. And of course if summation doesn't even make coherent sense, then a key assumption of the Traditional View is false anyway.

We need to exercise due care. There are many related but distinct issues in play in such examples. For instance, cases of this sort may uncover individual preferences for one's own life, which may differ between people or even for a single person over time. But we need the cases to reveal intuitions about normative facts that support some individual preferences rather than others. Still, many do have the relevant intuitions. The dominant pattern of intuition seems to be that at least some concern for each reasonably long period of one's life is rationally required, that there is at least a floor beneath which, other things equal, each period shouldn't go, that there is at least that very weak egalitarianism of long periods present in commonsense intuition and uncovered by these cases. But for the moment, let's rest with the weaker and less controversial claim that distribution intuitively matters some.

More interesting cases involve trade-offs between distribution and maximization. There are apparently well-founded intuitions that imply that distribution should matter even at some cost to the total sum of well-being in a life. John Mackie has uncovered some:

Suppose that as a young adult one could look forward to a fairly long life, and had some rough idea of the various satisfactions and frustrations likely to be experienced as a result of each of several alternative choices of a plan of life. Suppose that one could also allow for probable changes in one's preferences and ideals as one grew older, and was able to detach oneself from one's present youthful purposes and values and to look fairly at the alternative plans of life from the points of view of all one's future selves as well as the present one. Is it obvious that if a reasonable person were able to do all these things, he would opt for whatever plan of life promised the greatest aggregate utility? Or might he try to ensure that no substantial phase of his life was too miserable, even if very great satisfactions at other times were to compensate for this? ... I am suggesting that looking after each substantial phase might be the sensible thing to opt for in its own right, not merely as a means to maximizing the aggregate.[11]

Distribution of good within a life intuitively matters even in this somewhat stronger way, whether we focus on our own lives or on the lives of others. And notice that it does so in a way that supports or reflects at least a weak egalitarianism of substantial periods of a life. Notice this intuitive rationale hovering within Mackie's case. It seems that each substantial period of a life has a kind of equal normative standing of the sort that

11   Mackie (1984: 93).

concerns us. But I will not rest heavily on this point. We haven't reached our conclusion yet.

The second step in our main argument is to notice that there are a number of different ways in which temporal distribution might matter, or, perhaps it is more accurate to say, a number of different explanations of how and why it does matter. So perhaps the appearance of an intuitive egalitarian rationale that Mackie provides is misleading. There are three discernible classes of possible views about the proper distribution of well-being through life.

The first class, which I will call Timeless views, have perhaps the greatest abstract similarity to the Traditional View, and reflect the rationale that Mackie invokes. On a Timeless view, the contribution of the well-being within a period of life to the goodness of the life doesn't depend on when in life that particular period occurs.

Egalitarian treatments of periods are such views. They endorse the thought that each period has a moral status, independent of its temporal place in a life, comparable to the moral status that individual people are customarily granted in familiar normative theories, whatever their spatial position in the world.

But notice that if a period matters just because it is a period of a life, we may be unable to resist the claim that any noticeable period matters. There is no obvious reason why a period of one length would be salient but a shorter period would not. Years or days, youth or age, seem quite arbitrary periods.

This is not to say that we do not treat different periods differently. Someone might be willing to have a horrible two weeks in order to gain a later but somewhat greater benefit, but not a horrible five years in order to gain a correspondingly larger benefit. But there may be no coherent rationale for such differences. And we can closely approximate a five-year horror by a succession of two-week horrors separated by days off. So if periods matter, we should be prepared for the real possibility that all periods will matter. An egalitarianism of periods slides quite naturally toward the distributional significance of relatively short periods, against Mackie's perhaps more intuitive claims about substantial periods.

For this reason, as well as for reasons of familiarity from the literature, it is natural to consider first two alternative classes of distributional conceptions. Both essentially involve time, but in different ways. They involve what I will call either objective or perspectival temporal patterning.

Temporal patterning in general occurs when the proper valuation of a life depends on the temporal pattern – for instance, the temporal order – of the well-being in that life. Objective temporal patterning, which the views that I will call Objective hold salient, is perhaps the most obvious and familiar sort. Objective temporal patterns in a life don't vary as now varies. Objectively, 2005 precedes 2006. But it won't always be now 2005, nor will 2006 always be in the future. Objective temporal patterns are patterns that a life can maintain throughout and beyond its own history and that don't themselves change when now moves on. Perhaps the best way to understand this is to consider notable examples.

Michael Slote and David Velleman are proponents of Objective views.[12] Both suggest that a life that gets better is, other things equal, better than a life that gets worse.[13] An alternative Objective view might be that what happens in the prime of a life and not in the last days of decrepitude is especially relevant to its evaluation. Ed Diener reports a paradoxical "James Dean Effect", in which people rate a wonderful life that ends abruptly as better than one with additional mildly pleasant years;[14] this also is an Objective view. After a life is over, it either will or will not have these temporal patterns, from the point of view of the universe. Before or during a life, as long as we assume that there are determinate facts about the future, it will be such that it is either going to have these patterns or not. The relevant patterns are in that sense objective; they do not change with now.

Some interesting difficulties attend Objective views. First, while objective patterns have some intuitive salience, still, as previously noted, different people have different preferences for the temporal pattern of their lives, and they may well not have stable preferences for that pattern over time. And of course there are familiar reasons to be wary of accounts of individual good that rest on uncorrected and unrefined individual preferences, anyway. The James Dean Effect may be another reason of just this sort. So some art would be required to deliver a plausible Objective account that at all closely respected individual preferences, even granting that we must discount some individual preferences as irrational. A nonegalitarian Objective view would more seriously conflict with many individual preferences than would a Timeless egalitarianism. A second difficulty is the plausible suggestion of Derek Parfit and Frances Kamm

---

12 Slote (1982); Velleman (1991).
13 Slote (1982: 23–24); Velleman (1991: 50). But notice that Velleman only claims that this would seem so to most people, and also qualifies the claim in certain ways by an insistence on the importance of one's narrative of one's life. He also argues that it is wrong to conceive of the value of a life as some sort of summation of the value of its periods.
14 Diener, Wirtz, and Oishi (2001).

that temporal patterning of this sort may be more intuitively salient for some goods than for others – for instance, more salient for achievements than for pleasures.[15]

But, there are other ways in which objective temporal patterning seems intuitively to matter to morality, and this may seem to lend indirect support to Objective views. Kamm, in her treatment of mortality, has revealed a number of these.[16] Hedonistic value theories traditionally follow Lucretius into the claim that death is no special harm that having been born is not. But Kamm more closely tracks our commonsense intuitions. She presumes that death is a special evil, asymmetrical with having been born, and asks why. Certainly death deprives us of familiar goods like more life, happiness, pleasure, and desire satisfaction. But so does not having existed prior to the moment of our birth, since if our lives had stretched infinitely into the past we would have had infinitely greater opportunities for happiness, pleasure, and desire satisfaction. The most natural explanations of this asymmetry in our attitudes toward birth and death, if we accept these attitudes as normatively probative at even the deepest level, involve objective temporal patterning. Kamm suggests as relevant in particular an Insult Factor, whereby death involves a loss of goods to a person who already exists, and an Extinction Factor, whereby death ends permanently all significant portions of a life. Objective temporal patterning might also explain why we think that the satisfaction of desires after death may at least reasonably be supposed relevant to well-being in a way that their unknown satisfaction prior to one's existence is not. So objective temporal patterning is not an isolated phenomenon in commonsense morality.

The third class of views about the normative salience of the distribution of good or well-being within a life also involves temporal patterning, but of a different sort. These views, Perspectival views, hold that perspectival temporal patterning – that is, temporal patterning dependent on when now is and hence that changes with time – is relevant. Parfit has developed some classic cases, cases that may also undercut the traditional conception of prudence, that serve to reveal the most intuitive forms of Perspectival views:

I am in some hospital, to have some kind of surgery[,] . . . completely safe, and always successful. . . . The surgery may be brief, or it may instead take a long time. Because I have to co-operate with the surgeon, I cannot have anaesthetics. I have

15   Kamm (1993: 36–37).
16   Ibid., 13–71.

had this surgery once before, and I can remember how painful it is. Under a new policy, because the operation is so painful, patients are now afterwards made to forget it. . . . I have just woken up. I cannot remember going to sleep. I ask my nurse if it has been decided when my operation is to be, and how long it must take. She says that she knows the facts about both me and another patient, but that she cannot remember which facts apply to whom. She can tell me only that the following is true. I may be the patient who had his operation yesterday. In that case, my operation was the longest ever performed, lasting ten hours. I may instead be the patient who is to have a short operation later today. It is either true that I did suffer for ten hours, or true that I shall suffer for one hour.

I ask the nurse to find out which is true. While she is away, it is clear to me which I prefer to be true. If I learn that the first is true, I shall be greatly relieved.[17]

There are complications that attend this case. For instance, some people follow Locke into the claim that amnesia interrupts personal identity over time. So Parfit presents an alternative case without amnesia but with fuzzy memory instead.[18] Also, one reason some may want to have an operation in the past is so that their life always gets better. But with greater specification of Parfit's case, we could assure that the overall pattern of improvement in the life as a whole is steadily upward in any relevant sense, however the local trouble about the operation is resolved. Despite these complexities, for our purposes the key point is Parfit's conclusion, which is that the preference elicited by these cases, which most of us share, is not irrational even though it is in conflict with the traditional maximizing conception of prudence.[19] It is a perspectival preference.

There are some alternative explanations of our intuitive response to this case that, if properly available, could eliminate the conflict between the Traditional View and this response. For instance, it might be that the past is unreal, indeed more unreal than the future, or that desires cannot work backward. But no such explanation is sufficiently convincing or widely held. If the Traditional View is incorrect because of Parfit's case, then that suggests a corresponding Perspectival view, according to which the normatively relevant quality of one's life turns on whether one's suffering is in the past or in the future.

The three classes of views that might explain our firm sense that temporal distribution of well-being within a life is normatively significant are now on the table. The third step of our main argument will involve two

---

17 Parfit (1984: 165–166).
18 Ibid., 167.
19 Ibid.

subarguments, which conclude that Objective and Perspectival views are incorrect. This will force us, since distribution within a life does matter, to Timeless views like an egalitarianism of periods.

We will begin with Perspectival views. Certainly the pattern of preference and intuition that Parfit has uncovered is deep and real. But it is also relevant that Perspectival views are in conflict with traditional philosophical conceptions of normative rationality in a striking way, conceptions that encompass both the Traditional View and Timeless views.

It has generally seemed to philosophers that a preference for goods rooted simply in their relation to now is a paradigm of irrationality. This very traditional and standard conception is, I believe, correct. The preferences or intuitions that Parfit has uncovered are not intuitively rational in the strong normative sense of that word, though perhaps because we all have them to one degree or another they are not wildly irrational. This is for exactly the reasons the tradition would have offered, and indeed that Mackie's case invokes, that they treat the relevantly alike differently.

But Parfit's cases may disturb our traditional certainty on this issue. For one thing, we may wonder if there *can be* nearly universally shared preferences of this general sort that are not fully rational.

But in fact we already know that there can be. Perspectival temporal patterning of the sort that Parfit has uncovered, a preference for future good just because it is future, seems very likely to have an evolutionary explanation. It is quite plausible that we have evolved to be more concerned about harms and goods to come than harms and goods gone by. In the common – and hence most evolutionarily salient – case, we can affect by our action and choice only harms and goods that are to come, and not harms and goods gone by. Still, it would be wrong to conclude quickly that because evolution makes these tendencies inevitable in us, it also makes them normatively probative. Some things for which we have plausibly evolved tendencies – for instance, certain forms of sexual jealousy or vengeful anger – are not by that very reason feelings that morality must endorse, as even sociobiologists and evolutionary psychologists are usually quick to admit. And certainly we aren't ineluctably forced to act in accord with these tendencies, or with those that Parfit has uncovered. Evolution is not in itself an adequate rationale. And tradition does offer the plausible and intuitive rationale for thinking these tendencies are irrational.

Still, consider possible resistance. Evolution may seem to provide more rationale than I admit. If there is an evolutionary explanation for the preferences in question, then it must be that we have such preferences because, other things equal, our ancestors were more likely to survive, thrive, and leave offspring than human beings who lacked such preferences. So it would seem that such preferences are generally in human interest.

But this resistance is mistaken. Individual interests often come apart from evolutionary interests. People can choose on grounds of self-interest to have no genetic descendants, and to ignore the descendants of their kin. People retain their interests once they can no longer breed, and even once they are no longer much use to their genetic descendants. And the pain felt by children is contrary to their interests even if they grow out of it and it never interferes with the descent of their genes. Evolution is not enough.

Even in light of traditional rationales, and even if evolution is an insufficient rationale, we still may feel uncertain in the face of Parfit's cases. The best way to undergird the traditional charge against Perspectival views is to consider analogous hypothetical cases, in which our intuition will not be tempted by familiarity into thinking a phenomenon is inevitable and natural in some normatively relevant way.

So imagine a set of sea creatures that evolved to have a tendency to favor benefits received on their right sides, as we favor benefits to come. And imagine that we are distributing benefits to one of these creatures. How should we do it?

Perhaps we would begin by taking their tendencies and preferences seriously. But we have already discussed some of the problems this presents. Bare uncorrected preference, we know, is not normatively probative, and may differ over an individual's life.[20] And it is important to remember that cases we use to test our intuitions about the relevance of these spatial distributions of well-being must incorporate into the relevant well-being any necessary corrections for the effects of anticipation and memory, and also for the effects of frustration felt if particular desires for spatial patterns aren't met. We must presume that the benefit we are distributing to our creatures is some sort of basic normative good, and we must choose between a pattern that fits their chiral preference and another with an equal or greater sum of good.[21] With those corrections introduced, their preferences do not seem so clearly decisive, and indeed seem irrational. Good is not more normatively significant if it is on the

20 It might, for instance, differ over an individual's life in our case as they undergo various forms of anti-evolutionary training to overcome their innate tendencies – in other words, as they grow up and mature.
21 Or (if it doesn't make sense to talk about sums of well-being) in which we must choose between a pattern that fits their chiral preference and the same pattern mirror-inverted but with perhaps some extra well-being thrown in here or there.

right. There are few things of which we have greater normative certainty than that.

Still, the fan of evolution may resist. If these preferences evolved, then it may seem that the preferences must be in the interest of the creatures in question. But this argument is no more decisive than before. By some odd twist of circumstance, only what happens on the right sides of these creatures is relevant to their breeding and their protection of their descendants, as only certain time intervals matter for us. The rest of such a creature hangs out unprotected by evolutionary history on the left side. Still, what's on their left sides plausibly matters to their interests.

One way to bring out the relevant strangeness of these chiral preferences is this: Notice that if we distribute goods in accord with these tendencies, which we will assume are fixed over time, that will reveal some practical strain in those preferences and in our consequent action. As a single individual moves around and about, what is on the right can become largely what is on the left.[22] A distribution that was correct no longer is correct; one that satisfied no longer satisfies. Perspectival temporal patterning, which pivots on the now, exhibits similar strains, since the now changes. While today you may wish that you had the longer operation yesterday rather than the shorter one tonight, tomorrow you may have a different and more objective view about what would have been best. And if you don't care about what happened in your past at all, still you may wish before any operation to have a shorter operation later, and yet retain the perspectival wishes that Parfit uncovered.

I believe that we need to be wary of arguments against normative theories rooted in practical self-defeat arguments,[23] though it may be relevant that Parfit himself favors certain arguments of this general class.[24] But my point in stressing these practical strains here, and also the analogy, is merely to generate a proper sense of the strangeness and irrationality of the preferences that Parfit's cases have uncovered in us.

Even if we have such preferences, which we do, and even if they evolved, which they did, that does not mean that they must be reflected in any proper normative theory. Nor does it mean that they are supported by a properly reflective normative intuition that has faced relevant facts. The fact that we have these preferences is aptly explained by evolution

---

22 Their left hand of course stays on the left.
23 For worries about self-defeat arguments, see Mendola (1986).
24 Parfit (1984: 3–114).

in a manner that is completely independent of their normative probity. And what relevant rationales we have rule against them. The very familiar and traditional argument that it is paradigmatically irrational to treat likes differently without a suitably differentiating reason shows that Perspectival accounts of well-being are problematic, and this is reinforced by practical self-defeat arguments and by my analogy, both of which show that they are strange. The traditional intuitive pull of Timeless views or the Traditional View, which remains even in the face of these cases, is one reflection of these facts. Suitably reflective and informed commonsense intuition certainly does not rule in favor of Perspectival views, and on balance rules against them.

What about Objective views, which endorse objective temporal patterning that does not pivot on the now? First, distinguish between Objective views that are temporally symmetrical – for instance, views that hold that what matters is what happens in the temporal center of life – and those that are temporally asymmetrical – for instance, views in which a life that improves is better than a life that declines at the same rate. Then consider cases, similar to those that we recently discussed, that uncover our views about analogous spatial asymmetries.

Imagine a creature that has evolved tendencies to pursue an arrangement of things A, and hence a world, that is an exact objective mirror inversion of another possible arrangement B, with everything switched on an east-west axis running through, say, its place of birth, even when B is available to it much more easily, more certainly, and at less cost. The creature likes good things to be piled up in the East. If one hand hurts, it strives to keep it in the West. Again, presume that this is for evolutionary reasons. Such a tendency or preference, even if evolved, like a preference for a world just like this one but displaced three feet toward Polaris in absolute space, seems a paradigm of irrationality. Indeed, it seems to be of roughly the same sort of paradigmatic irrationality as Parfit's famous cases of intrinsically irrational desires. For instance, there is Future-Tuesday Indifference, in which one prefers agony on Tuesday to mild pain on any other day.[25] (Parfit's Within-a-Mile Altruism, which leads one to care greatly about the well-being of all those within a mile but not at all about those who are a mile and a quarter away, is perhaps analogous to Perspectival views, since what's within a mile changes as one moves around.)

25 Ibid., 124–125.

We can imagine someone with these tendencies; we can imagine someone evolved to be like that. But that is insufficient to provide such hypothetical tendencies intuitive probity. They do not suffer from the same kind of practical incoherence as the chiral preferences we previously discussed, since what is in the East doesn't shift as we move around in the way in which what is to the right can shift. For this reason, not Within-a-Mile Altruism but rather Within-a-Mile-of-Cleveland Altruism is a proper analogue of objective asymmetrical patterning. But such tendencies are still quite strange and paradigmatically irrational.

We are a temporal analogue of this spatial inversion case. Just as we evolved to have Parfit-style perspectival tendencies, so we evolved, and for much the same reasons, to focus especially on what happens later in a life at the expense of what happens earlier, to prefer a life that gets better to a life which gets worse, even if we correct for the pleasures and pains of anticipation and memory and equalize sums of well-being over a life. Our imaginary creature has preferences between different lives that reflect a tendency to favor benefits to the East. That tendency and those preferences are not normatively probative. Neither are our objective asymmetrical temporal preferences.

There may even be a way in which our objective asymmetric preferences are worse than those of the creatures we just considered. Those with asymmetrical temporal preferences of the ever-upward sort can always be led to delay some gratification up until the moment of their unforeseen death in a strange and ultimately unintuitive way. It is not that they will need to delay all gratification, of course, but that they will need carefully to husband resources to assure a continuous and ever-upward trend on into the unforeseen future and hence on beyond their uncertain death. They must strive to escape any final cadence, even though the time of their death may be very indeterminate. Indeed, they may even need to choose today a somewhat lesser well-being over a greater well-being available at the same cost so that tomorrow things can still get better. This is at least an analogue of practical self-defeat. These preferences, like those of our analogous creatures, are strange. Evolved preferences like these are not automatically probative, and the traditional rationale against asymmetrical temporal preferences remains. Treating different cases differently without reason, as in Future-Tuesday Indifference as well as in objective asymmetrical temporal patterning, is paradigmatically irrational.

There is no more difference in the quality of a life, all other things being equal, due to temporal inversion in good things in that life than to objective mirror inversion in such good things. This is perhaps obscured by the fact that it is hard to remember that we must control for effects of anticipation and memory and for the satisfaction of preferences about the shape of a life when considering sums of well-being to be fixed in appropriate temporal inversion cases.

We have yet to consider objective symmetrical temporal patterning, which would be preserved under temporal inversion. But no patterns of this sort have much to be said for them even on immediate and unreflective grounds. And indeed, we have already noted a troubling spatial analogy for these cases in Within-a-Mile-of-Cleveland Altruism. We should conclude that no Objective view is appropriate.

So we come to the end of our main argument. Distribution within a life does matter, so the Traditional View is incorrect. But there are three ways in which it can matter, and we have seen it cannot properly matter in the ways favored by Perspectival or Objective views. So we are left with Timeless views like an egalitarianism of periods, which, unlike the Traditional View, grant periods of lives equal normative status of the sort favored by many for persons as wholes. And this view has an intuitive and traditional rationale, which Mackie's discussion invoked. Periods matter. And we have already noted that this suggests that short periods matter too.

III

We have traversed our first stage in defense of flecks, from lives to periods, and indeed to short periods. It appears that a properly chastened and reflective commonsense intuition would favor short periods of lives as the basic moral patients, the basic subjects of properly egalitarian moral and rational concern. Or something like that.

I aim in this section to improve on this approximation. But first note a possible generalization. Asymmetric objective temporal patterning, and specifically temporal order, is relevant in many ways in commonsense morality. I have attacked the normative significance of temporal order only for one specific set of issues. Nevertheless, my argument in the last section suggests a generalization that would have other important ethical implications. Consider this possible generalization of my main claim: Moral claims that depend crucially on temporal order are incorrect. And then notice that deontological views often violate this constraint in various ways.

First, this general constraint supports traditional hedonist arguments against the special intrinsic evil of death, contrary to the normative asymmetry of death and birth embraced, for instance, by Kamm. It undercuts intuitions that projects completed after death matter to individual well-being in a way that desires satisfied before birth do not. And it would rule out McMahan's recent suggestion of Time-Relative Interest Accounts of the wrongness of killing and of the badness of death.[26]

Second, the constraint suggests that it is wrong to focus normative judgment on the causal and temporal consequences of acts in particular, as opposed to the alternative states of affairs identified with alternative actions independent of temporal order. This may be of significance because of Newcomb's problem and the conflict between causal and evidential decision theory.[27]

Third, certain sorts of harms and benefits are such only by essential reference to temporal order. They are essentially a making worse or a making better. There are some harms, which we might call modal harms, which are such independent of temporal order. Presume that if you do X, then Y occurs also, and if you don't do X, then Y will not occur, with temporal order irrelevant. If Y leaves someone worse off than they otherwise would be, then we might call doing X a "modal harm". Modal harms are defined as such against a modal and not a temporal baseline – what happens if you don't do X, not what was true before you did X. But modal harms and benefits do not necessarily deliver all the features of harm and benefit on which deontological critics of consequentialism rely. For instance, it may be that modal baselines are indeterminate, so that it is a firmer and more determinate fact that you ran over somebody than that if you had tried you would have avoided them.[28] And the acting/refraining distinction is not, even if modally available, necessarily the same as the harming/not helping distinction, which more crucially involves temporal order. Consider Heidi Malm's case: If you are headed downstream in a canoe and will run someone over if you fail to paddle aside, your failing to paddle may be your killing someone.[29] Modal harm and benefit seem insufficient to deliver the difference between killing and letting die. Of course, MAC can deliver this difference, but only by appeal to a particular sort of general group act that may in fact have more beneficent relevant alternatives.

In general, a sensitivity to temporal asymmetries, of the sort we have seen here to have plausibly evolved in us but to be without probative

---

26 McMahan (2002).
27 For discussion of such issues in a normative context, see Tännsjö (1998: 140–152).
28 Mendola (1987).
29 Malm (1989).

normative weight, runs very deep in deontology. It may ultimately tell against certain features of our commonsense morality. But of course these matters are complex, and these remarks merely suggestive.

It is a different extension of our argument that is most relevant in this context. So far in this chapter, I have concentrated on defending as properly intuitive the claim that brief periods of lives are a central locus, if perhaps not exactly the most central locus, of proper distributional concern. I have concentrated on the first stage of our two-stage discussion. Brief periods are in a certain sense midway between the lives that concern many contemporary theorists and the flecks that are our ultimate concern. This has allowed us to engage at once contemporary literature and intuitions, on the one hand, and our own specific concerns, on the other. But we must close the gap. We must traverse the second stage of our journey, from short periods to flecks. Some brief temporal periods are longer than even the finite phenomenal moments that flecks persist, and entire phenomenal moments of experience contain many flecks.

Still, it would seem that any rational considerations that constitute brief periods as distributionally significant also constitute briefer but phenomenally distinguishable periods as significant also.

And it is important to remember that real painfulness in our world does not come one fleck at a time, or for that matter one moment at a time. Almost all real pains involve many flecks at any single moment and indeed at more than one moment. So there is a limit to the practical significance of the focus of HMP on flecks rather than moments or even somewhat longer periods.

My third point is that in the context of the other elements of HMP, some structural relationships among the worst fleck, worst moment, and worst life further undercut the depth of the differences at issue here. If we ignore for the moment details introduced by ties between flecks of value and by the lengths of lives, then the worst-off life by the direct light of HMP would be that which contained the worst-off moment, irrespective of what else goes on in it. And the worst-off moment by the direct light of HMP would be that which included the worst fleck. This argument deploys structural relationships that depend on maximin distribution and not merely a focus on flecks. And to tie the value of a life so closely to its worst fleck, especially in the context of a hedonist value theory, may seem itself dangerously unintuitive. But in section VI and Chapter 8, we will explore the detailed interaction of a focus on flecks, maximin, hedonism, and plausible duties regarding murder and suicide. We will see that this interaction is properly intuitive. Still, there are some complications that can unlink flecks and moments and lives. There are some cases in which HMP does suggest that we should benefit a better-off life (in its worse moments) at the expense of a worse-off life (in its better moments). It is better to make a relatively worse moment in a better life better at the expense of a relatively better moment in a worse life. And a similar structure informs the relationship between moments and flecks. The worst moment by direct application of HMP might properly be made worse to the benefit of a worse fleck in a better moment. But yet these particular complications are relatively unimportant and limited, and also hard to bring to direct confrontation with common sense. If I have convinced you that short periods of lives are intuitively close to the proper primary locus of distributional concern, then that should be adequate to show that the apparent intuitive difficulty of HMP that is now under consideration is in fact not a difficulty at all, but rather almost an intuitive advantage.

My fourth and perhaps most important point is that we have already considered some direct arguments that spatial distribution of well-being within a moment of a person's life matters. It makes no coherent sense to build up suffering on your left side to allow for greater happiness on your right side. It is intuitively absurd to maximize the sum of well-being in a moment of your life by trading a searing pain in your left index finger for a mild pleasure across the rest of your body. Your finger intuitively deserves some distributional concern. That is a quite intuitive and commonsensical point, though one ethicists have generally overlooked. If the spatial distribution of well-being within a moment of life matters, and it intuitively seems that it does, then this suggests an egalitarian spatial distribution, for reasons analogous to those we considered in the last section. And once spatial bits matter, it is hard to believe that tiny spatial bits do not matter.

There is another conception of phenomenal hedonic value that is a lot like the conception I have suggested here, in fact a conception that I once favored,[30] which is inconsistent with some of these claims. It is not unreasonable to suggest that your experience of physical pleasure and pain presents itself as a general overall feeling about the state of your body. That would involve no troubling extension of distributional concern beyond moments of lives to mere flecks. But I have moved to the conception deployed here as a result of what seems the most plausible account of the

---

30   Mendola (1990b).

nature of phenomenal hedonic value. And though that forces us to flecks, we have now seen that such a conception is not forcefully unintuitive.

Of course, my arguments here have not been sufficient to force us on intuitive grounds to a focus on flecks as the basic locus of distributional concern. But we can properly conclude that the focus of HMP on flecks lies at least in the rough direction suggested by a properly reflective common sense, where a rough direction is all common sense can provide on these complicated matters. We cannot properly expect more detailed resolution from our vague common sense than that. And indeed, I merely insist on a doubly negative claim. We do not know on intuitive grounds that flecks don't matter. So my claims here are even weaker than the claims I made for hedonism on the basis of intuition in Chapter 4.

You may retain contrary intuitions about flecks. But it is important to remember that the intuitive detailed normative implications of HMP rest partly on MAC. As we will see in the next part, that matters.

IV

We next will trace the interaction of commonsense intuition and maximin principles for ranking outcomes. The literature on maximin presumes that lives, and not moments or flecks of lives, are the central moral locus, the proper basic unit of distributional concern. But in this section I will prescind from that detail, and trace the interaction of intuition and maximin whatever the central moral patients happen to be. We will return to the interaction of maximin and a focus on flecks in section VI.

HMP differs from classical utilitarianism in its extreme concern for the worst-off, and there are apparent intuitive objections to any view of that sort, whether the worst-off be moments or flecks or lives. Maximin principles provide an obvious route to the unification of plausible concerns with maximization and with distributional equity. And yet it has seemed that maximin principles are not really a plausibly intuitive way to dispose of the objection from distribution to traditional utilitarianism. Almost no one believes that *direct* application of such principles is remotely plausible. John Rawls was the most prominent proponent of maximin principles.[31] But even he cushioned the effects of maximin in certain ways that are not available to maximin consequentialism. For Rawls, maximin principles govern only expectations for primary social goods of representative

31   Rawls (1971).

members of basic social groups in just societies, and indeed merely in regard to economic expectations inside a fixed context of political liberties and equality of opportunity. Rawls, himself, suggested that maximin principles will be in conflict with common sense when applied in a more straightforward way.[32]

Still, maximin consequentialism would, in fact, be found intuitive by properly informed and reflective common sense. Or, at the very least, we do not know on intuitive grounds that it is mistaken. We will get to that conclusion in two steps. The first step will be to notice the truth of a certain conditional claim. But it will take a moment to do even that. My initial point is this:

There are certain concrete cases that seem intuitively to favor maximin, at least relative to traditional competitors, and certain concrete cases that seem intuitively to count against it. Yet any legitimate difference between those cases must rest on the deep moral significance of the difference between acting and refraining from action, or, to be more exact, between failing to aid and harming. But the moral significance of that distinction is itself quite controversial. It is not beyond commonsense dispute, and is, indeed, one of the central outstanding issues between consequentialism and its deontological and other critics.

In its simplest forms, consequentialism does not support any moral difference between failing to aid and actively harming when they have the same consequences. Even in sophisticated forms, consequentialism often does not support any deep such difference. Many, of course, consider this yet another objection to consequentialism. But my first goal in this section is merely to link two standard objections to standard forms of consequentialism, and to support a conditional claim: If consequentialism can legitimately undercut the apparently intuitive objection that there is a deep difference between failing to aid and harming, then it can evade the objection from distribution to classical utilitarianism by adopting a maximin principle.

We will return to the antecedent of this conditional in the second step of the argument of this section. But it is easy to prefigure: I believe that the difference between acting and refraining doesn't have the deep moral significance suggested by some elements of common sense. Nor does that between harming and not aiding. I believe that there are some differences here, just not deeply significant ones. That, in fact, is the implication of the

---

32   Ibid., 153–157.

treatment of these very distinctions we developed in Chapter 3, though we will need to come back to that point to see it properly. I believe that these differences aren't significant enough to support a differential treatment of the cases we will face here. Because there is no sufficient moral difference between the cases that suggest maximin and those that seem initially to intuitively count against it, we are forced to choose between our intuitions, between those in accord with maximin and those that count against it. I furthermore believe that the very facts that show that there is not the requisite difference between the cases also favor the intuitions that suggest maximin and undercut the intuitions that apparently constitute objections to it.

But my first job here is merely to establish the truth of a conditional, and not the truth of its antecedent. My first job is merely to probe the interaction of, on one hand, the intuitive status of maximin and, on the other, the significance of the difference between harming and failing to aid. Maximin will be seen to be suitably intuitive *if* that distinction is not of sufficient normative significance. So let me begin my argument for the truth of that conditional. For the moment, try to forget about Chapter 3 and the antecedent of the conditional.

We will begin by considering several cases that pull in different directions. The first case favors maximin relative to familiar competitors, at least if such a case can tell us anything about how to evaluate alternative outcomes. Consider the intuitive force of Ivan's claim in *The Brothers Karamazov* that he, unlike God – that he *against* God – would not consent to the torturing of one child to create great happiness for the rest of mankind. The suffering of that consequently worst-off individual intuitively trumps a concern for the well-being of the rest. Ivan says to his brother:

"[I]magine that you yourself are building the edifice of human destiny with the object of making people happy in the finale, of giving them peace and rest at last, but for that you must inevitably and unavoidably torture just one tiny creature, [a] child who was beating her chest with her little fist, and raise your edifice on the foundation of her unrequited tears – would you agree to be the architect on such conditions? Tell me the truth."

"No, I would not agree," Alyosha said softly.[33]

Many share Ivan's and even Alyosha's intuition that there would be something morally and humanly reprehensible in such an act.

_____

33 Dostoevsky (1990: 245).

Of course, the child isn't just worst-off. The case involves torture, indeed torture of an innocent. So many ethicists will claim that this case doesn't reveal anything about the relative evaluation of outcomes. The outcome Ivan considers may be a better one, they think; it is just not appropriate to get there by torturing someone. Part of my job must be to show that the torture isn't a distracting and misleading feature of the case, or, rather, that it isn't a distracting and misleading feature of the case if there isn't a deep distinction between harming and failing to aid. Please suspend for the moment your belief that I cannot possibly do that.

First consider other cases, in certain ways closely analogous cases, that seem to pull against maximin. The most thorough negative discussion of maximin is Larry Temkin's. Like Rawls's, Temkin's discussion is specifically focused on the relative justice of circumstances, as opposed to other virtues. But this seems a detail that we can properly ignore here.

Temkin begins with a situation he calls S, with one well-off group, one not so well-off group, and one still less well-off individual. Here are Temkin's main contrasting cases and his main conclusion rooted in intuitive reactions to those cases:

A, B, and C are alternatives to S. In A, the worst-off person would remain unchanged, the better-off group would be slightly lowered, and everyone else would be dramatically raised. In B, the worst-off person would be slightly raised, but everyone else would be lowered, and while the others who initially fared poorly would still not be as badly off as the worst-off person, each of them would lose more than the worst-off person gained. In C, the worst-off person would be raised slightly more than in B, the better-off people would be raised significantly, and the others would be lowered to the worst-off person's new level, each (again) losing more than the worst-off person gained.

On a Maximin Principle of justice focusing on the worst-off person, B and C would both be more just than A, with C most just. Many find this unacceptable.[34]

I admit the force of these intuitions. Indeed, let me be yet more concessive. Temkin's analysis plausibly captures not only our initial intuitions about these cases, but also the intuitive reasons for these reactions. Maximin is intuitively incorrect for two closely related reasons, according to Temkin. Here is the first:

Although considerations of justice may focus our attention on the worst-off person, and we may even be *most* concerned about her situation, surely her plight is not our *only* (significant) concern regarding justice. . . . [I]t is implausible that

---

34   Temkin (1993a: 103).

we should be deeply and genuinely concerned about benefitting the worst-off person, but not concerned at all about benefitting those who fare very poorly but are (ever-so-slightly) better off than she. In bringing about B or C rather than A, members of S would be directly harming, as well as failing to *significantly* benefit, many who are themselves quite badly off – all for the sake of slightly benefitting the worst-off person.[35]

Here is Temkin's second reason:

Let A* and C* be large populations. . . . Let A* be perfectly equal with everyone faring very well, C* very unequal with the worst-off group faring very poorly. Finally, assume that in Rawlsian terms A* is *perfectly* just, and C* terribly unjust. Clearly, the committed judgment of Rawlsians . . . would be that regarding justice A* would be much better than C*. But notice, A* and C* might be represented by A and C . . . , except for the worst-off person. Yet . . . focusing on the worst-off person, Maximin would rank A and C the exact reverse of A* and C*. This seems implausible. . . . [F]ocusing on the worst-off person . . . may seriously distort our judgment because the worst-off person's condition may not accurately reflect the situation's overall justness. . . . [It] may simply by an anomaly or fluke.[36]

So where are we? Temkin's cases and the general rationales he cites have some genuine intuitive force. But we also face Ivan Karamazov's in some ways very similar case, which seems to pull our intuition in the other direction. We must reconcile these apparently conflicting intuitions.

So our question becomes: What is the difference between Temkin's cases and Ivan's? Temkin himself notes what I take to be the key *surface* difference between the cases:

Although some might think it would be unjust to *bring about* A if one *started* in B or C, many believe A would be more just than B or C, and that starting in S justice dictates bringing about A rather than B or C.[37]

In other words, it apparently matters what situation we start with, because it apparently matters whether a situation is brought about by one's action or merely remains the case because of one's inaction. It apparently matters whether someone's horrible situation is a result of active torture by Ivan or is merely something we ignore in order to favor the interests of better-off others. It also apparently matters whether we will have to actively harm those others so as merely to aid the truly worst off. The intuitive difference between the cases rests, as I suggested earlier, on the apparently

---

35 Ibid.
36 Ibid., 103–105.
37 Ibid., 103.

intuitive difference between harming and failing to aid, indeed perhaps on more than one such difference.

Temkin's discussion is accompanied by relevant footnotes that reinforce this point:

If we learned that A's situation resulted from the (concealed) presence of a tortured slave, whose tormented struggles enabled everyone else to fare so well, we might completely revamp our judgment regarding A's justness.[38]

So in effect he grants the intuitive force of Ivan's case. And he says this about the difference:

The relevance of the starting point to our judgments may reflect two important strands of moral thinking. The first corresponds roughly to a distinction like that between the good and the right to which many nonconsequentists adhere. The good or just situation cannot always be rightly or justly brought about. The second corresponds roughly to the asymmetry many see between harming and not helping. Although it may seem unjust to harm those already worse off than everyone else so as to benefit others, it may not seem (as) unjust not to help those already worse off than everyone else so as to benefit others.[39]

Temkin is certainly no friend of maximin. His work represents its most thorough criticism. But the friends of consequentialist maximin should accept that this part of his analysis of what is going on in these cases is essentially correct. Our intuitions about these various cases depend directly for their probity on the presumed deep significance of the difference between harming and not helping, or on analogous presumptions that otherwise better situations cannot justly be brought about. The friends and enemies of maximin should agree so far.

But the rub is this. Many consequentialists and at least some strands in common sense do not accept that these factors have the significance that Temkin presumes. We certainly have no normative consensus that the paradigmatic consequentialist view of these issues, the view that these alleged differences are not deep differences, is incorrect. If consequentialists can properly insist that there is no deep difference between harming and failing to aid, then the intuitive case against maximin is not so obvious.

Certainly if the moral difference between aiding and not harming is deep, then maximin is intuitively implausible. I grant that. But what if it

38 Ibid., 105.
39 Ibid., 104.

is not? If it is not legitimate to treat Temkin's and Ivan's cases differently on such a ground, then what are we to conclude? The worst that could reasonably be said against maximin on that presumption is that common-sense intuition cannot resolve its plausibility, I believe. But in fact on such a presumption we can do better than that.

If, for simplicity's sake, we presume that there is *no* morally signifi-cant difference between acting and refraining, or between harming and not aiding, that would not intuitively serve to *remove* moral responsibil-ity for the effects of one's action, but rather to extend it to effects of one's nonaction. Consequentialists characteristically think we are morally responsible for more that happens. And it is one's responsibility for the suffering of the child in Ivan's case that so deeply evokes our intuitive concern.

Deontologists think that torturing someone is specially and grievously wrong in a way that letting someone be tortured is not, and some ethicists think that it is worse if someone is tortured than if a tree falls on them and does comparable harm. But consequentialists characteristically argue that letting someone be tortured is as bad as torturing, and that letting a tree fall on someone may be as bad as letting them be tortured, *not* that tor-turing is as normatively insignificant as some deontologists presume that letting someone be tortured is, *not* that letting someone be tortured is as normatively insignificant as some believe letting a tree fall on someone is. That indeed is the intuitive implication of a collapse of the customary distinction between harming and not aiding, to *extend* responsibility – in other words, to undergird our normative response to Ivan's case and sug-gest a generalization, and to undercut our normative response to Temkin's cases. It is not the torture in Ivan's case that misleads our intuition, but rather the lack of responsibility presumed in Temkin's cases, and indeed generally presumed by unreflective common sense when it confronts such cases.

Since this is the key point, we should pause to consider natural resis-tance. Temkin does at least sometimes suggest a situation of choice among the options he provides, and speaks of harms from and gains from a given baseline, and that may invoke responsibility of at least a weak sort. But his goal is proper intuitions about the justice of outcomes, independent of whether or not anyone has responsibility for them. And you may think that the way to uncover these intuitions is to remove as much responsi-bility from the situations to be considered as possible, not to heighten it dramatically in the way that torture does. In other words, you may think that Temkin's procedure is basically right, but that he should purify his cases yet further to remove those elements that may even weakly suggest responsibility for the outcomes in question. It may seem that our intuitive aversion to maximin in cases when we compare outcomes over which we know we have no control is quite revealing.

But consequentialists should disagree. They should insist that our real and unconfused evaluation of outcomes is revealed when the full weight of our responsibility for anything that happens because of our choice is felt.

Of course, things are not quite that simple and clean. There are complications. First of all, there is a series of differences between Temkin's cases and Ivan's torture that I mostly lumped together in the previous paragraphs. There is the difference between torturing and letting someone be tortured by someone else. And then there is the difference between someone's being tortured and their being otherwise harmed in the same way. And then there is the difference between their being harmed and their starting out in a bad situation from which they might be rescued.

Moreover, there can be *some* moral difference between harming and not aiding with the same consequences, even if there is not a deep and significant difference. As I said, I believe that the facts in the end are that there is *some* difference between harming and not aiding, and indeed that there is some difference along each of the steps we might distinguish between Temkin's cases and Ivan's. Chapter 3 showed why. But, as we will shortly see, these are not sufficient differences, nor indeed the right kind of differences, for us to conclude that the torture present in Ivan's case is intuitively misleading while the lack of responsibility in Temkin's cases is not. It is still rather the presumed lack of responsibility in Temkin's cases that misleads our intuition in the crucial way. And my own analysis is not idiosyncratic for a consequentialist. Paradigmatic consequentialists who grant some difference between the cases will still attempt to extend our responsibility for outcomes. According to this whole class of views, not the many small but real moral differences between torturing someone and leaving them in some equally painful state, but rather the general false presumption that we would not be responsible in Temkin-style cases, is what dominantly drives our false intuition of a normative difference between Temkin's cases and Ivan's. We are responsible for the effects of our actions and inactions in the most morally relevant sense, consequentialists think. If properly purged of the errors underlying the belief that there is a deep moral difference between harming and not aiding that eliminates our responsibility for the effects of not aiding, an alleged deep moral difference that does not in fact exist, commonsense intuition would favor maximin. The general tendency of consequentialists to extend responsibility suggests that even if there is some morally relevant difference between Temkin's and Ivan's cases, it will be relatively minor, and that it will indeed be such as to undercut our intuitions about Temkin's cases and to support our intuitions about Ivan's.

With the complications or without, this extension of responsibility is a controversial feature of consequentialism. Deontologists and others will object. They do not admit an extension of responsibility beyond the surface commitments of common sense. But for the moment, remember, our focus is merely a conditional claim, that if there is no deep difference between harming and failing to aid, then maximin is intuitive in the proper way. If this is right, then what have seemed two distinct objections to standard forms of consequentialism – the objection from distribution and deontology's objection to consequentialism's characteristic extension of responsibility – are connected in an unexpected way.

There is one further complexity that must be addressed even in our first and conditional step. Consider Temkin's first rationale against maximin, which stresses that maximin would somewhat sacrifice the well-being of many pretty badly-off persons in order to benefit the very worst-off. We haven't directly discussed that objection. And his second rationale against maximin reinforces the worry that it is inappropriate to focus, like maximin, merely on the worst-off individual. We haven't yet considered these central elements of Temkin's alternative explanation of what is going on in these cases.

But note that if we prescind from the elements of Temkin's cases that evoke questionable intuitions about the normative significance of the difference between harming and not aiding, and assume that the agent in question has moral responsibility for everything in the various options, some recent and quite intuitively sensitive deontological accounts suggest a treatment in accord with maximin consequentialism.

For instance, Scanlon has granted that

in situations in which aid is required and in which one must choose between aiding a larger or smaller number of people all of whom face harms of comparable moral importance, one must aid the larger number. On the other hand, [the correct view] does not require, or even permit, one to save a larger number of people from minor harms rather than a smaller number who face much more serious injuries.[40]

40 Scanlon (1998: 238).

In a situation where one is responsible for saving large numbers from small harms or a few from larger harms, save the few. That may suggest that we should generally focus on helping the few worst-off people at the expense of larger numbers of badly-off people.

Naturally, there are complications. Perhaps the course Scanlon suggests will still seem plausible even if those facing the larger injuries will end up all-told better-off in one way or another, whether they are injured or not. But at the very least that possibility leaves our intuitions less clear.

A second complication is that maximin requires other tough conclusions. Imagine that a million people are going to be tortured for fifty years, and one person for fifty years and a day. And remember that for the moment we are forgetting that mere flecks are the true basic locus of moral concern. Maximin suggests that it would be better to reduce the torture of that one person by a day than to eliminate everyone else's torture completely, and this may seem quite implausible.

But note that in cases of that sort that are intuitively clearest, it is correspondingly unclear whether the one day out of fifty years would make any difference whatsoever to the person about to be tortured, who may seem worst-off in only an abstract and mathematical sense. When the difference to the worst-off is obviously significant, then individual intuitions may well differ. And of course to focus solely on cases of saving people from harms and tortures may somewhat mislead common sense in the ways we have already discussed. If we are not to be misled, the consequentialist may plausibly insist, perhaps we should consider a case in which we ourselves would have to administer the extra day of torture to the one victim in order to relieve the sufferings of the others. Deontologists should think twice before embracing that course of action, even in a conditional way.

Of course, there are other cases. Two otherwise identical individuals A and B are struggling to obtain some scarce medicine, which would enable A to live to a ripe old age rather than die peacefully now, and B to live for another month rather than die in severe pain now. Maximin suggests that it would be better for B to get the medicine, while it may seem intuitively better for A to get it, since then it will do more overall good. There are various elements of this case that, in light of other elements of HMP, are misleading, and on which a reply might conceivably rest. Still, if we focus on a situation in which you, as a third party, would have transparently full responsibility for both these outcomes, in which you would have to torture B to death now so that the medicine would extend A's life for so long, we can see that there are some intuitions engaged even by this case that pull in accord with maximin.

I do not claim that maximin can make us happy in the face of all hard cases and tragic choices. No view can do that without illusion, at least if we are responsible for all the effects of our choices. And we have no consensus that we are not. I do not even claim that Ivan's case, or other similar cases, suffice to show that a maximin principle is to be intuitively favored over other relatively close and hence relatively unfamiliar competitors – say, a sufficientarian principle that requires the minimization of the number of individuals who fall below some critical threshold of well-being – though I also believe that we have uncovered a general pattern of analysis for cases that pushes towards maximin. Rather, my point is this. Maximin is at least in adequate accord with our intuition, if consequentialism is generally right about the nature of our moral responsibilities.

We have traversed our first step, and can turn now to the second. We have reduced the issue of whether maximin is suitably intuitive to the issue of whether or not there is a deep distinction between harming and failing to aid, at least according to properly reflective commonsense intuition. That is one central issue between deontology and consequentialism.

I have been largely pretending that we haven't already addressed this issue at some length, but we have. We saw in Chapter 3 that MAC delivers, in a manner appropriately consistent with commonsense intuition, a sufficient difference between harming and failing to aid. But it is not a *deep* difference of the sort relevant to the particular topic at hand. Still, MAC retains the characteristic consequentialist tenet that we are in the deepest moral sense responsible for the effects of our actions and our inaction, because it retains the familiar rationale of all direct forms of consequentialism. The moral propriety of actions rests directly on the value of their consequences. It is merely that the application of this claim to particular issues and cases is complicated in MAC by the fact that there are actions of groups as well as of individuals. MAC delivers the antecedent for our conditional.

Still, I have cheated just a little, because torture is worse, according to MAC, than letting someone be tortured, at least if we have cooperative practices that are group agents that are properly beneficent and support that distinction. Yet Ivan's case is properly revealing. Still, the proper perspective from which to assess our commonsense intuitions about the ranking of outcomes relevant to basic consequentialist assessment, which is after all our concern here, is a situation in which we feel full responsibility for the outcomes. That is the kind of responsibility an omnipotent

259

and omniscient god would have (without recourse to a robust theodicy and the free will defense), and which Ivan's case invokes. MAC does suggest that the violation of reciprocity that torturing involves may make it worse than full responsibility for such an outcome of the sort relevant to proper consequentialist assessment. But still, invoking torture remains an appropriate device to trick our recalcitrant intuition into accepting the responsibility for outcomes that we have in these cases and that we would at all costs deny. It is a kind of corrective rhetoric. It is not misleading. It just keeps one's nose to the relevant grindstone.

This extension of responsibility may seem terrifying. But of course we are not responsible for all the facts, as some omnipotent god would be. And we saw in Chapter 3 that our individual responsibility is defused and delimited in certain ways by the group agents in which we participate.

Temkin provides the most thorough and careful negative treatment of maximin we possess. And he speaks for many who believe that they know maximin is false. But they know no such thing, at least on the relatively abstract structural grounds that we are now considering.

V

HMP is quite risk-averse, at least in one sense of that ambiguous term. It evaluates lotteries by reference to their worst possible outcomes, even if such outcomes are very unlikely. This may seem quite counterintuitive, but in fact it is not.

That is largely because commonsense normative intuitions do not support any detailed, coherent treatment of normative risk. We don't have very determinate intuitions about how to handle risks in normative situations, and there are lots of unclarities and confusions in our intuitive thinking about them.

First point: On the one hand, we reward and blame people – with moral praise and opprobrium, among other things – at least largely on the basis of the particular outcomes of their actions that happen to turn up, rather than on the risks they were running. Even when we blame someone for running a huge risk with someone else, the judgment seems mitigated if they were lucky. Think, for instance, of the way we feel about people who pilot a boat drunk and manage to get home safely as opposed to those who in such a state actually kill someone. Or think of the different ways we feel about politicians who take dangerous risks in foreign policy, or doctors who take dangerous risks in treatment, when they are successful and when they are unsuccessful. And yet, on the other hand, we seem to have a strong intuition that normative evaluation should be at least largely independent of just that sort of luck, that agents should be morally evaluated on the basis of what is within their knowing control.

Second point: Worst possible outcomes, in particular, receive no very clear treatment by unreflective intuition. While we often ignore genuine but small risks of horrible outcomes in our commonsense normative evaluations of actions, that may well be because we don't think of them, or because we don't think that the worst risks really differ much between one relevant option and another. When there is an intuitively significant greater negative risk on one option rather than another, what we might call a salient risk, either a greater probability of a very bad outcome or a worse very bad outcome, that does seem intuitively to matter, though not to any clear or certain degree.

Of course, there are other grounds for worry about a highly risk-averse principle, even if common sense is not clear and decisive on these matters. If lots of agents act in individually risk-averse ways, then it is very likely, as the product of many individual likelihoods, that we will end up with an outcome that is normatively worse than if the agents hadn't so acted. Sometimes there are single and significant choices – say, social choices of institutional arrangements – where there are no iterated probabilities of many actions to worry about, or for that matter to save us if we have one very bad shake of the practical dice, and in that case worst possible outcomes seem more intuitively significant. But still it is likely that if we act in accord with a risk-averse principle in such a case we will end up with an outcome that is normatively worse than if we had not been so risk-averse. Whatever the confusions of common sense on the topic of normative risk, still HMP may seem to be intuitively unacceptable on these grounds.

Let me put the same objection in another way. Maximining over risks is generally rejected in favor of maximizing expected utility. That seems like paradigmatically rational behavior regarding risks, just as prudently maximizing one's total individual utility may seem like a paradigmatically rational response to the temporal distribution of goods within one's life. After sections I, II, and III, we should hesitate in the face of that parallel, and maximizing expected utility does require a valuation of outcomes that is not available in our ordinal construction. Still, Ramsey, von Neuman, Morgenstern, and Binmore have suggested a way to work backward, a way to construct quantitative individual utility that reflects what they take to be intuitively rational preferences over gambles.

But, I reply, this sort of allegedly "rational" expected utility maximizing is quite a dramatic idealization of real human behavior, just as individual utility maximizing within a life is an idealization. It is hence open to suitable normative question and manipulation. And it isn't in fact rational in the fully normative sense of that ambiguous word. It matches neither the way we in fact behave, nor the way we ought to behave. Risk-averse behavior is constituted as properly rational in the full normative sense by the argument of the previous chapter. Largely because the basic value that happens to be found in our world comes ordinally, we can only develop an ordinal valuation of outcomes, and hence an ordinal valuation of risks over those outcomes.

Still, it might be countered, agents who act in accord with risk-averse decision principles are irrational in the different sense that they will probably lose out according to their own valuation of outcomes, especially over the long run. But of course at issue here is what is the nature of the most important way of losing normatively, even in the long run.[41] The individual losers in any forced lottery that promises to max-imize expected utility overall, even if there is an overall lucky outcome for that lottery, do not intuitively lose their grounds for complaint just because expected utility was maximized. And of course the complaints of the losers if there is an unlucky outcome may intuitively be even stronger.

I have made two clusters of points. Common sense is vague on issues of normative risk, and the theoretical advantages of more traditional con-ceptions are not decisive, just because it is not obvious that they are the particular theoretical advantages that must intuitively count most. But there is also a third set of significant points.

The most practically relevant implications of HMP regarding norma-tive risk are mediated by the Proposed Code and hence by Multiple-Act Consequentialism. And the complexity of this mechanism of application serves to blunt some intuitive worries about the risk aversiveness of HMP. Remember that many of the most weighty acts according to MAC are very large one-off group acts, which are not relevantly iterated. And while the nature of the Proposed Code will turn on the nature of our options in various ways, still it will involve a generality that will engage salient general risks and features of outcomes at the expense of particular details. Salient and striking general risks do seem to matter to common sense,

---

41 Here one reason for distrusting self-defeat arguments against normative principles will be evident. For another, see Mendola (1986).

though not, as I've said, in any very precise way. And the salient worst possible outcomes of many of the relevant general risks properly in question in evaluation of the Proposed Code are effectively identically evil. Then what matters according to our principle is a greater probability of that worst outcome, which, when it rests on sufficiently general grounds, is likely to be intuitively salient to choice.

To summarize: It is impossible to develop any very determinate account of normative risk on the basis of unclear commonsense intuition. Standard theoretical advantages of standard theories are not decisive. And where commonsense morality has clear commitments on these issues, they interact with HMP only through the mechanism of Multiple-Act Consequentialism, which cushions remaining conflict.

VI

The three controversial structural elements of HMP – its focus on flecks, its maximin form, and its risk aversion – interact in intuitively relevant ways. They also interact with the hedonism of that principle. Some of the most obvious of these interactions may seem intuitively unfavorable. Let me put such an objection starkly and summarily.

HMP pays little heed to the way happiness is distributed among distinct lives, and to the degree that only a single life is at issue, it implies that no life at all is better in the most basic sense than one containing a moment of pain. It implies, for that matter, that no sentience at all is better than a situation in which one creature is momentarily in pain. Indeed, it is better that there be nothing at all than that there be the slightest chance that a creature will feel one fleck of pain. That there be nothing, and certainly none of us, would be better than any situation that we could plausibly achieve, let alone any risk we could plausibly run. What's more, there is another way, despite all this, in which HMP may seem to give pain too *little* heed. It suggests that it is better to have a situation in which everybody is always pretty miserable than a situation in which one moment, indeed one fleck, of one person's life is worse than that and everybody else is quite a bit better off.

Despite the fact that congruence with common sense is important, HMP is not so refuted. I will develop three replies to the contrary conclusion.

First of all, we have already considered some points that blunt elements of this objection, which we can see by focusing on one sort of pressing and troubling case. Recall our discussion of Temkin and Scanlon in section IV,

263

and consider in that light a particular case that may seem quite problematic for HMP.

Presume that we must rank two worlds. In the first, there are ten billion happy people. Not only are they happy on the whole, they are happy all the time – except that one of them has an accident, and crushes a finger, and feels an hour or two of physical pain. In the second world, there is no sentient being whatsoever. HMP says the second world is better, and that is not what we intuitively think.

However, remember that our intuition is misled by the lack of responsibility presumed in this case. The properly intuitive normative evaluation of outcomes is revealed only when we feel full responsibility for those outcomes. So instead assume that you must torture an innocent by breaking his finger against his will in order to bring the other beings into their happy existence. That is something many of us might do anyway, but it is not confidently commanded by commonsense moral intuition. Deontologists, in particular, may find it intuitively problematic. Of course, the innocent whom you torture may thank you next year, just as Ahab may thank you in the morning for excising his leg against his will. But in sections I and II we saw that commonsense intuition is also sometimes misled by a failure to notice the morally relevant difference between a person at one time and the same person at another time, even though on full reflection that difference is of real intuitive weight.

My second reply will focus in part on the kinds of details, presumed or stated, that make alleged counterexamples that involve the extinction of sentience, or pain of one for the sake of general pleasure, intuitively powerful. Hovering in the background of such cases are the possible conditions that would make such choices available to us – for instance, doomsday machines to certainly exterminate all life, or contraptions to increase someone's pain just a bit and certainly eliminate much other pain. And my point is that those details are not located at the level of abstraction that we currently engage. They cannot be properly discussed until we consider the interaction of HMP with the mechanism of Multiple-Act Consequentialism and understand details of the Proposed Code that it helps support. On these topics, I must now request your patience.

Still, there are some relevant considerations that we can properly see even now. The concrete conditions presumed in the background of such objections must be very unrealistic, and in a specially problematic way. No realistic situation gives us these options. For instance, none of us is ever going to be in a position to choose an outcome in which there is certainly no further sentience, as opposed to a wild thermonuclear option on which there are lots of risks of very painful future sentience. Even most science fiction extrapolations wouldn't give us that certainty. And it is also relevant that the certainty is a very precise detail of the cases, but one crucial to their intuitive force. Ivan's case is unrealistic, and so too are the spatial inversion cases we considered in section II. But their unreality doesn't infect very precise details of the cases that very significantly drive our intuition – for instance, a difference between certainty and near certainty. Our earlier cases were in that sense appropriately abstract, and our relatively abstract intuitions are all that we can now properly consider, without the full mechanism of Multiple-Act Consequentialism and the Proposed Code. Such abstract intuitions are also least subject to disruption by highly hypothetical cases. Detailed cases and very specific normative details, such as that on one option there will *certainly* be no sentience at all, can be properly engaged only through the mechanism of Multiple-Act Consequentialism and the Proposed Code.

Those are also the locations where the value of human life is most obviously and directly reflected in the overall account developed here. It is perhaps a little disconcerting to call murder or death a detail. But the general significance of murder and of death is underwritten at a different place in my overall account than we now engage, through the mechanism of Multiple-Act Consequentialism. Perhaps, to reinforce this point, it is worth remembering that there are literatures charging plausibly that average and total utilitarianism, not to mention negative utilitarianism, also have murderous or genocidal implications when deployed in conjunction with act consequentialism,[42] but that is not taken as conclusive refutation of utilitarianism. In light of MAC, it should not be.

The kinds of interaction of the structural elements of HMP that we can directly confront with commonsense intuitions at the level of generality and abstraction that is now appropriate point in fact to a confluence of HMP and those intuitions. This is partly because of the first aspect of HMP: its hedonism. As we have seen, HMP directs a maximin distribution not over lives but over flecks of lives. And it gives pain central importance. According to HMP, significant painful injury in an otherwise very successful life will be more morally significant than, for instance, a general deadening of pleasant possibilities in a relatively unsuccessful life. It is downside risks of that particular sort, risks of significant pains, that have special salience given the overall form of HMP. And note that we do

42 Henson (1971); Carson (1983).

265

intuitively cede to significant salient risks of such painful physical injuries and tortures a special normative weight. Torture and other great physical cruelties and dangers, physical disease and injury and other things closely related to physical pains, do engage intuitive moral concern in an immediately powerful way. And even salient risks of such things are taken very seriously in our commonsense evaluations. As we tend to the wounded, we forget about how rich or poor they are, and focus on their immediate suffering. And if someone is in immediate danger of being slashed or tortured, if that is a salient risk, then that is also of great intuitive concern, whatever their overall prospects in life. I have already argued that a focus on cases of torture is not intuitively misleading in our current argumentative context.

Of course, there are other sorts of goods, such as life and health and property, that have intuitive normative weight, and that engage different intuitions than those that best support my hedonist principle. And some of the goods I deployed in the last paragraph, like injury per se as opposed to the pain it causes, are only indirectly though still closely related to the basic value that HMP reflects. But we should expect intuitions about those other goods, given the structure of my proposal, to be fully engaged only at a different point, through the mechanism of Multiple-Act Consequentialism. We will look at some of the relevant details in the next chapter. And it is also relevant that we saw in the last part that the hedonic theory of basic value on which we rely here is itself in fact suitably intuitive.

Let me summarize the main elements of this second reply: The principal abstract structural interaction within HMP suggests a special normative salience for risks of certain urgent needs, because pain is closely associated with intuitively urgent needs. And that is an intuitive feature of my view. When there is sudden physical and painful danger to someone, it is intuitively absurd to pause and worry about how their lives are going as a whole. The intuitively pressing nature of pain, which we also considered in the last part, undergirds the most salient interaction of the three structural elements of HMP. While my attempt here to link the quality of flecks with the intuitive urgency of need must be qualified, since some cases of intuitively urgent need involve death or physical debilities that are not painful, still those other cases are appropriately and naturally reflected in this account by the extended conception of the good incorporated in the Proposed Code, supported partly by the mechanism of Multiple-Act Consequentialism. In my second reply, I also invoked the unreality of the details of some of the obvious intuitive cases that seem to tell most against HMP.

We are moving toward a consideration of interactions that also involve MAC and not merely the various aspects of HMP, and they are the proper business of the next chapter. But still, there may seem to be other telling cases of the general sort under consideration now that are not at all unreal and that cannot be evaded by the mechanism of MAC, and hence are untouched by my second reply. So let me develop a third reply, in which considerations deployed in my first two replies interact, and in which some new ones come into play.

Consider choices between long-term policies that affect population. We really have such choices, and they seem unregulated by common-sense morality and hence by the group agents on which MAC relies to block unintuitive suggestions of consequentialism. So they may seem to be plausibly relevant intuitive counterexamples to my proposal.

If applied directly to some population cases, HMP implies instances of what Parfit has called "The Repugnant Conclusion".[43] Say there is a choice between a population of ten billion people, each with a very happy life, and a larger population involving lives that are barely worth living in the sense suggested by HMP. HMP implies that the second situation is better. Indeed, if the choice is between situations without physical pain, in which there are no flecks of negative hedonic tone, then it will always be better according to HMP to have more individuals with longer lives and hence more flecks. That may seem quite unintuitive.

But, I reply, there are two mitigating factors.[44] First, remember that our commonsense intuition is misled when we consider a case for which we do not feel full responsibility. And if the choice were actually given us to eliminate someone in order to increase the quality of other lives, then we wouldn't have such a definitive contrary intuition. And the second mitigating factor is that this particular population case is also unreal in one crucial way, in fact in a way that suggests some intuitive problems for HMP from the opposite direction. That is because in reality any additional persons in the world will inevitably suffer some physical pain. So other things equal, it seems, any increase in the population would be bad according to HMP. Remember that it would be better that there be no one, according to HMP, than that there be anyone who feels or even risks a fleck of pain.

This in itself may seem quite intuitively problematic, of course. But remember that there are also no realistic cases in which we are faced

43   Parfit (1984: 388).
44   For a classical utilitarian reply to Parfit, see Tännsjö (1998).

with the certain extermination of all sentient life. And in any case, the extermination of the sentient invokes the mechanism of MAC and hence the details of the Proposed Code.

Still, if some population policy, or even indeed a group act that constitutes part of commonsense morality, enables the human population to be larger than it otherwise would be, then the population implications of HMP may suggest that such an intuitive policy or group act is morally problematic.

Because this particular worry applies not just to population policies but to the crucial group acts deployed by MAC, I will directly discuss it in the first section of the next chapter, where we trace the interaction of HMP, MAC, and commonsense morality. For now, let me simply discuss a key case that puts some of the apparent population implications of HMP in a proper and better light.

The real population-based worry about HMP is that it suggests that a population of zero would be better than any realistic larger population. But there are other things that many of us believe that suggest that also. Many of us believe that the world as it is includes sufficient evil to show that a beneficent, all-knowing, and all-powerful god does not exist. Indeed, whatever we moral agents do, our world will likely always be sufficient to reveal that, even if we ignore the ugly history of the world. It is clearly not the best world there might be, according to HMP or any plausible principle for ranking worlds. But the theist can plausibly remind us that there might not be a best possible world. It might always be possible to create another world that is better than any given world. And if we reply that a world created by a benevolent being would yet need to be better than this one, there is yet a reasonable question about how good a world would really have to be to reveal the beneficence of a creator, if there is no best of all possible worlds. So what, then, is our complaint? Surely we have one. The real problem of evil that many of us feel, it seems, is that the world in fact is worse than nothing. Remember that the true evaluation of outcomes is revealed in conditions of full responsibility for those outcomes, and it plausibly seems to Ivan Karamazov that any god who would erect a fabric of human happiness on the torture of one child would be morally problematic. And so the creation of our world, in which many children are tortured each day, would have been, many of us think, morally problematic. Remember also that traditional theological responses to the problem of evil often invoke an implausible afterlife that is supposed to make up for the earthly suffering of the innocent. And recall that in our discussion in the first part of this chapter we saw that suitably reflective intuition suggests that even a happy afterlife could not fully recompense the intense suffering of a child.

Our real world is in fact worse than nothing, even according to much less pessimistic principles than HMP. So our contrary intuitive reaction to the key population implication of MAC does not really undercut the pessimism of HMP. That intuition is distorted. It fails to acknowledge pretty obvious facts about the overall value of the world, facts that don't even drive deep enough to engage the particular pessimism of HMP. What may seem the central counterintuitive implication of HMP is in fact true, though it is hard not to avert our happy eyes from that unpleasant fact.[45]

Still, some may insist, while much of the world is dark, it is not immoral to have a child and hence to create another life, or to extend your own, even though the child's life and the extension of your own will surely involve some pain. But HMP does not imply that all realistic individual lives are on balance bad for the whole. Any life or segment of a life will be on balance a good thing if the most intense pain it involves is less than the most intense pain of others that it assuages. It is easy to have a worthwhile life, though that does require that you do something for suffering others.

We must consider yet the detailed interactions of HMP and MAC. But insofar as we can confront HMP and abstract and properly rectified commonsense intuition directly, we may conclude this chapter in this way: We have seen that a distributional focus on moments or flecks or something close is appropriately intuitive. We have seen that maximin is appropriately intuitive, since after Part One we can properly assume that there isn't a deep moral difference between harming and not aiding. We have seen that risk aversion is not intuitively inappropriate, at least if the Proposed Code is suitably intuitive in detail. And we have seen that the abstract structural interaction of these three elements is at least roughly intuitive in the further context set by what we already know to be the hedonism of our principle and the properly intuitive form of Multiple-Act Consequentialism, at least if the Proposed Code is properly intuitive, and if the one-off group agents that it deploys are in fact suitably beneficent according to HMP.

Still, we do face another abstract intuitive worry about the interactions of the various elements of my proposal. That involves a key interaction of MAC and HMP. In Part One, I defended the intuitive plausibility of

---

45   1 have company in these sorts of claims. See Fehige (1998: 521–523).

269

MAC by appeal to the plausibly beneficent consequences of various group acts. But I did that before I developed the somewhat unconventional value theory expressed by HMP. I have ordered the book in this way so that I move sequentially from the least to the most provocative elements of my proposal. But it is reasonable to worry that my earlier arguments in defense and support of MAC will look considerably more problematic in light of HMP. So we will need to reexamine those arguments in the next chapter. I have already promised to examine the population implications of the relevant group acts anyway.

Nevertheless, we can now conclude that we do not know on the basis of relatively abstract commonsense intuition that HMP alone is false in its structural features. And we can plausibly conclude that its three structural elements are indeed positively supported by properly reflective intuition, if the Proposed Code implied by a conjunction of HMP and Multiple-Act Consequentialism in our world has an intuitive detailed form. We are almost home.

Part Four

Advice for Atomic Agents

.

8

A Code

The conjunction of Multiple-Act Consequentialism and the Hedonic Maximin Principle modulates a traditional utilitarian concern about hedonic good through a focus on two sorts of justice: distributive justice and the avoidance of unjust means such as murder. I will refer to this marriage as the just good theory, or JGT.

JGT has been directly vindicated on the basis of ordinal hedonic value, and we have seen that each of its elements is intuitively appropriate at an abstract level, subject to some reservations about how the details work. We face one more argumentative burden. This chapter argues that, in the world we inhabit, the just good theory supports a moral code that I will call the Proposed Code, or PC for short, and that PC is a properly intuitive detailed morality.

PC is a relatively concrete set of normative directions. I will argue that it is within the range of contemporary reflective normative intuition of the same level of detail. You easily may have forgotten how JGT, which is a form of direct act-based consequentialism, can support a fixed moral code at all. The answer is that it supports such a code in the context of the actual group acts in which we participate. It is a code for us in those somewhat contingent circumstances.

PC has two major components, which reflect major components of the just good theory and also of contemporary reconstructions of commonsense morality. First, there is a conception of the good or well-being, the focus of section II. Second, there is a conception of duty and virtue, the focus of sections III and IV. Section I articulates various presumptions of our discussion, and section V considers the differences that total utilitarianism would introduce.

I

We must trace here the detailed confluence of commonsense morality and the just good theory. Commonsense morality makes a number of presumptions that can appropriately narrow our focus.

First, commonsense morality presumes that there is a single morality that is appropriate to the condition of at least the range of readers of a book like this. Application of MAC naturally takes the form of recommendations about reasons for atomic agents to accept. But our first commonsense presumption implies that this advice not only must be single and coherent for a particular atomic agent, regardless of the many overlapping agents in which it takes part at a moment, but also must be generally applicable across people in our roughly contemporary and local conditions. So we will seek a single and relatively general code of properly accepted reasons for atomic agents like us. That is the kind of code with which we can confront common sense.

Second, commonsense morality presumes that the background conditions of our lives – for instance, the existence of friendships, families, and property, and the relatively contingent features of our psychologies required if we are to accept reasons – are at least roughly appropriate. They might be appropriate if they are natural, inevitable, and unalterable, and hence not really optional. Or they might be appropriate if, though optional, they are legitimate in some adequate normative sense. I don't confidently believe either of those things. I have already registered worries about the particular case of the practices of risk sharing that underlie our intuitive reactions to the Trolley Problem. But any reasonably close confluence of any ethical theory and commonsense morality can plausibly be sought only within the bounds of this presumption. It may seem that such background conditions of our lives would be more problematic according to the highly risk-averse and distribution-sensitive HMP than according to more familiar normative principles for ranking outcomes. But while that issue is too complex to treat fully here, we will return in a moment to analogous and more pressing possible differences between HMP and familiar normative principles, during discussion of my eighth claim, and see that they are less dramatic than they might first appear.

Third, commonsense morality presumes that any moral code will have a certain abstract form. PC will be not only an articulation of appropriate reasons, but also an articulation that constitutes distinct conceptions of the good, of virtues, and of duties and obligations. Some aspects of that traditional organization are theoretically underwritten by JGT, but the necessity of the full traditional form is not obvious. Still, such a form seems largely a matter of emphasis and organization, and will aid in our attempt to gauge the confluence of the just good theory and commonsense morality. Otherwise, things are too complex to handle tractably.

Our fourth presumption is a commonsense conception of our options and alternatives and of the attendant salient risks. We can plausibly seek a confluence with commonsense morality only within this constraint. Perhaps by sufficient cleverness we could make the world an Eden for everyone, and in a way that would be very morally salient according to JGT. But I will put such radical possibilities aside here.

A fifth presumption is less within than about common sense. Our actual morality is quite complicated, and the various normative theories rooted in commonsense intuitions, and also various philosophers' attempted reconstructions of commonsense morality, are perhaps oversimplified. But I will presume that philosophical reconstructions and intuitionisms are at least roughly correct characterizations of commonsense morality. We will cleave close to the detailed range of intuition-based normative theories and attempts to sketch commonsense morality that have been developed by philosophers, as if they were each at least roughly adequate reconstructions of local commonsense morality. They are, I believe. This presumption implies, along with the variety of reconstructions and intuitionisms reflecting even contemporary common sense, something that might also be expected independently. Our commonsense morality, even if we focus relatively locally on our own morality now, is indeterminate, vague, and incoherent in various ways. That makes it easier for JGT, since it need underwrite only a specific coherent code somewhere within that range. But while some philosophers are confident that their own detailed and idiosyncratic normative intuitions capture common sense, while many of their close colleagues' do not, that is very unlikely. Still, I take the test of common intuition to be more restrictive than some do. I think that the just good theory is false if it has to bite too many bullets.

The sixth constraint on our project here, of course, is JGT. It is the conjunction of the Hedonic Maximin Principle and Multiple-Act Consequentialism. Let me recapitulate. The Hedonic Maximin Principle is this: First, of two lotteries over feasible worlds that consist of the same number of equally probable outcomes, the better lottery is the one that has the better worst-possible outcome. If they have equally bad worst-possible outcomes, then the better lottery is the one that has the better second-worst-possible outcome, and so on. Given the method developed in Chapter 6 for turning lotteries with different numbers of differently probable outcomes into equiprobable lotteries with the same numbers of possible outcomes, this yields a complete ordering of lotteries over worlds, which implies that of any two lotteries over worlds, the better lottery is the one that has the better worst-possible outcome. Second, of two feasible worlds that contain the same numbers of flecks of experience, the better world is the one that has the better worst fleck. If they have equally bad worst flecks, then the better world is the one that has the better second-worst fleck, and so on. And any world is equivalent in value to another that has the same number of flecks at each level of positive or negative ordinal value as the first plus any number of flecks of null value. So this provides a complete ordering of feasible worlds.

According to Multiple-Act Consequentialism, atomic agents accept reasons that constitute, govern, and balance an overlapping multiplicity of group agents. MAC applies a basic normative principle like HMP to rank available options. It holds that the most choiceworthy is the best. But this direct evaluation is performed all at once on the options of all the multiple agents that overlap in a given atomic agent. There will be practical conflicts among the various agents that overlap. In a case in which an atomic agent can defect from a group agent with a proper project, and hence achieve additional good consequences on the side while not undercutting the project of the group agent, we are to compare a first counterfactual situation in which the atomic agent achieves what it can by the defection but in which the various other atomic agents that constitute the group agent do not constitute such an agent, to a second counterfactual situation in which the group agent acts as it does and the atomic agent does not defect. If the first situation is better, then MAC says to defect. If the second situation is better, MAC says not to defect. That is the principle of Very Little Defection, or VLD. In a case in which we must assess the relative importance of two forms of overlapping but conflicting group agency for an atomic agent that is part of both, we also compare two counterfactual situations: In the first situation, the first group agent doesn't exist because the atomic agents in question fail to properly constitute such an agent, but the second group agent has its actual form. In the second situation, the second group agent doesn't exist, but the first has its actual form. If the first situation is better, then the second group agent is more normatively significant, and MAC says to defect from the first group agent in favor of the second. This is the principle of Defect to the Dominant, or DD.

Our seventh and crucial presumption is that there are in fact the group agents that I will deploy in my remaining remarks in this chapter. Remember my argument in Chapter 2 that our cooperative normative practices are characteristically one-off group agents, supported by entwined reciprocity and beneficence.

I will also repeatedly rely here on an eighth claim, that these cooperative normative practices are proper by the strictures of HMP. That may seem wrong, since HMP is unusually distribution-sensitive and risk-averse. And remember that I defended the intuitive cogency of MAC in Chapter 3 by appeal to the intuitively beneficent consequences of various group acts that constitute our deontic moral practices. So if HMP ranks these acts in a different way than more familiar normative principles, those arguments may need to be revisited. On this matter, I shouldn't rest on mere presumption. So let me make three replies to various aspects of this objection.

One part of the worry can be put this way: VLD, incorporated in MAC, implies that we shouldn't defect from a group act with good consequences unless by defecting we can achieve more good than the entire group act achieves. And I claim that many of our deontic practices are group acts with good consequences, from which we should rarely defect. But while this may seem suitably plausible if we presume a familiar utilitarian basic normative principle, HMP seems quite different. It suggests that we focus on the worst risks of intense pains that attend the group act and the individual act of defection. And since group acts have a considerably greater impact on the world than individual acts, they may hence seem to carry a much greater risk of harm. MAC may seem always to counsel defection from group acts when conjoined with HMP.

But, I reply, in a situation where defection is at issue, according to MAC we need to consider not merely the risk attendant on the group act in question, but the risk attendant on its absence. And because it is a group act, both risks are correspondingly large. According to VLD, we compare, on one hand, the world with the defecting act and without the group act, and, on the other, the world without the defecting act but with the group act. Even if the positive act of defection in itself risks little, the absence of the group act might risk a lot.

Still, it may seem that our moral practices generally, and hence the group acts on which I rely here, may be problematic according to HMP. They may increase some risks of great local evils. And recall our truncated discussion of population issues in the last chapter. If our common moral practices aid the stable survival of very large societies, if they allow the

277

human population to be much larger than it would be in some alternative state of nature, then the pessimism of HMP may suggest that they are inappropriate group acts.

But, I reply, in the cases under consideration the pessimism of HMP is focused through the mechanism of MAC on the worst risks for intense pain presuming, on one hand, individual defection from a group act and the absence of the group act versus, on the other hand, the worst risks for intense pain of the group act itself. And that helps with part of this worry. It is undeniable that some very large cooperative group acts – for instance, robust mass movements – may be quite relevantly dangerous according to JGT. They may increase the risk of organized and effective torture, for instance. It might risk less intense pain if they did not exist. But the deontic moral practices on which I rely here are one-off group acts that characteristically alleviate individual suffering. The risk of their misuse is not that of some massive and generally capable group agent that can be deflected toward evil ends.

There are possible worries about this reply. Apparently Goebbels complained that the Italians lacked sufficient honesty to effectively administer the Final Solution. Perhaps our one-off practice of not lying is a mechanism that can be put to a variety of evil uses. But, I reply, the common moral practice of refraining from lies involves plausible exceptions for disasters. A more general worry is that if there are unforeseen interactions between even a group act that is inherently beneficent and various contingencies, the group act can end up not only risking but also achieving an unforeseen bad end. But the group acts constituting our standing moral practices are so vast that almost all relevant eventualities and remote likelihoods will in fact show up across their range, and would show up across the vast range of their absence. There are no relevant unforeseeable contingencies.

To summarize the first two parts of my reply: There are great risks that attend any group act, but so too its absence. And the general and inherent nature of the very large one-off group acts which constitute our common moral practices is to weaken risks of intense pain. If life threatens to be nasty, brutish, and short without commonsense morality, then HMP would be very responsive to that increased nastiness.

There remains the worry about populations, the worry that because the group acts that constitute commonsense morality support larger human populations, they are contrary to HMP. But the sensitivity of HMP to locally intense nastiness would trump its limited pessimism about larger populations. One torture is more significant than lots of mild pain. And in any case there is the next point, my third reply. Recall that the group acts relevant to MAC are timeless. They include actual future cooperators. So to a large degree relevant populations are presumed fixed in the evaluations relevant to MAC. All of the population inside a group agent constituting a moral practice will be held fixed in the key evaluations by MAC of defection from that agent.

We face worries not only about the beneficence of the group acts that constitute commonsense morality, but also about the population polices that HMP suggests. At the end of the last chapter, we noted some factors that mitigate these worries. But the three replies we have just discussed also suggest that when population policies constitute widespread one-off group acts, they should be more optimistic than HMP alone may suggest.

With all presumptions and clarifications now in place, we face two questions: Given a commonsense view of our salient alternatives and risks, assuming the legitimacy of the background institutions in which our lives take place and that help to form our psychologies, specifically including the beneficence of the group acts that constitute many of our moral practices, and presuming a familiar code form that involves a conception of the good, of virtues, and of duties and obligations, what reasons should be accepted by all atomic agents in our more or less contemporary circumstances according to the just good theory? PC is the answer to this question. Our second question is whether PC is within the range of contemporary reflective commonsense morality that is revealed by the range of plausible intuitionisms and other philosophical renditions of that commonsense morality. To prefigure, it is.

II

The first element of PC is a specification of the good or well-being. One conception of the good natural to PC is of course the conception of fundamental good sketched in section I of Chapter 3. First, there is basic hedonic good, enshrined in HMP. Second, Multiple-Act Consequentialism implies that other sorts of good are also fundamental. In the first place, there are agency goods, conditions necessary to the existence of effective agency, which when in the service of proper projects become genuine agency goods, and hence one sort of fundamental, though not basic, good. These include true belief, life and health, physical and mental abilities, freedom from injury, and freedom from imprisonment and manipulation, when those things are in the service of proper projects. And there are also other ways in which agency goods can become fundamental goods that are neither "basic" nor "genuine", when they are protected by one-off group agents that are properly beneficent and yet that extend respect to agency goods that are not in the service of proper projects.

There are other sorts of goods that, while not quite fundamental, yet are entwined in characteristic close ways with fundamental agency goods or basic goods. This suggests a relatively central role even for these goods within PC. They have stable but contingent instrumental relationships with fundamental goods. I will call these tertiary goods.

There are tertiary goods closely related to agency goods. Social and economic power and position are goods that extend intuitive capacities for agency, and as a matter of general but contingent fact are relevant to our relatively general code. These are what I will call *genuine* tertiary goods only when they support fundamental agency goods. In other words, two tests must be met by genuine tertiary goods. They must have stable instrumental relationships of the right sort, as a matter of general fact. But they also must have in their particular case a proper relationship to the right sort of project in fact.

There are also tertiary goods that are closely related to basic good. Frustration of desire is sometimes painful even in the very concrete sense invoked by HMP. Remember our quasi-experience of physical pain. Certain general forms of desire frustration probably have enough of even a stable relationship to pain to count in some instances as genuine tertiary goods, to meet our twinned tests for such goods.

There are plausibly also cases in which tertiary goods – for instance, the absence of frustration or having wealth – are important but not genuine. This status can be delivered by the same indirect mechanism that generates analogous fundamental agency goods.

There are also more complex entwinings due to instrumental relationships that may be relevant. For instance, agency goods are general means to the satisfaction of the agent's desires. And sometimes stable instrumental relationships reinforce other sorts of status as a good. For instance, many forms of death or illness are also painful for the victim in a suitably general way.

In summary, PC includes a three-level conception of good or wellbeing, which I will hereafter call TLC (for three-level conception), and which incorporates (i) basic good – positive hedonic value and the absence of negative hedonic value; (ii) fundamental goods, including both genuine agency goods – true practical belief, life and health, physical and mental abilities, freedom from injury, and freedom from imprisonment and manipulation – when these things support proper projects, and also those agency goods not in service of proper projects that are yet protected by beneficent one-off group acts; and (iii) important tertiary goods – which include genuine tertiary goods like wealth and position that support proper projects and desire satisfaction linked with hedonic value, and other such goods that are yet protected by proper projects. Agency goods that are not fundamental and tertiary goods that are not important might be said to be goods in an extended though not normatively relevant sense. Within even this three-level conception, the class of basic goods is primary in an important sense, and tertiary goods in third place, because of the structure of JGT.

That is a sketch of the conception of the good to be included in PC. Of course, there are complications. I've already said that agency goods are genuine only when in service of proper projects; likewise for tertiary goods. But notice that this implies that the conception of the good rests on a conception of proper projects. As noted in Chapter 2, there are complexities regarding the general nature of proper projects beyond the obvious fact that they are at least roughly in accord with HMP. And TLC suggests an obvious extension of our initial notion, so that proper projects in a secondary but real sense also include those increasing fundamental agency goods and important tertiary goods.

TLC would seem to require some way to balance off various possible increases and decreases in agency goods or tertiary goods. But notice that even the primary normative balancing delivered by HMP has not yet been incorporated into the conception of the good I have sketched here, at least in any direct way. We have not yet developed a specific conception of when one thing of one type is better than another of another type; we have only a vague conception of the elements of the good in a rough normative priority suggested by JGT.

There is another large and related complexity. Basic hedonic value is the primary good of the primary moral patients, the primary objects of moral concern, which includes all the suitably sentient. But we saw in Part One that MAC suggests that some humans, those with whom we cooperate in beneficent projects or who engage in beneficent projects on their own, have a second status as another sort of moral patient. They are owed different types of respect. What's more, other forms of respect for agents beyond the group may be mandated by beneficent group acts. And notice that the existence of group agents suggests that some agency goods accede to groups themselves. Some organizations are richer or more powerful than others. When pursuing proper projects, even group agents become moral patients in a secondary sense. This status, as a matter of contingent but relatively stable fact, accrues only to things composed of atomic agents that are moral patients in the primary sense. But obviously, distributions of goods to one sort of moral patient can conflict with those to another.

So there are various complications that involve trade-offs and balances among goods that PC has not yet addressed. The structure of JGT naturally suggests that such conflicts and balances should ultimately be assessed by HMP, and our discussions of MAC have given us some additional mechanism to that end. But for the moment I will ignore these complexities, and leave TLC vague. That is for two reasons. First, it is largely through its deployment mediated by conceptions of duty and virtue, to which we will shortly turn, that this conception of the good is practically significant. In other words, proper consideration of balances and trade-offs will be our concern in sections III and IV. Second, the commonsense conception of the good is hardly more determinate than my vague conception in these ways. We can see this if we turn to a confrontation of TLC with common sense.

My first argument that this first element of PC is suitably intuitive is simply that it closely tracks the range of reasonably intuitive views of the good that have been developed by and are still discussed by philosophers, and that we considered in Chapter 4. Hedonism is one classical view, but so are desire-satisfaction views, and also objectivist views that make much of what we know now to be agency goods. And that suggests the very range of goods recognized by PC.

There are complexities. First, wealth and power are not parts of most philosophers' conceptions of the good. But they are, on the other hand, very intuitive goods. Second, only agency goods entwined with proper projects are genuine goods according to PC, and this may seem at least somewhat unexpected. But it does not violate any clear and certain commonsense intuition. For instance, TLC is more moderate in this respect than Kantian accounts that would grant the happiness of the vicious no basic value at all. And of course, some agency goods are fundamental but neither basic nor genuine.

It is also relevant, as we saw in Chapter 4, that the various conflicts among the differing philosophical accounts of the good are best resolved, and on intuitive grounds, in the direction of hedonism, a fact that is reflected in the basic status of hedonic value even in PC. We saw in Chapter 4 that hedonism alone is adequately intuitive, adequately within the range of rectified commonsense intuition. But the conception of good in PC merely organizes in a certain manner the basic elements recognized by all traditional competitors to hedonism and also by common sense, a manner that reflects the properly dominant role of hedonic value. It captures more of the subtleties and conflicting tendencies of our commonsense conception than hedonism alone, though we saw earlier that hedonism is, even on its own, at least adequately intuitive.

My second argument that TLC is properly intuitive is its close confluence with Scanlon's recent sensitive and intuition-based account. He notes that any plausible theory of well-being would have to recognize at least the following fixed points:

First, certain experiential states (such as various forms of satisfaction and enjoyment) contribute to well-being, but well-being is not determined solely by the quality of experience. Second, well-being depends to a large extent on a person's degree of success in achieving his or her main ends in life, provided these are worth pursuing. This component of well-being reflects the fact that the life of a rational creature is something that is to be *lived* in an active sense – that is to say, shaped by his or her choices and reactions – and that well-being is therefore in large part a matter of how well this is done – of how well the ends are selected and how successfully they are pursued. Third, many goods that contribute to a person's well-being depend on the person's aims but go beyond the success of achieving those aims. These include such things as friendship, other valuable personal relations, and the achievement of various forms of excellence, such as in art or science.[1]

TLC recognizes all these elements, with a certain characteristic spin. Corresponding to Scanlon's first fixed point, we have basic hedonic value. The spin is that hedonic value is what is involved in the relevant experiential states. Corresponding to Scanlon's second fixed point, we have proper projects helping to constitute genuine tertiary and agency goods. The spin is that what is worth pursuing is proper projects. Corresponding to Scanlon's third fixed point, we have agency goods, and proper projects relevant to certain forms of group agent. The spin is that friendships and personal relations aiming at evil are not genuine goods, though they may be fundamental. Certainly this spin on Scanlon's intuitive fixed points is well within the range of determinacy of our reflective common sense.

Scanlon is an important recent non-consequentialist foil to whom we will return in our discussion of duties and virtues. But he is also an immediately useful foil in two other ways. First, it may help to soften

---

1 Scanlon (1998: 124–125).

some resistance to the first element of PC to note that, despite my consequentialism, I agree with Scanlon's theoretical contention that well-being and the good are not "master values". I agree that the conception of one's good or well-being doesn't play much role in one's individual practical reasoning, though its components often do, so that it can be a kind of translucent Trojan horse: While it doesn't do much work beyond that which its obvious contents do on their own, yet it can introduce a certain element of distortion. And I also agree that for different third-person distributional judgments in various contexts, different detailed forms of well-being are normatively salient.[2] I don't suggest that the post office consult TLC to determine where to deliver a piece of mail. Still, despite the fact that the good and well-being are not "master values", a rough conception of individual well-being or good like TLC, or indeed Scanlon's relatively similar alternative, does play a general and necessary role in underwriting and specifying the duties and virtues that we will shortly trace.

Scanlon is also an immediately useful foil in another way. PC specifies a set of accepted reasons. So we face the question of how proper reasons as specified by PC can encompass a conception of the good such as the one we have just traced. Part of the answer is that it is refracted through the duties and virtues we will soon discuss. But there is another part of the answer, which we can take from Scanlon.[3]

Scanlon contrasts his view on this matter with what he calls the teleological view of value, the view that what "we have reason to do ... (at least as far as questions of value are concerned) ... is to act so as to realize those states of affairs that are best – that is, have the greatest value."[4] He complains, against the teleological view, that we value friendships and worthwhile activities from the inside in a different way, as things to be respected. This suggests a broader account of value.

To value something is to take oneself to have reasons for holding certain positive attitudes towards it and for acting in certain ways in regard to it. ... They generally include, as a common core, reasons for admiring and respecting it, although 'respecting' can involve quite different things in different cases. Often, valuing something involves seeing reasons to preserve and protect it (as, for example, when I value a historic building); in other cases it involves reasons to be guided by the goals and standards that the value involves (as when I value loyalty); in

---

2   Ibid., 108–143.
3   Ibid., 78–107.
4   Ibid., 80.

some cases both may be involved (as when I value the U.S. Constitution). To claim that something is valuable (or that it is "of value") is to claim that others also have reason to value it, as you do.[5]

This seems at least roughly correct. To have a conception of the good such as we have sketched here is at least in part to accept reasons to admire and respect basic goods, fundamental agency goods, and important tertiary goods, in the relevant ways that Scanlon notes. As Scanlon would not deny, this includes in some cases familiar teleological respect. As he probably would deny, this teleological respect has the kind of organizing role suggested by the primary status of hedonic value in PC. But, as I said, we will return to these issues of trade-offs and balances of goods shortly.

There is also a second layer in this translation between conceptions of the good and accepted reasons. To have such a conception of the good is also to accept higher-order reasons that specify that one should accept the first-order reasons, whoever one is. This way to treat claims to universality, such as that made in the last sentence of the quotation from Scanlon, is familiar from Allan Gibbard's work on the acceptance of norms.[6] One final complexity: PC must recommend acceptance of these reasons as agent-governing reasons, which govern the kinds of projects agents are to adopt. But it also must recommend acceptance of these reasons at a lower order, as the kind of agent-constituting reasons that constitute individuals and groups to have in fact certain sorts of projects rather than others.

III

The second component of PC is a specification of virtues and duties. It will be tailored for comparison to commonsense morality.

There are a number of axes on which plausible coherent reconstructions of our diverse and marginally coherent commonsense morality may reasonably differ. We can develop at least a rough sense of plausible positions on these axes by an historical survey of detailed formulations, reconstructions, or reformulations of commonsense morality by philosophers and religious figures, beginning with views that helped to form our normative tradition, and then moving on to more recent views that reflect it. My discussion reflects three historical waves of such reconstructions.

5   Ibid., 95.
6   Gibbard (1990b: 153–170).

I will not here attempt a general summary of these accounts, but they will inform the axes of difference that we will later consider. While my dominant concern is the contemporary commonsense intuition of Western ethicists, the historical elements of this survey will allow us to consider some of the various tendencies our common sense inherits, and will also serve to suggest a broader possible consensus.

The first historical wave consists of four religious documents. First, there are the nonreligious commandments of the Decalogue.[7] Second, Buddha's famous sermon in the Deer Park at Benares includes a crucial statement of his Middle Path, rooted in the Four Noble Truths that include a specification of the Eightfold Way to the cessation of craving.[8] In China, there is an important Buddhist tradition, and the Taoist tradition also incorporated a revisionary normative element allied with the Buddhist extinction of craving.[9] But Confucian doctrine developed a third tradition of moral theory, which is easier than Taoism to bring into contact with our main concerns. Whereas the Decalogue is deontological, and Buddhist ethics perhaps largely deontological though with some virtue-like elements, the *Analects* of Confucius suggest a largely virtue-based account, leavened with some deontological elements.[10] Our fourth religious document, the *Qur'an*, includes nonreligious ethical formulations that seem evenly deontological and virtue-based.[11]

The classical tradition represents a fifth alternative to the four religious accounts. But it is best represented by philosophers. Our second historical wave encompasses the three detailed reconstructions of commonsense morality by world-famous Western philosophers, by world-historical philosophers of great influence whose works are taught in standard normative theory courses. These are Aristotle's account in the

---

7 Exodus 20: 12–17, King James Version. These were traditionally thought – for instance, by Maimonides and Aquinas – to be subsumed under a single general principle, though there are some differences about which general principle. See, for instance, Donagan (1977: 57) and Luke 10: 25–37. It is interesting that Matthew 5: 21–22 suggests apparent extensions that seem quite revisionary. But even the tenth commandment seems to be a revisionary directive.

8 Buddha (1955). See also Pratt (1928: 59–64). The fourth step of the Eightfold Way is right action. This is generally selfless and charitable, but more specifically circumscribed by the Five Precepts, which bind lay people as well as monks. See Smith (1958: 119).

9 Lao-Tzu (1993).

10 Confucius (1979). Particulary relevant are *Analects* IV, 14; VI, 30; XII, 1; XII, 22; XIV, 4; and XV, 24. For background, see the introduction by Lau in Confucius (1979) or Smith (1958: 179–191).

11 Arberry (1955) or Dawood (1974). Particularly relevant are Surāh 70 (The Ladders), 22–35; and Surāh 13 (Thunder), 20–23.

Nicomachean Ethics,[12] Aquinas's in *Summa Theologica*,[13] and Kant's in the relatively neglected but also relatively detailed *The Metaphysics of Morals*.[14] This second wave to a degree reflects its contemporary common sense, but also helped to form ours.

The third historical wave consists of the detailed reconstructions of commonsense morality that have been proposed by more or less contemporary philosophers, which is to say, by philosophers who may reflect our roughly contemporary common sense, but who haven't formed it. It encompasses the reconstructions of Bernard Gert,[15] Alan Donagan,[16] W. D. Ross,[17] and Henry Sidgwick,[18] and the suggestive partial reconstructions by Charles Fried[19] and Thomas Scanlon.[20]

Each of the third-wave reconstructions, and to a large degree each of the second-wave reconstructions, captures in one coherent way various normative tendencies in our complex contemporary common sense, a common sense that is the complex heir to the tradition of the Decalogue and each of the second wave reconstructions, and to much more besides. None is obviously false to common sense. It is somewhat fashionable to deploy piecemeal deontological intuitions as decisive negative tests against moral theories, and they may be deployed against all of these reconstructions. But that would be inappropriate. That is in part because our commonsense intuitions are in obvious tension in various ways, between individuals and within individuals. And that in turn is in part because there are conflicting normative traditions that our common sense inherits, and also real normative tensions between intuitive duties and virtues and between goods achieved by individual and group action. These tensions must be resolved in some coherent way by a coherent ethical theory. There is no assurance that individual intuitions deployed piecemeal against a particular theory will not of necessity be abandoned when forced into a coherent and reflective system with other intuitions. So the only test that even our reflective normative intuition can provide spans the range of the third-wave coherent reconstructions, and probably also the second-wave

---

12 Aristotle (1980).
13 Aquinas (1915–38).
14 Kant (1996b).
15 Gert (1998).
16 Donagan (1977).
17 Ross (1930: Chapter II, 16–47).
18 Sidgwick (1907: Book III, 199–361; and Book IV, Chapter III, 423–459).
19 Fried (1978).
20 Scanlon (1998).

reconstructions. I will argue that PC is in the rough middle of the space encompassed by the third-wave and second-wave reconstructions.

We will now survey various axes of difference among the plausible reconstructions of commonsense morality, and locate PC along each axis, concentrating first on matters of general structure, and then on matters of specific content. We will take all the threads that comprise JGT, and run them together through various axes on which the various reconstructions differ. Or, to put it the other way around, we will develop a new reconstruction of commonsense morality recognizably related to the others, but with an eye to the theoretical framework of JGT. We will hence end up with a detailed code that is well within the range of our contemporary reflective common sense. That is the Proposed Code, or PC.

The first set of axes trace differences among the ways in which the reconstructions deploy very broad normative categories. Some reconstructions are primarily duty-based, some primarily virtue-based, and some mix those resources. Some recognize duties to oneself, and others do not. Some recognize special as well as general obligations; others do not.

On these matters, the general framework of MAC developed in Part One, at least in the context of our commonsense presumption about the proper general form of any moral code, implies that PC will occupy a middle-ground position. It will recognize all of these things – virtues and duties, duties to self, and special and general obligations. First, at least some intuitive virtues and duties to self support one's own proper agency over time, because continuing action in pursuit of proper projects is a kind of group activity in which various temporal segments of one's life cooperate. Some agent-constituting, agent-governing, and indeed agent-balancing reasons enjoin respect for such virtues, in the sense of "respect" we adopted from Scanlon in section II, and such self-regarding duties are themselves agent-constituting reasons. Second, special and general obligations are also intuitively captured, at least in general form, by MAC. Group agents with proper projects normatively constrain the atomic agents that make them up. Proper agent-constituting reasons help to create one-off group acts that are forms of normative cooperation supporting some general duties. Such reasons also help to create group agents with other proper projects that engage or support special obligations. And proper agent-governing reasons also support those types of special and general obligations. All this is familiar from Part One. In addition, proper respect for genuine agency goods and tertiary goods already incorporated in PC requires that there are agent-governing reasons that support some general constraints on behavior toward others with proper projects.

A second cluster of structural axes reflects the various mechanisms that reconstructions deploy to treat conflicts among duties or virtues. There are commonsense tensions between commonsense duties. Coherent accounts must resolve these in coherent ways, and different reconstructions use different mechanisms to do this. Kant distinguishes perfect and imperfect duties, where perfect duties can never be violated but imperfect duties prescribe goals too broad and imperfectly attainable for their full achievement to be absolutely required, and where negative duties, duties to refrain, are characteristically more perfect. Gert stresses negative duties, with even positive duties to act being duties to prevent harms, and also allows for exceptions. Fried suggests that there are absolute or categorical prohibitions against lying and doing physical harm to an innocent person, which reflect more general individual negative rights to life, liberty, and property. He thinks there is also a limited positive duty for concern and beneficence. This is made consistent by his adoption of a very stringent Doctrine of Double Effect. The DDE suggests that we are specially responsible for the intended consequences, but not for the foreseen but unintended consequences, of our actions. Another analogous intuitionist mechanism is Kamm's Principle of Permissible Harm, that it is permissible for greater good to produce lesser evil.[21] Donagan's reconstruction rests on the Pauline Principle, Paul's suggestion that evil should not be done that good may come of it.[22] He also deploys tacit exceptions, a limitation of positive duties to otherwise permissible acts, and a complex mixture of negative and positive duties. Ross grants all duties, negative and positive, mere prima facie status, but with the prima facie dominance of non-maleficence over beneficence. Sidgwick claims that ordinary duties are vague and conflicting, and that the vagueness and conflict are properly resolved by appeal to a higher-order principle, indeed a utilitarian principle.

The basic mechanism by which JGT resolves normative conflicts is its mechanism for balancing the demands of overlapping forms of group agency, especially DD and VLD. This mechanism must hence be reflected in the proper agent-balancing reasons, which in turn should be governed by analogous but higher-order agent-governing reasons. And the effect of this is rather ecumenical along the axes now in question. The important normative status of HMP in JGT provides an analogue to the methods

21   Kamm (1996: 172).
22   Romans 3: 8.

suggested by their partisans for resolution of Ross-style prima facie status and Sidgwickian vagueness and conflict. And while the direct consequentialist form of our account to a degree undercuts the intuitive depth of the difference between positive and negative duties, still we saw in Part One that MAC in fact undergirds and explains the normative relevance in certain situations of the difference between omission and commission, the difference between negative and positive duties, the Pauline Principle, and the Principle of Permissible Harm. Even the DDE can be given a similar treatment if our commonsense practice really takes that form. Actual and normatively weighty forms of group agency have a significant normative status according to JGT, and this includes group practices of distributing risk and harm.

A third sort of structural axis reflects the degree to which a reconstruction of commonsense morality includes an account of appropriate punishment, sanction, or blame. Though there are obvious restrictions on proper forms of punishment or blame that flow from general moral duties and virtues, some reconstructions give certain forms of blame or punishment special status, while others do not. Gert, for instance, builds a concern with punishment into the basic moral attitude toward his moral rules. Donagan's reconstruction instead deploys second-order precepts governing blame. Our concern here is above all with what we should objectively do and be, not with what people can properly do to us if we fall short. But still, the mechanism of JGT suggests an intuitive treatment of punishment, noted in Chapter 3. We are enjoined to cooperate in normatively weighty one-off group acts like that of not murdering other humans. But if someone violates such a cooperative practice, JGT implies a change in their normative status. Depending on the existence of other weighty group actions in which the perpetrator continues to engage, and the details of our group acts, the propriety of their individual punishment may then even turn directly on the consequences of such punishment as evaluated by HMP. In effect, MAC implies a kind of normative punishment for those who violate certain forms of normatively weighty cooperation, which is a change in normative status. This may in turn defeat a normative presumption against a more concrete form of punishment. This conception of punishment is an intuitive advantage of the just good theory.

The fourth cluster of structural axes reflects the fact that reconstructions differ in the kinds of higher-order principles or other forms of higher-order structure that they deploy. Still, these various forms of higher-order structure seem related, so that differences along the fourth set of axes are

mostly more apparent than real. Confucius, the tradition of the Decalogue, Buddhism, the *Qur'an*, Aquinas, Kant, Donagan, and Sidgwick all
recognize a basic role for either a negative or a positive Golden Rule,
an injunction to love others as ourselves, or benevolence. All in this way
suggest a basic normative role for harms and benefits to individuals. And
there are, at least arguably, three general sorts of harms and benefits that
are intuitively relevant to such basic precepts. They are (i) direct harm
or benefit to someone, as in giving them goods or taking them away;
(ii) just or unjust relative harm or benefit to someone, as in giving them
their just share of goods or less than that; and (iii) respecting or violating cooperative practices with those individuals. Various forms of more
detailed or even apparently cross-cutting higher-order structure suggested
by some reconstructions in fact track this three-part development of the
traditional general precepts. They provide relevant interpretations of these
three factors. Gert's reconstruction naturally suggests a division of his ten
moral rules in which the first five correspond to a certain interpretation
of (i) and (ii), while the second five correspond to (iii). The interpretative
element is that all of Gert's rules grant special salience to harm. Ross's
reconstruction seems to elaborate each of the three categories in other
ways. The first category becomes the prima facie duties of benevolence
and malevolence and self-improvement. The second becomes the prima
facie duty of justice. And category three becomes what Ross, somewhat
unusually, calls the category of special obligations, which encompasses the
remaining prima facie duties, which include not only duties of gratitude
and reparation but also the very general duty of promise keeping, incorporating the duty not to lie. Sidgwick also recognizes the existence of an
analogous structure within his general virtues of Benevolence and Justice.
Scanlon's analysis deploys an implicit structure with analogues of (i) and
(ii) in his Chapter 5 and of (iii) in Chapter 7.

JGT suggests a somewhat similar and hence appropriately intuitive
general higher-order structure. Categories (i), (ii), and (iii) correspond
roughly and respectively to Parts Two, Three, and One of this book.
HMP incorporates a conception not merely of the good but of a properly
moralized just good, reflecting a conception of justice as equality. And
we have MAC with its emphasis on a certain sort of cooperative activity,
and hence another sort of justice. There is spin in this interpretation of
(i) through (iii). But in earlier parts, we saw these various sorts of spin to
be intuitively correct in a general way.

There are other sorts of general structure present in some reconstructions. We have already discussed the division of duties into duties to self

and others, and into special and general obligations. And of course we have talked about virtues and duties. But some accounts recognize various intellectual and practical virtues and duties. These virtues and duties help to support effective action in accord with the basic moral duties and basic moral virtues whose organization we discussed in the preceding paragraphs, or even, in the case of some conceptions of wisdom, incorporate such moral duties and virtues. MAC naturally implies such supporting and encompassing virtues and duties, which are at least not determinately unintuitive, and indeed seem to have been neglected by some reconstructions simply as a matter of oversight or difference in focus.

We must translate the positions of JGT along our fourth cluster of axes into the language of accepted reasons. What of the element of higher-order structure represented by that theory? How can that be incorporated into PC? The answer is, very simply, as agent-governing reasons (presuming that class to include general rules about the proper balancing of forms of agency), which govern the proper acceptance of particular agent-balancing reasons as well as particular agent-constituting reasons. This constitutes a set of higher-order principles in PC to which particular decisions can be referred. We will get to its lower-order echo in agent-constituting reasons quite shortly.

But let me sketch this higher-order component of the translation in a little more detail. First, there are three principles that constitute the normative core of JGT. They are HMP, VLD, and DD. They direct us to weight options for choice in accord with HMP and to act in accord with that weighting, and yet first and foremost to act in accord with cooperative forms of group activity as directed by VLD and DD, though of course the implications of these tenets rest in turn on HMP. HMP may not tell us which is the suitably right option if that is less than the best option from some set of alternatives, but it will tell us which options are better than others, and that is what is most practically salient in the application of MAC to moral questions.

Second, there is a little more higher-order structure that we have already squeezed out of JGT. For one thing, an atomic agent is instructed to join beneficent group acts of which it is not already part on direct consequentialist grounds, as assessed by appeal to HMP, as long as that is not otherwise forbidden by the constraints of MAC. For another, TLC, the three-level conception of the good, extends our sense of when, if other things are equal according to HMP, one option may be better than another. It hence extends our weighting of options and also the conditions relevant to the application of VLD and DD. The respect for these goods already incorporated in PC involves the acceptance of agent-constituting reasons of various sorts, at a lower level than is now our concern, but also of higher-order agent-governing reasons that support this lower-order content. TLC is incorporated into PC as agent-constituting reasons of some weight, supported by higher-order agent-governing reasons. These constitute respect for fundamental agency goods and important tertiary goods.

But the general and for-the-most-part instrumental relationships that help to constitute genuine tertiary goods and agency goods also provide a second set of for-the-most-part agent-constituting principles that should have some weight, though not an indefeasible weight, in PC, and which in turn seem properly supported by relatively concrete agent-governing reasons of similar weight. These make PC yet more intuitive. Let me explain. HMP implies in practice that greater risks of greater pains are most normatively weighty. As a matter of general fact, these are caused by acute physical injuries and constraints, starvation, disease, and death above all, of animals as well as of humans. So PC should incorporate fairly weighty agent-constituting reasons that enjoin us to relieve or prevent those things, as long as that positive action doesn't involve a worse downside risk. And PC should reflexively support that with higher-order agent-governing reasons. But to pursue positive projects of this sort by means that involve or threaten serious physical injuries or constraints, starvation, disease, or death almost always involves downside risks that are unlikely to be countenanced by HMP. So PC should also incorporate fairly weighty agent-constituting reasons against means that threaten or involve such things, and second these with agent-governing reasons. Hence there would be some analogue of priority for principles of nonmaleficence over benevolence in this weighty but defeasible agent-governing layer of PC, and directed more broadly than the hedonism of HMP suggests on its surface. There are also at least arguably general and for-the-most-part instrumental relationships that run in the other direction relative to phenomenal value. While agency goods or certain tertiary goods are only genuine when in support of proper projects, and while any general commitment to respect or favor agency goods or analogous tertiary goods must be hedged by a qualification that makes the projects in which they are deployed quite normatively salient, still PC should probably include at least prima facie reasons to respect and favor such goods, both agent-constituting and agent-governing. This serves to reinforce and amplify the effects of the mechanism delivering respect for fundamental agency goods and important tertiary goods that are not genuine that I have already discussed, which involves the existence of beneficent group agents extending such respect.

That is more than enough complexity on the fourth axis. Our fifth and sixth axes begin to edge from abstract structure toward specific normative content. Now a recognizably familiar moral code will begin to emerge.

Scanlon argues that obligations of truth telling and promise keeping are largely independent of convention, while his antagonists on the fifth axis cede great weight to convention and hence introduce a significant degree of relativism into basic duties. The normative significance of actual normatively weighty group acts according to MAC introduces some element of conventionality and relativism, though group action does not stretch to cover all conventions. Still, MAC also recognizes that, other things equal, truth should always be told in support of proper projects. And MAC characteristically cedes dominance to the largest group act and hence to the broadest conventional practice. So on this axis the just good theory occupies a kind of middle and hence appropriately intuitive ground. We will return to the details of truth telling in a moment.

A sixth axis of difference that tracks what is at least very close to being a matter of content rather than structure involves the degree of revolutionary overthrow of customary forms of life that a code requires. Some reconstructions of common sense are quite conservative, while the ancient religious codes apparently require revolutionary psychological changes that would leave covetousness, unrighteous anger, and even desire behind us. The revolutionary elements of those ancient codes may be only fitfully reflected in contemporary common sense. But even commonsense morality may be in some tension with ordinary life. Since we presume here that our background institutions are appropriately correct, including those that support and help constitute familiar psychologies, this will not in the end be relevant to the details of PC. But nevertheless it is clear that PC should recommend in a general way at least conditional concern about the propriety of background institutions as evaluated by HMP.

Because of the sensitivity of PC to actual forms of group activity, and because of its sensitivity to their normative propriety, and given the obvious facts that forms of group activity may be unstable over time but are also partly constituted by reasons whose acceptance under local cooperative conditions may be mandated by PC, PC must specify acceptance of both a first and more general set of reasons that is relatively independent of local and current conditions, and a second and more specific set that is not. Clearly, the agent-governing reasons that reflect the higher-order structure in PC and that we have recently surveyed should be reflected in otherwise identical agent-constituting reasons of some weight, and this is at least a crucial part of that component of PC that is independent of local conditions. But there are also more detailed agent-constituting and agent-governing reasons, some which are relatively independent of local context and some of which are not, that are important according to the just good theory. We will see some effects of this in the next section. Clearly also, JGT requires that PC specify significant agent-governing and agent-constituting reasons to examine background institutions and other forms of actual cooperation in light of alternative possibilities and HMP, and to be aware of actual forms of cooperative action and also possible better alternatives. Such an examination may make revisionary activity very weighty according to JGT. Still, as I said, our general presumption in this chapter that the background conditions of our lives are appropriate makes these ultimately very important issues largely irrelevant for now.

IV

The seventh, last, and very large set of axes on which reconstructions of commonsense morality differ concern relative details of normative content. The location of PC on these relatively concrete axes provide it with a recognizable and appropriately intuitive shape. Aside from the familiar higher-order structure of PC, the guts of it are found here.

Differences on these axes are differences about the relatively detailed form of agent-constituting and agent-governing reasons, and sometimes also agent-balancing reasons, to be properly incorporated into a code. Because we must compare and contrast content aspects of both duty-based and virtue-based reconstructions that deploy different sorts of higher-order organization, I will organize our review by the particular set of categories they occupy according to the framework of JGT.

Benevolence and justice are already reflected in the higher-order structure of PC. But various reconstructions of commonsense morality deploy various other individual virtues that help to constitute successful continuing agency. Temperance, fortitude, prudence, courage, good temper, moderate ambition and pride, Confucian *chung* (doing one's best), patience, and a lack of servility are one set, which provide affective conditions of effective agency. I will call these agency virtues. There is also the intellectual group of intelligence, Buddhist right views, and practical wisdom. The latter incorporates the Confucian wisdom of knowing others' hearts and Kantian knowledge of one's own motives. These are also arguably agency virtues for the most part. There is also a traditional set

295

of socially attractive virtues, like Aristotelian friendliness and ready wit and Confucian natural and beautiful qualities. They have a less obvious relationship to continuing agency.

We can expect PC to incorporate a duty to cultivate the agency virtues. But the various reconstructions also deploy other duties to self that otherwise reflect the agency virtues. Some are correlative duties to these virtues. Some add greater detail or extend our responsibilities. Some of these possible duties forbid drunkenness, gluttony, unchastity, and even the use of intoxicants. Others help to constitute continuing agency in other ways – for instance, by forbidding suicide, self-mutilation, and reckless impairment of health, or by enjoining us to further our own perfection and develop our gifts. There is also the Buddhist precept of right effort.

PC will incorporate agent-constituting and agent-governing reasons that support all of these agency virtues and duties, at least to the degree that they create effective individual action for proper goals. This gives normative spin to this class of intuitive duties and virtues. For instance, courage directed toward evil ends is not a virtue in this way according to PC, nor is deviously evil intelligence, and it is implausible to think that chastity is an agency virtue in most contexts. But this is spin that leaves PC well within the broad confines of commonsense morality. And there is also a second level of support for agency virtues suggested by the structure of JGT, and the corresponding treatment of fundamental agency goods that are not genuine, which, depending on the details of our beneficent group acts, may enjoin support for agency virtues even beyond those in support of proper projects. This makes PC even more intuitive. It also implies that PC is in one way dependent on relatively historically contingent details of our current common sense. Normative conflicts that involve these duties and virtues are to be decided, and vaguenesses resolved, by reference to the higher-order structure already incorporated in PC.

Despite the fact that PC is adequately intuitive with respect to these traditional elements, there are evident complications that attend the interaction of the general structure of JGT and such traditional duties and virtues. Some of the traditional virtues are perhaps not, and others are not merely, agency virtues in the strict sense, but still support effective cooperative group agents in other relevant ways. For instance, fortitude, patience, and temperance can support one's role in group action involving other people. And socially attractive virtues like Aristotelian friendliness and ready wit are effective general means to the success of individual projects, and perhaps necessary in some degree if one is to be a candidate in the eyes of others for many forms of group action. These social virtues have a place in PC when deployed in pursuit of proper projects, though their place may be dependent on local convention to a large degree. Another complication is that absence of even some of the traditional temperance-like agency virtues and violation of some of the correlative duties does not really undercut one's effective agency, at least in the absence of local conditions that make them socially attractive virtues. These unnecessary virtues include the elements of chastity in the reconstructions that extend beyond ordinary temperance and also the strict avoidance of intoxicants. There are also duties and virtues not on the standard lists that are quite like the standard cases under discussion from our specific perspective, including physical strength and correlative duties to develop that virtue. But these complications also seem well within appropriate commonsense range.

The next class of duties to consider are general obligations. There are also allied virtues that are fixed dispositions to fulfill such general obligations and to have supporting sentiments, and also allied duties to cultivate those virtues. But it should be enough for us to focus on the basic duties of general obligation.

Most reconstructions of commonsense morality recognize abstract general obligations like benevolence and justice. Benevolence and justice are not merely virtues, but duties. A certain interpretation of these duties is already included in PC, in agent-constituting reasons that mirror the agent-governing reasons constituting the higher-order normative structure of PC sketched in the last section. HMP, DD, and VLD, the reasons constituting acceptance of TLC, and the prima facie reasons that encode acceptance of what we might call for-the-most-part goods, represent one plausible interpretation of benevolence and justice, not just as virtues but also as duties.

But let me focus on very intuitive general obligations of a slightly less abstract sort. It is clear that commonsense morality is very concerned with certain goods and evils other than pleasure, which are intuitively relevant to filling out concretely our obligations of benevolence and justice, or alternatively in expanding the class of general obligations beyond them. And it is also clear that common sense generally cedes special normative significance to avoiding direct harms of these sorts. The various reconstructions of common sense exhibit much concern with general obligations against lying, killing, causing injury, imprisoning, and causing the frustration of desire.

These concerns may seem a long way from HMP. Still, there is a variety of general mechanisms that link these intuitive general obligations to the higher-order structure of PC. TLC and the for-the-most-part goods include the central goods in question, and the risk-averse and maximin form of HMP creates a kind of natural normative salience for physical injuries. But the main way in which JGT incorporates intuitive respect for standard deontological restrictions on action is through the mechanism of MAC, as we discussed in Part One. This is already abstractly reflected in PC, because of its incorporation of DD and VLD, given the contingent existence of the group acts that I earlier deployed. Violation of the standard deontological prescriptions is in fact often defection from a one-off group act with a weighty project, and hence a violation of DD or VLD. But here we are concerned with the lower-order structure of PC.

PC incorporates agent-constituting and some relatively concrete agent-governing reasons that reflect deontological restrictions. We already saw this in a general way in Chapter 3, but let me apply that general model to all the cases we now face.

Lying is forbidden to one degree or another by almost all reconstructions of commonsense morality. There are lots of differences in detail about when and how. For instance, this negative duty is much less defeasible according to Kant than according to Sidgwick. Ross makes it a species of promise, and Confucian *hsin* suggests that it is part of a very general virtue that extends as far as accurate predictions. Scanlon thinks that we often have a positive duty to provide the truth, and some think that actively misleading true speech is as bad as lying, while others disagree.

But we already discussed this case in Chapter 3. The following four relatively concrete tenets are quite general directives of MAC, which in the context of our actual group practices and the truth of HMP are quite significant, though they are phrased in such a way as to make them appropriate beyond our specific current conditions: (1) Do not lie, and more generally, do not create false expectations or fail to deliver relevant information, within a group agent with a properly beneficent goal that lies outside of the practice of cooperation itself,[23] unless a violation of that duty is sanctioned by VLD or DD, or the lie serves the project of the group, or the lie is acceptable in the practice. (2) If other things are equal, do not lie, and more generally, do not create false expectations or fail to deliver relevant information, to another agent or group agent with a properly beneficent project. (3) Do not lie, and more generally, do not

---

23 This phrase distinguishes this obligation from that expressed by (3).

298

create false expectations or fail to deliver relevant information, whenever you are within a one-off group agent creating a sphere of truth-telling of some sort that is itself a proper project, unless a violation of that duty is sanctioned by VLD or DD, or unless the lie is acceptable in the practice. (4) Join such groups whenever that is required on direct consequentialist grounds, except when that is forbidden by MAC.

You and I are in fact within a widespread one-off group agent such as mentioned in directive (3), which is quite weighty according to HMP. The collapse of our one-off practice of truth telling would present salient downside risks of intense physical pain. So the fourth phrase of the third precept will be omitted from a yet more specific precept that PC will also incorporate in our still quite general situation. Because this practice is so weighty, VLD and DD will very seldom sanction exceptions. The practice itself, of course, specifies some appropriate exceptions from rigorous truth telling. It does not forbid some lies and allows a certain amount of misleading speech. But, roughly speaking, you should lie in a way forbidden by that practice only when you can gain as much value by that defection from our general group act as that whole vast cooperative practice creates. That will require quite unusual circumstances.

Notice that I have framed the general precepts in the preceding paragraphs to encompass implicit and explicit promises as well as lies. So while promise keeping is a concern of some reconstructions of commonsense morality, we needn't give it specific attention here.

A precept forbidding killing is found in most of the reconstructions of commonsense morality, but there are differences about killing animals. Here again, we can rely on our earlier discussions. JGT suggests that animal pain is normatively significant, but that killing nonhuman animals is not specially problematic, given the capacities of most of the nonhuman animals with which we interact, unless there are proper group acts that forbid such killing. Killing humans is another matter. Killing others with whom one is engaged in group activity of course eliminates the possibility of cooperative activity. Even in the unlikely event that the project of the group is favored by the murder of a single member, still this involves a violation of cooperative activity in pursuit of that goal, unless that possibility is specifically endorsed by the whole group and in particular by the member murdered. And of course there is a general group act among humans of not murdering one another, though with some exceptions, which is a one-off group agent with a weighty proper project. It is also relevant that participation in this general form of cooperation is a likely precondition for admission into most forms of group activity, and that killing others will undercut their individual proper projects and those of the group agents of which they are part.

With those links understood, we can see that the following analogues of our earlier precepts governing lying will be found in PC as weighty reasons: (1) Do not kill human or nonhuman cooperators within a group agent with any properly beneficent project having a goal that lies outside of that practice, unless a violation of that duty is sanctioned by VLD or DD. (2) If other things are equal, do not kill humans or other agents who have (or are parts of group agents that have) proper projects. (3) Do not kill whenever you are within a one-off group agent creating a sphere of nonmurder that is itself a proper project, unless a violation of that duty is sanctioned by VLD or DD, or is sanctioned by the practice as an appropriate exception. (4) Join such groups whenever that is required on direct consequentialist grounds, except when that is forbidden by MAC.

You and I are within such a practice as the third precept invokes. Since we have a general cooperative practice forbidding murder under most conditions that is a group act that is quite normatively significant by the tenets of JGT, PC largely forbids murder outright. You may murder to save the entire world from destruction, but you cannot murder an innocent even to stop most wars, because a generally brutish state of nature has worse downside risks than most specific wars.

Stealing is forbidden by nearly all reconstructions of commonsense morality. Still, Donagan introduces intuitively relevant questions about the justice of property arrangements. These questions are outside of the space of our presumptions in this chapter, but still conditionally quite significant according to the just good theory. In general, stealing will be forbidden by PC when it violates conditions necessary for the existence of effective group agents with proper projects of which one is part, at least when those agents and projects are sufficiently weighty according to JGT. It will also be forbidden when other agents' proper projects of sufficient normative weight would be undercut, or when it directly violates HMP or extensions allowed by TLC and the conception of for-the-most-part goods. So far, this would provide greater normative protection for property that is deployed in support of proper projects. But if an institution of property itself constitutes a one-off group agent with a proper project, then members of the group agent will be forbidden to steal except when that is sanctioned by VLD or DD. Those on the outside of that group agent, who may not necessarily include all those without property recognized in that practice, would have no special obligation to respect that property, unless they have a direct consequentialist obligation to join it.

It seems to me an open question whether our own practice of property meets these various propriety conditions.

Many of the relatively recent reconstructions of commonsense morality involve extensions of traditional concerns about killing, lying, and stealing toward more general prohibitions against injuring, disabling, depriving of freedom, causing pain or depriving of pleasure, manipulating, and causing emotional upset such as that inflicted by calumny, mockery, ridicule, disparagement, and even impoliteness.

Physical and phenomenally analogous pain and pleasure have, of course, a special status in JGT, but one that may be reinforced and refined in various ways by the role of those feelings in supporting cooperative behavior. One certainly relevant point about at least physical injuries is that they are generally connected to pains that HMP makes especially salient. But it is also relevant that the agency of others in support of proper projects is undercut if I cut off their feet at every opportunity.

And what of the other cases under consideration? First, the gradual historical development within common sense of prohibitions against injury, imprisonment, and even emotional pain seems to track an historical development in the forms of important group acts. If you beat me up every time we meet, we cannot function effectively together as a group agent in pursuit of certain proper projects, which is unfortunately not to say that oppressive group arrangements are not quite stable and capable of providing groups with opportunities for effective group action – for instance, in war. Still, if you cut off my feet, then I can't run to your assistance or run off to perform my task in a group project. And if you imprison me, I cannot effectively perform my role either. Even manipulation may undercut my cooperative abilities. Abstention from various harms and from manipulation of certain sorts preserves the conditions necessary for the existence of certain forms of group agent, in which the various atomic agents involved are able to act effectively in their individual roles. These can be very effective forms of group agent in pursuit of proper projects of weighty sorts. Indeed, mutual abstentions from injury and manipulation may themselves constitute proper one-off group actions, which have grown historically in a way that also tracks the development of these elements in commonsense moral codes.

In light of these links, PC includes the following precepts as weighty reasons. (1) Do not injure, disable, deprive of freedom, manipulate, or cause pain or deprivation of pleasure to those who are cooperating members of a group agent, in any manner that undercuts the effectiveness of that group agent, when that group agent has a proper project that lies outside of that cooperative practice, unless a violation of that duty is sanctioned by VLD or DD. (2) If other things are equal, do not injure, disable, deprive of freedom, manipulate, or cause pain or deprivation of pleasure of a sort that undercuts the effectiveness of the agency of those who are cooperating members of group agents with proper projects or who are acting on proper projects themselves. (3) Do not injure, disable, deprive of freedom, manipulate, or cause pain or deprivation of pleasure whenever you are within a one-off group agent creating such a cooperative sphere that is itself a proper project, unless a violation of that duty is sanctioned by VLD or DD, or unless an exception is allowed by the practice. Of course, we now have cooperative practices of just this sort. (4) Join such groups whenever that is required on direct consequentialist grounds, except when that is forbidden by MAC.

But there is another set of cases under consideration. Mockery, impoliteness, ridicule, and disparagement may be capable of a similar treatment. But when constrained by proper truth telling and various special obligations – for instance, to children – it seems that commonsense morality does not determinately rule them immoral in any special way. Certainly according to JGT there will be a limit to the normative weight of any relevant general group acts that eschew them. But the deontic avoidance of these forms of "emotional injury" is not recognized as a constraint of commonsense morality by most reconstructions.

On the other hand, there are some limited ways in which emotional injuries have a derived status in PC. A tendency to inflict such injuries may violate some of the socially attractive virtues. And physical pain deeply matters in an intrinsic way, so if ever "emotional pain" is suitably similar and involves negative hedonic tone, that will matter. Most important, perhaps, the infliction of emotional pain will matter when it undercuts effective agency in pursuit of proper projects. So avoidance of some sorts of mockery is required even by the duty not to manipulate. And special obligations to avoid such things may reflect, protect, or constitute small and intimate spheres of cooperation that are weighty. They are our next topic.

The last set of content differences among various reconstructions of commonsense morality involves special obligations. There is some arbitrariness in how we draw the line between these and general obligations. For instance, promise keeping is a kind of special obligation that is yet naturally covered by our earlier discussion of truth telling. Many accounts recognize a general duty not to break laws and also related obligations of citizenship that are recognizably special obligations, but which are naturally treated by JGT in much the same way that it treats stealing. But whatever their proper classification, we need to give some attention to at least the duties of gratitude and reparation as recognized by Ross, as also to obligations among friends and to family. These are obligations that constitute an important feature of many traditional codes.

The just good theory naturally treats special obligations to friends and family as arising from relatively small-scale group agents with proper projects. The acceptance of certain reasons that are not accepted by others outside of the group agent helps to constitute its existence. If I accept your directives as reasons, that may help make me a member of a group agent in which you have a certain role of authority. But of course it is important according to JGT that the group agent in question have a proper project, and of course we must balance this form of group agency against other conflicting forms.

Consider key cases. We have already discussed MAC's analysis of family obligations in Chapter 3, and the case of friends is quite similar. Families and friendships may be normatively weighty forms of group agent, with proper projects. But a grasping and powerful family or friendship may not have a proper project. And destructive families and friendships generate no special obligations by this basic mechanism. And JGT delivers no natural role for differences in hierarchical status within families or friendships unless they help to constitute effective forms of group agency for proper goals. So the hierarchical forms of family relations and even of friendly relations expressed in some of the traditional reconstructions have no natural place in PC.

But it may also be relevant that even hierarchical or somewhat destructive families or friendships are instances of effective forms of actual group cooperation with proper goals – say, the care of children – to which there is no locally salient alternative, and that they may reflect quite general normative one-off group acts, general conventions stabilized by accepted reasons and establishing social forms for families or even friendships, which, while not the best possible, are still weighty according to JGT. Still, these excusing conditions seem largely absent in the contemporary situation of academic ethicists.

We have also already discussed duties of gratitude and reparation. Specific duties of reparation are sometimes duties to restore forms of group action that one has violated, or more specifically, to make it be that in fact one hasn't in the end really violated a reciprocal obligation in the manner one's past activity alone would suggest. Duties of reparation can be in this way a present shadow cast by the combination of one's former cooperative obligations within a group agent and one's past action in apparent violation of those obligations. And duties of gratitude are sometimes duties to avoid the failures that occasion duties of reparation, as well as straightforward cooperative obligations within group agents that root later duties of reparation.

But gratitude and reparation are arguably also general duties that serve to foster the existence of a variety of effective group agents, rooted in a proper one-off group act, although the propriety of this practice is also arguably as suspect as our general practice of risk sharing. Another relevant point is that, like the socially attractive virtues, a tendency to fulfill duties of gratitude and reparation makes one a likely candidate in others' eyes for effective forms of group action.

The special normative status of gratitude and reparation is real but limited according to JGT. For instance, unless a group agent within which gratitude and reparation may exist has a proper project, such gratitude and reparation have no automatic special normative status. They also have no such special status unless they are of a form really necessary to the existence of that effective group agent. And in conflicts between small group agents and weightier group acts constituting deontic practices, DD will not sanction violation of general duties. But it may also be, as I said, that there is a general and proper group agent that generally prescribes gratitude and reparation of certain sorts.

V

PC as so far specified is somewhat complicated, but so is commonsense morality, and in analogous ways. PC is a house in which we could live, a boat in which to sail. It is suitably intuitive in detail. In many ways, it is near the middle of the various reconstructions of commonsense virtues and duties in the second and third historical waves, and even in the first. Even when it is not in the middle, it is still appropriately intuitive. It has a role for most of the normative elements recognized by any of the reconstructions, and all of the elements recognized by the majority of the reconstructions in the most relevant second and third waves. And we saw in section II that it incorporates a properly intuitive conception of the good.

This confluence of the just good theory and common sense presumes the existence of specific group agents. But it is clear that there are corresponding group practices, and they seem to exhibit the entwined benevolence and reciprocity characteristic of group acts. This confluence also presumes that the background institutions of our lives are suitably legitimate. As I said, I am not confident that that is true. And if it is false, then all bets are off about the confluence of JGT and commonsense moral intuition. But that is no *special* objection to JGT. If common sense is wrong about that, then all moral bets are off anyway. The confluence further and more crucially presumes that the key normative one-off group acts that I have deployed here are appropriately beneficent according to HMP. But so they seem to be, with the possible exceptions I have noted, which if improper themselves constitute illegitimate background institutions.

The dragons are dead and the just good theory is true, at least if there is natural ordinal hedonic value. You may think that they are only snoring away, but remember that conclusions in ethics are by necessity boring. Commonsense morality and JGT properly coincide, and so philosophical ethics is legitimate.

But there are possible alternatives to this happy outcome still in play. If there is no hedonic value of any sort, then no direct vindication of a basic normative principle is possible, and so philosophical ethics fails. Probably there are no genuine practical reasons at all. The world is grey in all its forking paths.

But what if hedonic value is cardinal, so that HMP is false and total utilitarianism true? As far as I can see, the key arguments I have deployed in this chapter are still, mutatis mutandis, mostly successful. HMP suggests that we look at worst-case scenarios, downside risks. And in particular, it suggests that we look at downside risks of intense physical pain, however fleeting or narrowly distributed. And the total utilitarian multiple-act consequentialist will rather ask about expectations for change in total utility. Still, the group acts we have crucially deployed here, commonsense moral practices, plausibly meet both tests. Our truth telling practice plausibly protects us against both expectation of overall loss of total hedonic utility and downside risks of great pain. It is not that we would always lie if there were no such practice, but the group act in question gets normative credit for all the lies that it prevents and their results. And that seems enough on either normative option.

Of course, a code implied by total utilitarianism in conjunction with MAC would look a little different. It would deploy a total utilitarian principle instead of HMP. And it would rank options differently and assess some conflicts adjudicated through DD and VLD in a different way. But the differences seem not to matter much in the situations we have faced in this chapter. If there is cardinal hedonic value, then total utilitarianism is true, and commonsense morality and the conjunction of MAC and total utilitarianism still sufficiently coincide so that ethics is viable.

There are certain features of PC that we haven't yet specified, because they address issues that are left unresolved by contemporary academic commonsense morality, except perhaps by reference to its vague and unsupportable selfishness, a selfishness that would be rectified in the more beneficent concentric group morality that eschews that unfortunate detail of our common sense. In such cases, total utilitarianism and HMP do sometimes pull in different directions, despite MAC. And we should consider at least some of these features anyway.

We might not like to wear life jackets in canoes, though there is a general group act of doing so. They are hot and uncomfortable. On balance, it might even serve utility if people generally didn't wear them. But if people generally didn't, there is a downside likelihood that someone somewhere would feel intense pain. Under such conditions, JGT says you ought to leave your life jacket on, even if it is a little uncomfortable, and even if you'd rather run the tiny risk of painful drowning. Utilitarian principles when conjoined with MAC suggest otherwise. So we can expect some precepts in a fully developed version of PC that would not appear in the total utilitarian analogue.

Would there be any interesting differences? I think so. But begin with another and still simple case that involves, if total utilitarianism is true, less a modification of PC than a surprise about its implications. There is a group act of desisting from torture. There probably wouldn't be a huge number of acts of torture even if there were no such group act. People aren't *that* nasty. But the acts of torture whose absence is due to the group act weigh very heavily against anything you might gain from a local deviation, according to both normative principles in play, no matter how well intentioned and well directed your use of torture might be. Still, perhaps you've never joined the group. You never publicly admit it, but you don't really accept the complex reasons constituting the group act of not torturing even for beneficent ends. You dissent in your classically utilitarian heart. No doubt there will be a day on which it will greater serve overall well-being for you to join the cooperative sphere of nontorture, and then you will be bound inside. But you can put off joining for a day. Under those conditions, the conjunction of MAC and utilitarianism would allow you to act toward some plausibly benevolent end today via an individual act of torture. Because HMP focuses on downside risks of intense pain, it does not yield the same result in the same circumstances. To use torture toward a benevolent end is always to risk, on the downside, that the torture might occur without the desired result.

I do not introduce this case to convince you that total utilitarianism is false even when conjoined with MAC. I think that if there is cardinal hedonic value, then total utilitarianism is true, whether I like it or not. I don't even introduce it to suggest that there are general intuitive advantages that stem from the fact that HMP requires risk aversion of those who defect from or abjure standard group practices, although I think there surely are. I introduce it rather to focus attention on the significance according to MAC of dissent in the heart, and because of its structural similarity to a case that commonsense morality does not adequately resolve but that we will shortly consider. Let me begin with the first point.

Violation of common normative practices such as that against lying will occasion criticism of someone even if in their heart they do not accept that lying is any big deal. And we certainly cannot conclude from the fact that you will be criticized for not doing something that you are participating in a group act of doing that thing. So perhaps quasi-deontological criticism of liars who in their hearts do not accept our antilying practice is unjust according to MAC. They can still be criticized for being outside the practice, of course, but that's not quite the same thing.

That is troubling. It is also troubling that while congenital liars will generally have straightforward act consequentialist grounds for joining such antilying practices, they might not always have such reasons. Perhaps this seems an objection to MAC.

But there is a mitigating complication. Remember that we accept reasons with different degrees of motivational efficacy. To be truly outside a group on such grounds, you cannot accept relevant reasons at all, in your heart or anywhere else. You cannot be a part of the group act of trying to avoid lies in even the slightest and most evanescent way. You must not be even disposed to complain on quasi-deontological reciprocal grounds if someone lies to you. For this to be true in the lying case, you would need to have a psychology unlike normal human psychology. Perhaps some do, but not many.

So you may be inside more group acts, and they may have more members, than it appears on the basis of gross behavior alone. And there is a second complication that swells the number of group agents to which you belong. Some might suggest that all the actual cooperators who are part of a group act must be here in the present, and in fairly close proximity. But that is not the correct conception of group acts. You and I can share projects on which we continue to coordinate while rowing off to different parts of the world, perhaps never to see one another again. And we can inherit a common project from the past even if we have never ourselves been close enough to be in communication. Indeed, no common cause of our acceptance of the relevant reasons is necessary. We may still be disposed to criticize one another in characteristic ways and to accept those characteristic sorts of criticism if we ever happen to run into one another. Perhaps our dispositions aren't focused on one other by name, but still they can be sufficiently focused on people in general, or on people of general sorts. And we might be disposed to actively coordinate activity, if only the opportunity arose. We can in this way recognizably share a common goal, supported by a kind of reciprocity and cooperation. So the spatial location of the cooperators is irrelevant. Nor are differences in time relevant. Remember that, according to MAC, individual prudence over time is one kind of group action in which you participate all by yourself. And while time asymmetries are important to some ethical theories, I have argued in Chapter 7 against their deep normative significance. Future cooperators are relevant as well as past cooperators, according to MAC. Of course, you don't know who the future cooperators will be, nor even that there will be any. But you don't necessarily know many of the relevant present cooperators either. And you probably don't know the relevant effects or indeed even the relevant objective probabilities of your individual acts. Ignorance is a kind of excuse, but ignorance does not in these particular ways affect what you should in fact do. Consequentialists should be used to that.

We are now in a position to properly consider an interesting normative question that cannot be consistently answered by commonsense morality in its unrefined state, but that would be addressed by a fully detailed development of PC, one that also reveals some differences between the implications of total utilitarianism and HMP when conjoined with MAC. It will still take us a while to get properly back to those differences.

Derek Parfit has plausibly suggested that commonsense morality was formed by pressures in small communities in a less technologically advanced world. In the past, we didn't need to deal with situations in which big nasty effects like ozone depletion or global warming are the result of huge numbers of individual actions that each make trivially small contributions to those large effects. We have little guidance from commonsense morality regarding our moral obligations in these situations, which are now quite important.

Common sense does not determinately suggest that it is grossly immoral to buy an SUV for idle urban use, or even a big yellow Humvee.

It is not customary to claim that an individual act can be grossly wrong when its negative effects on other people are imperceptible. But consider also Parfit's analogous case:

A thousand torturers have a thousand victims. At the start of each day, each of the victims is already feeling mild pain. Each of the torturers turns a switch a thousand times on some instrument. Each turning of the switch affects some victim's pain in a way that is imperceptible. But, after each torturer has turned his switch a thousand times, he has inflicted severe pain on his victim.[24]

The negative effects of each act are imperceptible, but every single act is wrong, even grossly so. Common sense does not, it seems to me, determinately resolve this apparent conflict in cases. But JGT and hence PC can resolve it. Even just MAC can resolve it.

If buying an SUV is part of a group act with horrendous consequences, it may be deeply immoral according to MAC. And that doesn't require a lot. Perhaps almost everyone who buys an SUV thinks that "it's my money and I can do with it what I want as long as it doesn't harm anybody in a significant way." Perhaps they participate in that normatively weighty practice, and indeed would criticize someone who started to think in a different way in support of a contrary practice, who fell away from that group. Then their individual action might be part of a horrendous group act, at least if it risks intense suffering that would otherwise not occur.

But presume there is no such group act. Presume that those who buy SUVs accept no supporting reasons, and that they wouldn't criticize any selfless fool who doesn't buy one. They aren't even disposed to criticize the selfless fool to themselves, in their mind's ear, as a fool. Presume that they aren't even part of some ideology that aims to take over public and political space to make the world safe for rapacious capitalism and the Rapture. Say someone just wants an SUV.

Still, there are other people out there, on the other side. They don't buy SUVs even though they want them and can afford them, and they are inclined to criticize those who fall away from their group as going over to the dark side. They are even inclined to criticize those always outside their group as inappropriately reciprocal, as insufficiently worried about the effects of many people buying SUVs.

They may be wrong about some of those other people on the outside, who may be so selfish as never to accept any reciprocal responsibility in such matters, even in some faint corner of their mind. Perhaps MAC

---

24 Parfit (1984: 80).

suggests that those outside get off too easy, though they still have their ordinary act consequentialist obligations to join group practices. We will come back to that point.

But you want an SUV, and you don't have that excuse. Inside there somewhere, you feel the sting. You accept the relevant reasons, along with other conflicting reasons in your conflicted self. You are disposed at least in part to make and accept the relevant criticisms rooted in reciprocity and beneficence. You are inside the group in the relevant sense, and to defect would be immoral in a quasi-deontological way, according to MAC, even if you usually do defect. There are others who do the right thing, and there are enough of them so that the group has some significant effects. If you were the only one in the world who ever worried about useless and wasteful consumption, then the world would be dark and you would have no group-based quasi-deontological obligation to refrain from your purchase. If the group of cooperators is tiny, the normative weight of the group is less. It is also insignificant if, though there are many who accept the relevant reasons in their heart, that never leads to real activity. But if the group is active and large, and not necessarily as a percentage of the total population, then the group act is significant. And remember also that relevant cooperators might be in the future and, given a certain abstraction in the project in question, in the past. Perhaps you and your ancestors accept reasons supporting the group project of leaving the world in as good shape when you die as it was when you were born. You are then inside a relevant and weighty group. You must reciprocate. Or perhaps everyone now is grossly selfish and always has been, but in the scary future when this problem is more vivid for all, many people will feel the pull to cooperative activity of the relevant sort. Then you owe it reciprocally to our descendants, even if you get nothing out of it, since you are, in at least some faint corner of your heart, inside the relevant group act.

I have presumed that the group act in question is beneficent according to HMP, and also total utilitarianism, but so it seems to be. Global warming risks intense pains that would otherwise not be risked, and misuse of resources to achieve trivial goals means that those resources will not be available to assuage other evident risks of great pain. Remember our discussions of population issues at the end of the last chapter and in section I if you think otherwise.

But what if you are in fact outside the group of do-gooders, and feel no pull at all to restrain your consumption, if you accept no reasons of that sort? Then your moral obligations are as ordinary act consequentialism suggests, to figure out whether joining the group would have a good effect

310

(presuming that it wouldn't violate more weighty prior obligations), and to accept or eschew the relevant reasons. And here a difference between total utilitarianism and HMP becomes salient. According to the just good theory, you should consider the downside risk of individual pain on each option. In the worst-case scenario, perhaps you are the crucial threshold, and without you the group fails to achieve its goal. Or perhaps in the worst-case scenario your child will die in a violent traffic accident because you join the group, and your joining will gain nothing. But most likely, in the worst-case scenario the group will fail to achieve its goal because you balk, and yet you will kill some other child with your big fat truck. Total utilitarianism will ask instead about expected total utility. And it is quite likely that, as in the case of torture we discussed earlier, a total utilitarian can find a special way to use a big truck to create more utility than that one truck will dissipate. If you have an act consequentialist obligation to join the group, according to MAC you are obligated to join, other things equal, and when you do, you will become bound by quasi-deontological duties to refrain from ruthless consumption. But total utilitarianism will not characteristically deliver an act consequentialist obligation to join, while HMP characteristically will. Issues like this one, I think, either will introduce explicit differences into any fully detailed code supported by the conjunction of total utilitarianism and MAC, or at the very least will give the code notably different implications.

There are other extensions of PC beyond the determinacy of commonsense morality. One case involves our obligations to the needy, and for that I can appeal to our earlier discussion, in Chapter 3. According to PC, you are obligated to give at least 2.5 percent of your annual income to the poor and starving if you are relatively badly-off for a reader of this book, and more lavishly if you are relatively rich. The poor and starving have a natural moral claim on us, and so do those who do their share. And you are inside the relevant group act, because you accept the relevant reasons to at least some degree, I claim. To one degree or another, you feel the sting.

Of course, this duty probably exists according to MAC even if HMP is false and total utility is our guide. And indeed, I earlier made the argument for this aspect of MAC without appeal to the peculiarities of HMP. That may itself occasion worry. But of course starvation is very painful, and our obligation is not merely to give charity, which may be misused to exacerbate standing evils, but rather to participate in a group act that actually feeds the starving. HMP may suggest that a little painful starvation now may be better than the risk of a lot later on, and starvation now may prevent the birth of more starving descendants. But still, that is not the plausible implication of the absence of the temporally and spatially vast group act of charity, which encompasses fixed participants across time. The absence of the relevant group act wouldn't buy a lot less starvation later for a little today, but rather a lot more spread out over time.

Direct obligations to do more for the needy depend, on straight act consequentialist grounds, on the normative weight of the generally beneficent group or individual acts from which you would hence defect or refrain. And it may be that HMP and total utilitarianism will assess these differently. But the basic obligation to the needy remains.

VI

Both modifications of traditional utilitarianism that I have proposed, the distribution sensitivity of HMP and its application through Multiple-Act Consequentialism, reflect what is in a sense a single thought, and not merely because they are rooted in two concerns about justice. There are moral agents and moral patients, beings who can act morally and beings whose condition is relevant to those acts. The perhaps now-dominant view of at least nonutilitarians is that individual people over their lives are both the primary moral agents and the primary moral patients. But that is wrong. Those three things – persons, primary moral agents, and primary moral patients – often come apart.

Derek Parfit has already developed this thought in a somewhat more classically utilitarian framework.[25] He has also argued that our reasons for acting should become more impersonal, but not quite in the way that objective hedonic value, flecks, or group agents are impersonal. So my version is somewhat different.

Consider first moral patients. I have argued that primary status as a moral patient is determined by sentience, and that how pleasure is distributed matters not only over individual lives but also within individual lives, that short periods of people's lives, indeed spatio-temporal bits of their experience, require moral consideration in something like an egalitarian way. The basic moral patients for HMP are flecks of experience. And MAC has obvious implications for the nature of moral agents. Neither individuals over their lives, nor individuals in moments of their lives, nor even both together, are the sole moral agents. They are not even

---

25 Parfit (1984).

312

the sole moral agents in which you at this moment take part. You also are part of various forms of group agent. There is more than one agent, indeed more than one type of agent, each with a distinct range of options, in which you at this moment take part, and of which your momentary behaviors are in various ways parts.

We ethicists should focus less on individual people over their individual lives. They are neither the sole and crucial agents in ethics nor the sole and crucial patients. On that relatively abstract point, common sense is mistaken. Ethicists should worry more about distribution within lives. And you and I at each moment of our adult lives are parts of agents that span the round earth's imagined corners.[26]

Our moral obligations depend on the true basic normative principle, and that depends on the concrete facts about hedonic value. If there is none, then there are no genuine normative truths. If it is ordinal, then HMP is true. If it is cardinal, then total utilitarianism is true. And if it is in between, then we are in between.

But our moral obligations also depend on the facts about group acts, including not only the reasons we accept at this moment, somewhere inside us, but also who is outside in the big world and in its future and past, and the reasons they accept. And our obligations depend on the effects of those group acts. And so ethics and something like politics are closely entwined. Our social practices cannot be ignored by morality. And they are not fixed objects for the ethicist to consider from the outside, big brassy blocks. We are inside, and there is writing all over our walls.

26   Donne (1950).

313

Bibliography

Adams, R. M. 1976. Motive Utilitarianism. *Journal of Philosophy* 73, 467–481.
Al-Shiekh, A. 1995. ZAKĀT. In J. Esposito (ed.), *The Oxford Encyclopedia of the Modern Islamic World*, vol. 4. New York: Oxford University Press, 366–370.
Aquinas, T. 1915–38. *The Summa Theologica of St. Thomas Aquinas*. Translated by Fathers of the English Dominican Province. London: Burns, Oates & Washbourne.
Arberry, A. J. 1955. *The Koran Interpreted*. London: Allen & Unwin.
Aristotle. 1980. *The Nicomachean Ethics*. Oxford: Oxford University Press.
Audi, R. 1997. *Moral Knowledge and Ethical Character*. Oxford: Oxford University Press.
Ayer, A. J. 1936. *Language, Truth, and Logic*. New York: Oxford University Press.
Baier, K. 1978a. Moral Reasons and Reasons to Be Moral. In J. Kim and A. Goldman (eds.), *Values and Morals*. Dordrecht: Reidel, 231–256.
Baier, K. 1978b. The Social Source of Reason. *Proceedings and Addresses of the American Philosophical Association* 51, 707–733.
Barry, B. 1965. *Political Argument*. London: Routledge & Kegan Paul.
Barry, B. 1989. *Theories of Justice*. London: Harvester.
Baumgardt, D. 1952. *Bentham and the Ethics of Today*. Princeton, NJ: Princeton University Press.
Bentham, J. 1970. *An Introduction to the Principles of Morals and Legislation*. London: Athlone Press.
Bergstrom, L. 1976. On the Formulation and Application of Utilitarianism. *Nous* 10, 121–144.
Blackburn, S. 1971. Moral Realism. In J. Casey (ed.), *Morality and Moral Reasoning*. London: Methuen, 101–124.
Blackburn, S. 1984. *Spreading the Word*. New York: Oxford University Press.
Blackburn, S. 1985. Supervenience Revisited. In I. Hacking (ed.), *Exercises in Analysis: Essays by Students of Casimir Lewy*. Cambridge: Cambridge University Press, 47–67.
Blackburn, S. 1988. Attitudes and Contents. *Ethics* 98, 501–517.
Block, N., and Stalnaker, R. 1999. Conceptual Analysis, Dualism, and the Explanatory Gap. *The Philosophical Review* 108, 1–46.

315

Boyd, R. N. 1988. How to Be a Moral Realist. In G. Sayre-McCord (ed.), *Essays on Moral Realism*. Ithaca, NY: Cornell University Press, 181–228.

Brandt, R. B. 1963. Toward a Credible Form of Utilitarianism. In H. N. Castañeda and G. Nakhnikian (eds.), *Morality and the Language of Conduct*. Detroit: Wayne State University Press, 107–144.

Brandt, R. B. 1979. *A Theory of the Good and Right*. New York: Oxford University Press.

Brandt, R. B. 1982. Two Concepts of Utility. In H. Miller and W. Williams (eds.), *The Limits of Utilitarianism*. Minneapolis: University of Minnesota Press, 169–185.

Bratman, M. E. 1987. *Intentions, Plans, and Practical Reason*. Cambridge, MA: Harvard University Press.

Bratman, M. E. 1992. Shared Cooperative Activity. *The Philosophical Review* 101, 327–341.

Bratman, M. E. 1993. Shared Intention. *Ethics* 104, 97–113.

Brink, D. O. 1989. *Moral Realism and the Foundations of Ethics*. Cambridge: Cambridge University Press.

Broad, C. D. 1930. *Five Types of Ethical Theory*. London: Routledge & Kegan Paul.

Broome, J. 1991. *Weighing Goods*. Oxford: Blackwell.

Buddha. 1955. The Sermon at Benares. In E. A. Burtt (ed.), *The Teachings of the Compassionate Buddha*. New York: New American Library, 29–32.

Byrne, A. 1999. Cosmic Hermeneutics. *Philosophical Perspectives* 13, 347–383.

Carson, T. L. 1983. Utilitarianism and the Wrongness of Killing. *Erkenntnis* 20, 49–60.

Carson, T. L. 2000. *Value and the Good Life*. Notre Dame, IN: University of Notre Dame Press.

Casell, E. 1982. The Nature of Suffering and the Goals of Medicine. *New England Journal of Medicine* 306, 11.

Castañeda, H-N. 1973. A Problem for Utilitarianism. *Analysis* 33, 141–142.

Chalmers, D. 1996. *The Conscious Mind*. New York: Oxford University Press.

Clarke, H. W. 1894. *A History of Tithes*, 2nd ed. New York: Scribner's.

Confucius. 1979. *The Analects*. Translated and with an introduction by D. C. Lau. Harmondsworth: Penguin.

Cummiskey, D. 1996. *Kantian Consequentialism*. Oxford: Oxford University Press.

Damasio, A. 1994. *Descartes' Error*. New York: Grosset/Putnam.

Darwall, S. 1983. *Impartial Reason*. Ithaca, NY: Cornell University Press.

Darwall, S., Gibbard, A., and Railton, P. 1992. Toward *Fin de Siècle* Ethics: Some Trends. *The Philosophical Review* 101, 1–114.

D'Aspremont, C. J., and Gevers, L. 1971. Equity and the Informational Basis of Collective Choice. *The Review of Economic Studies* 44(2), 199–209.

Davidson, D. 1980. *Essays on Actions and Events*. Oxford: Clarendon Press.

Davies, M., and Humberstone, L. 1980. Two Notions of Necessity. *Philosophical Studies* 38, 1–30.

Dawood, N. J. 1974. Translation of *The Koran*. Harmondsworth: Penguin.

Diener, E., Wirtz, D., and Oishi, S. 2001. End Effects of Rated Life Quality: The James Dean Effect. *Psychological Science* 12, 124–128.

Donagan, A. 1977. *The Theory of Morality*. Chicago: University of Chicago Press.

Donne, J. 1950. Holy Sonnet VII. In J. Hayward (ed.), *John Donne: A Selection of His Poetry*. Harmondsworth: Penguin, 168–169.

Dostoevsky, F. 1990. *The Brothers Karamazov*. Translated by Richard Pevear and Larissa Volokhonsky. New York: Farrar, Straus and Giroux.

Duncker, K. 1940–41. On Pleasure, Emotion, and Striving. *Philosophy and Phenomenological Research* 1, 391–430.

Edgeworth, F. Y. 1881. *Mathematical Psychics*. London: C. K. Paul.

Edwards, R. 1979. *Pleasures and Pains*. Ithaca, NY: Cornell University Press.

Fehige, C. 1998. A Pareto Principle for Possible People. In C. Fehige and U. Wessels (eds.), *Preferences*. Berlin: de Gruyter, 508–543.

Feldman, F. 1975. World Utilitarianism. In K. Lehrer (ed.), *Analysis and Metaphysics*. Dordrecht: Reidel, 255–271.

Feldman, F. 1986. *Doing the Best We Can*. Dordrecht: Reidel.

Feldman, F. 1995. Adjusting Utility for Justice: A Consequentialist Reply to the Objection from Justice. *Philosophy and Phenomenological Research* 55, 567–585.

Feldman, F. 2004. *Pleasure and the Good Life*. Oxford: Clarendon Press.

Fischer, J. M., and Ravizza, M. (eds.). 1992. *Ethics: Problems and Principles*. Fort Worth, TX: Harcourt Brace Jovanovich.

Foot, P. 1967. The Problem of Abortion and the Doctrine of Double Effect. *Oxford Review* 5, 5–15.

Foot, P. 1978. *Virtues and Vices and Other Essays*. Berkeley: University of California Press.

Frankena, W. 1973. *Ethics*, 2nd ed. Englewood Cliffs, NJ: Prentice-Hall.

Fredrickson, B. L., and Kahneman, D. 1993. Duration Neglect in Retrospective Evaluations of Affective Episodes. *Journal of Personality and Social Psychology* 65, 45–55.

Fried, C. 1978. *Right and Wrong*. Cambridge, MA: Harvard University Press.

Gauthier, D. 1986. *Morals by Agreement*. Oxford: Oxford University Press.

Geach, P. 1958. Imperative and Deontic Logic. *Analysis* 18, 49–56.

Geach, P. 1965. Assertion. *The Philosophical Review* 74, 449–465.

Gert, B. 1998. *Morality*. Oxford: Oxford University Press.

Gibbard, A. 1965. Rule-Utilitarianism: Merely an Illusory Alternative? *Australasian Journal of Philosophy* 43, 211–220.

Gibbard, A. 1990a. *Utilitarianism and Coordination*. New York: Garland Press.

Gibbard, A. 1990b. *Wise Choices, Apt Feelings*. Cambridge, MA: Harvard University Press.

Gibbard, A. 1992. Reply to Blackburn, Carson, Hill and Railton. *Philosophy and Phenomenological Research* 72, 969–980.

Gilbert, M. 1989. *On Social Facts*. London: Routledge.

Gilbert, M. 1996. *Living Together*. Lanham, MD: Rowman & Littlefield.

Gilbert, M. 2000. *Sociality and Responsibility*. Lanham, MD: Rowman & Littlefield.

Gilchrist, J. 1969. *The Church and Economic Activity in the Middle Ages*. London: Macmillan.

Goldman, H. 1978. Doing the Best One Can. In J. Kim and A. Goldman (eds.), *Values and Morals*. Dordrecht: Reidel, 185–214.

Goldsworthy, J. 1992. Well-Being and Value. *Utilitas* 4, 1–26.

Griffin, J. 1986. *Well-Being*. Oxford: Clarendon Press.

Hammond, P. J. 1976. Equity, Arrow's Conditions, and Rawls' Difference Principle. *Econometrica* 44, 793–804.

Hanna, R. 1992. Morality *De Re:* Reflections on the Trolley Problem. In Fischer and Ravizza (1992), 320–336.

Hare, R. M. 1952. *The Language of Morals.* Oxford: Oxford University Press.

Hare, R. M. 1963. *Freedom and Reason.* Oxford: Oxford University Press.

Hare, R. M. 1981. *Moral Thinking.* Oxford: Oxford University Press.

Harman, G. 1975. Moral Relativism Defended. *The Philosophical Review* 84, 3–22.

Harre, R., and Madden, E. 1975. *Causal Powers.* Totowa, NJ: Rowman & Littlefield.

Harris, J. 1975. The Survival Lottery. *Philosophy* 50, 81–87.

Harrod, R. F. 1936. Utilitarianism Revised. *Mind* 45, 137–156.

Haslett, D. W. 1990. What Is Utility? *Economics and Philosophy* 6, 65–94.

Heidegger, M. 1996. *Being and Time.* Translated by Joan Stambaugh. Albany: State University of New York Press.

Henson, R. 1971. Utilitarianism and the Wrongness of Killing. *The Philosophical Review* 80, 320–337.

Hooker, B. 1995. Rule-Consequentialism, Incoherence, Fairness. *Proceedings of the Aristotelian Society* 95, 19–35.

Hooker, B. 1996. Ross-style Pluralism versus Rule-Consequentialism. *Mind* 105, 531–552.

Hooker, B. 2000. *Ideal Rules, Real World.* Oxford: Oxford University Press.

Horgan, T. 1984. Supervenience and Cosmic Hermeneutics. *Southern Journal of Philosophy Supplement* 22, 19–38.

Horgan, T., and Timmons, M. 1990–91. New Wave Moral Realism Meets Moral Twin Earth. *Journal of Philosophical Research* 16, 447–465.

Horgan, T., and Timmons, M. 1992. Troubles on Moral Twin Earth: Moral Queerness Revisited. *Synthese* 92, 221–260.

Hospers, J. 1961. *Human Conduct.* New York: Harcourt Brace Jovanovich.

Hurka, T. 1993. *Perfectionism.* Oxford: Oxford University Press.

Hutcheson, F. 1968. *A System of Moral Philosophy.* New York: Augustus M. Kelley.

Jackson, F. 1987. Group Morality. In P. Pettit, R. Sylvan, and J. Norman (eds.), *Metaphysics and Morality.* Oxford: Blackwell, 91–110.

Jackson, F. 1998. *From Metaphysics to Ethics.* Oxford: Clarendon Press.

James, W. 1950. *The Principles of Psychology.* New York: Dover.

Kagan, S. 1989. *The Limits of Morality.* Oxford: Clarendon Press.

Kahneman, D., Fredrickson, B. L., Schreiber, C. A., and Redelmeier, D. A. 1993. When More Pain Is Preferred to Less: Adding a Better End. *Psychological Science* 4, 401–405.

Kamm, F. M. 1993. *Morality, Mortality,* vol. 1. Oxford: Oxford University Press.

Kamm, F. M. 1996. *Morality, Mortality,* vol. 2. Oxford: Oxford University Press.

Kant, I. 1996a. *Groundwork of the Metaphysics of Morals.* In Mary J. Gregor (trans. and ed.), *Practical Philosophy.* Cambridge: Cambridge University Press, 37–108.

Kant, I. 1996b. *The Metaphysics of Morals.* In Mary J. Gregor (trans. and ed.), *Practical Philosophy.* Cambridge: Cambridge University Press, 353–603.

Kim, J. 1979. Supervenience and Nomological Incommensurables. *American Philosophical Quarterly* 15, 149–156.

Kim, J. 1984. Concepts of Supervenience. *Philosophy and Phenomenological Research* 45, 153–176.

Kitcher, P. 1979. Phenomenal Qualities. *American Philosophical Quarterly* 16, 123–129.

Korsgaard, C. 1996a. *The Sources of Normativity*. Cambridge: Cambridge University Press.

Korsgaard, C. 1996b. Personal Identity and the Unity of Agency: A Kantian Response to Parfit. In her *Creating the Kingdom of Ends*. Cambridge: Cambridge University Press, 362–397.

Kripke, S. 1980. *Naming and Necessity*. Cambridge, MA: Harvard University Press.

Lacan, J. 1971. *Ecrits*. Translated by A. Sheridan. New York: Norton.

Lao-Tzu. 1993. *Tao Te Ching*. Translated by S. Addiss and S. Lombardo. Indianapolis: Hackett.

Lewis, C. I. 1946. *An Analysis of Knowledge and Valuation*. La Salle, IL: Open Court.

Lewis, D. 1980. Mad Pain and Martian Pain. In N. Block (ed.), *Readings in Philosophy of Psychology, Vol. 1*. Cambridge, MA: Harvard University Press, 216–222.

Lewis, D. 1989. Dispositional Theories of Value. *Proceedings of the Aristotelian Society* 89, 113–136.

Lewis, D. 1994. Reduction of Mind. In Samuel Guttenplan (ed.), *A Companion to the Philosophy of Mind*. Oxford: Blackwell, 412–431.

Lyons, D. 1965. *Forms and Limits of Utilitarianism*. Oxford: Clarendon Press.

Mackie, J. L. 1977. *Ethics: Inventing Right and Wrong*. Harmondsworth: Penguin.

Mackie, J. L. 1984. Rights, Utility, and Universalization. In R. G. Frey (ed.), *Utility and Rights*. Minneapolis: University of Minnesota Press, 86–105.

Malm, H. 1989. Killing, Letting Die and Simple Conflicts. *Philosophy and Public Affairs* 18, 238–258.

McDowell, J. 1978. Are Moral Requirements Hypothetical Imperatives? *Proceedings of the Aristotelian Society,* supplementary volume 52, 13–29.

McDowell, J. 1979. Virtue and Reason. *Monist* 62, 331–350.

McDowell, J. 1981. Noncognitivism and Rule Following. In S. H. Holtzman and C. M. Leich (eds.), *Wittgenstein: To Follow a Rule*. London: Routledge & Kegan Paul, 141–162.

McDowell, J. 1985. Values and Secondary Qualities. In T. Honderich (ed.), *Morality and Objectivity*. London: Routledge & Kegan Paul, 110–129.

McMahan, J. 2002. *The Ethics of Killing*. Oxford: Oxford University Press.

Mendola, J. 1986. Parfit on Directly Collectively Self-Defeating Moral Theories. *Philosophical Studies* 50, 153–166.

Mendola, J. 1987. The Indeterminacy of Options. *American Philosophical Quarterly* 24, 125–136.

Mendola, J. 1988. On Rawls's Basic Structure: Forms of Justification and the Subject Matter of Social Philosophy. *The Monist* 71, 437–454.

Mendola, J. 1990a. Bernard Williams and Ethics at the Limit. *Australasian Journal of Philosophy* 67, 306–318.

Mendola, J. 1990b. Objective Value and Subjective States. *Philosophy and Phenomenological Research* 50, 695–713.

Mendola, J. 1990c. An Ordinal Modification of Classical Utilitarianism. *Erkenntnis* 33, 73–88.

Mendola, J. 1997. *Human Thought*. Dordrecht: Kluwer.

Mendola, J. 1999. Hart, Fuller, Dworkin, and Fragile Norms. *SMU Law Review* 52, 111–134.

Mendola, J. 2004. Justice within a Life. *American Philosophical Quarterly* 41, 125–140.

Mendola, J. 2005a. Consequences, Group Acts, and Trolleys. *Pacific Philosophical Quarterly* 86, 64–87.

Mendola, J. 2005b. Intuitive Maximin. *Canadian Journal of Philosophy* 35, 429–439.

Mendola, J. In print a. Intuitive Hedonism. *Philosophical Studies*.

Mendola, J. In print b. Multiple-Act Consequentialism. *Nous*.

Milgram, S. 1974. *Obedience to Authority*. New York: Harper and Row.

Mill, J. S. 1979. *Utilitarianism*. Indianapolis: Hackett.

Moore, G. E. 1903. *Principia Ethica*. Cambridge: Cambridge University Press.

Moore, G. E. 1912. *Ethics*. New York: Henry Holt.

More, H. 1997. *An Account of Virtue*. Bristol: Thoemmes Press.

Murphy, L. 2000. *Moral Demands in Nonideal Theory*. Oxford: Oxford University Press.

Nagel, T. 1970. *The Possibility of Altruism*. Princeton, NJ: Princeton University Press.

Nagel, T. 1979. What Is It Like to Be a Bat? In his *Mortal Questions*. Cambridge: Cambridge University Press, 165–180.

Nagel, T. 1986. *The View from Nowhere*. Oxford: Oxford University Press.

Nagel, T. 1991. *Equality and Partiality*. New York: Oxford University Press.

Nussbaum, M. C. 2000. *Women and Human Development*. New York: Cambridge University Press.

Overvold, M. 1980. Self-Interest and the Concept of Self-Sacrifice. *Canadian Journal of Philosophy* 10, 105–118.

Overvold, M. 1982. Self-Interest and Getting What You Want. In H. Miller and W. Williams (eds.), *The Limits of Utilitarianism*. Minneapolis: University of Minnesota Press, 186–194.

Parfit, D. 1984. *Reasons and Persons*. Oxford: Oxford University Press.

Parfit, D. 1995. *Equality or Priority?* Lawrence: University Press of Kansas.

Perry, D. C. 1967. *The Concept of Pleasure*. The Hague: Mouton & Co.

Plato. 1975. *Philebus*. Translated by J. C. B. Gosling. Oxford: Clarendon Press.

Pogge, T. 2002. *World Poverty and Human Rights*. Cambridge: Polity Press.

Popper, K. 1966. *The Open Society and Its Enemies*. Princeton, NJ: Princeton University Press.

Postow, B. C. 1977. Generalized Act Utilitarianism. *Analysis* 37, 49–52.

Pratt, J. B. 1928. *Pilgrimage of Buddhism and A Buddhist Pilgrimage*. New York: Macmillan.

Quine, W. V. O. 1960. *Word and Object*. Cambridge, MA: MIT Press.

Railton, P. 1984. Alienation, Consequentialism, and the Demands of Morality. *Philosophy and Public Affairs* 13, 134–171.

Railton, P. 1986. Moral Realism. *The Philosophical Review* 95, 163–207.

Rawls, J. 1971. *A Theory of Justice*. Cambridge, MA: Harvard University Press.

Rawls, J. 1980. Kantian Constructivism in Moral Theory. *Journal of Philosophy* 77, 515–572.

Rawls, J. 1985. Justice as Fairness: Political Not Metaphysical. *Philosophy and Public Affairs* 14, 223–251.

Rawls, J. 1993. *Political Liberalism*. New York: Columbia University Press.

Regan, D. 1980. *Utilitarianism and Co-operation*. Oxford: Clarendon Press.

Ross, W. D. 1930. *The Right and the Good*. Oxford: Oxford University Press.

Ross, W. D. 1939. *Foundations of Ethics*. Oxford: Oxford University Press.

Rovane, C. 1998. *The Bounds of Agency*. Princeton, NJ: Princeton University Press.

Ryle, G. 1954. *Dilemmas*. Cambridge: Cambridge University Press, 54–67.

Sartre, J. P. 1953. *Being and Nothingness*. Translated by H. Barnes. New York: Simon and Schuster.

Sayre-McCord, G. 1988. Moral Theory and Explanatory Impotence. *Midwest Studies in Philosophy* 12, 435–457.

Scanlon, T. M. 1973. Rawls' Theory of Justice. *University of Pennsylvania Law Review* 121, 1020–1069.

Scanlon, T. M. 1982. Contractualism and Utilitarianism. In A. Sen and B. Williams (eds.), *Utilitarianism and Beyond*. Cambridge: Cambridge University Press, 103–128.

Scanlon, T. M. 1998. *What We Owe to Each Other*. Cambridge, MA: Harvard University Press.

Scheffler, S. 1982. *The Rejection of Consequentialism*. New York: Oxford University Press.

Scheffler, S. 1988. *Consequentialism and Its Critics*. Oxford: Oxford University Press.

Sen, A. 1986. Social Choice Theory. In K. Arrow and M. D. Intriligator (eds.), *Handbook of Mathematical Economics*, vol. 3. Amsterdam: North Holland, 1073–1181.

Sen, A. 1987. *On Ethics and Economics*. Oxford: Basil Blackwell.

Shoemaker, S. 1975. Functionalism and Qualia. *Philosophical Studies* 27, 291–315.

Shoemaker, S. 1984. Causality and Properties. In his *Identity, Cause, and Mind*. Cambridge: Cambridge University Press, 206–233.

Sidgwick, H. 1907. *The Methods of Ethics*, 7th ed. London: Macmillan.

Singer, P. 1972. Famine, Affluence and Morality. *Philosophy and Public Affairs* 1, 229–243.

Singer, P. 1993. *Practical Ethics*, 2nd ed. Cambridge: Cambridge University Press.

Slote, M. 1982. Goods and Lives. *Pacific Philosophical Quarterly* 63, 311–326.

Smart, J. J. C. 1973. An Outline of a System of Utilitarian Ethics. In J. J. C. Smart and B. Williams, *Utilitarianism, For and Against*. Cambridge: Cambridge University Press, 1–74.

Smart, R. N. 1958. Negative Utilitarianism. *Mind* 67, 542–543.

Smith, H. 1958. *The Religions of Man*. New York: Harper and Row.

Sophocles. 1984. *Oedipus the King*. Translated by R. Fagles. In *The Three Theban Plays*. Harmondsworth: Penguin.

Stalnaker, R. 1978. Assertion. *Syntax and Semantics* 9, 315–332.

Stevenson, C. L. 1937. The Emotive Meaning of Ethical Terms. *Mind* 46, 14–31.

Stevenson, C. L. 1944. *Ethics and Language*. New Haven, CT: Yale University Press.

Strasnick, S. L. 1975. Preference Priority and the Maximization of Public Welfare. Ph. D. dissertation, Harvard University.

Sturgeon, N. 1985. Moral Explanations. In D. Copp and D. Zimmerman (eds.), *Morality, Reason, and Truth*. Totowa, NJ: Rowman & Allanheld, 49–78.

Sumner, L. W. 1996. *Welfare, Happiness and Ethics*. Oxford: Clarendon Press.

Tännsjö, T. 1985. Moral Conflict and Moral Realism. *Journal of Philosophy* 82, 113–117.

Tännsjö, T. 1989. The Morality of Collective Actions. *Philosophical Quarterly* 39, 221–228.

Tännsjö, T. 1998. *Hedonistic Utilitarianism*. Edinburgh: Edinburgh University Press.

Temkin, L. S. 1993a. *Inequality*. Oxford: Oxford University Press.

Temkin, L. S. 1993b. Harmful Goods, Harmless Bads. In R. G. Frey and C. Morris (eds.), *Value, Welfare, and Morality*. Cambridge: Cambridge University Press, 290–324.

Thomas, E. J. 1935. *Early Buddhist Scriptures*. London: K. Paul, Trench, Trubner & Co.

Thomson, J. J. 1976. Killing, Letting Die, and the Trolley Problem. *The Monist* 59, 204–217.

Thomson, J. J. 1985. The Trolley Problem. *The Yale Law Journal* 94, 1395–1415.

Tuomela, R. 1995. *The Importance of Us*. Stanford, CA: Stanford University Press.

Unger, P. 1996. *Living High and Letting Die*. Oxford: Oxford University Press.

van Roojen, M. 1996. Expressivism and Irrationality. *The Philosophical Review* 105, 311–335.

Velleman, J. D. 1988. Brandt's Definition of 'Good'. *The Philosophical Review* 97, 353–372.

Velleman, J. D. 1991. Well-Being and Time. *Pacific Philosophical Quarterly* 72, 48–77.

Vischer, L. 1966. *Tithing in the Early Church*. Translated by R. C. Schultz. Philadelphia: Fortune Press.

von Neumann, J., and Morgenstern, O. 1944. *Theory of Games and Economic Behavior*. Princeton, NJ: Princeton University Press.

Weiss, H. (ed.). 2002. *Social Welfare in Muslim Societies in Africa*. Stockholm: Nordiska Afrikainstitutet.

Wiggins, D. 1987a. Truth, Invention, and the Meaning of Life. In his *Needs, Values, Truth*. Oxford: Oxford University Press, 87–138.

Wiggins, D. 1987b. Truth, and Truth as Predicated of Moral Judgments. In his *Needs, Values, Truth*. Oxford: Oxford University Press, 139–184.

Wiggins, D. 1987c. A Sensible Subjectivism. In his *Needs, Values, Truth*. Oxford: Oxford University Press, 185–214.

Wigoder, G. (ed.). 2002. *The New Encyclopedia of Judaism*. New York: New York University Press.

Williams, B. 1973. A Critique of Utilitarianism. In J. J. C. Smart and B. Williams, *Utilitarianism, For and Against*. Cambridge: Cambridge University Press, 75–150.

Williams, B. 1985. *Ethics and the Limits of Philosophy*. Cambridge, MA: Harvard University Press.

Index

moral intuitions
  abstract, 18, 226–270
  concrete, 18–19, 273, 275, 305
More, H., 206
Multiple-Act Consequentialism, 3–4, 18,
  23–102, 265, 266, 273, 274, 276
  demandingness, 93–102
  duties to self, 95–96
  general duties, 65–87
  principle for joining group acts, 51, 292
  special obligations, 87–91
  virtues, 295
murder, 86, 153, 299–300
Murphy, L., 96–98

Nagel, T., 7, 87, 155, 227
natural good, 13, 14–15, 139–182
naturalism
  analytic reductive, 147
  constitutive, 140, 148, 182
  nonconstitutive, 150–153
negative group act, 58
negative utilitarianism, 208
Newcomb's problem, 246
non-naturalism, 140, 144, 160
Nozick, R., 113, 119

objective temporal patterning and
  well-being, 237, 243–245
objectivist conceptions of well-being, 110,
  117, 124–126, 282
obligations from summation of small effects,
  308–311
obligations to the starving, 96–102, 311–312
one-off group agents, 58, 66, 82, 262, 277,
  278, 280, 288, 298
open-question argument, 157
orderings, 187, 191
ordinality, 165–167, 192, 204
organic unity, 193, 198, 199, 203

pain and pleasure, see also hedonism
  externalism versus internalism, 107–108
Parfit, D., 110, 227, 237, 238, 240, 242, 243,
  267, 308, 312
Pauline Principle, 78
PC, see Proposed Code
perspectival temporal patterning and
  well-being, 238, 240–243
pessimism, 263–269, 278
Plato, 115, 126, 128, 171, 230
Pogge, T., 98
Popper, K., 208
Postow, B., 32
principle of Defect to the Dominant, see DD
Principle of Sufficient Reason, 205, 212
principle of Very Little Defection, see VLD

Prisoner's Dilemma, 28
private language argument, 163
Problem of Evil, 268
project-constituting reasons, 56
promises, 299
proper projects, 66, 90, 95, 281, 283
Proposed Code, 9, 19, 262, 264, 270,
  271–312
prudence, 227, 229, 230
  traditional view of, 231
punishment, 92, 290

quality of pleasures, 170, 172, 222
quasi-experience, 170, 173, 178
questionable cases, 205, 207, 214, 219

Railton, P., 25
Ramsey, F., 261
rationality, 141
Rawls, J., 5, 91, 124, 125, 135, 147, 249,
  252
reciprocity, 12, 37, 58, 141
Regan, D., 26
religious codes, 286, 291, 294
restrictions on ordering worlds
  A (Abstraction), 192, 196–201
  B (Null Addition), 193, 201–202
  C (Generality), 193, 201–202
  D (Value Responsiveness), 194, 201–203
  E (Weak Pareto), 194, 201–202
  F (Separability), 195, 201–202
  G (Strong Ordinality), 195, 204–205
  H (Weak Equity), 196, 198, 205–213
    Argument from Value for, 207–209,
      220
    Argument from Equity for, 209–213,
      220
  O (Completeness), 191, 196, 205
risk aversion, 226, 260–263
Rohrbaugh, G., 33
Ross, W. D., 9, 10, 19, 109, 128–138, 287,
  289, 291, 298

Sartre, J. P., 172
Scanlon, T., 7, 11–12, 19, 135, 257,
  263, 283–285, 287, 288, 291, 294,
  298
Scheffler, S., 7, 70, 188
Schelling, T., 118, 230
self-defeat arguments, 242
sensibility theories, 151, 181
Sidgwick, H., 7, 8, 12, 19, 107, 164, 223,
  227, 287, 289, 291, 298
Singer, P., 99
Slote, M., 237
Stevenson, C. L., 145
Sturgeon, N., 148

325